Seeking Modernity in China's Name

Seeking Modernity in China's Name

CHINESE STUDENTS IN THE
UNITED STATES, 1900–1927

Weili Ye

STANFORD UNIVERSITY PRESS

STANFORD, CALIFORNIA 2001

Stanford University Press
Stanford, California

© 2001 by the Board of Trustees of the
Leland Stanford Junior University

Printed in the United States of America
on acid-free, archival-quality paper

*Figure 15 reproduced courtesy of The Columbia University Archives &
Columbiana Library.*

Library of Congress Cataloging-in-Publication Data
Ye, Weili.
    Seeking modernity in China's name : Chinese students in the
United States, 1900–1927 / Weili Ye.
        p.   cm.
    Includes bibliographical references and index.
    ISBN 0-8047-3696-0 (alk. paper)
        1. Chinese students—United States—Biography.   2. Chinese—
Education (Higher)—United States—History—20th century.
3. Returned students—China—Biography.   4. China—
Civilization—20th century.   I. Title: Chinese students in the United
States, 1900–1927.   II. Title.
    LB2376.6.C6 Y42   2001
    378.1'9829951073—dc21   00-046383

Typeset by BookMatters in 11/14 Adobe Garamond

Original Printing 2001

Last figure below indicates year of this printing:
10   09   08   07   07   06   05   04   03   02   01

For my mother, Bai Tian, and father, Fang Shi

Contents

12 pages of photos follow page 152

Acknowledgments

My teachers, colleagues, and friends have been enormously kind and encouraging to me throughout the research, writing, and revision of this book. Their help is especially meaningful to me because a major personal crisis almost stopped my work on the manuscript in its later stages. The completion of it represents not only my own success over trying circumstances, but also the unfailing support of all these good people. I am grateful to them beyond words.

A deep bow (as an appreciative student would do in China) to Jonathan Spence, my teacher and role model in the craft of history writing, and to all my other professors at Yale. My profound thanks also to Chris Gilmartin, a great friend and a strong believer in me; to Jean Humez, a caring colleague who carefully read the entire manuscript and offered detailed suggestions; to Joseph Esherick and Marilyn Young, two sharp yet always encouraging critics of my ideas and writing; to Ann Cordiliar, Kate Hartford, Jonathan Chu, Malcolm Smuts, Ann Froines, and Michael LaFargue, my steadfast friends and colleagues at University of Massachusetts, Boston; to Kandice Hauf, Esther Stieman, and Kethelean Cleaver, my fellow graduate students at Yale who cheered me along; to William Kirby, James Watson, Paul Cohen, and Leo Ou-fan Lee, whose interest in my work and sensible advice made my one-year visit at the Fairbank Center of Harvard University both pleasant and gratifying; to the two very thoughtful and constructive anonymous reviewers of the manuscript; and to Muriel Bell of Stanford University Press, who has been a staunch supporter of my project for several years. I also owe an indirect but great debt to Kwang-ching Liu, whose bibliography guidebook, *American and Chinese*, introduced me to extremely useful primary sources.

I have been blessed with many other wonderful friends in the United States and China who have been invaluably helpful in my completing the book: in the States, Kathy Klyce, Ma Xiaodong, Zhong Xueping, Lin Chun, Zhu Hong, Anping Chin, and Ann and John Watts; in China, Li Rolin, Wang Hui, Yu Ling, Liu Naiyuan, Yu Miao, Feng Jinglan, Lu Xiaoqin, and Zhang Youyun. These people have shown me, in their own unique ways, what the saying "A friend in need . . ." is all about. A big hug to each and every one of them.

I also want to express my sincere appreciation to a small number of veteran "returned students" whom I was privileged to meet and interview in Beijing in the winter of 1985. Chen Hansheng, Zhang Yuanshan (Djang Yuan-shan), Li Jinghan, Chen Daisun, and Zhou Peiyuan, as well as Meng Zhi (Chih Meng), whom I met in White Plains, New York, taught me more than I could ever hope to learn from books. Except for Chen Hansheng, all of these people have since passed away. I will forever cherish the memories of my meetings with them. My thanks also go to E-Tu Zen-Sun, Li Weige, and Pan Naimu, for their willingness to help me with information and insight about their parents, Chen Hengzhe and Ren Hongjun, Li Jinghan, and Pan Guangdan, respectively; and to Wen Liming, for his help about his grandfather Wen Yiduo. Three members in my extended family—my uncles Ye Duyi, Ye Duzhuang (who has since passed away), and Ye Duzheng— either helped me locate sources of information or shared with me personal knowledge about Luo Longji, Li Jinghan, and Zhu Kezhen, respectively. Thank you all, my uncles.

I am deeply grateful to the American Association of University Women, the Whiting Fellowship Foundation, the Yale Center for International and Area Studies, the postdoctoral fellowship program at the Fairbank Center of Harvard University, the Professional Development Grant program at SUNY Fredonia, the Institute for Asian American Studies at U. Mass.–Boston, and other internal funding programs at UMB for their generous support at various stages of my work on this book.

I am thankful to people at the archives at Columbia University, Cornell University, Yale University, Harvard University, and Wellesley College, the Chih Meng Collection at the Mansfield Freeman Center for East Asian Studies at Wesleyan University, the General Commission on Archives and History, the United Methodist Church at Madison, New York, the China

Institute in New York City, the Rockefeller Foundation Archives in Tarrytown, New York, Beijing Library, Beijing University Library, the Social Science Library of the Chinese Academy of Sciences, and the Weston Returned Scholars' Association in Beijing for their professional assistance.

Finally, my deepest thanks must go to my family, especially my extraordinarily loving parents and my always giving sister. My mother, who passed away in the spring of 1996, has always been a major source of strength and inspiration for me; her spirit has lightened some of the darkest moments in my life. My last word is reserved for my son, who has lived a large part of his young life during the conception and growth of this book. I thank him for being there with me in my long intellectual journey, and I hope he will understand someday his mother's passion for Chinese history.

A Note on Romanization

I have used pinyin romanization for most personal names, including those long familiar in the West, such as Wellington Koo and Hu Shi. I have retained Wade-Giles romanization only when a person's identification is unknown, and for Chiang Kai-shek and Sun Yat-sen.

Seeking Modernity in China's Name

Introduction

A photograph of about seventy young Chinese men, presumably taken right after they passed the selection examination for the Boxer Indemnity Scholarship Program in August 1910, shows almost all of them wearing long gowns, their queues having only recently been cut. Less than a month later, as they prepared to embark on the voyage to America, their looks had changed entirely: they wore Western hairstyles and all were dressed in Western suits made by tailors in Shanghai.[1]

F. L. Chang, a Chinese student in America at about this time, recounts in the *Chinese Students' Monthly*[2] just how traumatic it was to undergo the transformations typical for the America-bound Chinese male student (presumably based on his own personal experiences). First, he had to lose his queue, "up to now a life-long friend"; next went his "soft silk garments and comfortable shoes," which were replaced by a "much less satisfactory" straw hat, a double-breasted suit, and a pair of heavy leather shoes. The shift from chopsticks to knife and fork impeded his "manual dexterity"; changing his diet from "small bits of seasoned pork" to "a large piece of raw steak" often resulted in "indigestion"; and switching from a cup of tea to a dish of ice cream required "a strong constitution." When all these changes occurred in rapid succession, Chang observed, an "Oriental" person became very much bewildered.[3]

People such as Chang, who ultimately became modern Chinese by coming to America to study in the early twentieth century, stood at the forefront of the nation's encounter with the West. They experienced a more dramatic, perhaps more thorough, and in many cases more conflict-ridden transformation into modern ways than did their peers in China. Their sojourn in America, which for the majority of them took place at a formative period in their lives, had a substantial impact on their political, professional, emotional, and even physical development. A fascinating yet until recently little-studied group,[4] this generation of American-educated Chinese, whose importance to China is just beginning to be fully recognized, produced some of China's most prominent leaders in diplomacy, industry, and finance, as well as China's first career women. From this group also came many of China's major modern educators and scholars, individuals who would set the tone and style of university and intellectual life in the first half of twentieth-century China.[5] The foundations these people laid in republican China, particularly in the areas of higher education, research, and, to a lesser degree, industry,[6] eventually provided the institutional base of the People's Republic of China. Still more pertinent for this study is the fact that they introduced new social customs, new kinds of interpersonal relationships, and new ways of associating in groups—in brief, they initiated a new way of life that contained key aspects of Chinese modernity. This is why our understanding of twentieth-century China and the process of cross-cultural social change can be greatly enhanced by a careful examination of their experience.

MODERNITY AS LIVED EXPERIENCE

The best known among this remarkable group was Hu Shi (Hu Shih), China's preeminent liberal in the Dewey tradition. Hu attended Cornell and Columbia universities and emerged as a chief spokesperson for the May Fourth New Culture Movement that began around the mid 1910s.[7] Yet Hu

Shi was only one among many of comparable talent.[8] In the same cohort that arrived in America with Hu Shi in 1910 (the group whose photograph I mentioned above) were the following, eventually influential men: Zhu Kezhen (Chu K'o-chen, known in the West as Coching Chu), a Harvard-trained meteorologist who would serve as vice president of the Academy of Natural Sciences in the People's Republic (and whose story after returning to China will be told in the Epilogue); Zhao Yuanren (Yuen Ren Chao), a pioneer in China in the fields of linguistics and musicology, whose Chinese-language textbooks are still being used by universities across America; and Zhang Pengchun (P. C. Chang), a Columbia-trained educator who contributed significantly to the development of both Qinghua and Nankai, two highly acclaimed universities in twentieth-century China, and who also helped introduce modern theater to China by enthusiastically promoting student drama at Nankai Middle School.[9]

Many others of equal brilliance came to America during this period, later bringing about a wide range of changes in modern China. For a long time, these people were marginalized and negated by the dominant school of "revolution-centered" modern Chinese historiography in the People's Republic. Their foreign educational background put them in the category of "bourgeois intellectuals," a political label that often led to their denunciation and persecution during much of the Mao era. This bleak situation has changed a great deal since the 1980s, when the "four modernizations" became official policy and a new wave of foreign study began in China. A rehabilitation of foreign-educated Chinese has taken place and a number of books have been published in China on the subject of the Chinese foreign-study movement.[10]

None of these books, however, focuses specifically on American-educated Chinese in the early twentieth century; nor do they adequately examine these people's multiple contributions to modern China. Fei Xiaotong, one of China's most revered social scientists and himself a student of the American-trained educators studied in this book, compares his recent efforts to introduce his teachers to contemporary readers to the "white-haired palace maid's" futile attempt to recount a past few people cared to listen to (an allusion to a poem written by the famous Tang dynasty poet Bai Juyi).[11] Fei's remark generates a question; namely, have the foreign-educated Chinese from the first half of the twentieth century been truly understood, now that they have been rescued from obscurity and political condemnation in the PRC?

Western-educated Chinese have not received adequate attention in Western scholarship either. Charlotte Furth, the author of a well-received book on the British-trained geologist Ding Wenjiang (Ting Wen-chiang),[12] contends that while the new intellectual class of the early twentieth century helped usher in an urbane and Western-oriented modern culture, "it was also threatened by a new estrangement from the rest of the Chinese society" because of its elitist Western education and its distance from the center of political power.[13] Y. C. Wang and Jerome Chen, each the author of an authoritative work on the foreign-educated Chinese, agree with Furth's formulation.[14]

While it is true that the elite foreign-educated class was relatively ineffective in twentieth-century Chinese politics, I believe that the politically oriented approach to their impact is overly narrow. The American-educated Chinese studied in this book belonged to the same generation that produced Mao Zedong, Deng Xiaoping, and Chiang Kai-shek—twentieth-century larger-than-life figures whose presence overshadowed their politically less prominent peers, even though the latter were significant historical actors in their own right. Born between the 1880s and the 1900s, theirs was a "special generation" in modern Chinese history, men who were "the last to have the world of Confucian learning etched into their memories as schoolboys, yet the first as a group to confront the intrusive Western world forcing itself into Chinese territory and Chinese minds."[15] To understand the historical roles played by this generation of American-educated Chinese, it is important to trace their intellectual genealogy and to compare them with people of the previous generation.

Several prominent thinkers in that earlier generation served as intellectual mentors for the people examined in the present study. As the first representatives of the "Chinese intelligentsia," those individuals in the older generation (who henceforth will be referred to as the "pioneer thinkers") emerged as a "visible group of new social types" toward the end of the nineteenth century.[16] Among those who fully embraced a recognizably "modern" mode of consciousness,[17] Liang Qichao and Yan Fu stood out as the most influential. Liang's acceptance of the nation-state as the "terminal community"[18] and Yan Fu's rational-technological approach, as well as his search for a "wealthy and strong" Chinese nation, exerted a profound impact on the younger generation.[19] Revolutionary as they were in their thinking, however, the pioneer thinkers "largely abided with the traditional life styles."[20] Furthermore, although the idea of a "modern man" as a "self-confident engineer, industrialist and professional" was first advocated by the pioneer thinkers,[21] it remained for the next generation, precisely Liang Qichao's own children and their peers,[22] to undergo specialized training as professionals in Western countries, in Japan, and within China itself.

Both the American-educated students and their mentors can be regarded as "transitional," but there were significant differences in the ways the two generations related to "modernity." To begin with, the pioneer thinkers came under Western influences only after they had reached adulthood, whereas the student generation received a more systematic modern education in their younger years. Furthermore, the dismantling of the civil service examination system in the early twentieth century compelled the younger generation to search for new career paths. And lastly, everyday life also began to show signs of change; in coastal cities in particular, some Chinese were choosing a "modern" lifestyle as early as the first decade of the twentieth century.[23]

If, as Myron Cohen perceptively argues, "being Chinese" for the elite classes in traditional China meant choosing particular lifestyles and ways of making a living,[24] then "being modern Chinese" similarly included aspects of both. The conventional approach to studying modern Chinese intellectuals, which often focuses only on their ideas and concepts, fails to capture their multidimensional experiences; for them, "modernity" was not just an intellectual issue, but an "existential" one as well. How one lived had become an increasingly important statement about who one was, since "the more post-traditional the settings in which an individual moves, the more lifestyle concerns the very core of self-identity, its making and remaking."[25]

It is my argument that although this contingent of American-educated Chinese were not the first generation of modern Chinese to begin to *think* differently, they were among the first for whom "modernity" became a *lived* experience. In terms of both lifestyle and livelihood, they made decisive strides toward a modern mode. Meanwhile, through reordering their own lives, they furthered the development of a Chinese modern identity, a historical project already begun by the pioneer thinkers. The study of the American-educated Chinese, therefore, challenges us to go beyond the conventional emphasis on political and intellectual history, and to embrace a broader social and cultural perspective. Then we can understand more adequately the historical roles of these people, men and women who gave daily content to the modernity that they sought in China's name.[26]

In this study, "modernity" is treated neither as a "pre-established sociohistoric" scheme and a one-size-fits-all ideal, nor as a "completed or synthetic whole."[27] No single universal definition is adequate to convey what "the modern" has meant in different periods and in various cultural settings.[28] There are and have been, as Benjamin Schwartz emphasized, many varieties of modernity within the "modern West" itself, with all the conflicts and tensions that make modernity a complex and unresolved state of affairs.[29] Moreover, Western-derived notions of modernity may be unable to capture sufficiently the peculiar adaptation of the "modern" mode in non-Western cultural contexts. In Wang Hui's critical study of the Chinese quest for modern identity, Wang, a highly regarded scholar in China, not only points out the tensions and paradoxes embedded in modernity, but also asks, "Whose modernity scheme is it?" to stress the Western origin of the term and to caution its application to the Chinese context.[30] The process of constructing Chinese modern identity, Wang argues, not only implies borrowing ideas, attitudes, and behaviors from various sources in the modern West, but also requires both critical reexamination of and a creative and selective reconnection to China's own history and tradition.[31]

Modernization for the Chinese people has not been a "natural" development, but a turbulent and painful process that involves the search for a modern yet still Chinese identity. In this context, the question of cultural continuity and discontinuity always arises when modern Chinese intellectuals are studied. Joseph Levenson, for instance, saw little continuity with Chinese tradition, aside from emotional attachments, among modern Chinese intellectuals.[32] More persuasive, in my view, is the notion that modern Chinese intellectuals favor a combination of continuity and discontinuity in their resolution of tradition and Western influence and their creation of new culture in China.[33] This is especially true about the generation studied here, a generation that was systematically educated in the West yet still sufficiently rooted in the cultural heritage of China.[34] Rather than being passive receivers of Western influence, the thoughtful people among this generation consciously searched for ways to regenerate Chinese culture by a careful selection and digestion of Western knowledge.[35] As Pan Guangdan, an unusually perceptive man who studied in the U.S. from 1922 to 1926, contended in the *Chinese Students' Quarterly*,[36] the purpose of foreign study was not to make the Chinese depend on the West intellectually, but to enable the Chinese to stand on an equal footing with the West, and to create, along with countries all over the world, an "equal yet diverse common cultural life."[37]

This study is largely focused on my subjects' years in the United States (although there are sections, such as the one in Chapter 2 about professional identity, where I discuss at length their activities after they went back to China). I explore what modernity meant to them and how they experimented in America with a modern mode of life. The vast majority of the students, it is important to keep in mind, returned to China after they finished their studies abroad.[38]

For the Chinese, modernity by its very nature involves cross-cultural interchange.[39] What is most intriguing about the students' experience is precisely that it occurred in a cross-cultural setting and in the dual historical context of China and America. The challenge is to contextualize the experiences of the Chinese students within the political, social, and cultural environments of both countries. A number of major political events and social and cultural movements marked the histories of both countries in this period and underscored the modern transformation they were undergoing. While China was at the threshold of a modern age and in a particularly stressful transitional period from the late Qing to the early republic, America was encountering its own, different modernization problems, arising from rapid industrialization and urbanization. Ultimately, it was the students' perceptions of the conditions and needs of China that guided what they would do with the stimuli and influences of America. America of the early twentieth century offered the Chinese students a particular version of modernity, which, of course, left its mark on the students' adaptation to modern ways, a style that might not have been as evident to the Chinese who did not have prolonged experiences of American culture. The unique American imprint on the students' experiences notwithstanding, the issues the students dealt with in their lives and discussed in their writings—factors such as nationalism, democratic participation and voluntary association, professionalism, romantic love, new forms of leisure, as well as race—were universal issues in the making of a modern Chinese identity, and are still relevant to today's Chinese.

THE FIRST AND SECOND WAVES

It is important to place this generation of American-educated Chinese within the larger context of the foreign-study movement in modern China. For over one hundred years, driven by an urge for social and political change, the desire for new knowledge, and a longing for more personal freedom and a better life, generations of educated Chinese have left home to study in almost every major country in the world. There have been both active and inactive periods in the foreign-study movement, in response to the fluctuations in modern Chinese history. In recent times, since the reform era began in the People's Republic in the late 1970s, hundreds of thousands of Chinese have gone abroad to study.[40] A new wave of Chinese foreign study has clearly and forcefully arrived on the world scene.[41]

The first major wave of Chinese going abroad to study consisted of a number of Qing-government-sponsored overseas educational missions in the 1870s and 1880s, during the era of the "Self-Strengthening Movement."[42] The best known were the one hundred or so Chinese youth of the "Yung Wing mission" to America (1872–81), referred to later as "China's first hundred."[43] This mission was terminated abruptly, in part because of the conservative Chinese officials' concern over the adoption of American lifestyles by the young students, and in part because of the rise of anti-Chinese sentiments and actions in America at that time, events that led the U.S. government to back off from its earlier agreement to let the Chinese students enter American military academies.[44]

The foreign-study students of the early twentieth century, including the American-educated group examined in this study, comprised the second wave, a new movement stemming from a political crisis in China. In the wake of the Boxer incident of 1900, the Qing government, motivated by the need for self-preservation, made an earnest effort to readjust China's position in the world. Among a series of political and social reform measures taken by the Qing regime, the most significant and far-reaching was the abolition of the imperial civil service examinations in 1905.[45] Henceforth Chinese youth were to be educated in a new way consonant with China's need to survive in the modern world. Zhang Zhidong, a governor-general and reform leader at the turn of the century, saw foreign study as a solution, even though he insisted at the same time that Western learning could only serve as the means (*yong*) while Chinese learning should remain the essence (*ti*).[46] His "means-essence" formula, proposed in the late 1890s, soon became outdated. Facing a crisis of "orientational order" as the Chinese intellectual world rapidly disintegrated,[47] people began to embrace not only Western technical knowledge, but Western learning in general, becoming, in fact, amazingly receptive to Western influences. It was in this generally open intellectual milieu in China that the second wave of the foreign-study movement began to rise. Compared with the Yung Wing mission's short-term and narrowly defined educational project,[48] this new wave enjoyed a much stronger and more enduring momentum, was endorsed by both state and society, and was marked with a self-conscious willingness on the part of the students to acquire broad learning from the West. It also became understood and largely accepted by the people involved that going abroad to study would imply a departure from traditional ways of life, in contrast to the resistance to Western cultural influences by the conservative officials on the Yung Wing mission.

Not all Chinese students in the second wave chose to study in the West. To many people in the first decade of the 1900s, recently modernized Japan was a shortcut to Western knowledge. In the peak year of 1906, the number of Chinese students in Tokyo alone amounted to over eight thousand,[49] much larger than that of the students in America in any given year. While most people in Japan studied subjects like education, law, medicine, or military science, the best-known students there were not the degree-seeking scholars but political dissidents such as Sun Yat-sen and his colleagues.

With the launching of the "work-study" program in the mid 1910s, France became an important center of foreign study in Europe, attracting over sixteen hundred Chinese youths between 1919 and 1921, many of whom went to Paris and Lyon. What came out of this academically dubious program was the formation of some of the earliest Chinese communist groups.[50] A number of other European countries such as England, Germany, and Belgium also attracted students from China.[51]

In contrast to the drastic rise and fall of the numbers of students in Japan and France, the increase of students in America between 1900 and 1927 was gradual and steady: in 1906, about 300 Chinese students were in America; the number grew to roughly 650 in 1911; by 1915, the number had passed 1,000; three years later, about 1,200 students were in America; and between

1925 and 1926, the estimated figure was around 1,600.[52] The Chinese tended to concentrate in schools in the East and Midwest, with a much smaller number of them in the West and the South.[53]

The cost of study in America was far beyond the economic capacities of most Chinese families,[54] so people of lesser means had to depend on financial support from various sources. Government sponsorships of different kinds furnished most financial aid, with missionary patronage a distant second.[55] Occasionally, some individuals were also helped by wealthy philanthropists. Generally speaking, Chinese students in America, even those on government scholarships, came from families that were relatively affluent by Chinese standards.[56]

A high percentage of the students came from just three provinces, Jiangsu, Zhejiang, and Guangdong.[57] The large number of students from the increasingly westernized seaport regions underscored the widened gap between the interior and the coast, a reality that had become noticeable since the mid nineteenth century. Elite missionary school graduates made up a considerable portion of the student body, a fact that was noted, with some alarm, as early as the 1910s.[58] Despite the Boxer Indemnity program and other government programs, the proportion of government fellowship students (*guanfei*) steadily declined over time; after 1910, self-supporting students clearly outnumbered government fellowship students.[59]

The Boxer Indemnity Scholarship Program was the most important scheme for educating Chinese students in America and arguably the most consequential and successful in the entire foreign-study movement of twentieth-century China. It enjoyed a good reputation because of its competitive selection procedure and high academic standard, especially after the founding of a specially designed preparatory school in Beijing, Qinghua (Tsinghua) College.[60] From the approximately thirteen hundred individuals sent by the program from 1909 to 1929,[61] there emerged some of modern China's best scholars and educators, as well as prominent leaders in other walks of life.[62]

The story of the American remission of the Boxer Indemnity reveals a complex, and fundamentally unequal power relationship between China and America. Overall, as Michael Hunt convincingly argues, the remission of the Boxer Indemnity in the form of scholarship aid to Chinese students in America was an act on the part of the American government to promote

American-directed reform in China.[63] It should also be understood in the context of contemporary international geopolitics, especially Americans' concern over the rising military and political influence of Japan after the Russo-Japanese War of 1904–5, and the subsequent large influx of Chinese students to that rapidly modernizing Pacific rival.[64]

For the Chinese, including those who benefited by the educational opportunity, the humiliating memory of the Boxer Incident remained a source of bitterness.[65] The West in the nineteenth and twentieth centuries represented to the Chinese intellectual class both the oppression of imperialism and the lure of modernity, and the American Boxer Indemnity program clearly embodied these paradoxical roles. An interesting footnote to the story of the American Boxer Indemnity remission is that two former students of the Yung Wing mission were highly instrumental in the development of the Indemnity program. Liang Cheng, the Chinese minister to the United States (1903–7), played a key role in pressing the American government to return the excess money to China;[66] meanwhile, Liang Tunyan, the Chinese minister of foreign affairs in 1909, was crucial in deciding what academic subjects should be emphasized in the program.[67] The connection between the first wave and the second wave of the Chinese foreign-study movement was nowhere more explicit.

SOURCES AND ORGANIZATION

This study intends to recapture and interpret Chinese students' daily life in America, and therefore draws extensively on voluminous publications by the students themselves both in English and in Chinese, as well as records in university archives, contemporary newspaper and magazine accounts, personal memoirs and diaries, oral histories, and interviews I conducted in China in the 1980s. In six topical chapters, the book explores various aspects of the students' experiences in their years in America, and in some sections, their activities after they returned to China.

A major conceptual adjustment many educated Chinese made at the turn of the century was to begin to see themselves as Chinese nationals, a primary marker of their modern identity. As such, they sought new ways of grouping with other Chinese nationals; Chapter 1 looks at the associational life of the Chinese students in America in these terms. Special attention is given to one particular organization, the Chinese Students' Alliance, the largest and most elaborately organized among all the Chinese student organizations in America at this time. In the late 1900s, when a vigorous constitutional movement was being launched in China, which upheld the ideas of self-government and political participation, the Chinese Students' Alliance embarked on its own comparable democratic venture.

The eventual waning of the democratic spirit among the students after the founding of the republic, accompanied by the decline of the Alliance, illustrates tellingly the political dilemmas China faced in her desperate struggle to survive as a new modern nation-state. Students' political attitudes and behaviors during the stressful transitional period from late Qing to the early republic provide important clues regarding the meaning of democracy to the Chinese in the early twentieth century and the changing political roles of the educated class. Despite the decline of the Alliance, the associational drive survived. Among other types of student organizations, Chapter 1 also looks at the development of student fraternities, an elusive and seldom studied subject that can help shed light on politics and organizational behavior in the republican period.

Chapter 2 focuses on the professional life of the students. The evolution of educated Chinese at this time from civil servants of the state to independent modern professionals was a significant historical phenomenon. American-educated Chinese constituted the mainstay of the first generation of Chinese professionals, a new intellectual force that began to become visible in China in the second half of the 1920s. The development of professional societies, which the students experimented with while in America, played a crucial role in implanting professional consciousness of these individuals. The presence of these professional organizations, modeled after ones in America, was another important expression of the students' associational drive. Overall, the students acquired a primarily technical, gradualist approach to solving China's problems, as opposed to the political and revolutionary methods of the Chinese Communist Party. After they returned to China, efforts were made by them not only to transplant Western disciplines and professional societies to their home country, but also to sinicize them, as the case of the sociologist Wu Wenzao (and his students) demonstrates. To a large extent, the Chinese professionals succeeded both in establishing the new authority of professionalism and in carving out a relatively autonomous space for themselves in the Nationalist period. The close connection between this subject matter and that of Chapter 1 was what led me to make it the second chapter, although the fact that it consists of the students' experiences after they returned to China could have been a rationale for placing it toward the end of the book.

Chapter 3 examines the question of race. Educated Chinese during the early twentieth century wrestled with Western-defined notions of race and constructed their own racial consciousness within the framework of Chinese nationalism. For the students in America, more than for their peers in China, the question of race was relevant and pressing since they found themselves in a country where Chinese immigration was banned. Through the students' ambivalent relationship with "backward" Chinese immigrant laborers in the United States, the difficult issues of race, class, and modernity all came to the fore. While limited efforts were made by some students to improve the conditions of the Chinese laborers through "general welfare" programs in the early 1910s, little concrete work was done in the 1920s by members of the May Fourth generation, even though these people were more ready to view the plight of the Chinese immigrants as a symbol of China's humiliating position in the world. From the May Fourth group, however, came individuals who began to study race and ethnicity as trained professionals in the social and natural sciences. As a whole, the students did not reject the Western-defined racial hierarchy, but rather sought to improve Chinese position in it.

The unique questions raised for female students in America is the subject of Chapter 4, which, covering the period from the 1880s to the 1920s, provides a fuller historical overview of the story of the *nü liuxuesheng* (female foreign-study students) since their first appearance.[68] Three rather distinct generational groups of women students can be identified in the four decades under review, each with its own share of problems and strategies for tackling them. Part of the general movement of students sent to study abroad, but also apart from them, the women students had perspectives and experiences which differed notably from those of their male counterparts. Modern meanings of domesticity and femininity, and the conflict between career and marriage—these were of special relevance to women students, and were wrestled with by the three generational groups in their respective historical contexts.

Chapter 5 probes the emotional world of the students, particularly the male students. Leaving behind a country whose social and cultural order was disintegrating, and coming to a sexually more permissive country with a different code of social behavior, many male students (a large percentage of them already betrothed in China) experienced initial shock and uncertainty about how to adjust to the new mores and, eventually, how to break away from the confines of traditional Chinese personal culture. Meanwhile, Confucian morality, while fading, had by no means lost all of its power. This culturally conflicted milieu was the setting for the students' new struggle with issues of gender relationships, love, sexuality, and interracial marriage.

Chapter 6 discusses the students' recreational activities, particularly athletics and theater, two important cultural arenas of modernity for students in the early twentieth century. Through participation in sports, the students developed an appreciation for physical fitness and nurtured a more rounded personality ideal. In particular, the male students embraced new notions of masculinity that emphasized action, competitiveness, and physical prowess. The theater, on the other hand, provided the students with a new way to relax and entertain, a convenient means for imparting positive images of China to the American audience, and an important medium for exploring issues of common concern. A number of individuals who first participated in theater while in America went on to play pioneering roles in China's modern theater.

My study's focus is the first quarter of the twentieth century, up to 1927, a period in which critical cultural shifts and political transformations took place in China. The year 1927 marked the beginning of a new Nationalist era. By then, most of the members of the generation examined in this study had completed their overseas sojourn and returned to China. The source materials about students during this twenty-seven-year period are abundant, interesting, and highly informative.[69]

A PERSONAL NOTE

I became curious about an earlier generation of American-educated Chinese after living a few years as a Chinese student in America myself. Having grown up in the PRC during a time when history books seldom mentioned

Western-educated Chinese, I knew nothing about my predecessors when I arrived in America in the early 1980s. Gradually, my own experience as a Chinese person studying in America made me wonder about them. In the winter of 1985 I went back to China to do research on the generation of the American-educated Chinese in the first decades of the twentieth century. I was able to meet a few survivors, all in their eighties and nineties.[70] The most valuable thing I gained from these interviews was not factual information, but a "feel" for this remarkable group.

I was especially drawn to Li Jinghan (Franklin C. H. Lee), who studied sociology at Columbia University in the early 1920s and returned to China to become an advocate of statistical research and an authority on the study of rural China. The old man had poor hearing and could not quite follow the questions I had prepared. His mind was still clear, though, and I let him wander in his own reminiscing. Twice I saw light shining in his ninety-one-year-old eyes: first, when he talked about how he had won first prizes for a tennis tournament and for a speech contest at a Chinese students' summer conference in America;[71] and second, when he told me that some of his works, out of print since after 1949, were to be reprinted soon by a Chinese university press. The sweet smile on his face was almost childlike. Li's story will appear in the Epilogue.

After I left Li's modest apartment in eastern Beijing and came out onto the busy street, I felt sad for Li Jinghan and sad for China's discipline of sociology. I was certain that few people in this undistinguished neighborhood knew that there lived amongst them one of China's most eminent sociologists in the twentieth century.[72] The ground work laid by Li and his colleagues decades ago had been undermined after sociology was denounced as "pseudoscience" in the early 1950s. As a result, a young generation of Chinese students had to go abroad again to "reinaugurate" sociology, instead of learning from their Chinese teachers at home.

Now that the twentieth century is past, a rethinking of twentieth-century Chinese history is inconspicuously but firmly under way both in China and in the West. Notable in this effort is an endeavor to rediscover and reevaluate those people and events that have been obscured by the "revolution-centered" modern Chinese historiography. Almost all of a sudden, Chinese history of the past one hundred years has started to be revealed in all its dazzling multiple colors and facets. This study was conducted within this historical current. It is a tribute to members of an earlier generation of American-educated Chinese from a person who followed in their footsteps more than half a century later, and who, until I started digging up long-buried materials, was totally ignorant of a vital group of intellectuals in modern Chinese history. It is my intention to trace the paths taken by this memorable group of people, to examine and reflect upon, in a comprehensive and critical manner, the making of Chinese modern identity in the course of the twentieth century, and to connect my own generation to our predecessors.

CHAPTER ONE

Student Associational Life and Chinese Nationalism

The Chinese students of the early twentieth century came to America not in tightly knit groups, like those in the Yung Wing educational mission, but as individuals, scattering throughout the vast country on many different college campuses. Against great odds (the geographical distance between them being just one of several barriers), they launched organizations that incorporated the majority of Chinese students in America. The organizations they created met a wide variety of needs: social, political, professional, and religious.

Associational life featured prominently in the experiences of Chinese students in America. Among all the associations, the Chinese Students' Alliance, whose predecessor organization was founded in 1902, was the largest, the most elaborately organized, and for a while the most influential. At its height around 1910, two-thirds of the Chinese students in America joined the Alliance,[1] many of whose officers and activists went on to become prominent figures in various walks of life in modern China.[2] In its heyday, it was an experiment in democratic organization, characterized by vigorous advocacy of self-government and serious concern for popular participation—an exciting political venture for Chinese in the early twentieth century. Through involvement in organizations like the Alliance and participation in American college campus life, Chinese students learned how to debate issues, conduct elections, and chair meetings—the essential skills for Anglo-American-style democracy.

Other types of associations also existed among the students, including local clubs and the Chinese Students' Christian Association in North America, the major organization for Chinese Christian students. In the 1920s, when the Alliance had largely declined into a social club, two alternative and much smaller societies were formed to attract politically active students: *Cheng-chih hui* (the Association for Accomplishing Ideals, or CCH), a secret fraternity, and *Dajiang hui* (the Big River Society), an alumni association made up of Qinghua College graduates of certain classes. The groupings of different types testify to the range and vigor of the associational drive among the Chinese students in America.

The question of how to mobilize the Chinese people in modern-style voluntary organizations occupied the thinking of individuals like Liang Qichao at the turn of the century. Liang wrote about the notion of *qun* (group or grouping, first given modern meaning by Yan Fu[3]), which he saw as a key to the success of the modern West. Liang Qichao believed that a broad mobilization of people was necessary for a strong and modern Chinese nation, and voluntary associations, in Liang's view, would serve as an important means for integrating the Chinese people into a cohesive and unified community.[4]

Voluntary societies mushroomed in China in the last decade of the nineteenth century and continued to thrive in the first decade of the new century,[5] demonstrating the urge among progressive-thinking Chinese to search for new ways of organizing and relating to each other. In the political context of the late Qing, the appearance of voluntary societies constituted an integral part of China's modern nation-state building. The associational drive of the Chinese students in America can best be understood in this context. For the Chinese born around the turn of the century, nationalism provided a "quasi-religious center of meaning" at a time when the old "symbolisms" of China crumbled.[6] Nationalism became meaningful also because personal memories of this generation were closely intertwined with the humiliating recent history of the nation. An essay written in 1915 by a student in America under the pseudonym Chung-hwa Sing ("China Prospers") expressed an intensely nationalistic sentiment commonly shared by many members of this generation:

> Most of us were born somewhere around the year 1894. Have you not been taught what a year 1894 was for China? It was the year of the Chino[*sic*]-Japanese war over the question of Korea. . . . All these humiliations of our country happened when we were just raising our first baby cries. Do you not realize that you were born in the time when your country was perishing? . . . Having realized that we are the people of a perishing nation, we instinctively want to know what we shall do to save China.[7]

For the Chinese at the turn of the century, nationalism was a central and definitive theme of modernity.[8] As a "widespread consciousness" and an "intellectual movement," its arrival in the 1890s marked a fundamental "turn" in modern Chinese culture.[9] The conversion by Chinese intellectuals to the nationalistic viewpoint was accomplished in roughly one generation.[10] If in the minds of some pioneer thinkers of the 1890s the pull of "universalism" still remained strong,[11] ambivalence toward nationalism largely disappeared for the early-twentieth-century generation of students, who decidedly relinquished universalism and accepted China as a "terminal political community."[12]

The "spatial change"[13] made by many Chinese at this time not only meant accepting China as "one nation among many"; it also meant, on a personal level, a shift of people's primary identification from a particular local region to the Chinese nation, and constructed a sense of Chinese national identity. The Chinese spatial adjustment to the modern world, therefore, contained both international and domestic dimensions,[14] with implications for each individual person. The two competing ideas during this period, "self-government" and "administrative centralization,"[15] reflected the tension of the domestic spatial transition. The differing viewpoints tested the resilience of Chinese nationalism, and raised the issue of how China should be ruled. The students in America consistently revealed a tendency to endorse a version of nationalism that upheld China as one unified political entity, despite their brief support of the ideal of "self-government." Perhaps more than their peers at home, they were self-conscious about being Chinese nationals, since their nationality was highlighted by living abroad.[16]

Regarding another polemical issue in late Qing—revolution versus reform—the students in America as a whole identified with the reformers and supported the reform-oriented constitutional movement. Their reformist politics created few political headlines, and was therefore overshadowed by the radical activism of Chinese students in Japan. Since the "revolutionaries" have attracted most of the limelight in much of the twentieth-century Chinese history, the students in America have been regarded as generally nonpolitical.[17] However, the difference between them and their counterparts in Japan was not that they "avoided politics,"[18] but that they avoided "radical" politics.

Three periods deserve special attention regarding the students' political attitudes and behavior: the late Qing (1906–11), when a constitutional movement was going on in China; the early republican era (1912–16), when Yuan Shikai dominated the political scene; and the warlord period following the death of Yuan (1916–27). The state of the students' associational life paralleled the turbulent political situation in China. Initial enthusiasm among the students for democratic practice during the late Qing gave way—after 1912, the year when the republic was founded—to doubt as to whether democracy would really protect the Chinese nation. Subsequently, their interest in democratic experiment within their own organizations declined. An examination of the students' political attitude and activity over a period of two decades will provide us with a richly textured sense of their associational life, and will also illuminate certain basic tensions within Chinese nationalism.

THE FOUNDING OF THE CHINESE STUDENTS' ALLIANCE

On an October day in 1902, twenty-three Chinese students gathered in a Congregational church in San Francisco to found the Chinese Students' Alliance of America.[19] The core members were people from the Beiyang School in Tianjin, the first group of government-sponsored students to come to America since the aborted Yung Wing mission twenty years earlier.[20] Interestingly, the same year also witnessed the founding of another overseas Chinese student organization: the *huiguan* (guild) in Japan, a rather traditional-sounding name. The students' association in Japan enjoyed sponsorship and financial aid from the Chinese legation in Tokyo.[21] There is no indication that the Chinese legation in the United States was behind the founding of the students' organization in America. The initial purpose of the organization was to instill patriotism in local, American-born Chinese youth, whose loyalty to China the students from the home country had found wanting.[22] A year later, in 1903, when Liang Qichao traveled on the west coast of the United States, he noted this organization, now boasting fifty members.[23]

Liang Qichao had good reasons to be interested in this voluntary organization, which conformed to his notion of *qun*, around which most of his sociopolitical thinking revolved at this time. America at the turn of the century was a place vibrant with all kinds of voluntary associations and clubs, and college campuses were enlivened by student governments and a variety of student societies.[24] These organizations usually had what Max Weber would describe as "a rational-legal authority," as opposed to the type of "traditional authority" characterized by a system of "statuses of persons" that the Chinese students were familiar with at home.[25] These voluntary organizations represented a significant aspect of what Jürgen Habermas has called a "civil society."[26]

Upon arriving in America, many Chinese students were intrigued by the existence of American student governments and societies. To C. Y. Chin, a student writing in 1913 in the *Chinese Students' Monthly*, these organizations helped "train men for moral independence, intellectual efficiency and physical capacities to take up the tasks awaiting them in the larger world." Certain qualities were especially valued by Chin, such as "the ability to organize, the method of self-government, the efficiency of expression—oratorical or journalistic, the ability to manage the various enterprises and physical endurance to cope with strenuous tasks." Above all, Chin maintained, the student governments and various student extracurricular events served as "the training camp of a hundred desirable traits of citizenship," through which the students would "get a broader scope of human activities, receive inspiration for unselfish exertion, develop a spirit for public work and be given a chance to show their real talent."[27]

Frequently when the American model was praised, the Chinese system was criticized. One student thus complained, "Something is lacking in the

Chinese home or school, or both. . . . We, most of us, are perhaps first graders in the school of cooperation and should have enough sense to admit it."[28] The American student voluntary organizations demonstrated to the Chinese the strength of Western approaches to associational life and served as models for the Chinese students' own group structures.

THE POLITICAL EXPERIMENT OF THE EASTERN ALLIANCE

Following the founding of the Alliance in San Francisco, organizations formed by Chinese students also appeared in Ithaca, Chicago, and Berkeley. Once several of the Beiyang students transferred to schools on the East Coast and a number of provincial educational missions arrived there, that area of the United States became the center for Chinese student associational life. In August 1905, a meeting of thirty-six students in Amherst, Massachusetts, marked the birth of the Chinese Students' Alliance of the Eastern States.

The Alliance of the Eastern States was organized under a constitution, in accordance with the customary practice of student governments in American universities and colleges. Written in 1905, the constitution was possibly one of the earliest legal documents drafted in the Western style by any Chinese. The objectives of the Eastern Alliance were threefold: to labor for the welfare of China, to keep Chinese students in America in close touch with each other, and to promote their common interest.[29] In contrast to the objectives of the West Coast group in its early days, the focus was now shifted from American-born Chinese youths to students from China.

In the fall of 1911, the various Chinese student organizations across America, including the Alliance of the Eastern States, were incorporated into one unified body: the Chinese Students' Alliance of the United States of America. This nationwide organization had regional sections in the East, the Midwest, and the West, each of which retained its own administrative structure and constitution. The next two decades witnessed the initial prosperity and eventual decline of the Alliance, and finally its dissolution in 1931.[30] Of the three geographically-based sections, the Eastern one, and its predecessor, the Alliance of the Eastern States, stood out as the most active and effective, and had the most complete records.[31] My study therefore focuses primarily on the Eastern Alliance.

The early years of the Eastern Alliance were filled with new ideas and inventions. In 1907, a unit was added to its governing body: the board of representatives. The creation of the new board was meant to curtail the power of the executives, to achieve a "better representation of the interests of the members as a whole," and to aim at "a more democratic government" for the organization.[32] At one point every five Alliance members were supposed to send one delegate to the representative board. The idea was obviously impractical, but the desire to maximize participation from the rank and file was tellingly demonstrated.

The board of representatives was entrusted with law-making power sufficient to override the resolutions of the board of executives: should a resolution presented by the board be disapproved by the chief executive officer, the resolution could be repassed and made into law by the representative board with a vote of a two-thirds majority. The notion of a strong representative board was fully endorsed by the executive officers. Wang Jingchun (Wang Ching-chun, or C. C. Wang), the president of the Eastern Alliance from 1907 to 1908, maintained that the function of the executive board was "purely and simply to carry out the constitution and the wish of the majority of the members."[33] His successor, Wang Zhengting (C. T. Wang), compared his office to "the switchboard of a telephone central station," whose function was merely to transmit the "voice" of the members back and forth.[34] The pages of the *Chinese Students' Monthly*, then the official organ of the Eastern Alliance, were filled with correspondence between officers of the two boards, displaying a serious attitude toward legal procedures as well as a transparent style in managing the business of the organization.

If the *Monthly* provided a public forum for the student community through printed words, it was the annual summer conferences that gave the "imagined community"[35] a sense of physical reality. The conferences usually took place in scenic college towns in New England, where, for a week or so, students from different schools gathered together. The format of the conference programs resembled that of the YMCA: business meetings in the mornings, sport events in the afternoons, parties and entertainment in the evenings. The annual meetings helped connect the students with one another, allowed them to share thoughts on issues of common concern, and gave them opportunities to show their artistic and athletic talents. They also boosted the morale of the student body, forged a communal feeling among the Chinese, and enabled people with leadership qualities to surface. For the local American residents, the gatherings provided a window into the life of the Chinese students. The conferences were often reported with interest in the local newspapers.[36]

A major feature of each conference was the "conference address." Invited speakers included Chinese government representatives to the United States, American educators, and occasionally American government officials.[37] The venerable Yung Wing, in retirement and residing in Hartford, Connecticut, appeared at the 1910 conference. In a "quivering voice," the old man gave his "advice and counsel."[38] Well-known American personalities in China, such as Edward Hume, director of the Yale-in-China program in Changsha, Hunan, also came to speak to the students. Many speakers expressed high expectations for the students. The conference addresses set the tone for the annual gatherings, giving the young men and women a sense of purpose and direction.

Until 1911, when students in China began to have summer camps,[39] there was no comparable activity in China; the Alliance summer conferences was therefore a uniquely "American" experience. From the beginning there were people who wished to emphasize the fun part of the conference, but a balance was maintained between the "seriousness" and entertainment in the early years. Many people left the summer gatherings reportedly feeling "spiritually uplifted, socially satisfied, and physically refreshed." One student remarked, "Can any one of us remember any other week in his or her whole life which has been better spent? Has there ever been any other week in which we could find this happiest and most charming combination of invaluable advice and fascinating entertainments?"[40] More important, as one *Monthly* editorial argued, the summer conferences offered a rare opportunity for the students to learn "practical democracy":

> No one can afford to leave America as an American-educated Chinese without having once been present at one of these conferences and shared with his compatriots under the influence of a practical democracy the experience of organization for self-government, and co-operation toward a common goal—

the welfare of China. Viewed from our [vantage] point, the Alliance is but a miniature republic, . . . in its structure and organization.[41]

Perhaps the best way to experience "practical democracy" was to participate in the elections of Alliance officers. According to the Eastern Alliance constitution, all officers were to be elected annually by direct vote. Gu Weijun (Wellington Koo), who served as the "conference historian" of the 1909 conference held on the campus of Colgate University, described vividly and at length how the aspiring candidates campaigned:

> Three days before the election, after the nominations were declared open, there were seen students hurrying around the town, stopping some fellow students on their way, perhaps to secure the permission to nominate them, or perhaps, to ask them to nominate themselves, for one position or another. As the election day was drawing nearer, and the nominations were closed, the atmosphere became rife with talks of the possibilities of the respective candidates, and the campus of Colgate University was dotted with groups of two and three, some of them with their soft hats tipped over on one side and lighted cigarettes between their fingers, engrossed in talking in a low voice, occasionally with a furtive look around, apparently to see if there was anybody overhearing their conversation. More likely than not, it was "political canvassing.[42]

On the election day, as it turned out, one hundred students packed the meeting hall, out of the one hundred and thirty-five attendants of that year's conference. The entire morning, reported Gu Weijun, was consumed in "electing."[43]

In November 1909, two months after the Eastern Alliance had elected its officers, eligible voters in China cast their first ballots in the election of provincial assemblies, an important first step in a nine-year plan toward establishing a full constitutional government. The constitutional reform, modeled after the Japanese-style parliamentary monarchy, composed a major aspect of the "new policies" (xinzheng) adopted by the Qing court in 1906 in an attempt to save the ailing Manchu regime. Was it a mere coincidence or was there some connection between the election held on the Colgate University campus and the elections held in the Chinese provincial capitals? To answer this question, it is necessary to first find out how well-informed the students were about the political situation at home.

Those who were interested in the political events in China were able to obtain up-to-date information. One important source was obviously the American press, which did provided coverage of major events in China. The *Monthly* also had a special column on home news, where significant events were reported promptly and analyzed carefully. Correspondence with relatives and friends in China furnished another channel, bringing to the students not only news but also a sense of the atmosphere and mood at home.[44]

What was happening in China at this time was truly historic. Although the elections of the provincial assemblies in 1909 involved only a small segment of the population, they marked an unprecedented new level of political participation from the nonofficial elements in the society.[45] The elected provincial assemblies enabled the locally rooted and nonofficial elite, some with modern and even overseas educational backgrounds,[46] to have a voice in local, provincial, and national politics. In the meeting halls of the provincial and national assemblies, these locally rooted elite advocated "self-government" and acted rather consciously as checks and balances on the executive powers both at the provincial and national levels.[47]

One central tension during this time was caused by "state-societal" conflict, to borrow a term used by Mary Rankin.[48] The presence of the new political actors not only enhanced the power of the "society," but also greatly augmented provincial autonomy. Yet, as "enlightened intellectuals," the new political elite did not simply advocate local interests, but sought to elevate national consciousness, promoting a kind of "nationalistic localism."[49] Soon their conflict with the Manchu central government, which had become increasingly autocratic and ethnically discriminatory against the Han Chinese, would reach a breaking point that would lead to the downfall of the Qing court.

Many students in America were encouraged by the constitutional reform at home. The *Monthly* followed its development closely and reported the activity of the constitutionalists with obvious approval. Praising the constitutional reform as one of the most significant achievements in China since 1902, Wang Jingchun, an important student leader at this time, remarked in 1910, "China during this short period of her real contact with Western civilization has done much more than Japan did under similar circumstances."[50]

In light of the constitutional reform in China, the political experiment of the Eastern Alliance should not be understood merely as an isolated incident or a pure imitation of the American political model. Rather, it should be viewed as an indirect participation on the part of the students in the political reality of China. The members' high regard for the Alliance constitution (which had undergone several revisions by 1912), their creation of the board of representatives in 1907 to restrain the power of the executive board, and their enthusiastic participation in Alliance elections, were all indications that the students were influenced and inspired by the developments of the constitutional movement in China.

For S. T. Lok, a woman student activist and a one-time vice president of the Eastern Alliance, the correlation with the constitutional reform at home was obvious. Urging people to join the Alliance, Lok confidently argued, "By joining the alliance we enter into the laboratory of self-government." In her view, the Alliance furnished "an ideal experiment . . . because it contains the fundamental principles that underlie all self-government of any form." Believing that "every student will be called upon to be the leader either in town self-government or in national constitutional government," Lok asked her fellow students "to seek every practical means to increase our knowledge and experience" in America so as to be ready for the political responsibility awaiting them in China.[51] The fact that this argument was made by a woman is particularly interesting, and it is worth pointing out that Lok was only one among a number of quite visible female student activists who maintained a high profile in the Alliance around this time.

The Eastern Alliance's identification with Chinese constitutional reform posed potential practical problems for the student organization. Whereas, in China, provincial representatives had good political reasons to distrust executive powers, the tension between the representative board and the executive board within the Eastern Alliance was artificially created. As a result, the checks and balances imposed onto the executive board often led to the delay of business, as each newly elected president found out when he tried to communicate with the huge and dispersed representative board. As we will see later, when constitutional reform disappeared in China after the fall of the Qing dynasty, the role of the Eastern Alliance's representative board also diminished and the power was once again concentrated in the hands of the executive office. This outcome, ironically, suggests that the democratic experiment of the Alliance before 1911 was shaped largely by the political agenda of the constitutional movement in China.

While the students generally identified with the constitutionalists in China, they tended to endorse a broader nationalism than did the provincially based reformers back at home. The convening of provincial assemblies in the fall of 1909 was used as evidence by the *Monthly* to dispute "foreign writers'" opinion that "each Chinese province is a small kingdom by itself." The provincial representatives, the journal emphasized, all had the "good of the whole country" in mind.[52] On another occasion, the *Monthly* cheered the emergence of "a new nationalism" while dismissing "localism, sectionalism and provincialism" as ideas of the past.[53] Meanwhile, the Alliance consciously fostered the "new nationalism" in their own organization. One purpose of the Alliance, in the opinion of a veteran member, was to bring "the many Chinese students who have come to the U.S. from different provinces, separated by great distances and diverse dialects and religions," into one unity, so that "they may become acquainted and recognize each other as brothers."[54]

New and modern ways to identify people were adopted as the students made the shift toward seeing themselves as Chinese nationals. Traditionally, Chinese literati had identified themselves primarily with their place of local origin (*jiguan*), which had served as a principal link among Chinese gentry-scholars.[55] In the registers of the Alliance, however, *jiguan* was conspicuously absent. Instead, university affiliation became a primary marker by which the students in America were categorized. The summer conference program committee encouraged the student participants to "wear their university colors, carry the university banners." School teams competed with each other in various conference activities. In group photographic portraits, which were taken as an important bonding ritual at the summer gatherings, the students were seen clustering around highly visible college banners. The emphasis on university affiliation clearly showed the influence of American college culture on the Chinese students. To further downplay regional differences, English was used as the "official" spoken language at the summer conferences. It was a noteworthy decision made by the Eastern Alliance, since in this manner the complex problem of Chinese dialects was avoided, regional uniqueness was minimized, and a sense of shared identity was forged. The irony was that a Western language had to be used to achieve this arguably nationalistic goal.

By comparison, for Chinese students in Japan before 1911, local origin was still a primary identification category.[56] The majority of the students in Japan stayed in Tokyo, where many of them lived in Chinese "ghettos,"[57] a circumstance that made it easier for people from the same province to band together. Since the students in America were scattered across a vast country it was much more difficult to find a fellow student from the same Chinese region. The situational difference between Japan and America notwithstanding, it is still significant that the students in America made deliberate efforts and took concrete measures to encourage a "new nationalism." The political rhetoric of the Chinese students in America might not have been as radical as that of their counterparts in Japan, but by consciously downplaying provincial distinctions, they departed markedly from the traditional Chinese mold of grouping, and deliberately forged a different sense of themselves. Saliently, they embodied the emerging Chinese national identity.

NEW BEHAVIORAL IDEALS

If the students' desire for self-government and democratic participation had its roots in China, America provided the script of democratic practices and furnished a stage upon which the students could rehearse their political act. Moreover, America also inspired a new set of behavioral ideals for individual Chinese. College campuses became convenient and suitable places where the students could observe and practice these ideals.

In the early twentieth century, student extracurricular activities became increasingly important on American college campuses.[58] Those who came to college only in pursuit of knowledge were often regarded as "grinds" and treated as outsiders, while an increasing number of others believed that "classes and books existed as the prices one has to pay for college life."[59] Perceiving college social life as a field of preparation for success in the competitive larger society, many American students threw their energy and enthusiasm into extracurricular activities, which existed as a world of the students' own creation. Against this backdrop, American educators and commentators of the time debated among themselves about the value of students' extracurricular activities.[60] Many Chinese students, despite coming from a tradition that equated learning with "classes and books," appreciated extracurricular activities, particularly their value in nurturing a "public spirit." The issue of public spirit had concerned Liang Qichao deeply at the turn of the century, who asserted that what China badly needed was "pub-lic morality" (*gongde*), as opposed to the traditionally overemphasized "pri-vate morality" (*side*). In order for China to survive in the modern world, Liang argued, it was essential for individual Chinese to participate voluntar-ily and actively in public life.[61] This new, assertive and public-oriented out-look contained the essence of Liang Qichao's ideas on "modern citizenry" and was an integral part of his concept of *qun*.[62] In espousing public moral-ity, Liang was in effect calling for a new set of behavioral ideals for the Chinese people.

Individuals aspiring to realize the new ideals began to emerge among the Chinese students in America. Gu Weijun and Hu Shi, in particular, exemplified the successful cultivation of the new behavioral traits. Both men would go on to become very influential figures in China, Gu as one of the most accomplished diplomats in the republican period, and Hu as a a cul-tural and political critic, and an important educator, first in the May Fourth New Culture Movement, then in the Nationalist period.

Gu Weijun was a founder of the Eastern Alliance. Making use of his aca-demic training in law, he exerted considerable influence on the shape of the organization's constitution, responsible both for its original drafting and sub-sequent revisions. Meanwhile, Gu also served in other capacities in the Eastern Alliance, including once as its president. If there were any "core" members in the early days of the organization, Gu was certainly one of them.

Gu also let himself be fully absorbed into the lively campus life of Columbia University, where he studied from 1906 to 1912, first as an under-graduate and then as a graduate student. He was on several sports teams, including being the coxswain on the rowing team, where he learned to swear in English; was a member of the Dramatic Society and performed a number of times on stage; and represented Columbia once in a debate with Cornell (his presence inducing the other side to include a woman student in order to "offset the novelty of a Chinese"[63]). He also made the editors' board of the most prestigious student journal at Columbia, the *Spectator*, first as an asso-ciate editor and finally, in his senior year, as editor-in-chief.

One of his most exciting experiences at Columbia took place in his junior year, when he ran for the Student Board of Representatives. Originally, Gu was not in the race, but after being approached by a number of candidates, Gu "began to see how things were done" and decided to run himself. Thereafter when other people came to solicit his vote, he would agree to it only if they agreed to give him theirs. With the help of his classmates, he was elected to the nine-member representative board of the university, much to his surprise and delight. It's worth noting that Gu believed that his victory was largely due to the fact that he was Chinese. At a time when there was a great deal of tension between Jewish and non-Jewish students at Columbia, Gu found himself in an advantageous position as an outsider to attract votes from both sides.[64]

Experiences like this taught Gu how American-style democracy worked at the local level. Gu was also interested in American national politics. He took a course on American government in 1908, a national presidential election year. One memorable event in this class was a mock presidential convention. The class was divided into a number of delegations, each of which had to nominate candidates for the president and vice president of the United States. Gu's nominating speech for his candidate, Joseph Cannon, then the Speaker of the House, received "vociferous and prolonged applause" from his classmates.[65]

Before coming to Columbia, Gu had thought that he would study to become an engineer, a popular career choice among Chinese students in America. Gu's experience at Columbia, both in and out of the classroom, opened up new horizons for him and eventually changed the course of his life. His acceptance as President Yuan Shikai's English secretary in 1912, before he completed his doctoral program in law at Columbia University, marked the beginning of his life-long career in public service.[66]

Like Gu Weijun, Hu Shi was immediately attracted to student activities upon his arrival in the United States in 1910; he served on the editorial boards of the *Monthly* as well as the *Chinese Students' Quarterly*. His articles frequently appeared in both, some triggering controversies.[67] Like Gu, Hu Shi did not confine himself to the Chinese student circle. At Cornell University as an undergraduate, Hu became interested in the Cosmopolitan movement, a youth movement advocating internationalist idealism that had spread to many American universities at this time.[68] From 1913 to 1914, Hu Shi was the president of the Cornell Cosmopolitan Club. His first experience of chairing the club meeting was a memorable event, which, in Hu's opinion, taught him more about practical democracy than months of book learning could have.[69] Reminiscing more than forty years later about his student life in America, Hu considered his experience in conducting those meetings to be his most valuable lesson in Western democratic practices.[70]

As the president of the Cornell Cosmopolitan Club, Hu Shi had ample opportunities for making speeches, an activity that he enjoyed tremendously. In a three-year period as a student at Cornell, Hu Shi gave more than seventy speeches across the East Coast, to church groups, social clubs, and women's organizations. His topics ranged from Chinese customs to cosmopolitanism and English poetry. Hu Shi and some students at Cornell also founded a society to practice oration in Chinese, anticipating that once back in China they would be in demand as public speakers.

Like Gu Weijun, Hu Shi was intensely interested in American national politics. During the presidential election of 1912, Hu got his fellow Cosmopolitan Club members to play an "election game." Everyone, regardless of nationality, was to select a candidate for the president of the United States. Hu himself chose to support Theodore Roosevelt and wore a Bull Moose button throughout the campaign. Four years later, Hu turned into a passionate Woodrow Wilson supporter. On the night when the outcome of the election was announced, Hu and some other Chinese students at Columbia University (Hu had come to study there as a graduate student in 1915) walked from the Columbia campus to Times Square to wait for the results. During his visit to Washington, D.C., he went to Capitol Hill to hear congressional debates.

American politics at the local level was equally fascinating to Hu. With American friends, Hu Shi went a number of times to observe the meetings of the Ithaca Common Council. Afterward he would carefully record both the procedures and the resolutions passed at the meetings. He was particularly impressed by the fact that the city council was composed of ordinary people, and that the previous mayor of the city was a laundryman by occupation.

Aware that few Chinese students were as involved in American society as he was, Hu Shi reflected in writing upon his own actions, justifying them on the grounds that China needed people with public spirit:

> Wherever I live I consider the local politics and the social causes as if they were concerns of my home town. . . . This kind of experience will help form in us a habit of concern for public affairs. If we don't care about the local causes here and now, how can we be ardent advocates for the interest of our home country when we return to China?[71]

Hu Shi paid special attention to intellectuals' roles in American politics. During the 1912 presidential election, for example, Hu was impressed by the serious attitude of two Cornell professors when they debated important issues of that year's campaign, and when the results of the election came out, Hu Shi was deeply touched by his professors' jubilation. In New York, Hu Shi observed a public rally for women's suffrage and was surprised to find that his teacher John Dewey was in the crowd. He described American intellectuals' attitude toward politics as "disinterested interest," meaning that the intellectuals' interest in politics showed a public spiritedness rather than a personal interest. He claimed later that his own attitude toward Chinese politics was very much influenced by these Americans.[72]

Not every Chinese student shared Hu Shi's high regard for American-style politics or his admiration for American intellectuals' political role. Mei Guangdi (K. T. May), a student at Harvard and a personal friend of Hu Shi, express his critical opinion in the *Monthly*. Mei was disturbed both by American politicians who knew "how to work a crowd" and by the "aloofness" of American intellectuals toward politics.[73] But Mei also saw merit in American democracy, and he gave the credit mostly to "brave-hearted and public-spirited citizens."[74] Believing that "a democracy must necessarily depend upon active and enlightened citizenship," and yet failing to find models in the American intellectual community, Mei proposed Confucius and Zeng Guofan (the latter a ranking Qing official and a leader of the Self-Strengthening Movement in the 1860s and 1870s) as "our best exemplar[s] of citizenship."[75] Mei Guangdi was in effect challenging Liang Qichao's assertion that Chinese tradition had failed to produce people with "public morality."[76] In the 1920s, after they returned to China, Mei Guangdi and a group of like-minded people, including the American-returned students Chen Yinke, Wu Mi, and Tang Yongtong, would continue to advocate positive aspects in Chinese Confucian tradition, directly challenging the radicalism of the May Fourth New Culture Movement.[77]

A large number of people were needed to make the Alliance and other student associations function properly. Public spirit, familiarity with legal and formal procedures, and the ability to conduct public affairs (including oratory) were not rare qualities among the Chinese students in America. What made Gu and Hu stand out among their fellow students was their intense involvement in both Chinese students' activities and American life. Not many Chinese students, as C. Y. Chin correctly pointed out, ventured outside the Chinese circles.[78] Racial discrimination was a major obstacle to the Chinese students' entrance into American life,[79] a factor that will be explored at length in Chapter 3. Both Gu and Hu faced the problem of racism, yet they managed to deal with it: Gu Weijun by turning his Chinese identity into an advantage during his campaign for the Columbia student board, and Hu Shi by countering racial division with internationalism.

EMBRACING "CENTRALIZED NATIONALISM"

The transition from the Qing dynasty to the republican period was a crucial historical moment for Chinese nationalism. The contention between the competing ideas of self-government and administrative centralization tested the principles of this emerging ideology. Among some leading intellectuals, notably Liang Qichao, there was a marked shift from earlier advocacy of self-government, in late Qing, to arguments for strong centralization, in the early republic.[80] As noted earlier in this chapter, the political attitudes of Chinese students in America largely paralleled changes in the home country; an examination of this relationship will not only cast light on the making of Chinese nationalism, but also will lay bare the implications of democracy to the Chinese at a critical historical juncture.

News of the anti-Manchu Wuchang Uprising in the fall of 1911 caught many students in America by surprise, as Gu Weijun admitted.[81] Earlier, when the debate between the revolutionaries and the constitutionalists was heatedly conducted elsewhere, the Alliance deliberately avoided engaging in the controversy. Support for Sun Yat-sen and his Revolutionary League was both limited and subdued among the students, even though Sun personally approached some of them.[82] In contrast with the frequent coverage of the constitutional movement in the *Monthly*, Sun Yat-sen and his revolutionary colleagues were hardly mentioned in the student journal.[83]

The students in America generally identified with the reform-oriented constitutional movement in China, shunning the revolutionary rhetoric that appealed to many of their peers in Japan.[84] Several factors were at work here leading the students to lean toward the reformists. The comparatively conservative political culture of intellectuals in America did not favor the rise of radicalism, and the missionary educational background, which marked a large number of Chinese students in America, was not in tune with radical politics. The fact that many students depended on large amounts of governmental financial aid also explained why they favored a politically more stable China.

As the situation at home became increasingly confrontational throughout 1911, the students' political attitudes appeared to resemble those of the gentry constitutionalists in China, who persisted on a reformist path until finally, in the fall of 1911, they accepted revolution as inevitable.[85] In his discussion of the Wuchang Uprising, published in the *Monthly*, Zhu Tingqi (T. C. Chu, a one-time president of the Eastern Alliance) did not see the event as a victory of the anti-Manchu revolutionaries, but as a result of conflicts between the central and provincial interests that failed to be resolved.[86] Zhu acted at this time as the *Monthly*'s chief analyst of political development in China and his opinion presumably had a following in the student community.

A few months after the Wuchang Uprising, some student leaders, notably Gu Weijun and Zhu Tingqi, founded the *Aiguo hui* (the Chinese Patriotic Union), an ambitious organization designed for "all the intelligent and patriotic people" in China. The founders described their political attitude as "conservative, [and] cool-headed" and described themselves as "non-political, non-interfering, non-revolutionary, non-partisan and non-sectarian." Meanwhile, the organization promoted "the educational, social, and economical [*sic*] interests of our people both at home and abroad."[87] Perhaps not accidentally, the *Monthly* published a series of articles on economic development in China around this time. Little was heard of the *Aiguo hui* thereafter, but its "non-revolutionary" and technical approach to solving China's problems is a noteworthy foreshadowing of the students' subsequent political posture.

By early 1912, it was clear to many students that "a republic was inevitable."[88] The February 1912 *Monthly* editorial stated that "a month ago we might have considered some other form of government, but now the fire of Republicanism is ablaze; the only way to save the situation is to direct but not to quench it."[89] Zhu Tingqi now saw the republican political organization as a "better system," since it would rescue the Chinese people from the likelihood of having "a baby emperor, a foolish emperor, and a wicked emperor."[90] A letter was sent in February 1913 from the secretary of the

Alliance headquarters to President Taft to urge the United States to recognize the Chinese republic.[91]

The students' support for a republican form of government was accompanied, significantly, by their endorsement of "a strong, central government." A March 1912 *Monthly* editorial marked the beginning of the journal's persistent call for strong centralization:

> The only way to safe-guard against these treacherous rocks that might wreck the ship, known as "the oldest empire and the youngest republic," is to establish with all speed a strong central government. . . . A republic to be successful in China must have a strong federal government. . . . A republic based upon the idea of state rights as an experiment would prove disastrous. Reality and not idealism is the sure basis of a modern state.[92]

As noted earlier, the tendency to deemphasize regionalism had already existed among the students in late Qing. When they promoted the "new nationalism" before the fall of Qing, however, the idea was not to sanction a strong centralized Manchu state, but rather to modulate it with checks and balances. This sentiment was expressed by a *Monthly* editorial in early 1911, when, upon reporting the convening of the National Assembly, the author made it clear that he hoped the legislative body would bring "great pressure to bear on the central government at Peking."[93]

The view that the central power should be restrained disappeared with the founding of the republic. Yoeh Liang Tong, a student at Yale University, gave a speech at the 1913 summer conference of the Eastern Alliance that represented the shift of positions. He criticized the newly formed National Party, and strongly opposed "party government" on the grounds that the new republic was not ready to cope with party politics:

> We can not have party government until the feeble and chaotic forces of our country can be consolidated on some other basis than the ambitions of faction. . . . Until China has passed through her present critical period of transition, the introduction of party government will do us more harm than good, result in discord rather than unity among our people.[94]

Several months before Tong's speech, it is worth noting, Song Jiaoren, the Nationalist Party leader, was assassinated, possibly by Yuan Shikai's people. Tong did not say anything about this brutal event. Besides party politics,

Tong also regarded labor unions and the women's suffrage movement in China as signs of "overprogressiveness," warning that a "sudden and abrupt departure from the beaten track of the past, . . . is fraught with serious dangers." By the same token, Tong was also critical of the press, charging it with showing an "undue emphasis on rights and the lack of an adequate sense of duty." "The prime need of China" at this transitional moment, Tong maintained, was "not dissension, but a real sinking of differences, a steadfast cohesion and union."[95] Tong's speech won the first prize of the conference's oration competition.

Why did students look at the central government differently, now that the Manchu dynasty had fallen and a republic was in its place? Why were they no longer interested in those practices that would restrain the power of the center and enable broader participation from the society? In a recent study, Prasenjit Duara examines the conflicts between the "centralists" and the "federalists" in the early decades of the twentieth century, linking the "federalist" cause to democratic reform and a potential grounding of a "civil society" in China.[96] A major argument used by contemporaries to boost the federalist movement was the American model.[97] Why did the Chinese students, living in the United States, doggedly urge centralism rather than "federalism" for the newborn republic?

The students' position reflected a fundamental change of attitude toward the power of the state at a critical historical juncture when the prospect of China's nation-state building suddenly became both hopeful and perilous. To many of them, the founding of the republic opened up great hope for China and at the same time exposed her to serious danger from foreign powers. Articles in the *Monthly* around this time constantly alarmed the students about the territorial ambitions of Japan, Russia, and England in Manchuria, Mongolia, and Tibet, respectively, all of which were viewed as endangering the integrity of China's territory and threatening the sovereignty of the new nation. Anti-imperialistic sentiment, already existing among the students in the late Qing, underlay the argument in the early republic for strong centralization in China.

The domestic situation did not look encouraging either, the financial incapacity of the central government being the most disturbing of the problems. An editorial of the *Monthly* regarded the restoration of China's financial credit as "the supreme task," expressing concern for the central government's difficulty of collecting sufficient taxes from the provinces.[98] The continuous "antagonism" between the provinces and the central government was viewed as another potential threat to the survival of the new republic.

With the founding of the republic, a vitally important question arose: how should China be ruled? Just as the Japanese during the Meiji period reinvented the institution of emperorship in their creation of a modern nation state, the Chinese needed something to embody a new nation. To many students in America, only a strong, centralized government was able to safeguard the feeble new nation. True, this "state-centered" attitude had a long history in China's imperial tradition, as some scholars rightly point out.[99] But the endorsement of centralization in the early days of the republic occurred in a rather different geopolitical context from China's imperial past, with the Western powers now being a factor the Chinese had to reckon with.

A sense of hope persisted despite the predicament. The founding of the republic gave a new birth to an ancient country, now celebrated as a "baby" republic and a "young" nation. The anxiety felt by some students about the perceived delay of recognition of the Chinese republic by the American government indicates that the students saw the founding of the republic as a singular event,[100] perhaps the defining moment that had marked China's entrance into the community of modern nation-states. As such, China needed acceptance from other countries, a need that had not been a factor in the country's imperial past.

Trying to persuade the American public to support the Chinese republic, the students often invoked the example of the American Revolution. Along with the United States, France was another country that was often applauded as a source of inspiration.[101] Most of the references to the Western experiences in the students' publications were brief and vague, but occasionally, the discussion of a Western model would become more specific. A case in point is a *Monthly* editorial on Alexander Hamilton. Consistent with the emphasis on centralization, the writer highly praised the American federalist, quoting his statement that "energy in the Executive is a leading character in the definition of good government." Calling Hamilton a "genius" and "our favorite author," the editorial recommended "everything from that man" to its readers as the "most profitable reading."[102] In the context of a rising "centralized nationalism" in the early republic, it was not an accident that the *Monthly* editorial favored Hamilton's centralism rather than James Madison's checks and balances and Thomas Jefferson's individual liberty and freedom. Not all the American founding fathers were treated equally by the Chinese.

The espousal of "centralized nationalism" by the students was consistent with a similar move by some prominent individuals of diverse political backgrounds in China at this time, such as Liang Qichao, Zhang Taiyan, Cai E, and Li Dazhao.[103] Liang Qichao had been an ardent promoter of the constitutional movement in the late Qing and the founder of a protopolitical party (*Zhengwen she*) that advocated judicial independence and the establishment of local self-government. After the republic was founded, however, Liang turned to support a centralized polity and opposed the federation of relatively independent provinces, which was favored by the Nationalist Party.[104] He was eventually drawn into government service as a cabinet member under Yuan Shikai's presidency, with the hope of helping implement an effective central power.[105]

In the early days of the republic, Yuan Shikai was regarded by many students as a person more capable of bringing about a strong and unified China than Sun Yat-sen,[106] and more likely to give the country a stable government. A January 1912 *Monthly* editorial held that it was safe to entrust the "constructive work" to Yuan Shikai of "unify[ing] the nation into one homogeneous whole."[107]

To be sure, not everybody supported Yuan Shikai. A group of students at Cornell University wrote a letter to the *Monthly* to voice their distrust of Yuan Shikai, on the grounds that Yuan had been "a traitor," an allusion to Yuan's betrayal of Emperor Guangxu during the One Hundred Days Reform in 1898.[108] In the same letter, they also questioned the pro-Yuan stand of the *Monthly*. Holding to their position, the *Monthly* editors replied, "Indeed, Yuan does not have a clean record in his political life, . . . but . . . the first thing to remember is [that] according [sic] to his own declaration aiming 'to save the nation from dissolution.'"[109]

The students' belief in the need for a strong central government led them largely to tolerate Yuan Shikai's autocratic style. Until the beginning of 1916 when rumors abounded that Yuan was heading towards a monarchical revival, the students seldom criticized Yuan's antidemocratic measures. The news of a revived monarchy was received by the students with disbelief and outrage. A petition was sent to China by the Alliance headquarters to protest against the scheme. Some students directed a great deal of their resentment against Frank J. Goodnow, Yuan Shikai's American adviser and a supporter of the monarchical plan.[110] The news of the sudden death of Yuan Shikai from a heart attack in June 1916 came as great relief to many students.

FROM IMAGINED PARTICIPANTS TO DISHEARTENED SPECTATORS

The failure of monarchical restoration in 1916 did not usher in an era of "constitutional efficiency, [and a] real government by the people," as some students had hoped.[111] Instead, China entered an age of division, chaos, and warlordism. Repeatedly the students made a request that by now sounded very familiar: for the sake of the nation, stop the internal feud. China's perilous international condition made it too risky to have a divided and weak Chinese government. Yet the situation in China continued to deteriorate and the students soon realized that there was little they could do. Meanwhile the Alliance itself was losing much of its political drive and organizational vitality. The democratic experiment of the Alliance now became largely an empty gesture. The election of the Eastern Alliance in 1920, for instance, attracted little interest from participants and took place only as a mere formality, in sharp contrast to the enthusiastic election of 1909. The apathy toward Alliance affairs in the student community was acknowledged in 1917 by Song Ziwen (T. V. Soong), then the president of the Alliance, who admitted, "The general prospect of the Alliance is not exactly favorable."[112] With approximately six hundred students on the membership register of the Alliance at this time (out of a total of twelve hundred Chinese students in America), only a little over two hundred paid their dues. The members' lack of commitment made it difficult for both the *Monthly* and the *Quarterly* to cover their expenses.

As the 1920s unfolded, the decline of the Alliance accelerated. Two comparable events, one at the 1909 summer conference, the other in 1924, tellingly demonstrate the extent of weakening morale within the student body. In 1909, the Eastern Alliance sponsored a competition for a "best student" award, the criteria for which were as follows: (1) scholarship; (2) active interest in Alliance work; (3) prominence in college life; (4) moral character;

(5) general popularity. The award eventually went to both Wang Jingchun and S. T. Lok.[113] A decade and a half later, at the 1924 summer conference, a different kind of competition was held. People were asked to choose "the most popular boy, the most popular girl, the most handsome boy, the most beautiful girl, the most girlish boy, the most boyish girl, the most talkative boy, the most reserved girl, the best dressed boy, the best dressed girl," and so on.[114] In the same year, at the summer conference held in the Midwest, only twelve people showed up at an invited speaker's talk on "the regeneration of China," while most of the other conference participants went to the "social gatherings and dances."[115]

Still, when the political situation in China became especially compelling, the Alliance was able to mobilize the students to some extent. In May 1919, the same month that the May Fourth movement broke out in China, the Alliance headquarters sent a cablegram to the Versailles Peace Conference protesting against its unjust decision regarding China's territory in Shandong, which was to be given to the Japanese instead of being returned to the Chinese following the German occupation.[116] Later, some student representatives went to Washington, D.C., to voice their discontent. During the Washington Conference in 1921, the Alliance created six committees to work on the Shandong question and asked the Chinese government to allow the student organization to participate in the conference. Eventually five student representatives joined the Chinese delegation and "contributed significantly" to the conference.[117]

The 1925 May Thirtieth Incident in Shanghai, which resulted in the deaths of thirteen Chinese demonstrators and the wounding of many more at the hands of the British, aroused angry reaction from the student community in America and stirred another wave of political activism in the Alliance. That year's summer conferences in all three sections were filled with anti-imperialist rhetoric. Even entertainment bore a political message: a play depicting the May Thirtiethth Incident, called "Nation's Wound," was put on at the Eastern Alliance's conference.[118] Significantly, Chinese was used for the first time as the conference's official language.[119]

The political enthusiasm turned out to be short-lived, however. At the 1926 summer gathering of the Eastern Alliance, except for a handful of people who "either had to or did not know any better," almost everybody else shunned nonsocial events. With sarcasm, one student suggested that in the future all conference addresses and discussions should be dispensed with, so as not to embarrass guest speakers. "The phenomenon was lamentable, I admit," he wrote, "But what could you do? Reconstruction of China. A program of organized cooperation. What the devil did these delegates care? They went there for a good time, and paid good cash for it too."[120]

Not everyone had a good time at the 1926 conference. At least some participants were embarrassed by a play called "The Bunk of 1926," which showed two men going out for a social event, one dressed and acting like a woman. The two actors went through "a series of [scenes of] petting and spooning" on the stage, and the audience waited "painfully for the worst to come."[121] Later, the episode was described as "intellectually stupefied and morally depraved."[122]

Reflecting upon the "bad taste" of the 1926 conference, one student wrote, "The Chinese students in this country, with few exceptions, are too light-hearted and light-minded to appreciate these things [serious subjects] anyhow." Instead of the "reconstruction of China," said the writer, "what was sorely needed was the reconstruction of their [certain students'] own mind, their own character, and their own soul."[123] The situation prompted some Alliance members to pass a resolution asking the Chinese educational directors in Washington to exert stricter guidance over the students, especially over the ones with government scholarships. The confidence in "self-government," so ardently expressed in the early years of the Alliance, was now being replaced, ironically, by a request for supervision from the authorities.

This negative self-assessment contrasted sharply with the earlier sense of pride and high self-esteem, which reached its peak right after the republican revolution, when a number of American-returned students received important appointments in the new republic.[124] By the second half of the 1910s, however, it was already clear that American-returned students were regarded more as a problem rather than a solution, both by the general public in China and by the students themselves. Gu Weijun, now the Chinese minister to the United States, discussed the "problems and difficulties of a returned student" at the Eastern Alliance's summer conference in 1917.[125] The unsatisfactory performances of returned students was a recurrent topic for the *Monthly*.

The decline of prestige of the American-educated students resulted partially from the negligence of the warlord government, which generally adopted a laissez-faire policy toward foreign education. It was not unusual for government students not to receive their stipends in the mail. The constant disruption of financial aid not only caused hardship to the people directly affected, but also harmed the morale of the student body as a whole. To some extent, also, the political apathy of the students in the 1920s merely reflected the general atmosphere of campus life in post–World War I America, a period when American college students, men and women alike, experimented with pleasure-seeking, "modern" lifestyles, and were generally inactive or even conservative politically,[126] in contrast with the activism of the Progressive era. The influence of the "modern school" of American life on the Chinese students was noted by a long-time participant of the Alliance conferences, who observed that "joy-riding, jazz dancing, and petting parties" in American society were regarded by some Chinese as "symbols of the new freedom, . . . inevitable to the new order which is sought for China."[127]

More crucial for the decline of morale among the students was the disappearance of a vibrant and cohesive political reform movement in the home country. Without it, the students' own political experiment in a foreign country lost much of its meaning and drive. Within a decade, the students had turned from imagined participants in China's political reform (in the late Qing) to disheartened spectators of warlord politics. Meanwhile, the students' attitude toward democracy also underwent a notable transformation. The initial enthusiasm for democratic forms and practices around 1910 was replaced by a loss of interest in democratic experiment and an endorsement of a strong centralized government after the founding of the republic.

In his study of the thinking of Liang Qichao, Hao Chang maintains that democracy for Liang was primarily a collectivistic and utilitarian tool, used to serve the interest of the Chinese nation-state in a world complying with Darwinian rules and dominated by economically superior Western countries.[128] This analysis can also be applied to the students in America, whose previous advocacy of democratic practices had not meant a commitment to democratic ideals, but rather had implied a distrust toward the Manchu government.

Here lies the fundamental dilemma of Chinese nationalism, which was conceived in the era of modern imperialism by a people with rich statist heritage. The overwhelming concern in the early republic was the building of a modern Chinese nation-state, in an environment perceived as perilous within and without. Centralization was viewed by many, including many Chinese students in America, as the only plausible way to hold the feeble new nation together; democratic ideals, tried during the late Qing constitutional movement, were now shelved. The students' overseas experience further intensified their nationalism along Liang Qichao's anti-imperialist lines. Yet the making of modern China involved not only the building of a modern nation-state, but also the creation of a modern "society."[129] The justification for centralization resulted in a tolerance of Yuan Shikai's antidemocratic measures, which included restriction on political participation by the people and persecution of political oppositions. In the end, the space for independent political activity was substantially reduced, which hindered the growth of a modern "society." The students by and large went along with Yuan Shikai's antidemocratic policies in China. Ironically, this was soon translated into their own political marginalization. Their transition from imagined participants in the constitutional movement of the late Qing to disheartened spectators of republican politics testifies to the shrinking of legitimate political activism in the later period, and a changing relationship of intellectuals with the state.

Yü Yingshih has discussed the process of the Chinese intellectuals' political marginalization in twentieth-century China.[130] As Yü sees it, the intellectuals were pushed passively to the periphery, while the "lower elements" in the society, whose number greatly swelled as a result of social disintegration, ascended and occupied the central stage with the help of party ideologies and tight organization.[131] While Yü's evaluation of the politics, society, and culture of twentieth-century China goes well beyond the scope of this chapter, his argument on the position of intellectuals is relevant: if political marginalization of Chinese intellectuals indeed occurred—as it seems to be the case, especially for the upper spectrum of the educated elite—is Yü right that the intellectuals were only passive victims of this process? The story of the Alliance suggests that the students played a part in their own political marginalization.

OTHER FORMS OF ASSOCIATIONAL LIFE

The decline of the Alliance did not necessarily mean the decline of associational life. As the number of students on each university campus grew, a great deal of activity was conducted at the local level; wherever there was a sufficient number of Chinese students, there was a local club. Like the three sections of the Alliance, many of the local clubs had their own constitutions and conducted their own annual elections, and some local clubs even had their own rented houses as regular meeting places.[132] For many students, local clubs represented the idea of self-government and were also the center of their social life. The clubs helped the students develop an identification with their schools and provided a link between the students and the larger communities. The condition of the local clubs depended on the people involved, and they were not much affected by either the prosperity or the decline of the Alliance. Local-club activities were reported regularly in the *Monthly,* yet local clubs never became subunits of the Alliance. In the long run, it seems, it was the "simple and practical" cooperation of the local clubs that maintained their vitality and made them an important resource for the Chinese students.

Besides the Alliance and the local clubs, there were four other kinds of associations: professional, religious, alumni, and fraternal. Professional associations will be discussed in detail in Chapter 2. In the following pages of this chapter we will look briefly at selected examples of the other three types, which reveal the changing dynamics within the student community, especially in the 1920s when the importance of the Alliance was diminishing.

The only student organization large enough to rival the Alliance was the Chinese Students' Christian Association in North America (CSCA). Formed in the summer of 1908 by six people, CSCA had grown into an organization with six hundred members by 1917. As a Christian organization, the CSCA claimed to uphold high moral ideals. An editorial in *Liu Mei Tsing Nien,* the official organ of the CSCA,[133] stated: "In this land of freedom and liberty, of progress and life, we, as students, should devote at least some of our time to the study of ethical principles, moral forces, and high ideals that are at work in achieving, maintaining, and in preserving the results of American progress."[134] In addition to regular Bible classes and other religious meetings, the CSCA stressed the importance of social service, including service to local Chinese communities, and assistance to new and returning students. Some of the work was conducted cooperatively with the Alliance, whereas other work, such as helping the Chinese laborers in France, was done with financial support from the International Committee of the YMCA of North

America. The Alliance and the CSCA maintained a friendly if distant relationship, and it was not uncommon for a student to join both organizations. It is hard to tell, however, the proportion of Christians among the students, since the CSCA did not require its members to be Christian converts.

The rise of a number of small, more tightly knit, ideologically more clearly defined, and largely exclusive or even secretive societies in the 1920s began to draw people's attention. Their prominence in this decade indicates that the "serious-minded" students were searching for alternative ways of socializing. *Cheng-chih hui* (CCH, the Association for Accomplishing Ideals), a secret fraternity, and *Dajiang hui* (the Big River Society), an alumni association made up mostly of Qinghua College graduates, are two cases in point. Although differing markedly in a number of ways, both societies attracted politically earnest people and both were intensely nationalistic.

Greek-lettered fraternities had existed on American college campuses since the early nineteenth century and were flourishing in the 1920s as an integral part of the zestful youth culture of that decade.[135] Against this backdrop, CCH came into existence in 1920 as an amalgamation of two earlier Chinese fraternities with Christian leaning: David and Jonathan, or D&J, and Cross and Sword, or "Cands,"[136] founded in 1907 and 1917 respectively. Both fraternities shared the motto "we unite for the uplift of China," and both were aimed at attracting people with "high qualities." In 1920, the two fraternities merged, and the new organization adapted the name the Association for Accomplishing Ideals, or CCH. In the following years, CCH became the leading fraternity among Chinese students, establishing local chapters in major cities in both America and China. As in American fraternities, members of CCH were expected to help each other in their studies and careers. Unlike many American fraternities that were primarily social, CCH had a clear ideological orientation: Chinese nationalism.[137]

By 1936, CCH had 270 members, most of whom were back in China. Members developed networks among themselves and helped further each other's careers, sometimes resulting in important political appointments.[138] Many CCH members held preeminent positions in republican China, in the areas of politics, education, banking, diplomacy, business, engineering, and Christian church organizations.[139] CCH held an interesting place in modern Chinese history that has not been fully understood and recognized, partly because the fraternity remained secretive throughout its history and few members have candidly recorded their experiences.[140] A careful study of CCH will shed light on an elusive aspect of the social and political life in the republican period.

While some people approved of fraternities among Chinese students because of their nationalistic focus,[141] others were critical of their divisive nature. Pan Guangdan, a student at Columbia, for instance, argued that students' attraction to fraternities reflected a lack of cooperative spirit among the Chinese students and an inability to work together as equals. By joining a hierarchically ordered fraternity, Pan contended, people became "big brothers" and "younger brothers" on the basis of age, thus avoiding competition based on ability and talent. Worst of all, Pan emphasized, was the estrangement created within the individuals themselves. By hiding behind the aegis of a fraternity, the average member escaped the responsibilities of true cooperation. Pan called on his fellow students to reject fraternities and to work together, not as "autistic and make-believe brothers," but as "able-bodied and intelligent social individuals."[142]

Pan Guangdan was likely to have had another model of student association in mind when he wrote his long article repudiating fraternities in 1925. Pan himself belonged to the Big River Society, which was founded in the fall of 1924.[143] "Big River" referred to the Yangzi River, a commonly understood symbol of China's greatness. The society was loosely knit and not secretive, but it was not inclusive either. Almost all the members were graduates of Qinghua College, mostly from the classes of 1921 and 1922 (two classes that were deeply affected by the May Fourth movement of 1919). A concrete result of the society's two years' existence from 1924 to 1926 was the publication of the journal *Dajiang jikan* (Big River quarterly). When its key members returned to China after 1926, the society dissolved.

Critical of the "slackness and decadence" of some Chinese students in America, the Big River Society aimed at demonstrating the "cooperative spirit" of Qinghua College and bringing "new interest and new spirit" to the Chinese student community.[144] Moreover, the society believed it had a message to convey. Intensely nationalistic, the society's members promoted a brand of nationalism they called *guojia zhuyi*,[145] which shared the core element of anti-imperialism with the "centralized nationalism" embraced earlier by many students in America. But there was a critical difference: *guojia zhuyi* did not advocate hope in a strong central government, but, rather, sought to raise the national consciousness of the Chinese people, who were seen as a passive mass to be educated and awakened by the intellectual elite. The shift from state-centered nationalism to a more populist rhetoric reflected the educated class's increased distance from the state.

Members of the Big River Society were among the most active in the Chinese student community in the 1920s. In the wake of the 1925 May Thirtieth Incident, members of the society were prominent in various student patriotic activities. In that year's Alliance summer conferences, they helped define nationalism as the central theme and dominated the platforms at all the regional meetings. A number of them were elected to Alliance regional offices. Luo Longji, who had been a charismatic political activist at Qinghua College, proved himself a capable leader once again and was elected as the president of the Alliance at this time. (Luo's story will be more fully told in the Epilogue.)

The rise of CCH and the Big River Society in the 1920s coincided with the accelerated decline of the Alliance. The days were gone when a big organization like the Alliance was able to incorporate a large number of students into a single association with a shared sense of purpose. Local clubs proved to be more effective and more capable of furnishing "simple and practical cooperation." Meanwhile, associations like CCH and the Big River Society provided organizational and political alternatives for "serious-minded" people. Perhaps the change was inevitable, given the increase of the number of Chinese students in America over the years, and the deepened political and ideological divisions in China at this time. The fact remains, however, that the democratic ideals of maximum participation, large-scale cooperation, and respect for legality, embodied by the Alliance in its early years, largely disappeared. Moreover, women, once a highly visible group in the activities of the Alliance, were almost completely excluded from both the fraternities and the Big River Society. The fraternities, in particular, were both secretive and hierarchical.

To summarize the main points in this chapter, the early twentieth century was a time when the Chinese, both in China and abroad, were searching for new ways of grouping in their quest for national unity and strength. The associational activities of the students in America occurred in this political milieu. After the decline of the Alliance, even though much of the early political idealism diminished, the associational life of the students survived in the form of smaller-scale groups that were still influenced by American models and continued to be intensely nationalistic. The political role of the intellectual elite was less certain and their relationship with the state was more ambivalent. In the following chapter, one more type of student association, the professional society, will be explored. This type of organizations aimed at a more autonomous relationship with the state and a primarily technical approach to solving China's problems.

CHAPTER TWO

The Professionals:
Predicaments and Promises

While the political activities of voluntary organizations occupied some Chinese students' time, a much larger proportion of many students' time was spent on academic studies. After all, the Chinese had come to America primarily and seriously in pursuit of modern knowledge. Some people who were studying the same subjects eventually came together to found societies defined by professional aspirations and alliances. After they completed their education, the vast majority of them went back home, many of them becoming founders of professional disciplines in China, building upon their experiences in America. Together with the Chinese who were educated in Europe and Japan, they constituted the mainstay of the first generation of modern Chinese professionals. Much of this generation's impact on modern Chinese history, in fact, was professional rather than political.

To be sure, an earlier generation had broken the ground in certain professional areas. Prominent in this early group was the Yale-trained engineer Zhan Tianyou (Jeme Tien Yau), known as "the father of China's railroads."[1]

Taken as a whole, however, the size of the early group was too small and the academic training of its members was generally inadequate to make it a significant new force in Chinese society.[2] The generation that came to America in the early twentieth century received substantially more solid and advanced modern education. The American Boxer Indemnity Scholarship Program alone turned out approximately 1,300 people with bachelor and other higher-education degrees from 1909 to 1929; and, from 1905 to 1929, at least 110 Chinese people were granted doctoral degrees in various disciplines from American universities.[3] Japan and countries in Western Europe also contributed to this human-resource pool, though to a lesser degree.[4] By the end of the 1920s and early 1930s, there were enough people systematically trained in modern professions to warrant regarding them as a new kind of influential force in China. American-trained professionals were the backbone of this emerging new force.

What qualified these people as modern professionals was not just the kind of training they received, but more importantly, the professional identity they acquired. The development of such a new identity was only possible after the ending of the examinations especially designed by the Qing court for returned students in the wake of civil service's demise.[5] This institutional change fundamentally altered the nature of the relationship between the state and the educated class. Officialdom, traditionally the main route to power and prestige for the Chinese literati, began to crack.

While students were in the United States, they were under the influence of the evolving culture of professionalism. After they returned to China, they worked hard to promote professional credentials and expertise as alternative sources of authority. The formation of professional communities in China in the 1920s and early 1930s fostered the cultivation of professional consciousness and professional identity, and helped turn the practitioners of modern crafts into truly modern professionals. Professional consciousness and a sense of autonomy from the state apparatus composed crucial aspects of the modern identity of the group of Chinese students examined in this study.

Scholars of modern professionalization generally agree that professions are typical by-products of an industrial society,[6] but in China, the emergence of the modern professionals did not reflect industrialization; rather, it anticipated it. Despite political strife, foreign invasion, and civil war, all of which marked the first half of twentieth-century China, the vision of industrialization persisted, particularly among the professionally trained people. In contrast to the ideological commitment of China's political activists, the professionals embraced a fundamentally pragmatic philosophy, adopted an essentially technical approach to China's multifaceted problems, and preferred gradual change to revolution.

Under the largely inhospitable circumstances of the first half of the twentieth century, many aspiring professionals found their roles circumscribed and compromised. Some fell back to the beaten track of officialdom. On the whole, however, this generation of Chinese professionals survived, despite incredible odds. They not only succeeded in transplanting many modern professions and disciplines to China, but at least in some fields, also consciously adapted their professions to the needs of their country, as the efforts of some sociologists to "sinicize" sociology demonstrated.

What were the social, intellectual, and political forces, both in China and in America, that nurtured and molded these people? How did the new educated class adjust their relationship with the state? How did the ideology and organization of professionalism emerge and evolve in the republican period? How did this group of American-trained professionals modify their disciplines to suit the needs of China? These are the questions that will be addressed in this chapter. The story of the Chinese professionals is not just about the tremendous problems they faced after returning to a country in the midst of political upheavals; it is also about their aspirations, abilities, and amazing achievements.

THE PRAGMATICS OF LEARNING

China's entrance into the modern world did not have to involve a drastic departure from its past intellectual resources: it could have been a rediscovery and reconnection with that past. The students seeking modern knowledge in America had been nurtured by a rich Confucian tradition that upheld the practical value of learning, even though the requirements of practical life changed over time. The question of what subjects the students should study underscored a pragmatic approach to learning, based on an understanding of what was needed for China's modernization. From time to time, the state played an important role in deciding what the needs were.

Until 1908, the Qing government did not specify what subjects overseas students should study; nor did it reward students majoring in technical subjects. On the contrary, as will be shown later, when a specially designed examination was first given by the Qing court in 1905, those with technical degrees were at a disadvantage because of the long imperial tradition of honoring only the literati. During his visit to the United States in 1903, Liang Qichao noted, with some disapproval, that the number of Chinese students majoring in technical subjects, such as engineering and so forth, was relatively small.[7] After 1908, the Qing government began to exercise substantial control over the students' choices of study, and technical subjects were now strongly emphasized. An imperial decree was issued that year that all government students should study such subjects as engineering, agriculture, and natural sciences. Self-supporting students would not be awarded scholarships unless they also enrolled in these disciplines.[8] A year later, the newly established Boxer Indemnity program required that 80 percent of the students should study engineering, agriculture, and mining.[9] In 1910, a series of regulations further stressed "practical subjects," while limiting the number of students in law and politics.[10] Consequently, technical disciplines dominated the fields of study for the America-bound Chinese who are the focus of this book. Among the first group of forty-seven Indemnity students in 1909, for instance, forty-three majored in disciplines within science and technology.[11] Similar patterns are found among Indemnity students in the following years.[12]

The Qing government's restriction on the study of law and politics undoubtedly revealed its displeasure with the politically active students in Japan, who tended to study such subjects. It also reflected the government's enhanced commitment to the building of the railroad and the opening of mines as a major part of its modernization scheme at this time. But there were deeper reasons for its favoring of technical subjects, reasons that can be traced to a pragmatic strand in China's intellectual tradition.

Hao Chang argues that the central motive of Confucianism, which fundamentally defined the place of learning for the Chinese, was pragmatism.[13] The term *shixue* (practical learning), which was in frequent use at the turn of the century, encapsulates this Confucian pragmatic tradition. The meaning of *shixue* underwent a series of changes in late imperial China. In the seventeenth century, it designated the "empirical" study of Confucian literature, the kind of learning that would enable the Chinese to address actual problems during the troubling Ming-Qing transitional period.[14] After the mid nineteenth century, when the power of the West was manifested forcefully in cannons and battleships, *shixue* began to acquire new implications. As China started to build shipyards, arsenals, and a modern navy, *shixue* was largely understood by the advocates of the Self-Strengthening Movement as the skills required for Western, particularly military, technology.

China's defeat in the Sino-Japanese War of 1894–95 exposed the inadequacy of the Self-Strengthening Movement's military emphasis. Consequently, a new generation of progressive-thinking Chinese, represented by Kang Youwei and Liang Qichao, advocated a more comprehensive and more thorough reform. *Shixue* now connoted any knowledge that could help the development of industry, defense, commerce, education, and the general improvement of China's standing in the world. To a large extent, *shixue* was now equated with multidisciplinary "Western learning." Even with a broader understanding of what Western learning contained, many people in the early twentieth century still equated it primarily with technical knowledge. From the seventeenth century to the early twentieth century, the term *shixue* was redefined a number of times. Despite the changes, its central significance remained: to qualify as *shixue*, the subject needed to have practical value.[15] By embracing seemingly "non-Chinese" subjects such as engineering, reformers such as Liang Qichao, and Western-educated Chinese, together with the Qing government officials, actually sustained and even enhanced the pragmatic strand in Chinese thinking.

Some prominent missionary educators also reinforced the tendency toward technical subjects. Liu Jingshan, who came to America in 1904 with a group of Beiyang University students,[16] recalled a telling incident. Before leaving China, the students had a meeting with Charles D. Tenney, a well-known missionary educator and the supervisor of the Beiyang mission. Tenney asked the students what they would like to study. Liu's reply, "railroad engineering," pleased Tenney, who responded, "Very good. China needs railroad. You should study hard." In contrast to the encouragement received by Liu, another student was scolded by Tenney when he expressed his interest in literature.[17]

After the fall of the Qing, especially during the warlord period, the government no longer dictated to Western-bound students what to study[18]—a change that reflected a more open attitude toward Western learning. Now that the students enjoyed a greater degree of free choice, an increasing number of them turned to social sciences and humanities. This led immediately to a diversification of academic studies among the students,[19] and would lead later to the development of social sciences in China in the 1920s and 1930s, a subject that will receive some attention later in the chapter.

The increased academic diversification at this time did not eclipse the basic dominance of technical disciplines. In 1914, for instance, three-fourths of the new arrivals from China said that they intended to study engineering. Nearly one-third of the Qinghua graduates throughout the period from 1909 to 1929 majored in engineering, more than those in social sciences and humanities combined. Together with the people in natural science and agriculture, they composed nearly half of the entire Qinghua student body.[20] This pattern was not appreciably different from the distribution of fields of study among all the Chinese students in the United States. Furthermore, the diversification did not indicate a less pragmatic view toward learning; students in social sciences also justified their choices by emphasizing the utility value of their disciplines, thus broadening the definition of "practical."

A TECHNICAL APPROACH

Knowing what to study implied an understanding of the process of modernization. To many Chinese students in America at the turn of the century, modernization was essentially the same thing as industrialization, and America was seen as the model. In an article written in 1910, a student explained the Chinese attraction to America and why so many of them chose to major in engineering:

> The key to England's success lies in commerce. The key to America's lies in industrialization. . . . America owes its prosperity to the vastness of its territory and the abundance of its resources. China's condition resembles that of America and differs from that of England. America relies on technology to cultivate its rich natural resources, therefore she has the most advanced manufacturing. [This is why] the majority of us Chinese students have come to America. [This is why] most of us in America are studying engineering and other subjects of *shixue*.[21]

The study of *shixue* was undertaken to promote *shiye*, or practical enterprise, and *shiye jiuguo* (rescuing China through practical enterprise) became the catch phrase of the day. As scholars of the twentieth-century Chinese economy point out, however, although the Qing government adopted measures to promote *shiye* of various sorts, the overall results during this period were inadequate. After the republic was founded, during both the warlord period and the Nationalist era, the modern industrial and transport sectors grew at a comparatively rapid rate, yet large-scale industrialization did not really occur, even though there were spurts of industrial growth.[22] The arrival of the Chinese professionals in the first decades of the twentieth century, therefore, was not accompanied by a surge of industrialization, as in the cases of Western Europe and America. Still, many professionally trained people cherished a vision of industrial China, which became an essential part of their world outlook and persisted despite often disappointing reality.

China's failure to achieve systemic industrialization in the first half of the twentieth century is a historical fact we now see clearly with hindsight. It was not self-evident, however, to many contemporaries. The Chinese students in America were especially hopeful about the arrival of an industrial age during the Qing-republican transitional period. A year or so before the republican revolution engulfed China, a student predicted that what was in store for China would be "essentially industrial," rather than "chiefly political."[23]

This statement, one of many similar expressions by Chinese students in America at this time, appeared to be confirmed by recent developments in China. In June 1910, a national exposition was held in Nanjing to display both domestically-made industrial and handicraft products and imported foreign goods. Inspired by similar foreign expositions, this was the first Chinese attempt to "study the economic resources and industrial conditions of the empire with a view to the more rapid development and promotion of the same."[24] To house the exposition, a total of thirty-eight buildings were erected, some in Western styles, a few even modeled after Gothic churches. The *Monthly* reported the exposition with enthusiasm: "The country is progressing faster than can be recorded."[25] A photograph of a glowing night scene of the exposition site was printed in the students' journal, conveying the impression that "everything is resplendent and the outlook is dazzling to the eye."[26] Those familiar with the splendid Chicago World Fair of 1893, known as the White City, would recognize something similar in the Chinese exhibition.[27] Clearly the message to the *Monthly* readers was that an industrial age for China was on the horizon.

The founding of the republic in 1912 further raised students' hope for an industrial China. Perceiving the birth of the republic as greatly enhancing the prospect for the development of *shiye*, the students happily turned their attention to "industrial, economic and educational subjects," for these were the "real problems that will arise and face us in the future."[28] Many students adopted a primarily technical approach to the problems facing China, and their writings underscore a celebration of both the utility and rationality of science and technology. An article written by Y. Tsenshan Wang, a student of mining geology at the University of Chicago, was typical of this way of thinking. In 1910, Wang accompanied his two American professors to survey the mining conditions in Shanxi and Sichuan and afterward wrote about this trip in the *Monthly*. Wang was both impressed by the abundance of the natural resources in the two provinces and astonished by the negligence and indifference of the local people and the governments toward such riches. Though he noted the appalling working conditions and was clearly sympathetic with the plight of the miners, Wang's primary concern was how to enable the Chinese to manipulate their natural environment. He believed that modern technology was the key to reducing poverty.[29]

Many other students viewed economic development as the most effective way to maintain social and political stability. "Industry," in the opinion of one student writing in 1913, was "the means to maintain the new republic and it has great effect upon the social conditions at large."[30] Even during the politically more gloomy period of warlordism, the students' confidence in the redeeming power of industrialization did not fade. Writing in 1919, a student insisted that industrial development was the only way to ensure "the prosperity of our people, the well-being of our society, the rehabilitating, invigorating, and rejuvenating, indeed, the very existence of our country, all depend, in the last analysis, upon this point."[31]

To be sure, American-educated students were not the only Chinese to adopt a primarily technical approach to solving China's problems. As noted above, these ideas were in part the products of a widespread pragmatic trend in progress since the late Qing. Yet unlike the general public, the students had a personal stake in the industrial development of China. The advance of their social and professional status would be directly linked to the progress of industrialization, so it is understandable that they were among the most zealous in promoting the vision of an industrial China. Amid the chorus of unreserved praise for industrialization, a critical voice like M. H. Li's sounded out of tune. In an article written in 1914, Li discussed the negative impact of industrialization: "With technical development, economic problems have become more complicated, and social evils have multiplied themselves in almost mathematical progression." The social evils he mentioned included industrial accidents and the deterioration of morality among the working class. Echoing the American middle-class reformers during the Progressive era, who were also critical of the problems caused by industrialization and urbanization, Li prescribed the following: "Modern parks, good pavements, pure food, adequate housing, community music, religious service and technical demonstrations are all factors to be considered."[32]

Those who embraced industrialization wholeheartedly envisioned a preeminent role for themselves in an industrial society, as exemplified by the following confident declaration: "Who are to be the captains and generals of industry in China? And who are the Chinese Edisons and Watts? It is expected that they are more likely to be found among returned students than any others."[33] Another student, a forestry major, imagined himself both as a "general" who would lead "armies" to subdue "the enemy that cut down mountains" and a "philanthropist" who would conquer "famine not by giving temporary relief, but by turning stretches of unused territories into luxurious gardens."[34] Many students demonstrated pride, even faith, in their chosen professions. John Wang, a mining engineering major, maintained that "it is only too plain to need any further proof that . . . a direct development of her [China's] natural resources, such as coal and iron, must occupy our first and best attention."[35] Similarly, C. L. Wu, a student of chemical engineering at MIT, opined that "of all the factors in the solution of these perplexing problems [poverty, backwardness, etc.], that of chemical engineering is of the greatest importance."[36] Clearly the students were promoting the authority of their own professions.

By its very nature, modern professions entail disciplinary specialization. To establish the authority of professionalism, the students had to challenge a deep-seated Chinese tradition: the gentry-official class's ideal of amateurism. In his penetrating analysis of Chinese intellectual tradition, Joseph Levenson considered the amateur ideal a "condition of Chinese thought."[37]

From Confucius's statement that "the accomplished scholar is not a utensil," to the Ming gentry artists' contempt for those who took painting as an occupation rather than as cultivation, there was a "long and continued" insistence in Chinese intellectual tradition upon treating learning as a symbol of high social and cultural standing. While the pragmatic strand in Confucianism modified this aloof tendency, especially at times of social and political crises, and allowed people to address urgent problems, it did not in itself nurture or sanction specialization in any field. Rather, being a Confucianist meant being a generalist.

The amateur ideal was challenged by the students head-on. In an article entitled "The Need of Experts," written in 1916, one student remarked, "The Chinese are a nation of amateurs. Whether in statecraft, education, industry or commerce, the conduct of affairs and the formulating of policies have been largely in the hands of amateurs—men without special training, knowledge, or skill in their particular fields of activity."[38] Old-fashioned literati were criticized by other students for being "too exclusively literary,"[39] and were called "burden[s]," "parasite[s]," and "weeds which take all the food from the soil." Meanwhile, values such as productivity, utility, and efficiency now became the new yardsticks by which things were measured. As one student put it, "The old theory that education is simply a matter of school teaching is losing its hold. It is now coming to be more clearly understood that the practical and physical side of [the] education is not less important than the intellectual. . . . We should remember that we study not to become educated but to do efficient work."[40] Some students regarded professional specialization as a key virtue of a modern person. One person contended that specialization, "the most fundamental principle," required that "each individual should select a profession for which he is specially trained." Without it, an individual's mind would be unsettled and unconcentrated, and time and energy would be wasted. "Such a life is bound to be a failure," the writer concluded.[41]

What the new educated elite brought to the Chinese intellectual scene, then, was not the ideas of utility and pragmatism, which had already existed in the Chinese tradition, but their belief in professional specialization, or, in the Chinese vocabulary, *zhuanye*. They insisted that a modern man (women were usually not included) should be equipped with specific professional expertise. The promotion of professional specialization and professional authority in turn further strengthened the pragmatic thread in Chinese thinking.

Some people, however, realized that professional specialization is inherently problematic. In an article written in 1912, entitled "Vocational Education Narrows," the author pondered the conflict between a narrowly defined professional specialization and the aspiration to play a leadership role.[42] Concerned with the same problem, another student urged his fellow engineering students to change the image of engineers as "machinery in human shape."[43] The concern about a decline in humanistic knowledge and skills was persistently expressed throughout the period. As early as 1908, one student suggested that students of technology should also take courses in "humanities, economic sciences and philosophy," since "we are supposed to lead, not to follow; we are supposed to replace foreigners; but responsible leadership and competent substitutions require a knowledge not only of things but of man."[44] The narrow technical education of many returned students was also noted by foreign observers. Writing in 1914, an American considered it the "fatal weakness" of returned students, saying, "What China needs more than foreign technology are foreign methods of administration."[45]

While the amateur ideal in the Chinese tradition was incompatible with a complex modern world, Western professional and technical education, with an emphasis on specialization, was inadequate to the task of equipping the students with broad humanistic values and skills. The profession of engineering, for instance, was believed to imbue its members with a "trained incapacity for thinking about and dealing with human affairs."[46] By insisting on technically oriented training as the new basis for authority, returned students often found that they were ill-served by the very ideal that they espoused.

An awareness of the inherent narrowness of professional specialization notwithstanding, this generation of Chinese students largely embraced the values of professionalism as vital to modern man. To a considerable extent, their conviction reflected the influence of the evolving culture of professionalism in America, which had emerged and matured in the years from 1870 to 1900 with the founding of professional societies and the elevation of professional standards. By 1900, professional authority had been firmly established in the fields of law, medicine, and many others. By and large, American universities came into existence to serve and promote professional authority in society.[47] The Chinese students came to American universities and colleges at a time when the culture of professionalism had thoroughly penetrated the places of higher learning. The ideology of professionalism in America nurtured in the Chinese students a professional consciousness that was an important prerequisite for the establishment of professionalism in China. But this was not enough by itself. A changed relationship between the professional practitioners and the state was also required. For the Western-educated Chinese, a more autonomous relationship with the state was only possible after the remnant of the civil service examination system completely disappeared, sometime around 1915.

A CHANGING RELATIONSHIP WITH THE STATE

In China's imperial past, classical education enabled qualified degree holders to hold government offices and gain the accompanying social status. For the American-educated Chinese, professional training was regarded as the new path to prestige and authority. Charlotte Furth argues in her study of the British-trained geologist Ding Wenjiang that the Western-educated intelligentsia were heirs to the scholar-bureaucrats of the old imperial system, in the sense that both groups derived their credentials from education and both aspired to leadership roles in the society. The old elite, absorbed into the state apparatus through the imperial examination system, "felt little sense that there need be any basic antagonism between their own highest values and state power."[48] How did the new intellectual elite relate to the state power?

According to a survey conducted in 1917 of 340 Chinese returned from America, the two most important fields of employment were education and government service, with the former accounting for 39 percent and the latter 32 percent[49]—a trend that persisted for the next twenty years.[50] Government bureaucracy, then, continued to absorb a large number of returned students. A closer look at where these people worked, however, reveals that a considerable proportion of them were employed in specialized agencies such as the Ministry of Transportation or the Ministry of Finance, where certain professional knowledge was presumably needed.[51] Y. C. Wang's figures also indicate that roughly half, and in some cases far more than half of the returned students in "government service" in 1925 were able to fully or partially utilize the training they had acquired abroad.[52]

Although the nature of government service might have been changing in the modern age, government posts (*zuo guan* in the colloquial language) had begun to lose their attraction to many people with modern education. These individuals—a friend of Gu Weijun, for example—started looking, therefore, for alternative routes to economic security and social prestige. Trying to persuade Gu to major in engineering, the friend based his argument not only on China's need for factories and railroads, but more forcefully, on his conviction that the engineering profession could provide more economic security and that an engineer would enjoy more autonomy from state power. As he put it, an engineer did not have to bow to government officials all the time. Gu was almost convinced.[53]

In the late Qing, the quest for different routes to social prestige and economic security was essentially an individual endeavor. Many a Western-educated Chinese, as Furth demonstrates in the case of Ding Wenjiang, still viewed the career of an educated man in the "Confucian perspective."[54] The relationship between the Western-educated elite and the state had not been immediately affected by the abolition of the civil service examination system in 1905, nor was it changed overnight by the fall of the Qing dynasty. The state, first the Qing court and then the Yuan Shikai regime, adopted a paternalistic policy toward the foreign-educated, and through the device of a specially designed examination system, treated them as a new kind of civil servant. The full impact of political and institutional changes on the foreign-educated became apparent only during the warlord period.

In the last decade of the Qing, both personal ties and institutional apparatus bound the Western-educated professional to the state. There even existed a kind of patron-client tie between some students and a number of powerful provincial governors. Because the cost of foreign study, especially in the West, was too great for ordinary Chinese, only people from very wealthy families or with financial aid from a sponsor could afford it. In an era when reform became fashionable, some provincial officials came out as powerful patrons of foreign-study students. A Shanghai journal commented in 1907 that sending students abroad had become "the favorite hobby of the enlightened viceroys and governors."[55]

Among the "enlightened" officials was Duan Fang, the governor-general of Jiangsu and Jiangxi provinces, who, in the summer of 1907, conducted a three-day examination in Nanjing to select students to study in America. Although tuition was going to be paid by the Americans (with scholarships offered by Yale, Cornell, and Wellesley), the ten male and three female students who had successfully passed the examination were referred to as "students sent by Duan Fang."[56] Yuan Shikai was another ranking provincial leader whose name was personally linked to foreign-study students. Liu Jingshan recalled a "pep talk" given by Yuan, then the governor-general of Zhili, before the Beiyang students left for America in 1904. Yuan told the students to study hard and not to get involved in "the nonsense of freedom and revolution." Yuan also promised the students: "After you finish and come back home, I will tell the emperor, no, I will petition to the emperor, to appoint you to official positions."[57] Later, when approached by Sun Yat-sen in America to join the revolutionary cause, Liu declined—a decision affected by Yuan Shikai's warnings about "freedom and revolution."[58] Liu Jingshan's case indicates that the relationship between the students and their official patrons, though often loose, not only gave the students a sense of affiliation, but could also influence their politics.

One critical device designed to forge a bond between the Qing state and the students was the specially designed examinations for returned students. The symbolic meaning of this device was more important than its practical purpose. Held annually from 1905 to 1911, the examinations aimed at drawing foreign-educated people into the state bureaucracy. Now that the age-old civil service examination system was dismantled for the population at large, studying abroad became the new—and the only—institutionalized route to government office.[59]

From the very beginning, the new wine in the old bottle (to borrow a metaphor that is both Chinese and Western) had a strange taste. The first fourteen returned students examined by the Board of Education in 1905 had all studied in Japan.[60] American-returned students followed suit the next year, accounting for sixteen out of a total of forty-two people that took the examination. The academic qualifications of the candidates this year varied from a Yale Ph.D. to a Japanese high school graduate, yet all were competing on equal terms. To make the situation worse, some examiners were simply not competent to judge the qualifications of the examined, and there was prejudice against people in technical subjects. Students of engineering, law, and medicine, for instance, were placed in the "fourth class" and were thereby unable to receive the *jinshi* degree. A chief examiner justified this discrimination by explaining that since time immemorial the degree of *jin-shi* had been conferred only upon literary men. One of the requirements of the examination was for candidates to write an essay, either in Chinese or in a Western language. The topic of the Chinese essay was "To respect those in authority, to love one's kin, to venerate one's elders, and to segregate the sexes; these are principles that will abide for all generations"—a typical Confucian theme. Thirty-two participants passed the examination out of the total of forty-two, five of whom were eventually awarded the *jin-shi* degree and the rest the *ju-ren* degree (*jin-shi* was the third or highest examination degree, won only by passing the metropolitan examination and palace examination in the civil service examination system in Ming-Qing China [1368–1911]; *ju-ren* was the second or intermediate degree won by passing the provincial examination). Ten people subsequently joined government service after several modern government agencies petitioned to have them.[61]

A major distinction between occupations and professions, a scholar of modern professionalism observes, is that only professions have the recognized right to declare "outside evaluation illegitimate and intolerable."[62] The returned students in the imperial examination subjected themselves precisely to such an "outside evaluation." Feeling humiliated by the experience, one obviously unsuccessful candidate remarked afterwards, "I am a poorer but wiser man, and nothing under the sun would make me undergo such an experience again."[63]

The process of fitting back into the old system with new credentials was frustrating. Despite many problems, however, the practice did not merely continue: it flourished. The number of successful candidates increased from 38 in 1907, to 107 in 1908, and 400 in 1911, many of whom would be hired by the newly established modern governmental agencies. One observer commented in 1911 that an increasing number of returned students were "flocking to Peking for government appointments."[64] The content of the examination might differ notably from that of the old civil service tests and the tasks performed in the new agencies by returned students might not bear much resemblance to those of scholar-bureaucrats, but by participating in the state-sponsored examinations, the students honored the same ritual and related to the state in the same way as their earlier counterparts. With court-granted literary degrees and official titles, it was hard for the returned students to develop an independent political and professional identity.

After the fall of the Qing, Yuan Shikai tried to retain some continuity with the Qing policy regarding returned students; in 1915 he personally ordered an examination for them. Out of the 192 candidates, 151 passed and subsequently received official appointments. This turned out to be the only examination for the returned students after the fall of the Qing.

The warlord period witnessed the final collapse of the examination system for returned students. The central government, itself in constant political and financial turmoil and unable to create an institutionalized and meaningful relationship with the educated class, adopted a laissez-faire attitude toward foreign education, no longer specifying what subjects students should study. In addition, neither central nor provincial governments were able to send stipends to the students on time.[65] The governments' financial difficulties further eroded the authority of state power. The Chinese Educational Bureau, a government agency established after 1900 to oversee the affairs of Chinese students except those on Boxer Indemnity scholarships, was permanently closed in 1925.[66]

Left to fend for themselves during this chaotic period, the Western-educated class found that an adjustment of their relationship with the state was both necessary and possible. When the Nationalist government established itself in Nanjing in 1928, it attempted and largely succeeded in reconnecting the state with the educated elite,[67] but the nature of the relationship was forever altered. Now the Nanjing government had to deal with a relatively autonomous intellectual class. The warlord period, therefore, had produced the unintended result of setting free the educated elite.

But freedom had a price; the process of transition was filled with confusion and frustration. For many people living in the midst of it, the dominant feeling was perhaps a sense of loss rather than of liberation. The termination of the recruitment mechanism left a void, keenly felt by many. Ren Hongjun, then a student at Cornell University, who would later become a highly respected educator in republican China, described a common reaction of the students to the new situation:

Previously, the Qing court set up the examination system to catch the returned students. At the time the students all fell into the trap of officialdom. Now that the political structure is transformed and the examination system abolished, there are among us people who are regretful of the changes, fearing that there won't be any channel of upward social mobility for themselves.[68]

The first concern of many returned students was finding a suitable job—a task, as they soon learned, which was not easy. Ren Hongjun noted an experience familiar to many students: "They take whatever jobs that can earn themselves money. Thus we see students of humanities employed to build railroads and students of mechanics in charge of education. . . . Many people have to give up what they've learned, and to take whatever job is available, 'putting Zhang's hat on Li's head' and 'cutting one's feet to fit the shoes.'"[69]

Even though the systematic route to government service did not continue, making a living as an official still seemed to be a relatively easy and ready way. To some people it remained attractive because of its immediate financial rewards and conventional respectability. Besides, as mentioned above, working for the government did not necessarily mean that the students could not utilize what they had learned abroad. During the republican era, however, an official life increasingly came to be perceived as a bad choice. One student bluntly called it a life for "parasites."[70] The same person suggested in another article that the students should "pay more attention to the direction of production or industrial development than to the hunting of government positions."[71] This student's criticism was echoed by Nathaniel Peffer, an American who claimed to have "rather intimate contacts with a wide circle of foreign educated Chinese." Peffer leveled his charge in 1922:

> Do they know how many of the returned students are among those corrupt officials, among the worst of them? Do they realize how many Chinese students . . . went back to China, fluttered tamely against conditions that confronted them at home, held out a fleeting while against temptation, compromised first a little, then a lot, went finally into official life and now are playing the same old mandarin game as it is played by those who never saw a foreign institution, are tainted with the age-old mandarin taint?[72]

The *Monthly* published Peffer's article, along with an editorial endorsing the American's criticism: "Mr. Peffer launches a relentless attack on the returned students. His facts are true; his charges undeniable."[73]

During this time, one of the criticisms of the returned students most commonly heard from the Chinese public was that they were no different from the old type of officials. This opinion reflected a certain reality, yet it also revealed an underlying anxiety, present in the public and among the students themselves, about what kind of role the new intellectual elite should and could play in a society where the old social and political arrangements were disrupted. The challenges confronting this generation of professionally trained and Western-educated Chinese were enormous and multifaceted. Discussing Ding Wenjiang and his fellow returned students, Charlotte Furth comments that the biggest problem Western-educated Chinese had to face after they returned home was the deprivation of research facilities and atmosphere in China,[74] a problem that indeed existed. But a much more serious problem for returning students was to adjust their relationship with the state and to negotiate with various political players—officials and institutions that were no longer paternalistic toward students—to find a place for themselves in a changing society.

As it turned out, with some assistance from the state, but mostly through their own efforts, the Western-trained professionals largely succeeded in creating a niche for themselves and in establishing professional authority in a society that had always esteemed officialdom. The process was far from smooth and the results were mixed, but the important thing is that these people made progress. Along the way they demonstrated courage, perseverance, and even vision. At the same time, they turned themselves into real, conscious professionals. The creation of professional societies was a key factor in their accomplishment. In the following pages, we will look at how the notion of professional societies was introduced to the Chinese, how the Chinese students experimented with this notion in America, and how professional societies became an established reality in China in the late 1920s and early 1930s, thanks largely to the efforts of returned students, a substantial number of whom were American-educated.

ORGANIZING ACCORDING TO PROFESSIONAL STANDARDS

An examination of the histories of thirty-seven professional societies in republican China shows that the majority of them were founded during the

1920s and the first half of the 1930s,[75] the period when professionalism took root in China. American-returned students played vital roles in this endeavor, both as founders of various professional societies and as leaders in the later development of these societies.

Professional associations are essential for the existence of the professions, since "a profession can only be said to exist when there are bonds between practitioners, and these bonds can take but one shape—that of formal associations."[76] Here the bonds refer to "a relatively permanent affiliation, an identity, personal commitment, specific interests, and general loyalties."[77] In America, the last few decades of the nineteenth century witnessed an upsurge in professional organizational activities. By the early twentieth century, professional associations had become well established.

American and other Western professional associations had inspired Kang Youwei and Liang Qichao to organize *xuehui* (study societies) in the 1890s.[78] In his essay, "Lun xuehui" (On study societies), written in 1896, Liang Qichao stressed the importance of *qun* (group, grouping), and praised the fact that in the West, "each profession has its own association."[79] Liang believed that the associations pulled together the people in the same profession, promoted knowledge, and more important, contributed to the strength and prosperity of a country. After a brief setback in the wake of the abortive One Hundred Days Reform in 1898, study societies reemerged with new momentum in the first decade of the twentieth century. Aiming at promoting modern education and reform, they generally lacked specific professional goals. The culture of professionalism in America and the anticipation of a modern, industrial China led the students in America to organize along professional lines. Their resulting experiences helped implant in them a sense of professional fellowship and taught them the rules and methods that would make a professional society work—skills that were invaluable to them when they went back to China.

The beginning of the students' professional activities in America was marked by the creation of the Chinese Academy of Arts and Science by the Eastern Alliance in August 1910. The academy was described as a "federation" composed of a number of professional clubs.[80] The organization's major goal was to promote "professional fellowship," and in fact, one hundred people joined the ambitious-sounding "academy" in the first year of its existence. Interestingly, the academy's founding also reflected a concern for the "fate of all the returned students," who could easily be engulfed by "the tidal wave of the Chinese teeming millions" if they weren't properly organized.[81] After 1913–14, the name of the academy no longer appears in the *Monthly*. It is possible that it was reorganized under the new rubric Arts and Science "groups." Less grandiosely named, the groups had a clearer idea of what they were up to:

> It is hoped that intellectual interest will be stimulated, broadened and nourished, and that something like a scholarly or professional spirit may arise and grow among us as students, and finally that the same scholarly spirit and intellectual interest may lead us, when we return to our fatherland, to establish learned societies for encouragement and promotion of learning in every field.[82]

The groups also had a more elaborate structure. Two parallel organizations were formed: the Engineering Committee and the Agriculture and Forestry groups. Within the Engineering Committee, seven different departments were set up, each organized along a specific division of engineering. A project of compiling a bibliography of engineering books was announced, and a list of all Chinese engineering students in China was compiled to help avoid an overconcentration of Chinese engineering students in some branches and a neglect in others.

In the summer of 1914, a number of Cornell students founded the Science Society (*Kexue she*), which people from other universities also eventually joined. The first issue of the journal *Kexue* (Science) was published in Shanghai a year later. In 1918, a number of core members having returned to China, the headquarters of the society was moved to Nanjing, and the journal *Kexue* became the leading publication of theoretical and applied sciences in the republican period. It not only devoted itself to serious articles on science proper, but also consciously promoted the adoption of a "scientific" worldview.[83]

In *Scientism in Chinese Thought*, Daniel W. Y. Kwok sees what he calls "scientism" as a new form of belief in China.[84] Based on the assumption that all aspects of the universe are knowable through the methods of science, Kwok writes, this ideology acted as a new philosophy of life capable of replacing Confucianism in the first half of twentieth-century China.[85] Such a way of thinking, though no doubt showing "the fundamental stirring of the Chinese mind in search of an integrated modern identity,"[86] failed to "distinguish between the critical attitude and methodological authority, between scientific objectivity and absolute rationality, and between scientific laws and irrefutable dogmas."[87] Some of the most ardent Chinese advocates of scientism examined by Kwok were members of the Science Society.[88] In the larger community of Chinese students in America, a "scientific" world outlook also had a great deal of appeal. The profound impact of "scientism" on twentieth-century Chinese thinking is a topic worthy of further investigation.[89]

Another phase of the students' professional activities began after the mid 1910s, when societies organized along specific professional lines sprang up more frequently. Both the Agricultural Society and the Chemical Society were founded in the early 1920s. Claiming to have seventy members in America and thirty-five members in China by the end of 1925, the Chemical Society was the predecessor of the Chinese Chemical Society founded in China.[90]

Engineering illustrates better than any other field the role played by American-educated people in promoting professionalization and the culture of professionalism in China. Engineering was the most popular subject of study among the Chinese students in America, accounting for some 30 to 44 percent of the student body between 1905 and 1924. Several attempts had been made to organize engineering students in America, but nothing was accomplished until December 1917, when a group of more than twenty engineering students, trainees, and engineers gathered in New York City to form China's Engineering Society. This group became the largest and the most influential of the Chinese professional associations that came into existence in America in this period.[91]

By 1923, a large number of its members having returned to the home country, the activity of the Engineering Society moved to China. The membership increased from 350 in 1923 to 1,730 in 1930 (this presumably included people trained in China and other countries as well). In 1931, China's Engineering Society merged with China's Engineers' Society,[92] the new hybrid association retaining the latter's name. The mission of the new society was threefold: to unite people in the fields of engineering, to develop China's engineering projects, and to promote research in the engineering professions.[93] Eventually, the society had fifteen subsocieties, each organized along a specific field of engineering and relatively independent of the others.

The Engineers' Society managed to have an annual conference almost every year between 1931 and its final year, 1950. During the Sino-Japanese War, the headquarters of the society moved to the war capital, Chongqing, where activities were conducted under extremely difficult conditions. Against all the odds, membership continued to grow: by 1949, the society claimed a total of 16,717 members. Throughout all these years, the participation of American-returned students was essential, in that so many society leaders came from their ranks.

The society maintained a high professional standard. Membership was based on strict academic criteria, and members abided by an ethical code, which included, among other things, "honoring professional dignity."[94] In 1940, the society passed a resolution to make June 6 a national holiday for engineers, the first holiday in China designated for people of a modern profession. The establishment of such a national holiday testified to the considerable prestige now enjoyed by engineers, which would not have been possible without the long and persistent efforts of the Engineers' Society to raise the status of the profession. The society's relationship with the Nationalist government raises interesting questions. A few high-ranking Guomindang officials, themselves graduates of American universities, had shown interest in the society since the early 1930s.[95] During the war, cooperation with the government was clearly strengthened: the society increased its attention to problems related to defense, and ranking Guomindang officials were elected to leadership positions in the society.[96] After all, what the Engineers' Society aimed to promote would help strengthen the Chinese nation, and therefore it was in the interest of the state to see its work prosper. During the Nanjing decade and the following wartime period, as E-tu Zen Sun has shown, the Chinese academic community maintained fairly close contact with the Guomindang government.[97] Even though some government officials were involved in the Engineers' Society's activities, and the endorsement of the state was indispensable, the society was able to maintain a considerable degree of autonomy, in part because a major source of the society's funds was membership fees.[98] On the whole, it is fair to characterize the society's relationship with the state authority as interdependence rather than dominance by the state.[99]

Scholars in the West generally believe that modern professions have contributed to the "restructuring" of society, by establishing a new differential system of education and credentials.[100] The professions therefore are closely bound to a social stratification system. In the context of republican China, the roles played by the professional communities in this respect were paradoxical, on the one hand helping to introduce a new hierarchical structure, and on the other hand helping to maintain some basic democratic elements in society. The existence of the relatively independent professional communities contributed to the cultivation of a kind of "public sphere," or, to borrow Philip Huang's term, a "third realm," in this period.[101] The presence of this "realm," small in size and vulnerable to political forces, was nonetheless remarkable if we consider the fact that after the founding of the People's Republic, all professional societies were incorporated into the state apparatus and placed under Party leadership.

THE SOCIOLOGISTS: A CASE STUDY

The formation and growth of professional communities in republican China indicate that the culture of professionalism made headway during this period, an observation that is also made by Y. C. Wang, an authority on the Chinese foreign-study movement of this period. Wang contends, however, that the Chinese professionals in general were poorly adjusted to the situation in China, and that they formed an elite disconnected from the life surrounding them and from the actual conditions in the country at large. Wang uses the example of returned students in the field of agriculture to illustrate the unsatisfactory performance of the Western-trained professionals.[102] One contemporary of the students, while acknowledging the allegedly poor performance of agriculture students, suggested that the training that the students had received in America should be held responsible. Because of the many differences between the "Chinese art of agriculture and the American science of farming," argued this person, their training was not quite applicable to the Chinese condition,[103] an argument that is confirmed by Hu Shi's brief experience as an agricultural student at Cornell.[104] Even Shen Zonghan, a "star pupil" of agriculture and China's preeminent agronomist, found that in some respects his education in America had not prepared him well for what was needed in China.[105]

Many Western-trained Chinese had to confront the challenge of how to apply Western learning most effectively to the situation in China. Their responses, in turn, would largely determine their success and failure as modern professionals in their homeland. While a comprehensive evaluation of the history of professions in modern China is beyond the scope of this study, it is my argument that Chinese professionals, at least in some fields, made deliberate and steadfast efforts to address national needs. Chinese sociologists will be the focus of my discussion in the following pages; their story is a case in point of how a Western discipline was transplanted from abroad and eventually took root in China. My choice of subject is partly intended to correct an imbalance in the historical narrative, since it is usually the engineers and natural scientists who have enjoyed the limelight in China, and partly because the sociologists' story illustrates the depth of their commitment and dedication to their country and to their profession.[106]

In 1947, of the 143 university faculty members teaching sociology in China, 71 had studied in the United States.[107] The preponderance of American-trained sociologists, and other evidence of American influence in the discipline, have prompted one scholar to describe sociology in the republican period as "American-oriented."[108] This characterization ignores the fact that the Chinese sociologists made conscious efforts, beginning in the 1920s and intensifying in the 1930s, to establish their own version of the discipline—efforts which, by the 1940s, had borne impressive results.

From the time sociology was introduced to China, it was linked to China's search for "modernity" and was associated with social reform. Originally translated as *qunxue* (the study of groups), a term with a classical resonance thoughtfully chosen by Yan Fu,[109] the Japanese word for sociology, *shehuixue*, was later adopted by the Chinese.[110] This choice of terminology not only reflected the influence of Japanese translations of Western terms at this time,[111] but also reflected the desire of the new intellectual class to break away from old concepts.

The first Chinese instructor of *qunxue* was Kang Youwei, who taught the subject at his academy in Guangzhou in 1891. No information is available on the content of Kang Youwei's lectures, though given the date we can confidently assume that it had little to do with Western sociology per se. A few years later, Kang's student Liang Qichao developed his own thinking on *qun* and wrote the famous article "Shuo qun," drawing inspiration from both Kang's lectures and Yan Fu's translation of Herbert Spencer's book

Study of Sociology. Sociology was first taught in China as a modern discipline in American Protestant missionary colleges. St. John's in Shanghai offered courses in 1905, followed by a few other Christian colleges. The instructors, of course, were Westerners,[112] as were the first people to conduct research in China. Western scholars dominated both the teaching of sociology and social research for the first two decades of the twentieth century.[113]

The May Fourth movement in 1919 and the subsequent Nationalist revolution in the 1920s made it relevant and compelling for progressive-thinking youth to understand Chinese society, and created a favorable atmosphere for Western social and political theories. The family system became a hot topic, written about by a number of Chinese scholars, most of whom had no systematic training in the social sciences.[114] For some people, "sociology" became synonymous with social change. Qu Qiubai, a communist leader and theorist, was head of the sociology department at Shanghai University, a place that attracted many communists and radical intellectuals in the early 1920s. Qu himself taught two sociology courses, which were remembered by a student as consisting primarily of Marxist thought.[115]

Sociology also became increasingly popular among America-bound students. In 1914, seven Chinese students majored in sociology in American universities, and the number went up to nineteen in 1920–21 and twenty-seven in 1927.[116] Wu Wenzao, a graduate of Qinghua College in 1923, credited the May Fourth New Culture Movement for inspiring him to choose sociology as his subject of study in America.[117] Three of Wu's fellow Qinghua students, Pan Guangdan, Wu Jingchao, and Wu Zelin, also made similar decisions. All of them eventually became renowned scholars in the fields of sociology and anthropology in China.[118]

In 1928, a sociology society was founded in the Shanghai-Nanjing region.[119] Soon, this society merged with a sociology society already in existence in Beijing to form a national professional society, the Sociology Society of China. Seventy-nine names appeared on the 1930 membership register, all Chinese nationals and most teaching in universities. The society published a professional journal and conducted annual conferences.[120] By this time, sociology as a discipline had clearly achieved professional status in China. The professionalization of sociology in the early 1930s was built upon institutional development in the 1920s, when a number of Chinese universities began to establish sociology as a legitimate academic discipline.[121] Two prestigious national universities, Qinghua University in Beijing and Central University in Nanjing, were known for their strong sociology programs. In the 1930s, sociology was not only an accredited major, but was even fairly popular among college students, drawing 7 percent of the total student population.[122] Fei Xiaotong, who discontinued his premedical study to enroll in the sociology department at Yanjing University, explained the appeal of sociology to college students at this time:

> It was at the end of the 1920s that China entered a period of political stability and reconstruction. Young students, after having participated in the previous revolution, began to settle down and think about more fundamental issues. It was clear that political enthusiasm by itself would be futile if it were not to be followed by a period of practical reconstruction of the country. But when practical problems arose, most of the responsible leaders were at a loss, not for courage or devotion, but for knowledge of the existing realities. Quite naturally, therefore, students of that period directed their attention to the social realities and demanded a better understanding of the situation about them.[123]

The growth of sociology occurred in the context of important political and cultural changes: the development of higher education and nation-building during the Nanjing decade. One objective of the Nationalist government was to standardize academic programs at the university level. In 1938, for example, the Ministry of Education made sociology a required course for majors in the humanities, natural science, law, and education.

Compared with the earlier dominance of Westerners in the field, a significant difference in the 1930s was that all the major teaching and research centers of sociology were now staffed and directed primarily by the Chinese. After the Sino-Japanese War, Chinese instructors had almost entirely replaced Westerners.[124] A number of prominent scholars emerged from the expanding ranks of Chinese sociologists, representing various schools of sociological theories and methodologies. The first step in establishing sociology as a modern academic discipline in China was to systematically introduce relevant Western theories to China. Among the people who labored diligently in this area, Sun Benwen stood out as the most productive and authoritative. Sun studied sociology in America from 1921 to

1926 and received his Ph.D. from New York University. After returning to China, Sun taught at the Central University in Nanjing and wrote more than ten books on sociology. His 1935 work, *Shehuixue yuanli* (The principles of sociology), a synthesis of major sociological schools in the West, was the most widely used college sociology textbook in the republican period.[125]

If Sun Benwen was an authority on theories, Chen Da (Chen Ta) and Li Jinghan excelled in empirical research. Chen Da was famous for his statement, "Let the data make the argument and let the figures speak for themselves."[126] After graduating from Qinghua College, Chen came to America in 1916 and received a doctoral degree in sociology in 1923 from Columbia University. Chen taught at Qinghua University after he went back to China that same year. In 1925, he took a group of Qinghua students to Chengfu Village, a rural community near Qinghua and conducted a social survey with them that was the first to be directed solely by a Chinese scholar.[127] Chen eventually established himself as an authority on population and labor; his 1946 study of Chinese population was a pathbreaking work in the field.[128] Li Jinghan, meanwhile, arrived in America in 1917 and, while attending Pomona College in California, conceived the idea of doing social surveys in China. After he returned to China, Li (whose story will be told more fully in the Epilogue) eventually developed a research methodology to suit Chinese conditions, with an emphasis on empathizing with the subjects.[129]

Perhaps more than any other Chinese sociologist of this generation, Wu Wenzao was the most conscious of the need to establish a "Chinese sociology" and was the most systematic in his efforts to achieve this goal. A devoted teacher, Wu spent a great deal of time with his students, cultivating them to become experts in the study of Chinese society. Among his students was Fei Xiaotong, who has been widely regarded as the finest social scientist in twentieth-century China.[130] Wu Wenzao was born into a peasant's family of modest means in Jiangsu Province in 1901, and began his education at a time when the modern school system had just become officially established. In 1917, Wu took the entrance examination of Qinghua College, partly to take advantage of the school's free tuition;[131] at Qinghua, Wu came under the influence of the May Fourth New Culture Movement. In 1923 Wu graduated from Qinghua and left for the United States.

In his first two years in America, Wu studied as an undergraduate at Dartmouth College. Besides taking courses in social sciences, Wu also took two natural-science lab classes. This experience later led him to advocate using natural-science methodology to study social phenomena.[132] After receiving a bachelor's degree from Dartmouth in 1925, Wu went to Columbia University, then a major center for advanced studies in sociology (another important center was the University of Chicago, which Wu's Qinghua classmate Wu Jingchao attended). At Columbia, Wu audited classes in the anthropology department, which in turn convinced him of the usefulness of an anthropological approach to sociological studies. Wu's dissertation for his Ph.D. (which he received in 1929) earned him Columbia's award for best foreign student. After returning to China in the same year, Wu began a decade-long teaching career at Yanjing University,[133] which turned out to be the most fruitful period in his professional life. Yanjing's sociology department was generally regarded as the finest in China.[134] Yet until Wu Wenzao joined the faculty, the department was best known for its "social service wing," which had its origin in the missionary concern for social work.[135] Wu built the "sociology wing" from scratch, with no departmental tradition and with limited resources, and soon attracted a group of admiring students, who with him developed the most dynamic research center in the field. Wu's relationship with his students, as one scholar describes it, resembled a kind of mentorship reminiscent of China's traditional teacher-student bond.[136] Wu himself once said that he had put far more energy and thought into mentoring his students than into raising his own children.[137]

At the time he returned to China, Wu found that sociology was still very much an imported discipline. In the classroom, students read about Chicago gangs and Russian immigrants in America, but learned practically nothing about Chinese gentry in towns or peasants in villages. Scholars in the field either depended almost entirely on library research, which was not much different from the traditional Chinese way of conducting scholarship, or emphasized only quantitative data. Wu's and his students' dissatisfaction with the state of sociology in China[138] motivated them to establish a more rigorous sociological discipline for their country. The sinicization of sociology was a conscious decision on Wu's part. To achieve this goal, Wu believed that it was necessary for sociological research to incorporate anthropology's concern with culture and its field-work techniques. To Wu, community study (*shequ yanjiu*) combined the advantages of both disciplines and "best fit[ted] the situation of China."[139] Wu applied British functionalist theory to community study, a viewpoint that conceived of communities as wholes and that viewed each social and cultural element as an integral part of a whole. Neither community study nor functionalism was Wu's invention, but his familiarity with the most up-to-date Western scholarship indicates that his selection of these two models, out of many other options, was a deliberate choice—an approach that was based on his understanding of China's needs.

Wu Wenzao's ultimate goal was to train his students as first-class researchers. For this purpose, Wu invited Robert Ezra Park, a sociologist from Chicago known for his community studies, and A. R. Radcliffe-Brown, a founder of British functionalism, to be guest lecturers at Yanjing.[140] Using his connections in China and abroad, Wu looked for the best scholars in the field for his students' advanced training. Wu was the main influence behind Fei Xiaotong's decision to study with the Russian anthropologist S. M. Shirokogoroff at Qinghua University and to go to London to study with the famous functionalist scholar Bronislaw Malinowski. Other students of Wu's received similar guidance. Fei Xiaotong once commented that Wu "had a master plan in his mind to groom his disciples."[141] Eventually, several of Wu's students emerged as the next generation's leading scholars.[142]

It is clear that Wu Wenzao and his students set their own research agenda and methodology, even though foreign grants and connections were very important to their work.[143] Not only did Wu Wenzao and his students decide what theories and methodologies to take from the West, they also had their own way of applying them to the Chinese context. Their use of functionalism is a good example of this; in their hands, it became a useful tool for understanding Chinese society and culture in order to promote social changes,[144] even though functionalism has been criticized in the West for perpetuating a conservative ideology opposing social change.

Many Chinese sociologists, including Wu Wenzao and his colleagues, had chosen their field of study with an urge to change China through gradual reform rather than revolution. More than a few of them were directly involved in reform projects and social work in the republican period, such as the famous Dingxian County rural reconstruction movement led by Yanyang Chu (James Yen) with the help of Li Jinghan and students and other faculty from Yanjing University.[145] Individual sociologists, too, sought ways to combine scholarship with practical work. Li Anchai (Li An-che), for example, a student of Wu Wenzao, gave up his professorship at Yanjing in 1938 to work as a local official in a Tibetan region in Gansu Province.[146]

During this period, the general public often mistook sociology for "socialism," since the two terms shared the Chinese term *shehui*—a misperception some sociologists were eager to correct. While socialism was an "ideology," sociology, insisted its practitioners, was a "science," drawing its conclusions through systematic empirical studies. In his authoritative work on the history of sociology in China, published in 1948, Sun Benwen declared that his book only looked at "pure" sociological theories and their applications and would not include any works of a "propagandist" nature. To make himself clearer, he specifically singled out works expressing a "materialist" viewpoint as not belonging to "pure" sociology.[147] "Materialism" was associated with Marxist ideology, which Chinese sociologists generally shunned.[148] Rejecting the revolutionary approach to solving China's problems, they were looking for an alternative, evolutionary, and "scientific" route to bring about the changes that China needed to become a modern nation. The victory of the 1949 Communist revolution, however, meant that sociopolitical approaches were the dominant means to change. Consequently, sociology withered as a discipline in the 1950s.

Chinese sociologists' vision, as well as their version of a modern China, were shared by many other Chinese professionals of this generation. It is not surprising that they have been seen by both their contemporaries and later scholars as an elite out of touch with the Chinese reality. There might be some truth in this view, as their concerns often did not speak directly to the survival struggles of millions of Chinese, but they played a vital role in laying the foundation in the areas of modern industry, higher education, and research in the first half of the twentieth century. When large-scale industrialization took place in China in the 1950s, these professionals, particularly those in the fields of technology and natural sciences, were readily put to use. Without them, industrial development in the early PRC "would have had to rely more heavily on foreign technicians"—a reliance that would have slowed, perhaps significantly, the pace of China's industrialization.[149] The story of the social scientists under the PRC during the Mao era was much less reassuring, as what happened to sociology in the 1950s reveals (more information about sociology during this period will appear in the Epilogue).[150]

Even when the professionals, especially in the fields of technology and natural sciences, were of practical use to the country, the professional authority they represented posed a potential threat to the political authority. One recurrent theme after 1949 was the "red vs. expert" dichotomy, and the repeated attacks on experts and specialization (*zhuan*) by the Communist leaders during the Mao era indicate that the perceived threat was taken quite seriously.[151] It is evident, then, that professional authority had indeed gained wide recognition in China by the mid twentieth century. The culture of professionalism, embodied by the first generation of Chinese professionals, constitutes a vital, if at times disparaged, aspect of Chinese modernity.

CHAPTER THREE

The Question of Race

On a June day in 1924, a commencement ceremony was taking place at Colorado College. The graduating class walked in pairs to receive their academic degrees, one male student alongside one female. The mixed-gender parade by the departing class was a long-observed tradition in that coed school. Marching in the very front, however, were three pairs of six Chinese men. Since no American women students were willing to walk next to a Chinese man, the school authorities had come up with this awkward arrangement. The black hair, black eyes, and yellow faces of the Chinese looked conspicuously different from the appearances of their white classmates.[1] The graduation day of these Chinese would be forever remembered not as a moment of glory and pride, but one of debasement and humiliation. At that ceremony, their "race" overshadowed everything else.

While people have been prejudiced about different skin colors since ancient times, the abstract conceptualization of it is a modern development that began to appear only about two centuries ago, as a result of the

European voyages of discovery, slave trade, colonialism, and world capital-
ism, as well as the developments of various branches of scientific inquiry. It
was the "white race" in Europe and North America that has been responsible for conceiving physical differences between humans as "racial" and for
inventing the concept of race.[2] In the nineteenth century, Darwin's discov-
eries were used to further reinforce the conception of race as a physical category that had already been widely accepted by Europeans and white
Americans.[3] The need to come to terms with the Western-defined notion of
race presented Chinese intellectuals with a significant challenge. Racial consciousness constituted an essential feature in the Chinese modern identity.
The formation of "the discourse of race" in modern Chinese history is an
important and complex topic that deserves careful, sensitive, and systematic
study that goes beyond the scope of this chapter.[4] Suffice it to say that the
late nineteenth and early twentieth centuries were a critical and even
definitive period, when Chinese intellectuals, wrestling with the Western
notion of race, were constructing their own racial identity within the broad
framework of Chinese nationalism. Two generations of Chinese intellectuals contributed to this endeavor. The first generation was represented by the
pioneer thinkers Liang Qichao and Yan Fu, who were among the first
Chinese to abandon age-old sinocentricity and cultural universalism, and to
adapt to Western-defined racial concepts. The second generation was
represented by the May Fourth people. Within this group, I will focus on a
number of American-educated Qinghua graduates, who not only helped
articulate racial sensibility in modern China, as the story of Wen Yiduo
demonstrates, but also began to treat the question of race as a "scientific"
subject, as the cases of Wu Zelin and Pan Guangdan show.

For the students in America, perhaps more than for their peers back in
China, the question of race was particularly relevant and compelling. The
early decades of the twentieth century were a time when Chinese laborers
were banned from entering the United States—a prohibition that made the
Chinese the only "race" openly discriminated against in American immigration laws. Upon arriving in this Western country, the students found themselves in a peculiar and precarious racial situation. As upper-class Chinese,
they were exempted, like merchants and diplomats, from the exclusion acts
and were granted legal protection by the American government;[5] as an intel-

lectual elite seeking Western learning, they were in general kindly received by educated Americans (although the 1924 commencement scene at Colorado College indicates that this was not always the case); yet as members of an "inferior" race, they were at the mercy of prevalent anti-Chinese sentiment and practices in broader American society.

Many students were bewildered by the presence of Chinese laborers in the United States, who tended to work and live under pathetic conditions in ghettolike "Chinatowns." Back in China, the students would have little to do with their lower-class compatriots except to act like masters commanding the latter's service. In the United States, the "masters" found out that, like it or not, they were bound to the "servants" by common racial and national identity. The question of "what could we do for our working class in this country" was eventually brought up by the *Monthly*.[6] From 1910 to 1912, a small number of students were involved in "general welfare work" in helping to improve the conditions of the Chinese laborers. This activity took place both in the context of the "Progressive era" in the United States, when white, middle-class social reformers were going about helping newly arrived immigrants, and in the context of the constitutional movement in China that stimulated the reformist impulse in some of the students in America.

Issues of race, class, and modernity were all implicated in the students' ambivalent relationship with the Chinese laborers in the United States. Some students blamed the lower-class Chinese and their traditional way of life for the poor image of China held by the American public, and strove themselves to project a new and westernized image. Being the Other to the laborers in terms of class and modernity, the students nonetheless found themselves inseparable from the lower-class immigrants around the issue of race. And race mattered in America.

The low racial status of the Chinese in America sharpened many students' nationalistic sentiment. Their heightened racial consciousness did not lead most of them to challenge the premises of racial inequality. Rather, they largely accepted the racial hierarchy in the modern world and sought to improve China's position in it. The "general welfare work" was conducted not merely to better the lives of the Chinese laborers, but ultimately to improve the image of China in America. For members of the patriotic May Fourth generation in particular, the plight of the Chinese immigrants symbolized China's lower-class status in the world and provided an emotionally provocative case for their already intense patriotism. On a daily basis, however, they had little contact with Chinese laborers.

RACIAL IDENTITY AS A MODERN CONCEPT

To the Chinese living at the turn of the twentieth century, racial identity was a newly acquired aspect of modern consciousness. Two major thinkers in late Qing wrote about human differences in ways which underscore the tremendous conceptual leap Chinese intellectuals made during this period, and testify to how the pressing presence of the West altered the Chinese perception of the human world.[7]

In Tan Sitong's "Views on the Management of World Affairs," written in 1889, China, along with Korea, Tibet, Vietnam, and Burma, formed the core of a civilized universe, called *huaxia zhi guo* ("the Chinese states"), superior both to the *yidi zhi guo* ("the states of the barbarians"), consisting of Japan, Russia, Europe, and North America, and to the *qinshou zhi guo* ("the states of beasts"), made up of India and Africa. Tan's usage of "beasts" demonstrates that in the minds of many sinocentric Chinese, the people in India and Africa were viewed as less than human. Nevertheless, in Tan's world order, physical differences were not employed as a central criterion for classifying peoples, hence he placed the Japanese in the same camp with the Europeans and North Americans. In 1902, less than fifteen years after Tan Sitong wrote his piece, Liang Qichao envisaged a world composed of five races of different colors, with the Chinese belonging to the "yellow race." Liang certainly did not invent the notion of a "yellow race," which had been brought to China from the West.[8] Accepting the premises of racial inequality, Liang perceived the world as divided into "historical" and "ahistorical" races, with the "yellow race," a lesser "historical" race, ranked above the three darker "ahistorical" races of "red, brown and black" and below the superior "historical" white race. Within less than fifteen years, the Western defined, skin-color-based racial world order had been internalized by leading intellectuals of China.

To what extent had the Chinese indigenous hierarchical model helped to prepare the Chinese to adapt so quickly to the modern racial hierarchy? To be sure, as Frank Dikotter maintains, "the discourse of race" did not emerge in China out of an intellectual void.[9] The Chinese had not been innocent of prejudice against non-Han peoples, particularly those ethnic groups around the fringes of ancient China, nor had they been ignorant about the existence of different skin colors and other physical characteristics among peoples. Yet until the second half of the nineteenth century, the Chinese differentiated peoples chiefly by "social customs," "place," and "atmosphere." This is demonstrated by the thinking of Wang Fuzhi, a committed anti-Manchu Ming loyalist in the seventeenth century, arguably one of the most self-conscious "Han Chinese" of his time. In Wang's writing, the differences between the Chinese and "barbarians" lay primarily in sociocultural factors, rather than in biological ones.[10] It was "culture" that had made the Chinese superior to the "barbarians."

China's entrance into the modern world necessarily meant an abandonment, on the part of the educated Chinese, of China's age-old sinocentricity and cultural universalism, and an adaptation to Western-defined racial concepts.[11] "Attitudes about skin color and physical characters" might have been of "great antiquity" among the Chinese,[12] but the notion of "race," as defined primarily by skin color, was largely imposed upon the Chinese by the ascending West. The intrusion of an all-powerful West into the Chinese physical and intellectual landscape in the mid nineteenth century should not be slighted in an examination of "the discourse of race in modern China."[13] It is important to locate the party who initially defined the concept of "race" in the modern world, since "power consists in originating definitions."[14] As it turned out, the people who defined "race" also held the power to determine "racial relations" on their terms.

Western notions of race arrived in China at a time when Chinese intellectuals were primarily concerned with China's national survival in a Western-dominated and severely competitive world. Against this backdrop, Yan Fu, a British-educated scholar, introduced social Darwinism to the Chinese, along with new vocabulary and new concepts, such as "evolution," "natural selection," and "survival of the fittest." Social Darwinism, interpreted and presented by Yan Fu,[15] portrayed the world simultaneously as an arena where fierce struggles for racial survival were waged and as a place which offered hope for those who were striving for self-strengthening. This new doctrine profoundly affected the way the Chinese intellectuals perceived race and racial relations and helped many Chinese make sense of a strange and unfriendly modern world. Awareness of China's "racial status" in the world was also a crucial component in Liang Qichao's nationalist thinking, and the Chinese intellectuals of the early twentieth century were greatly influenced by both Liang Qichao and Yan Fu. The Chinese students who came to America at this time acquired a particularly acute understanding of China's racial status, as they found themselves in a country where Chinese were openly and legally discriminated against.

AMERICAN RACIAL DISCRIMINATION AGAINST THE CHINESE: A HISTORICAL REVIEW

In May 1882, in response to mounting anti-Chinese sentiments in the country, the United States Congress passed the Chinese Exclusion Act, prohibiting the entrance of Chinese laborers into America for ten years and reinforcing a provision of the 1868 Burlingame Treaty that denied naturalization to the Chinese already residing in the United States.

The early decades of the twentieth century witnessed two waves of renewed anti-Chinese sentiments. The first wave resulted in two acts by the Congress, in 1902 and 1904, in which the exempt classes of merchants, students, and in some cases even diplomats, were also affected. The second wave came in 1924, when Congress attempted to "plug the loopholes" of the exclusion laws. Chiefly targeting Japanese immigrants, the new act was known to the Chinese as the Second Exclusion Act, because it also hit them hard. Since the early 1880s, the anti-Chinese exclusion acts remained the cornerstone of official American policy toward the Chinese for six long decades, until they were finally repealed in 1943 after America and China became allies during the Second World War.[16]

Accompanying the discriminatory laws was a grossly unfavorable representation of the Chinese people as dirty and sly. The roots of this unfavorable image can be traced back to the late eighteenth century and the first half of the nineteenth century, when American traders, missionaries, and diplomats made their first contacts with the Chinese empire. Together these people developed categories, generalities, and stereotypes that became powerful determinants of public opinion. China was portrayed as politically despotic and socially static, and dishonesty and uncleanness were said to be characteristic traits of the Chinese people.[17]

The majority of early Chinese immigrants in the United States were poverty-stricken peasants from the Pearl River Delta in Guangdong Province. Their arrival in the mid nineteenth century coincided with the culmination of the slavery controversy between the North and the South, thus making the Chinese laborers an easy target as a permanent servile class and earning them the label "coolie." It was also the time when "scientific racism" was being advanced and race as type was being conceptualized and popularized.[18] After the Civil War, encouraged by rapid industrial development, Americans embraced ideals of progress and liberty more enthusiastically than ever before, while China by contrast appeared to represent the opposite of such ideals.

In the first decades of the twentieth century, popular entertainment, especially the rapidly developing movie industry, helped sustain and popularize impressions of mystery, peculiarity, backwardness, and dishonesty already associated with the Chinese. Hollywood began to portray China and the Chinese in feature films as early as the mid 1910s. Until the 1930s, when a more sympathetic depiction of China and the Chinese people began to appear, the American screen was largely dominated by unflattering images of the Chinese.[19] The best-known Chinese character in American popular culture during this period, both in fiction and on the screen, was Dr. Fu Manchu. Wearing a queue and long nails and attired in a dark long gown, Fu Manchu personified the Chinese villain as a well-educated and cultured man with mysterious and destructive powers.[20] Pulp magazines, short stories, novels, and plays also contributed to the "yellow peril" image of the Chinese.[21] The Chinese students in the United States were well aware of the negative image of the Chinese persistently held by the American general public. Four years after the 1911 republican revolution, as a student observed, caricatures and illustrations in American magazines and newspapers still made "Chinamen" wear queues. "If we had not been trained to appreciate the high art of American journalists," the student wryly remarked, "we would not have been able to recognize ourselves in the illustrations. . . . Thus thinks the American editor, the Chinaman must have a queue—forthwith it stands straight as an arrow on the top of the Chinaman's head, defying wind and the law of gravitation."[22]

The bound feet of women were another enduring feature associated with the Chinese, to the dismay of a student who had watched a slide show given at a church gathering by a returned American missionary. The show included the image of "a bare bound foot of an old Chinese woman [which was] placed on a piece of white cloth and enlarged many times." "The materials they [the returned missionaries] provided," the student observed, "tend to represent the lowest level of culture in their 'missionary land.' . . . The American women present were all shocked. . . . As for myself, I was impressed by the magic effect of the American popular education. I would rather see no popular lecture on the subject than distorted and misleading ones like what I attended to."[23] This kind of event led one student to lament, as late as 1925, "It seems that yellow teeth, long queues, and a few other unmentionable things are in the unconscious part of the American mind [about the Chinese]."[24]

THE STUDENTS' EXPERIENCE AS AN "EXEMPT CLASS": INFERIOR RACE OR SUPERIOR CLASS?

Legally, the students were exempted from the provisions of the exclusion acts. However, they were inevitably affected by the acts and the anti-Chinese sentiment prevalent in America. Racial tension in the early 1880s had led to the abrupt withdrawal in 1881 of the Yung Wing mission from the United States. To be sure, other factors had contributed to the sudden termination of the mission, yet the anti-Chinese zealotry of the American policy makers as well as the American government's refusal to admit Chinese students into U.S. military academies had given the conservative Chinese officials a convincing excuse to call back the educational mission.[25]

The early 1900s witnessed a new phase in the American exclusion effort that went beyond the barring of lower-class laborers to also include the "exempt class."[26] Students arriving in the United States around this time found that harassment by immigration officers was commonplace. Chen Guangfu, who came to America in 1904 and would later become a pioneering banker in China, was once ordered by immigration officers to leave a classroom in order to be questioned about his legal status.[27] In some cases, even Qing government representatives were not spared from abuses by

American immigration officers.[28] A massive boycott of American goods occurred in major cities across China in 1905, in part as a protest against the mistreatment of the upper-class Chinese in America.[29] The experience of Kong Xiangxi (H. H. Kung), who later became the minister of finance in Chiang Kai-shek's government, was a case in point. In September 1901, Kong and another Chinese young man were brought by Luella Miner, a Presbyterian missionary, to attend Oberlin College in Ohio. It took them a whole year to reach their destination, a delay that was due to their detention in San Francisco, which included a week in a filthy dockside shed, an experience that badly damaged Kong's health.[30] Perhaps not coincidentally, Song Ailing (Ailing Soong), the eldest of the famous Soong sisters who later married none other than Kong Xiangxi, also encountered humiliating treatment upon landing in America. In the summer of 1904 she was detained on a ship for more than two weeks before her influential father used his connections to get her released.[31]

Clearly the cases of Kong Xiangxi and Soong Ailing conveyed a sense that all Chinese, regardless of social class, were unwelcome. One writer expressed in 1907 the fear many students felt upon landing in the country: "To all of us, the most trying time is when we first land our feet in this country. . . . Instances have occurred time and again that some students have, during such times of trivial trouble, given up all their ambitions and actually returned home. . . . the difficulties of gaining admission into this country are always in dread of [*sic*] more or less by every new comer."[32] Consequently, many Chinese students shunned the United States and went to other countries instead. It was reported that in 1904 comparatively fewer overseas-bound Chinese students had "the courage to select the United States as their destination."[33] Note that this was the very period when a new wave of "studying abroad" movement began to rise.

The tendency of the Chinese students to stay away from the United States alarmed some Americans. In a letter in 1900 to John Hay, then the secretary of state, an American missionary in China argued that the presence of Chinese students "would not only give us an educational ascendance here, but it will also increase our prestige and stimulate commercial as well as intellectual intercourse."[34] In 1904, more than two hundred Americans in Shanghai, mostly "missionaries and educators," signed a petition expressing concern over the drift of "desirable classes of Chinese to other countries."[35]

Some American diplomats in China were also disturbed. Wilbur T. Gracey, vice-consul of the American consulate in Nanjing, observed that the exclusion laws were "one of the greatest points against which we have to contend in endeavoring to promote American trade and good feeling."[36]

These Americans comprised what Michael Hunt calls the "open-door constituency." Interested in promoting a good-will relationship with China for the benefit of America, they propagated a paternalistic attitude of wanting to defend and reform China[37]—an attitude represented by the State Department, which was engaged in a battle with the proexclusion Congress. The outcry of the open-door constituency caught the attention of President Theodore Roosevelt, who had previously been a supporter of the exclusion policy. To calm Chinese protest, which was forcefully expressed by the 1905 boycott of American goods, and to appease the open-door constituency, Roosevelt decided in 1906 to reform the Immigration Bureau by dismissing the notoriously racist Victor Metcalf, then the secretary of commerce and labor (the Bureau of Immigration at that time was under the jurisdiction of the Department of Commerce and Labor). Roosevelt told the new secretary to "do everything to prevent harshness being done to merchants and students," while still strictly ensuring the barring of the laborers.[38] Subsequently, a class-oriented "exclusion of Chinese laborers only" policy was reinstated; the Chinese "exempt classes" were reassured of respectful treatment.

There continued to be obstructions, however, at ports of entry and also during the residence of Chinese exempt classes in the United States. A recurrent problem was confusion over the definition of "students." Before 1906, only a person who came to enroll in a college-level educational institution was a "student." The new student category defined in 1906 loosened the requirements, so that, subsequently, a larger number of Guangdong peasant boys entered the country as students but eventually settled to work as laborers.[39] Meanwhile, real students were often suspect in the eyes of immigration officers. It was not until 1924 that this situation was effectively changed by the "Second Exclusion Law," which again tightened the regulations for students.[40] Another frequent hassle for the students was having the validity of their travel papers questioned. Both Kong Xiangxi and Song Ailing were charged with possessing improper documents. The process of issuing passports in China was not standardized until the end of 1911, when the U.S. Immigration Bureau began to issue them to Chinese citizens in both Hong Kong and Shanghai, a practice reportedly resulting from a recommendation by Wu Tingfang, a two-time Chinese minister to America. Yet abuses of students by the immigration authorities did not disappear. In a report to the Ministry of Education in Beijing in 1917, an official in charge of students' affairs at the Chinese legation in Washington maintained that there were "countless" cases of students being detained by the American immigration officers. Sometimes this official had to go all the way from Washington, D.C., to San Francisco to personally assist the students with the entrance procedure.[41]

Having been admitted into the country did not mean that racially-related harassment was over for the students. Chen Da, who arrived in America in 1916 to study sociology, once found himself openly insulted because of his race. Riding in a car with some American friends in Seattle, he was spotted by people in a truck coming from the other direction, who shouted at him in one voice, "John Chinaman! Chin Chin! Chinaman!" On another occasion, this time in Oregon, Chen Da went to a restaurant to eat. The waiter refused to serve him by replying that the restaurant had run out of every dish Chen ordered from the menu. A couple of years later, in response to a student's article on racial discrimination, Chen Da shared his own grievance in a piece entitled "Listen to Me Pouring Forth My Bitterness."[42] Another student, Chen Guangfu, was told by an American professor that, considering his grasp of English, he should not have been a student at all. Memories like this tended to linger painfully. Years later, Chen Guangfu frankly admitted that he had suffered from an inferiority complex when he was a student in America.[43] And racial prejudice could affect the students' everyday life in even more serious ways. In 1904 when Cheng Guangfu was looking for a place to live in St. Louis, he was told openly that colored people were not welcome.[44] Similarly, a "Miss Xue" had to move out of a summer resort lodging after her landlady found out that this pleasant "Oriental young woman" was not Japanese but Chinese.[45] Apparently, for the landlady, Japanese were superior to the Chinese, even though both belonged to the "yellow race." As late as 1919, newcomers from China were advised by the *Monthly* to inform their prospective landlords about their nationality to avoid potential embarrassment.[46]

It was not uncommon for Americans to mistake Chinese for Japanese or even non-Asian nationalities. One student living in the South once bitterly commented, "The people here seldom see upper-class Chinese, hence they always mistake us as [*sic*] Hispanics."[47] To some Americans it seemed an odd idea that a Chinese could be anything other than a laundryman or a restaurant worker. More than a few students were asked if they worked in a laundry. To some sensitive people, even the overtly benevolent attitude of American religious communities could carry hidden racist messages. In a letter to a friend in China in the early 1920s, a Christian student revealed his dismay:

> The people here, as a whole, have a strong sentiment against Chinese, so it is rather hard for a young chink to make acquaintances in refined society. . . . I don't feel at home at all. The hearty welcome I get from the church people makes me feel the more that I am among the strangers; they greet me so much more warmly than they greet each other, it makes me feel I am different.[48]

On college campuses, where the students spent most of their time, the atmosphere was generally more friendly. At the 1907 summer gathering held in Andover, Massachusetts, Alfred E. Stearns, principal of the Phillips Academy and the guest speaker of that year's conference, apologized for the "prejudice and selfishness" that had "dictated policies and actions at variance with the American ideals and against which the true Americans cry out in protest." Stearns assured the students, "In her higher institution of learning you will find American ideals best exemplified. . . . Into these institutions your students are gladly welcomed."[49] Students appreciated the respect paid to them by the American-educated elite, which was in sharp contrast to the contempt frequently found among the general public. One student jokingly compared the different perceptions of the Chinese held by the different social classes in America: "American conception of the Chinese—the average Americans: 'They are Japs.' The uneducated class, 'Well, the Chinaman's chop-suey is some class.' The middle class: 'Chinaman eats rats and bird nests!' The intelligent class: 'The Chinese Revolution! Premier Kai and Dr. Sen.'"[50]

Sometimes, however, the students found that their trust in educated Americans could be misplaced. The 1924 Colorado College commencement was such an instance. On another occasion, a play called "Tickled to Death" was staged by a theater group in 1925 at the University of Michigan. The play depicted the absurdity and cruelty of a Chinese "high priest" in a Buddhist temple, whose behavior clearly resembled that of Fu Manchu. After finding out that an American archaeology student had fallen in love with his young female charge, the priest decided to tickle the American man to death. The woman, incidentally, was a "white girl" who had been raised by the priest and whose ultimate fate was to be a sacrifice to the Sun God on the monastery's dreadful altar.[51] This play aroused an unprecedented wave of protest from the Chinese student community. Besides a strong letter from the president of the Alliance to the president of the University of Michigan, the *Monthly* published a bitter and unusually lengthy editorial devoted entirely to the incident, in which the editor wondered if "the mind of the American in a university is different from that of one who has never entered it."[52] Subsequently, a Chinese graduate student withdrew from the university in order to demonstrate to the Americans the Confucianist moral principle that "a gentleman might be killed, but he can never be humiliated."[53]

In 1927, an American social scientist surveyed 1,725 Americans and found that only 27 percent said they would accept Chinese as fellow workers, 15.9 percent as neighbors, and 11.8 percent as friends.[54] Clearly, racial discrimination against the Chinese was a reality of life in American society. Such a reality, interestingly, was only frankly acknowledged by a small segment of the Chinese students, the majority of the students, it seems, either keeping silent or downplaying the significance of racial discrimination. Kong Xiangxi, for example, never in his life openly discussed his detention at the San Francisco dockside shed.[55] This kind of attitude puzzled some contemporary observers. One person expressed his bewilderment to a fellow student:

> There is one problem I can not solve. . . . When I was in China, the returned students I met all talked about how well-received they were by the American society, and how they were treated with special favor by the Americans. Few mentioned the humiliation and discrimination they experienced abroad. Did Americans treat us Chinese better then than they do now? Or did the earlier students not mix up as much with the Americans as we do today? Or else they simply were good at hiding the unpleasant facts and spreading the pleasant facts, in order to avoid mockery from our compatriots? As for myself, I would rather be laughed at by my compatriots than be humiliated by foreigners.[56]

Note that this conversation took place in 1919, a time when educated youth in China had reached a new level of nationalist consciousness. As it turned out, the students baptized by the May Fourth movement appeared to be more ready to take issue with racial discrimination than people before them. (This subject will be further explored in a later section of this chapter.)

In sum, the Chinese students found themselves living in a racial environment that was delicate and contradictory throughout the period this book is examining. As Chinese, they lived under the heavy shadow of overt racial discrimination existing in American society; as members of an exempt class, they were protected by the American law; as students seeking Western learning, they were generally well-received by the American-educated elite. Their self-image as members of a superior class frequently clashed with the American general public's perception of the Chinese as an inferior race. Racial discrimination drew some students closer to the Chinese laborers, but for others, this largely imposed racial binding aroused resentment. A built-in ambivalence existed in the students' relationship with the laborers.

AN UNEASY BOND WITH THE "FELLOW COUNTRYMEN"

There was a tendency among some students to emphasize their class status so as to differentiate themselves from the resident Chinese. One person, studying in the South, reported in the *Quarterly* that the resident Chinese there were "almost all laundry workers," who dressed improperly and acted awkwardly in public. "No wonder," the student remarked, "they fail to gain respect from other people."[57] In reality, however, not a small number of the resident Chinese in one southern state, Mississippi, for instance, were in the grocery or retail business.[58] The student's perception of the resident Chinese as "almost all" laundry workers, ironically, conformed to the stereotype held by the American general public. Similarly, in a letter to a friend in 1915, Chen Hengzhe, a student at Vassar College who later became the first female professor at Beijing University, did not hide her disdain for the resident Chinese: "After two months' careful observation [since I arrived in the U.S.], I have found that though there are Americans who respect China, perhaps a greater number of the people . . . tend to consider our country only half civilized and our people all like the long-queued, ignorant San Francisco workers."[59]

It is interesting to note that Chen Hengzhe objected to the representation of China by the "San Francisco workers" not only because they were "lower class," but also because they embodied an "antimodern" way of life, signified conspicuously by their "long queues." By contrast, Chen Hengzhe and many other students saw themselves representing both the "upper class" and the "modern way." The story told by a student about how he had helped a young laundryman illustrates the point: under the student's influence, the young worker cut his queue, changed into Western-style clothes, and made his laundry a "clean and well-kept" place only a week after the two got to know each other. Pleased with the result, the student asked, "Who shall guide them [people like the laundry man]—we students or their old-fashioned and conservative friends and relatives?"[60]

While class and education placed the students above the Chinese laborers, race pulled them back together. The possible views a student might take regarding the question of Chinese laborers were never starkly binary, but were often mixed and ambivalent. Many students were made to realize that, regardless of how they perceived themselves, they were inseparable from their lower-class compatriots in the mind of the American general public. Like it or not, they had no choice but to identify to some extent with the laboring Chinese immigrants. Eventually, some students began to refer to the resident Chinese as "fellow countrymen," a term that acknowledged a bond. How much contact did the students have with lower-class Chinese residents? Available sources do not provide an adequate answer, since few students recorded their experiences in this respect. Hu Shi, for example, did not mention in his diary any personal encounter with resident Chinese during his seven long years in the United States, which included three years in New York City.[61] Similarly, nothing can be found on this issue in Zhao Yuanren's reminiscences of his student days in America.[62] The lack of visibility of the resident Chinese in students' accounts suggests that the subject was of an unpleasant nature for students and probably indicates that the actual contact between the two groups was minimal.

One reason for the apparent lack of contact lay in the differences between the two groups' spoken languages. While the majority of the resident Chinese spoke various dialects of Guangdong Province, a large percentage of the students came from other parts of the country and therefore would find the Guangdong dialects unintelligible. Jiang Menglin, a native of Jiangsu Province, once found himself surrounded by a group of curious people in a Chinese grocery store in San Francisco's Chinatown. Unable to make the shopkeeper understand his speech, Jiang had to write down in Chinese what he wanted, which prompted an old woman to ask, "If this Chinese can not speak Chinese [meaning Cantonese], how can he write it?"[63] Jiang was relieved when he was finally able to leave the store with a bottle of soy sauce and other Chinese groceries. This kind of experience was likely to be repeated by other non-Cantonese speaking students. Yet, despite language barriers and other obstacles, the two groups did occasionally cross paths. When that happened, in more than one instance, the people involved found the experience mutually gratifying. Xie Bingxin (Wanying), who received her M.A. degree from Wellesley College and went on to become one of the most accomplished woman writers of her generation, recorded such an encounter.

In the summer of 1923 Xie and other Chinese students, mostly Qinghua graduates—the largest group of Chinese students to travel to America that year—boarded the ocean liner *President Jackson*. In order to avoid being mistaken for laborers by American immigration officers, the students all took first-class cabins. This arrangement, calculated to protect the students from racial discrimination by American immigration officers at the port of entrance by deliberately stressing their class status, delighted the cabin boys and bartenders on the ship, most of whom were from Guangdong Province. They were pleased to see so many Chinese traveling first class. During the voyage, the service people "really cared a great deal about how the Americans on board thought of the Chinese students." Before the ship landed at Seattle, they wrote an open letter to the students, in which they talked about their bitter life as "ocean-crossing Cantonese" often at the mercy of difficult Western passengers, and expressed their wish to see the students "make it" for the sake of China. Touched by the letter, the students replied with equal earnestness.[64]

Liang Shiqiu, who was on the same voyage, recalled another moving story that took place after the ship landed. Traveling east, their train made a stop at a station in Wyoming to allow the passengers to eat. Liang and his friends found a small restaurant run by an elderly Asian-looking man and ordered food there. When the old man learned, through an exchange of Chinese words on paper, that these young *tangren* (people of Tang dynasty, used by Guangdong people to refer to people from China) had come to this country to study, he suddenly looked very serious, and gave the students the thumbs up. When Liang and his friends went to pay their bill, the old man refused to accept it and uttered something in Cantonese, which Liang figured out meant "We are all *tangren*!" More than half a century later, these words still rang in Liang's mind.[65]

It was not unusual for Chinese laborers in America to remind their more fortunate compatriots of their responsibility for China, as did the service people of the *President Jackson*. On another occasion, a student in the South met an American-born Chinese laundryman, who had served in the U.S. Army during the First World War. He gave the student a gas mask he had used in the military, hoping that the student, who majored in chemistry, would study the mask for the benefit of China.[66] Chen Guangfu had a similar encounter with a Chinese waiter in St. Louis, which prompted Chen to remark, many years later, that "the Chinese laundrymen and restaurant workers in the U.S. were very kind to Chinese students. Although uneducated, they were more patriotic than the educated class."[67] One place where the two groups might cross paths was the Chinatown in a big city. For many students, however, Chinatown generated ambivalent feelings, representing both a symbol of home and a reminder of racial and national disgrace. In the early twentieth century, "filthy streets, dingy shops and opium dens" in a Chinatown symbolized to the American middle-class reformers the evils of urban poverty; they were places that attracted "sociological classes and slum parties" and were vulnerable to harsh police regulations.[68] On the other hand, the special scenery, smells, and sounds of a Chinatown were the closest things to home in a foreign country. On a Chinese New Year's Eve, Jiang Menglin and his friends went to San Francisco's Chinatown, where they admired shop-window decorations and enjoyed the noise of firecrackers. Jiang felt as if they were celebrating the New Year in China.[69]

The ambivalence many students felt toward resident Chinese did not affect their basic position on the issue of Chinese immigration. When Mary R. Coolidge's pioneering study, *On Chinese Immigration*, first came out in 1912, the *Monthly* recommended it to its readers and printed the entire last chapter in one of its issues, an unprecedented act by the *Monthly*.[70] Coolidge was sympathetic to Chinese immigrants and argued for an end to the exclusion laws.

Articles on the history of Chinese immigration and the conditions of Chinese immigrants appeared quite frequently in students' publications. Two themes dominated the articles: defending the Chinese immigrants, who were portrayed as law-abiding and hard-working people, and criticizing the exclusion legislation, which was viewed as chiefly responsible for both the pathetic conditions of Chinatowns and the difficulties of Chinese residents' assimilation into American society.[71] A common argument in the articles was that the exclusion laws also hurt America, both economically and politically. Racial prejudice was named in several articles as the essential cause of the exclusion laws. Notably, none of the articles emphasized the class differences between the students and the resident Chinese; some even identified the three major groups of Chinese in America, the laborers, the merchants, and the students, as one entity.[72]

Hu Shi's position regarding the question of race contrasted with the generally nationalistic approach taken by other students. During Hu's years as a student in America, the cosmopolitan movement occupied a significant place in his life. Embracing internationalist idealism, this movement had significant support on American college campuses before World War I. By espousing universal human values that transcended national and cultural boundaries, it rejected nationalism narrowly conceived and belligerently expressed.[73] The spirit of the movement was best summarized by the saying "Above all nations is humanity," which became Hu Shi's favorite motto.[74] Participation in the cosmopolitan movement allowed Hu Shi to become acquainted with a large number of international students, including people from Central and South America, Asia, and Africa, some of whom Hu Shi maintained friendships with for decades. The movement also helped make Hu Shi sensitive to racial injustice in America and led him to pay attention to the situation of African-Americans. Once Hu wrote a strong letter on behalf of two black female students at Cornell who had been barred from a white dormitory.[75] On another occasion, using the opportunity of a party held to honor him as the retiring president of the Cornell Cosmopolitan Club, Hu Shi gave a speech that "stirred every man present," in which he challenged anti-Semitism and racial discrimination against blacks within the cosmopolitan community itself.[76] Though more broad-minded than many of his fellow Chinese in his approach to racial issues, Hu Shi was conspicuously silent about the specific situation of Chinese immigrants.

THE "GENERAL WELFARE WORK"

The question "What could we do for our working class in this country?" was officially raised by an editorial in the *Monthly* at the end of 1909.[77] This question of "great delicacy" was finally brought into the open after the *Monthly* had received "numerous letters" from its readers touching upon the issue, and after the editors of the journal realized that "other nations are striving to improve the conditions of their workmen." To ward off possible negative responses from those who might say "we have nothing to do" with Chinese laborers, the editorial referred to a clause in the constitution of the Alliance: "to labor for the general welfare of China both at home and abroad."[78]

Responses to the editorial were encouraging and revealing. One student remarked that the issue "ought to touch the heart of everyone of us who have [*sic*] seen the deplorable conditions under which some of our countrymen live."[79] A political science major at Harvard University wrote that he and his friends in the Boston area had given "a great deal of serious attention" to the problem of Chinese laborers in the city and had in the past sought support from influential Chinese merchants in Boston's Chinatown. What they received from the merchants, however, was "indifference." Now that the *Monthly* was taking up the issue, he and his friends had new hope.[80] Overall, the editorial was regarded as long overdue by the student community.

An American woman was also encouraged by the editorial. Writing to the *Monthly*, Mrs. Harry E. Mitchell said that she had worked among Chinese laborers in America for many years, but had in the past chosen to keep silent on the subject because of what she described as "the seeming indifference of other Chinese" and because, as an American, she was afraid of "being misunderstood" for raising a "delicate question." Apparently a Christian, Mitchell emphasized the importance of love, sympathy, and brotherhood in the relationship with the Chinese laborers.[81] In all probability, Mrs. Harry Mitchell was a "progressive," a kind of middle-class social reformer in early-twentieth-century America who set out to right the wrongs caused by a rapidly expanding urban and industrial society. Some progressives were involved in the settlement house movement in cities, which aimed to help recent immigrants. Many progressives were motivated by a strong sense of moral righteousness.[82] Mrs. Harry Mitchell conveyed this sense of high moral ideals in her letter to the *Monthly*.

Soon after the publication of the editorial, a "general welfare committee" was set up by the Eastern Alliance, with the intention of encouraging students to organize local branches to help Chinese laborers. The committee was subsequently endorsed by the Joint Council of the Eastern and Western

Alliances. The fact that general welfare work was launched by the Alliance in 1909–10, in the midst of the American Progressive era, is significant. The Progressive movement helped highlight the plight of recent immigrants and may very well have made some Chinese students more sensitive to the predicament of the Chinese laborers. The reference to "sociological tours" to Chinatown in a *Monthly* editorial indicates that the editors were well aware of the American public's attention to the crowded living conditions and poor sanitation in Chinese neighborhoods. The middle-class nature of the American social-justice movement also assured the students that their own work would be respectable. Yet in contrast to the frequently moralistic motivation of the American progressives, the Chinese students were concerned primarily with nationalistic issues. Lui-ngau Chang, an editor of the *Monthly*, articulated this well:

> Before the eyes of the world, China has been in a large measure misrepresented, misconceived and misjudged. She is largely represented abroad by a class of people, undesirable in bearing and unprepossessing in occupation. . . . The whole Chinese race is sure to be discredited and be held accountable for the misconduct of one of its ignorant, humble members. . . . Unless something is done to eradicate this great source of humiliation, our efforts are incomplete, and our activities are rendered slow in progress.[83]

This was a reluctant argument for the "general welfare" cause. It was unfortunate, as Chang saw it, that China was "misrepresented" by its "ignorant, humble members" in America. What was at stake was not these miserable creatures per se, but the reputation of the "whole Chinese race." Chang might sound more contemptuous of the Chinese laborers than some of his fellow students, but his nationalistic concern was commonly shared by other people and served as the main justification for the launching of the general welfare work by the Alliance.

In March 1910 a general welfare association was founded in Boston, consisting of ten people, eight from Harvard and two from "Boston Tech" (MIT).[84] Students in the Boston area had responded warmly to the *Monthly* editorial, but when it came to taking action, many people found excuses, citing the difficulties of language, money, and time. It is not surprising that among the ten men who set out to do the work, all but one spoke

Cantonese. Having a language in common with the lower-class laborers made it much easier for the students to "imagine" a sense of fellowship.[85]

As the first local endeavor by the Chinese students, the Boston general welfare work set an example for similar projects in other cities. The students chose teaching as their way of helping the laborers. Through Mr. Mei, a "young and patriotic" teacher at the Boston Chinese School in Chinatown, the students made connections with the local Chinese community. Realizing that they needed understanding and support from "influential men," the students reached out to the Chinese Merchants' Association, which subsequently donated fifty dollars to the general welfare work. The students also contacted the Chinese Reform Association, an organization affiliated with Kang Youwei and Liang Qichao's loyalist Constitution Association.[86]

It is worth pausing here for a moment to take a brief look at politics in Chinese immigrant communities in America around this time. Two dissident and opposite political organizations had a presence in America: Tongmenhui (Revolutionary Alliance) and Xianzhengdang (previously called Baohuanghui, better known in English as the Imperial Reform Party), led respectively by Sun Yat-sen, and Kang Youwei and Liang Qichao.[87] The Revolutionary Alliance, generally appealing to the "common man" and associated with secret societies, advocated anti-Manchu revolution, whereas the Reform Party, attracting mostly community leaders and merchants, originally fought for the restoration of Emperor Guangxu and later supported the constitutional movement in China. The two political organizations intensified their competition in America after 1905, which led to an increase of political division in Chinese communities along ideological lines.

The Chinese Reform Association was apparently a branch of the Reform Party in Boston, while the Revolutionary Alliance probably also had established a chapter in Boston by 1910.[88] The city, however, was not a stronghold for either party. It is hard to tell how much the students knew about the political divisions in Boston's Chinatown, though it is unlikely that they were totally unaware of them. When it came time to choose between a Christian church and the meeting hall of the Chinese Reform Association as the site for the general welfare school, the students rejected the idea of a church, lest the school be "misunderstood for religious purpose,"[89] and settled for the meeting hall. The danger of having their work perceived as being linked to the loyalist cause was dismissed on the grounds that the Reform Association advocated both a constitutional government for China and the idea of citizenship for the Chinese people. The students' association with the Chinese Reform Association could be regarded as a deliberate choice, consistent with the Alliance's reformist inclinations around 1910, examined already in Chapter 1. Meanwhile, the students were eager to emphasize the independent nature of their endeavor, insisting that "the school is to be managed by us, and their help [that of the Reform Association] is welcome as we welcome the help from any other person or body of persons."[90]

On the opening day of the school, to the delight of the students, the meeting hall was packed with people, many having been recruited by Mr. Mei. Most of the pupils were young men, "dressed like us," in Western-style clothing. The school organizers envisioned that the current body of pupils would become the "leading spirit of our laboring classes" in Boston's Chinatown. The school leaders promised that after "three to five years," when the pupils successfully completed the entire program, "certifications" would be granted. The dual goal of the school was to make the pupils "more efficient workmen" and "better citizens." The idea of the "new citizen" enjoyed a high currency in the ongoing constitutional movement in China, and the promotion of "citizenship" was high on the students' agenda, "the very thing which our movement stands for."[91] Not surprisingly, the general welfare school was named the Citizenship School of Boston.

The classes were scheduled on Sundays, the afternoon section devoted to developing "efficient workmen," with classes on English, mathematics, and Chinese (Mandarin), while the evening section aimed at developing "better citizenship," with classes on Chinese geography and history, general information about the United States and the situation of Chinese immigrants in America, which included "the Chinese people as seen by others, and their reform and betterment." Last but not the least, lessons on personal hygiene were offered. The inclusion of this topic in the curriculum is noteworthy, since it echoed the concern of American progressives regarding recent immigrants and reflected the students' awareness of the Chinese immigrants' reputation as carriers of germs.[92] It was also a way of bringing "modernity" to the "laboring class."

In early 1912, roughly two years after the Citizen School of Boston began, the secretary of the school reported to the *Monthly* that the school was still operating on the same scale and still following the same format as it was two years previously.[93] When the Chinese republic was founded, the students and the Boston Chinese community celebrated the occasion together. The report asserted that the conditions of Boston's Chinatown had improved since the founding of the school.[94] The apparent success of that endeavor led to the establishment of general welfare work among Chinese laborers in at least two other American cities: New York and Philadelphia. In November 1910, the Chinese students' club at Columbia University launched its general welfare school.[95] Like the Boston group, the students in New York insisted at the outset that their endeavor was "strictly secular, non-religious." They managed to obtain support from the Chinese Merchants' Association, which donated fifty dollars, and from the Chinese consulate in New York. Finding a proper site for the school proved to be a challenge, since the school had to be located in a "neutral territory" to avoid friction with opposing factions (*tongs*) in New York's Chinatown.[96] The curriculum of the New York school resembled that of the Boston school.

It is noteworthy that students in both Boston and New York insisted on the nonreligious nature of general welfare work. Before the launching of general welfare work by the Alliance, some Chinese Christian students had already made efforts to set up Sunday schools in a number of cities to help the Chinese laborers. One such school, in New Haven, founded during the first decade of the century, was associated with a local Baptist church, and taught only religious subjects at first. Later, lectures on current events, mathematics, geography, and English were added, possibly reflecting the influence of the general welfare work.[97] The school was still in existence in 1916, reportedly having as many as one-third of the Chinese laborers in the city enrolled in its programs.

While the general-welfare schools were aimed only at male immigrants, at least one student paid attention to the situation of resident Chinese women. Living in Pittsburgh, Be Di Lee was bewildered by "the strong resentment of the American people toward our countrymen" and was especially concerned with the ideas "entertained by these Americans as regards Chinese women." Her academic training in sociology, with an emphasis on social work, gave her a professional angle from which to view the problems of Chinese immigrants. She decided to interview families in Pittsburgh's Chinese community, and in the process found that the courses she had taken at school were "immediately useful." She claimed that she was gaining respect from the Chinese immigrant women in Pittsburgh, but did not give details about what she had done besides interviewing people.[98] Resident Chinese youth also received help from the Chinese students, mostly through the organization of Boy Scout Troops, which began to appear in Chinese communities around the time that the general welfare work was launched. In early 1916, the *Monthly* reported the existence of Chinese Boy Scouts in several large cities, formed under the auspices of Chinese students' local clubs.[99] The first unit registered at the American Boy Scouts' national headquarters was Troop 50 of the Manhattan Boy Scouts, organized in May 1916. Led first by Americans, it was taken over a year later by Chen Heqin (Chen Ho-chin), a student at Columbia who later became a renowned educator in China. As the only officially registered Boy Scout troop "entirely run by the Chinese themselves," Troop 50 upheld the ideals of "initiative, co-operation, and service," which were considered "three essential things" "badly needed among our Chinese people." Instead of "merely training our scouts for good citizenship," Chen Heqin wanted his boys to become "future leaders in their community."[100]

It is difficult to evaluate the effectiveness of the students' general welfare work and other programs, since the stories in available documents have been told only from the point of view of the "teachers."[101] It is fair to say, however, that the general welfare work never achieved the scale of a real movement. Nor was it ever considered a priority on the agenda of the Alliance. The number of people actually involved in the general welfare work was very small and, if the Boston school is an indication, most of them spoke Cantonese. The life span of the general welfare work was apparently rather short: after 1912, little information about it appeared in the Chinese students' publications.

THE MAY FOURTH GENERATION

After 1912, with the disappearance of general welfare work from the agenda of the Alliance, meaningful interaction between Chinese students and resident laborers in America largely came to an end. Concerns for "fellow countrymen" continued to be expressed by the students, but little concrete work was pursued.[102] On a daily basis, therefore, little contact occurred between the two groups.

When young people of the May Fourth generation arrived in the United States, some showed a keen racial sensibility and readily viewed American racial injustice against the Chinese in light of China's national humiliation. Their heightened racial consciousness constituted an extra dimension in their passionate nationalism. Members of this generation also began to pursue "scientific" inquiries about the question of race. In the following pages, we will look at a few individuals who arguably best represented the May Fourth spirit, to examine how they confronted the question of race in America.

Wen Yiduo (Wen I-to), who later would become a renowned poet of the modern style and an acclaimed scholar of Chinese classics, perhaps embodied the keenest racial sensibility among his peers. His biographer described his life in America (1922–25) as "lonely" and concluded that "homesickness led him to over-idealize his country and prejudiced him against anything non-Chinese."[103] In Dikotter's recent work, Wen is used as an example to illustrate how, in order to compensate for feelings of alienation derived from living abroad, many Chinese intellectuals tended to project "superior feelings on to the homeland."[104]

Wen Yiduo is an intriguing phenomenon in modern Chinese intellectual and political history, and the present brief account cannot do him full justice. Suffice it to say that during his days as a student in America, Wen could not be described simply as a narrow-minded cultural nationalist. On the contrary, Wen demonstrated a "cosmopolitan" spirit and was engaged in a more intense intellectual inquiry about Western culture than most of his peers. His ultimate concern was how to absorb the best in Western culture in order to create a new Chinese culture.[105] To this end, Wen chose to study Western art, a rare subject for a Chinese student in America. He was an admirer of van Gogh, Cézanne, and Matisse, and was also attracted to the poems of Keats, Byron, and Shelley. His mastery of English verse impressed his American schoolmates. In his daily life, he dressed like a Bohemian, wearing long hair, a black tie, and a paint-stained studio smock—a far cry from the elegant image of a classical Chinese scholar.

Wen was not isolated from American society either, at least not in his early student days in Chicago, when he sometimes appeared at gatherings of American intellectual and artistic elite. Wen was particularly drawn to and made friends with those people who appreciated Chinese civilization.[106] Eventually, however, Wen had less and less contact with Americans. Twenty years after his return from America, Wen explained that his withdrawal from American society was a deliberate decision to avoid racial humiliation.[107]

Wen was a delicate and sensitive person and a poet by nature, yet Wen's racial sensibility should not be attributed to this factor alone. He was a product of the May Fourth movement, when China's humiliation at the hands of the Western powers raised to a new height the nationalistic consciousness of a whole generation of Chinese youth. It was against this background that Wen wrote his article "Qinghua has become too Americanized," shortly before his departure for the United States. In this article, Wen criticized American culture for its materialism, mediocrity, shallowness, vainness, impulsiveness, and extravagance.[108] Racial prejudice was missing from the list of failings, but it would soon be recognized and eventually loom very large in Wen's critique of America. In one of his first letters to his family from America, Wen commented on his observations of racism. He noted that "skin color" was the basic criterion Americans used to differentiate people: "In America only white people are respected. The colored people (here the yellow, black and red people are called colored) are barbarians."[109] Six months after his arrival in America, he dwelt on the same subject with enhanced bitterness in this letter home:

> The experiences of a sensible Chinese young man in America defy description. Wait till the end of the year after next, when I come home to spend the New Year with you around the fire. Then I will cry and tell you [about the humiliation I have experienced here] so that to let out my accumulated anger. I am not a man without a country. We have a history and a culture of five thousand years. In what are we inferior to the Americans? Should we say that because we can not manufacture guns and cannons for massacring people, we are not as brilliant and superior as they? In short, a few words can not adequately describe how we Chinese are being discriminated against here in America. After my return I would rather advocate friendship and alliance between China and Japan against the Americans than advocating friendship between China and the United States against Japan.[110]

For the rest of his life, Wen would think about the "alliance between China and Japan," but his indignation against racial discrimination retained its intensity. The available material does not provide us with sufficient information on how Wen personally experienced racial injustice in America. He could have been one of the six Chinese men walking in the commencement parade at Colorado College.[111] What we know mostly is how he reacted to incidents of racial humiliation encountered by other Chinese, some of whom were his fellow Qinghua schoolmates.[112]

There is no indication that Wen had much personal contact with Chinese laborers either, yet he was possibly the first student to portray the lives of the resident Chinese in America in a literary form. In his famous poem "The Laundry Song," the first of a "series of sketches" Wen intended to write about "how the Chinese people are being bullied in America," Wen let a laundryman tell his grievances in a first-person voice. Washing dirty clothes "year in year out" with "a drop of homesick tears," he received only racial ridicule from people whose appearances he helped keep clean.[113] In the preface to the poem, Wen wrote that since laundry work was such a common occupation for Chinese in America, Chinese students here were frequently asked, "Is your father a laundryman?"[114] "The Laundry Song" was first published in the Big River Quarterly. The race-related experience of the overseas Chinese was a common subject matter in a number of literary and scholarly pieces in the two issues of the Quarterly.[115] In these writings, however, the Chinese laborers were presented largely in symbolic terms and their plight was incorporated into the larger narrative of Chinese national humiliation to promote nationalism, the ultimate concern of the Big River Society.

The first serious academic study of racial problems in America by a Chinese student was undertaken by Wu Zelin, a member of the Big River Society, who chose the topic "Attitude[s] toward Negroes, Jews, and Oriental[s] in the United States" for his doctoral dissertation.[116] Using quantitative methods, Wu studied how his subjects were treated "in various fields, political, economic, educational, social, and religious, by white Gentile Americans." In Wu's view, "a race problem is after all a problem of attitude." Since attitudes were "so deeply conditioned both ontogenetically and phylogenetically," they were "extremely difficult to change within a short time."[117] Regarding the situation of black Americans, Wu pointed out that racial discrimination was a political, economic, and social reality for blacks in both the North and in the South, even though "under law and in the court, Negroes are equal to white men." With an increasing number of blacks migrating to Northern cities, "threats, violence, and legislative measures are being resorted to keep the white section from being contaminated." The problem for Jewish people, on the other hand, was primarily "social isolation." Jewish students, for instance, confronted "various forms of discrimination" on college and university campuses "along social lines." The status of "Orientals," meanwhile, was somewhere between that of the blacks and the Jews. Discrimination in the job market was common and there was little opportunity for the groups studied by Wu to mingle with the rest of the society. On the whole, however, Wu found that "the bitterness toward the Chinese has been greatly softened and the attitude toward the Japanese is tending to be more conciliatory."[118]

What is significant about Wu's study was not its great depth and acute insight, which it did not really possess, but rather the choice of topic, the analytical tone, and the "professional" posture. Here, a Chinese scholar was examining racial problems in America, not with the sentiment of a member of a victimized race, but with the cool gaze of a trained social scientist. Wu Zelin's contribution to the study of "race" will be further explored in the next section.

THE PREMISES OF RACIAL INEQUALITY

By coming to the United States, many students acquired a heightened racial consciousness, yet few of them questioned the notion of racial hierarchy. When defending the rights of Chinese immigrants, they based their argument largely on the grounds of treaty agreements and common interests for both China and America. Some Chinese students, while opposing racial discrimination against the Chinese, held prejudices against other races, particularly African-Americans. A 1910 *Monthly* editorial exemplified such an attitude:

> Now it must be remembered that the Chinese and the Negroes are entirely different peoples and the consideration of them must be on entirely different lines. The one came under the bondage of slavery, the other as citizens of a treaty nation; the one cost his country five hundred dollars a man, the other cost her nothing; the one came without a preliminary discipline and therefore not qualified for immediate advancement into higher forms of school, the other with a civilization and culture of more than four thousand years. And yet the Negroes have been given privileges of ballot while the Chinese laborers are not even allowed to come. Americans may have much to fear from the Negro race, but from the Chinese she needs fear nothing.[119]

Among the few people who did challenge the premise of racial hierarchy, Wu Zelin stood out as one of the most articulate. He continued his study on the question of race after he returned to China and published an important work on the subject, the first of its kind in Chinese. His view on innate racial equality was questioned by Pan Guangdan, his Qinghua schoolmate and friend, who was leaning toward a conditional acceptance of racial hierarchy. Both Wu and Pan employed contemporary Western theories to support their arguments. Together, they represented the most serious and well-informed inquiries into the question of race in republican China.

Wu Zelin went back to China in 1928 with a doctoral degree in sociology from Ohio State University. In 1931, he published his first book in China, *Xiandai zhongzu* (Modern races), a topic that had already commanded much of his scholarly attention in America.[120] While his dissertation, an examination of racial "attitudes" in America, did not explicitly address the issue of whether some races were inherently or biologically superior to others, in this book he confronted the question head-on. Acknowledging the importance of "race" in modern times, Wu began by raising a number of questions: What is race? How should races be classified? Are different races equal? Is there "scientific evidence" to support the theories of racial hierarchy?[121]

Drawing upon recent studies conducted by Western scholars to support his argument, including an influential study by Franz Boas of Columbia University in 1911,[122] Wu argued that none of the current criteria used to define and describe racial differences—skin color, eye color, skull size and shape, height, and so on—were scientifically satisfactory,[123] and hence the physical differences between various "racial" types were relative, not absolute. There was also no proof, Wu maintained, that one racial group was innately more intelligent than another. Moreover, it was extremely difficult to objectively measure the intelligence level of one group against another, since the currently employed methods could hardly be free of cultural and linguistic bias.[124] His conclusion, therefore, was that there was no scientific evidence to support theories of racial hierarchy, even though at the same time it should not be denied that races did differ physically, psychologically, and culturally. These variations, however, resulted from differences in environment and had nothing to do with the innate qualities of the races.[125]

Wu Zelin's position on race adequately summarized the revolt against racism in academic disciplines in the West since the 1920s, led in particular by Franz Boas.[126] There was a gradual shift around this time from explaining human societies in terms of heredity and biology to emphasizing cultural factors.[127] The rise of cultural anthropology substantially sustained this academic revolt. On the other hand, challenges to racist theories by no means led to an immediate repudiation of the premise of racial hierarchy. Racism was still respectable among a large number of people eminent in sciences and social sciences.

Wu Zelin's views on race were challenged by Pan Guangdan, who, in his overall positive review of Wu's book *Modern Races*, questioned Wu's "total rejection" of racial hierarchy.[128] A rare phenomenon among scholars of his generation, Pan Guangdan was able to discourse comfortably in natural sciences, social sciences, and humanities. Coming to the United States in 1922, Pan majored in biology, zoology, and genetics, earning his bachelor's degree from Dartmouth College and his master's degree from Columbia University. After returning to China in 1926, he worked on a wide range of topics, including the study of Chinese family system, Chinese population, genealogy, and human sexuality.[129] Pan's broad intellectual interests notwithstanding, the central concern throughout much of his scholarly career was eugenics. Seeing it as a science of *qiangzhong yousheng* (strengthening the race and improving birth), Pan promoted eugenics in China as the calling of his life.

"Eugenics" as an intellectual and social movement first emerged in late-nineteenth-century Britain and soon spread rapidly to other industrialized nations.[130] The mainline eugenics theories assumed that intellectual capacity and behavioral traits were inherited,[131] and that certain races, nations, ethnicities, and classes were more civilized than others, hence justifying their domination over the lesser ones. Western civilization became the ultimate standard against which other peoples and their cultures were measured. Eugenics in this context, as Juliette Chung maintains in her recent study, "was considered as the science or technology of human betterment through the application of genetic laws to measure up the civilizational standards or to restrain the deplorable tendency of racial and national degeneration."[132] Since the mid 1930s, when certain concepts derived from eugenics were intimately associated with Nazi ethnic cleansing, eugenics began to acquire an extremely negative reputation and has never regained its intellectual respectability among the general public.[133]

Although eugenics can be used to promote extreme racial and class prejudices, it is important, as Chung convincingly argues, not to see eugenics merely as an immoral movement, but to examine it in different local contexts where it was adjusted and modified, especially in developing and underdeveloped countries, to serve their own needs, some of which could be reformist and progressive under the local circumstances.[134] Translated as *youshengxue*,[135] the Chinese term for "eugenics" contains much ambiguity.[136] Dikötter has rightly maintained that the popularity of eugenics among intellectuals in republican China reflected both a concern for national revival and the influence of the traditional hierarchy that sharply distinguished educated scholars from uneducated peasants.[137] It is also important to point out, however, that the rise of eugenics in China was closely related to the May Fourth New Culture Movement and that some ideas were taken up by radical thinkers of that movement to promote social reform and to attack Confucian familism and other perceived evils of out-dated Chinese social tradition.[138]

Pan Guangdan became seriously interested in eugenics after he came to America in 1922.[139] Upon learning about his friend's newly acquired interest in eugenics, Wen Yiduo allegedly remarked that "if the result of your study leads you to the conclusion that the Chinese [as an inferior race] should be eliminated, I would have to kill you with a gun."[140] Evidently, Wen Yiduo saw eugenics primarily as a ranking of the value of different races. One major attraction of eugenics for Pan, on the other hand, lay in its treating humans as both social and biological beings, hence placing the study of humans upon a "scientific" basis.

Pan Guangdan wrote a number of articles on eugenics in Chinese between 1924 and 1926, while he was in America. Pan's early articles laid out what were to become the dominant themes of his thought,[141] namely, faith in the leadership responsibility of the intellectual class,[142] distrust of Western individualism, and confidence in the family as the basic unit of the nation-race. Among all the articles he wrote in this period, only one, published in the *Big River Journal*, directly addressed the issue of racial hierarchy.[143] Racism, Pan maintained in this article, consisted of two basic aspects, the first focusing on "race" as defined largely by skin color, the second on "ethnicity." Prejudice of both kinds was chiefly advocated and supported by the "Nordic," the allegedly most superior ethnic group in the "white race."[144]

Pan Guangdan discerned four existing schools of thought regarding the question of racial and ethnic differences. The first of these views held that there were no differences whatsoever between various racial and ethnic groups, a view that tended to be entertained, in Pan's words, by "sentimental priests and ministers and idealists out of touch with reality." The second perspective saw differences, both physiological and psychological, as rather insignificant, and believed that differences were not inherited but were rather changeable as the environment altered. A representative of this opinion was Franz Boas, whose work Pan was apparently familiar with. The problem with this approach, in Pan's view, was that it downplayed the importance of the biological basis of human life. The third school held that the differences were both inherited and absolute, hence denying individual members within an allegedly inferior race any sense of worthiness and any possibility of improvement. The Ku Klux Klan, as Pan saw it, best exemplified this way of thinking. The fourth school, however, incorporated elements from both the second and third approaches to come up with a number of tentative propositions: it would not draw absolute conclusions but would look at the qualities of different racial and ethnic groups individually and comparatively. One racial [or ethnic] group might score higher in one aspect but lower in another; overall, however, while some racial and ethnic groups were indeed "superior" to others, it did not follow that any given racial and ethnic group should be treated as a categorical whole. Rather, the basic unit was not the "group," but the individual.[145] Out of these perspectives, Pan believed that the fourth was the most balanced and therefore the most convincing.

Written in 1925, after Pan was converted to eugenics, "Jindai zhongzu zhuyi shilüe" shows where Pan stood on the question of racial hierarchy. The "fourth school," though adhering to racial superiority of certain groups over others, served as a modification and even a critique of what Pan called "absolute racism," represented by the Ku Klux Klan. By focusing on individuals rather than the group, this school gave hope to the relatively "inferior" racial and ethnic groups. The hope, as Pan perceived, lay with members in the educated class, who held the key to the improvement of their race.

Wu Zelin and Pan Guangdan were among a number of American-trained Chinese who adopted "scientific" approaches to the question of race, although, as we've seen, they ended up with very different conclusions.[146] Both of them continued their study on race and ethnicity after they went back to China. They did not merely introduce to the Chinese the most up-to-date Western theories on the subjects, but used the theories selectively and critically in their analysis of the Chinese situation. Later in his life, Wu Zelin devoted a large part of his time to the study of ethnic minorities in southwest China. In 1940, he put together in Guizhou Province three exhibitions on minorities' arts and artifacts, the first of its kind ever held in China, at a time when the minority peoples were regarded as inferior, and the Nationalist government pursued a chauvinist policy by forcing them to assimilate into Han Chinese social customs. Wu's fascination with and respect for minority arts and artifacts eventually led him to become China's most highly respected museologist in this field. His devotion to the cause lasted until the end of his long life, despite the many hardships and sufferings he encountered.[147]

As for Pan Guangdan, after returning to China in 1926, he continued to contemplate and write about eugenics, and launched a campaign to promote eugenics in China, which, in the opinion of his daughter, was almost like a "one-man operation," at least in institutional terms.[148] A comprehensive examination of Pan's rich, complex, and continuously evolving thinking in this and related areas is beyond the scope of this study.[149] It is worth mentioning, however, that during the Sino-Japanese War (1937–45), Pan was a firm critic of the Nazi version of racial ideology; he was also promoting interethnic mixture between the Han Chinese and the frontier minorities in order to rejuvenate the national stamina and improve the genetic makeup.[150] In the early 1950s, his sympathy toward ethnic minorities was expanded into a cultural critique of the sinocentric Han Chauvinism.[151] After 1953, when he was assigned to work at the Central Institute of Chinese Minority Nationalities (after the sociology department at Qinghua University, where he had worked for many years, was dissolved), he began to conduct research on Tujia and Yu, two minority groups in southwest China. He also spent many years going over the voluminous "Twenty-four Histories" (Ershisishi) for any information on *minzu* (ethnicity) in Chinese history. By 1966, he had gathered five thousand index cards containing such data, clearly in preparation for a major book. He died in 1967, at the height of the Cultural Revolution. The book was never written.[152] In sum, people like Wu Zelin and Pan Guangdan were vitally important in formulating the "discourse of race" and the notions of ethnicity in modern China, and they deserve sufficient acknowledgment and careful reexamination.[153]

CHAPTER FOUR

The Women's Story, 1880s–1920s

In 1885, Jin Yunmei (Yamei King) received her medical degree from the Women's Medical College of the New York Infirmary,[1] becoming the first woman from China to graduate from an American institution of higher education.[2] Before the end of the nineteenth century, at least three other women from China had followed suit,[3] and there would be hundreds more as the twentieth century unfolded. In the year 1922 alone, it was estimated that more than two hundred women students were in the United States, comprising a highly visible minority in the Chinese student community.[4]

There were three fairly distinct cohorts of American-educated Chinese women from the mid 1880s to the mid 1920s, each influenced by changing notions of womanhood in China and in America. The first group overlapped chronologically the first wave of Chinese coming to study in America. Made up of a tiny band of doctors, these women all graduated from American medical schools in the last two decades of the nineteenth century. All of them had been educated by missionaries, and like their mentors and associates, saw their work in terms of pious dedication and regarded their medical profession as an ideal form of feminine service. Their accomplishments impressed reformers like Liang Qichao, who used their example to advocate female education as a means to revive the ailing Chinese nation.

The second and third groups both were part of the new wave of the Chinese foreign-study movement in the early decades of the twentieth century. The second group was educated in America from about the turn of the century to the mid 1910s. As beneficiaries of the new, official endorsement in China toward female education, this group stressed the compatibility of modern education and domesticity, trying to live up to the modern version of the good mother–virtuous wife ideal (*xianqi liangmu*). These women tended to internalize the anxiety of male-dominated Chinese society about the potential threats posed by women's education. Yet within acceptable ideological confines, they asserted themselves, mainly by entering the field of teaching, and promoted new concepts of home life, helping to bring "modernity" to the urban domestic sphere in China.

The May Fourth New Culture Movement, beginning to unfold around 1915 with the publication of the journal *New Youth*, influenced the formation of the third group, which arrived in America starting in the late 1910s. The more iconoclastic individuals in this group sought to break the boundaries set by their male compatriots and took the initiative to define their own roles. They began to enter professional fields conventionally deemed "masculine," justifying their career aspirations on the grounds of individual fulfillment and women's right to economic independence. Meanwhile, they found the emerging feminist movement in America relevant and inspiring. Like their Western peers, they were troubled by the dilemma common to modern women everywhere: the conflict between career and marriage.

The distinctions between the three cohorts are not clear-cut, especially for the second and third groups. The third group distinguished themselves from the second not by what they actually accomplished later in life, but by what they aspired to accomplish. Their rhetoric bore a clear imprint of both the May Fourth New Culture Movement in China and the feminist movement in America, and their entrance into a number of "masculine" fields, insignificant as it might be numerically, was indeed remarkable because of the historical context in which it occurred. In brief, these cohorts are not so much identifiable in terms of defining characteristics; rather, they were each forerunners of important trends characteristic of their era. For the sake of convenience, I will refer to the first group as "the doctors," the second as "modern-day good mothers and virtuous wives," and the third as "the May Fourth generation."

Part of the general movement of students sent to study abroad, but also apart from it, the experiences of women students differed notably from those of their male counterparts. Women students not only faced the question of what it meant to be a modern Chinese, but more specifically, what it meant to be a modern Chinese woman. Domesticity, femininity, and the conflict between career and family—these were among the bewildering issues they had to grapple with. Nationalism, a defining ideology throughout this period, justified education for women and the broadening of women's roles, yet when the women in the third group began to make their own demands, they found their feminist agenda did not neatly fit the male nationalistic framework. At all points, even if sometimes unacknowledged, gender was an essential factor shaping the women's experience.

The women's story leads us to confront several largely unexplored topics in modern Chinese history, such as the outcome of missionary girls' education, the development of a "modern" home life in urban China, the emergence of career women,[5] and the middle-class women's reform movement. The American-educated women enjoyed extraordinary advantages unthinkable to the majority of the Chinese female population. In this sense, their experience was not representative. Being elite and exceptional, they were nevertheless pioneers in the pursuit of female higher education and professional careers, demonstrating along the way extraordinary courage and commitment. In the past, their experience has been heavily overshadowed by the politically oriented women's movements and therefore has been largely overlooked. It is time to see their experience as an integral part of Chinese women's ongoing struggle for emancipation in modern times.

THE DOCTORS

When Jin Yunmei (1864–1934) received her medical degree in 1885, she was soon to be joined by three other Chinese women: Xu Jinhong (Hü Kingeng, 1865–1929),[6] Shi Meiyu (English name Mary Stone, 1872–1954), and Kang

Aide (English name Ida Kahn, 1873–1931).[7] The 1880s and 1890s witnessed the establishment of medical education for women in America.[8] This was also a period when most college women, as the first of their sex to enjoy the privilege of higher education, had strong aspirations to do something useful with their learning.[9] This context likely had a lasting impact on the educational experience of the four Chinese women I am discussing in this section, and on their commitment to purposeful pursuits.

All of the women except Jin returned to China soon after they completed their education in America.[10] It is truly amazing that these women presented themselves as doctors in China before the end of the nineteenth century, when few Chinese men had a higher Western education and the vast majority of Chinese women were not educated at all. What were the social and intellectual origins of these women? How did they find the necessary support for such pioneering careers? All four of the women shared similar family backgrounds and educational experiences: they were either adopted children of American missionaries or daughters of Chinese Christians, and they were born in the 1860s and 1870s in various treaty ports. Jin Yunmei became the responsibility of an American couple in Ningbo, as her father, a Chinese Presbyterian pastor, had requested on his deathbed. Ida Kahn, the unwanted sixth daughter of a Chinese couple in Jiujiang, was given away by her parents when she was two months old to the American missionary woman Gertrude Howe.[11] Adopted at a tender age, each was reared personally by the Americans, quite unusual for Chinese children in similar situations.[12] Xu Jinhong and Mary Stone, on the other hand, were the daughters of Chinese Christian parents, and both of their fathers were pastors of Protestant churches in the treaty ports of Fuzhou (Xu Jinhong) and Jiujiang (Mary Stone).

Jin Yunmei was mostly educated in Japan and America while living with her foster parents,[13] but the other three went to mission girls' schools in China before they came to America. In the early twentieth century, missionary publications liked to present such women as testimonies of missionary achievement in China, attributing their successes to their missionary upbringing. Christianity certainly affected their upbringing decisively. But rather than attesting to the normal state of mission girls' education in China at the time, these women's achievements resulted from extraordinary circumstances. In fact, the doctors' education took place before foreign mission schools were reformed in response to the late-nineteenth-century "social gospel" movement in American Protestantism, after which they provided a more liberal education.[14] It is therefore fair to say that the accomplishments of the doctors not only defied the patriarchal Chinese society that held women in a lowly position, but also challenged the conventional wisdom of missionary educators. Individual initiative and efforts were more crucial in the making of the doctors than institutional support, at least in the early stage. A number of individuals—Chinese and Americans, parents and teachers—helped prepare the women physically, emotionally, spiritually, and academically. In the process, these educators and mentors demonstrated singular vision, courage, and commitment. The stories of the doctors would not be complete without them.

All the four women had natural, unbound feet, a necessary physical precondition for their future vocation. If it is not surprising that the two women with American adoptive parents did not have their feet bound, it was indeed unusual that Xu Jinhong and Mary Stone were spared the disabling custom, largely because their fathers were against it at a time when most Western missionaries did not seriously take issue with footbinding.[15] One important reason to have young girls' feet bound was to ensure their future marriageability. This is why one American missionary woman expressed her surprise when she noticed that Mary, already five years old, still did not have bound feet.[16] Given the pressure to conform with tradition—felt by parents and daughters alike—the decision of the parents demonstrated extraordinary courage. Years later, Xu Jinhong was still able to recall the ridicule from her neighbors, who liked to say, "Rather a nice girl, but those feet!"[17] Mary Stone grew up with similar teasing from the local community.

Missionary sources tell us that both Xu Yangmei, Xu Jinhong's father, and Mary Stone's father (Shi; given name not known), belonged to the rare breed of gentry converts. Shi was a descendent of an "aristocratic" family, while Xu was the son of a "military mandarin."[18] Studies on other educated Chinese Christians in this period show that these people, likely from lower gentry backgrounds and possibly having failed the civil service examinations, tended to be critical of certain Chinese social customs, such as polygamy, concubinage, and footbinding.[19] As some scholars point out, these men might have already been prepared for a revolt against unjust social practices even before they became Christians, carrying on an indigenous feminist tradition associated with Yuan Mei, Yu Zhengxie, and Li Ruzhen. Buttressed by Christianity, they were able to appeal to a new set of values as a basis from which to attack the old evils, and to express their opinions with firmer conviction.[20] There are reasons to believe that Xu and Shi may well have shared intellectual similarities with their contemporary fellow gentry Christians. Besides insisting on their daughters' having natural feet, both Xu and Shi sent their daughters to local mission schools, thereby (in Shi's case at least) contemplating drastically different lives for their daughters. When Mary Stone was seven years old, Shi took her to see the local mission school teacher in Jiujiang, and asked that the little girl be trained to be a medical doctor. The idea was so extraordinary that after nearly half a century Mary Stone still felt amazed at her father's remarkable vision: "In those days there was not even a man doctor in China [practicing Western medicine]," she explained. "Here was a Chinese wanting his little *daughter* to study medicine!"[21] If, as Jessie Lutz argues, mission education emerged out of the needs of the missionaries rather than as a result of the demands of the Chinese,[22] then Shi presents us with an unusual case in which a Chinese made a demand. In her recent study, Dana Robert argues convincingly that Chinese pastors were indeed the ones who pushed higher education for girls.[23] Shi was presumably impressed by the Western female physicians who were just beginning to enter the field in China in the late 1870s.[24] What is incredible is how powerfully the few women doctors, an extremely rare breed at the time, caught Shi's imagination and convinced him about the future of his own daughter.

Shi probably did not realize that the goal of conventional mission girls' schools at this time was not to train the pupils for higher academic studies. Rather, they focused on indoctrinating the young women into Christianity so that they could bring the Gospel to Chinese homes. At this time, the student body was largely made up of girls from poor families, many of whom were in schools for the free tuition, and perhaps other material rewards offered by the eager missionary educators. In order to lighten the financial burden, girls' schools tended to engage their pupils in "self-help" activities like needlework and embroidery.[25] Such assignments would also serve to reinforce the ideal of domesticity, to which the female missionaries themselves adhered.

As it turned out, the regular mission education Mary Stone received in school was not what prepared her to become a doctor. Rather, together with Ida Kahn, also a native of Jiujiang, she was provided with a specially designed program offered primarily by one individual, Gertrude Howe (1847–1928), without much institutional support from the local missionary establishment in China. The way Howe learned about her adopted daughter Ida Kahn's wish to become a doctor is rather interesting. When told by Howe that a man in Shanghai was interested in arranging for Kahn to marry his son, who had been educated in America and therefore did not mind her "big feet," Ida, then twelve years old, reacted furiously, "I don't want to be betrothed. I want to study medicine."[26] Among Howe's four adopted Chinese daughters, Ida was the only one who would become a doctor.[27]

Gertrude Howe had come to Jiujiang in 1872 and taught a girls' mission school with another American woman, Lucy Hoag. The academic level of the school was rather low and English was not in the curriculum, realities that reflected a common suspicion among missionaries about the ability as well as the motivations of the Chinese to learn Western languages.[28] Howe reportedly smiled when she heard that Shi wished to have his little daughter study medicine, and said, "Your daughter would have to study English first."[29] Consequently, Howe investigated how feasible it was to teach English to Chinese, making a special visit to the students on Yung Wing's education mission during her furlough in America. Convinced that the Chinese were able to learn, Howe began to teach her students not only English, but other serious academic subjects as well. By engaging herself in such unusual teaching activity and spending most of her time with Chinese, Howe aroused "a great deal of opposition in the mission."[30] When most of the other missionaries went to the beautiful resort of Kuling for the summer, Howe stayed in the "little hut-like home in the hot foothills" with the "flock of her [Chinese] grandchildren." Such action could mean, as Mary Stone later remarked, "ostracism from close [missionary] circles."[31]

The education of Xu Jinhong was more typical for a mission school graduate, in that Xu did not acquire much academic knowledge through her schooling. A native of Fuzhou, Xu worked as an assistant in a local mission hospital after her graduation. Her diligence impressed Dr. Trask, an American female physician and the head of the hospital, who recommended Xu to her home mission board for medical training in America. Dr. Trask's confidence in a young Chinese woman was very unusual. What is even more significant is that the Chinese pastors made a strong request on Xu's behalf.[32] The Women's Society of the Methodist Episcopal Church helped finance Xu Jinhong's medical education. Later, a different branch of the same society also helped fund the education of Mary Stone and Ida Kahn. This society was one of many Protestant women's mission boards that emerged after the Civil War in the United States. Driven by the same evangelical zeal that had carried many male missionaries to the "heathen" lands, the women's boards were formed to bring the Gospel to the people of their own sex. Dominated by evangelical concern, the work of the women's boards was in many respects socially conservative. Yet by supporting the higher education of the Chinese women, the women's boards of the Methodist Episcopal Church embarked on a far-reaching enterprise.[33]

Xu Jinhong was eighteen when she came to America in 1884, and her parents were hesitant about letting their young daughter take such a long journey. They had good reasons to be concerned: for one thing, Xu did not speak a word of English; nor was she sufficiently prepared academically. Consequently, it took Xu eight years to complete her studies, four years as an undergraduate at the Ohio Wesleyan University and four years at the Women's Medical College of Philadelphia, an impressive achievement given the inadequacy of her educational background. The treatment Xu received from her American schoolmates was friendly, if somewhat condescending. She was remembered as "a dainty little foreign lady, a sort of exotic blossom, . . . gentle, modest, winning, her heart was fixed on a goal far ahead, she was an example to the earnest Christian girl and a rebuke to any who had self-seeking aims."[34] In 1894, Xu Jinhong graduated from the medical college with honors.[35]

In 1892, when Xu Jinhong was in Philadelphia, Mary Stone and Ida Kahn came to Ann Arbor, Michigan, along with three Chinese male students, all accompanied by Gertrude Howe. Howe not only stayed for two years with the Chinese girls to help them adjust to the new environment, but also personally helped finance their studies. Having been better prepared than Xu Jinhong, Mary Stone and Ida Kahn were enrolled directly in the medical department at the University of Michigan. In their junior year, the two Chinese girls "shocked" everybody by earning the highest scores in their class, and in 1896, they successfully completed their studies. After a brief internship, they headed home the same year. By this time, Xu Jinhong had been back in China for one year, working at the Fuzhou Women's Hospital. Jin Yunmei, who received her medical degree in 1885, had presumably stopped practicing medicine after she got married.[36]

It turned out that the doctors' return to their home country was well-timed: when they landed in Jiujiang, Mary Stone and Ida Kahn were welcomed by an enthusiastic crowd with noisy firecrackers and shouts of *hao! hao!* (good! good!). Patients began to line up the next day, before the doctors even had a dispensary. Xu Jinhong was also warmly accepted by the people in Fuzhou after she proved that she was as capable as "a foreign doctor."[37] More important than coming back to hospitable local communities, the doctors entered upon a favorable national scene. In 1897, only one year after they returned to China, Ida Kahn and Mary Stone were "discovered" by Liang Qichao. In one of a series of articles he wrote before the One Hundred Days Reform in 1898 to advocate female education, Liang used the examples of the doctors to illustrate his argument that Chinese women were intellectually capable and that China as a nation needed to mobilize its female resources in order to survive in the modern world. Downplaying their Christian background, Liang depicted the women as patriots who were determined to help their troubled country.[38] Gertrude Howe believed that the examples of Stone and Kahn also inspired Liang and his comrades to take a firm and open stand against footbinding.[39]

The 1890s was the first time since the Jesuit missions of the seventeenth century that formal contacts were acceptable between missionaries and mainstream Chinese officials and scholars.[40] Some evidence suggests that Howe was eager to make the doctors known to the reformers' circle.[41] Ida Kahn and Mary Stone were brought to Liang's attention possibly by two progressive Jiangxi men who had come to Jiujiang to pay a visit to the two women physicians earlier in 1897. At about this time, Xu Jinhong was also asked by Li Hongzhang, the most powerful Qing official in charge of diplomacy, to represent China at an international conference on women.[42]

After a temporary setback resulting from the Boxer Incident, the doctors appeared once again on the public scene in the first decade of the twentieth century. When the Qing government began to pursue a reform course, which included an official endorsement of education for women, the doctors attracted wide attention and were sought after by important Qing officials and the general public. The powerful governor-general Zhang Zhidong reportedly asked Mary Stone and Ida Kahn to head the medical department of a women's university he wanted to establish in Shanghai around the mid 1900s.[43] For a while, the doctors enjoyed a celebrity-like status and were often invited to appear at graduation ceremonies of girls' schools. To the young audiences, they symbolized an inspiring new ideal. On one such occasion, in 1909 at a girls' normal school in Nanjing, Mary Stone met the daughter-in-law of a provincial governor. The young aristocratic woman told Stone that she wished to give up all her luxuries to lead a useful life like that of the doctor. And at the commencement exercises of Xu Jinhong's hospital, with many upper-class individuals and teachers of the government schools on hand, one man decided that his daughter should go to school to study medicine.[44] In some circles, the doctors were quasi-legendary: "When our schoolgirls learn of anything 'the doctors' did when they were pupils," Gertrude Howe proudly reported, "they seem to think they have found solid ground on which to set their feet."[45] Starting at about this time, missionary literature presented the doctors as the prototypes of mission success stories in China. Of the four doctors, Mary Stone and Ida Kahn were especially praised and their stories were frequently told.

It is remarkable that the doctors' reception in China at the turn of the century did not seem to be seriously hindered by gender bias. Compared with the discrimination experienced by the early American women physicians at the hands of the medical establishment,[46] the Chinese seem to have met far less resistance from Chinese male medical practitioners. Several factors might account for this difference. Traditional Chinese doctors, practicing a totally different type of medicine, were not in a position to judge the qualifications of the women. It seems clear, then, that the women doctors were empowered by modern Western science. It is also important to remember that the presence of women healers was not a total novelty in Chinese society: childbirth, for example, was considered unclean and ominous and therefore the exclusive domain of midwives.[47] By confining their work to treating women and children, observing a strict gender division, the female doctors not only met the medical need of a large portion of the population, but also diminished potential causes of controversy.

Furthermore, both in public and in private, the doctors behaved carefully and appropriately, in strict accordance with the norm of Chinese etiquette. There is one anecdote about two men who had heard about Mary Stone and

Ida Kahn and subsequently traveled a long way to visit them in Jiujing, after the two doctors had just returned from America. Believing that it was "wise to adopt a conservative attitude in regard to receiving calls from young men, lest their influence with the women they were to work with should be weakened," the doctors declined to appear. The men had to satisfy their curiosity by just seeing the doctors' diplomas from the American university, which Howe showed them.[48] It is likely that these two men are the ones who brought the female doctors to Liang Qichao's attention. It's worth noting here that at least for Mary Stone, following Chinese social norms meant that she had to modify the behavior that she had acquired in America, where she had been socially active, befriending both women and men. One last factor helps account for the apparent absence of hostility in the local Chinese society toward the female doctors: we should not forget that some Western women had already been working in the field of medicine and that people therefore were somewhat desensitized to "the newness of the new, making it less conspicuous and more palatable."[49]

Eventually, all four of the female doctors excelled in their profession: Jin Yunmei, having returned to China at the turn of the century after her husband's death, was asked by Yuan Shikai in 1907 to supervise a women's medical department in Tianjin; Xu Jinhong managed the missionary Woolston Memorial Hospital in Fuzhou; Mary Stone headed the Elizabeth Danforth Hospital in Jiujiang, holding the post from 1900 until she went with her close friend Jennie Hughes to Shanghai to found the Bethel Mission in 1920;[50] and Ida Kahn was in charge of the Nanchang Women's and Children's Hospital, where she spent most of her working life.[51] Both Stone's hospital in Jiujiang and Kahn's hospital in Nanchang were large, impressive-looking, and well-equipped modern facilities. The doctors' daily work included seeing a large number of patients, training medical students, who were to become the first generation of China's professional nurses,[52] and in addition to all this, taking care of the administration of the hospitals—professional and administrative responsibilities that were indeed rare for Chinese women in the early twentieth century.

The doctors perceived themselves and the unusual working life they led, however, not as a self-fulfilling career in the modern sense, but as an essentially feminine service and a Christian duty. Their sense of identity was derived from a complex combination of their nationality, gender, religion, and profession. Nationality had been an important factor in the doctors' lives from childhood on, since, given their early contact with Westerners, they no doubt became aware of this issue at a young age. Mary Stone's reminiscence of Gertrude Howe reveals a young Chinese woman highly sensitive about the way Westerners treated the Chinese.[53] The doctors appear to have had an unshaken Chinese identity, which their missionary mentors and colleagues tended to help reinforce.[54] On the other hand, being Chinese could also be advantageous professionally for the doctors. A missionary journal attributed the warm welcome that Mary Stone and Ida Kahn had received upon their return to Jiujiang from America to the fact that the doctors were Chinese nationals.[55]

The Chinese populace was less tolerant about religion, especially in areas beyond the doctors' home bases and in the years before the Boxer Incident. Ida Kahn once found herself and an American missionary woman in a mob-like situation in Nanchang, surrounded and chased after by a big crowd eager to see the "foreign devil."[56] Kahn had made the trip to treat the wife of a prominent upper-class man. After the woman recovered, some local literati offered to fund Kahn to work in the city, under the condition that she give up the "foreign religion." Kahn refused the condition but decided to open a dispensary in Nanchang anyway. The worst outburst of hostility occurred during the Boxer Incident, when both Western missionaries and their Chinese converts became the targets of attack, and both Kahn and Stone had to flee to Japan.

While Jin Yunmei worked in a government hospital from 1907 on, the other three doctors were regular medical missionaries[57] and frequently corresponded with the missionary headquarters in America, their letters containing both medical reports and descriptions of their evangelical work. To them, as to their Western colleagues, medical work was a means to serve an evangelical end. Xu Jinhong fully believed that "A mission hospital is a part of the church."[58] The doctors saw to it that regular religious ceremonies were conducted in their hospitals and that "Bible women," the specially trained Chinese female Christians, worked among their patients. In Mary Stone's words, their job was to "win every patient for Christ."[59] The doctors' value to the missionaries was well recognized. Ida Kahn was once regarded by the missionary community as "one of the most efficient agencies for the Gospel in all that region."[60] Christianity both defined the doctors' medical work and justified their unconventional departure from the domestic sphere. Following a nineteenth-century American tradition, women's supposedly superior spirituality especially qualified them for service in the wider world. Although service to God was required of all missionaries, nurturing and caring for the sick could easily be associated with women's traditional responsibilities. In this sense, the doctors' profession, religion, and gender blended well: both Christianity and the medical profession encouraged the doctors to retain their femininity.

During the transitional period between the Qing and the republic, when Chinese society was undergoing profound changes and traditional values and norms were being challenged, the doctors consciously emphasized service-oriented femininity as an important virtue for women. In a piece entitled "As We See Ourselves," written in 1907, Jin Yunmei offered her opinion on what education should do for women. Upholding the belief that "the dominant note in a Chinese woman's life is service," Jin insisted that "the most advanced experience does not conflict with the broad outlines of our fundamental ideas," but would only add "strength and keenness to the usual feminine virtues." To buttress her argument, Jin told her readers that American women, educated as they were, were indeed "very rigid" in their "standards of purity." She further clarified the "usual feminine virtues" by criticizing "the violent agitator of equality."[61] Jin was vague about who the "agitator" was. She could either have been talking about the relentless women suffragists of England or people closer to home. Beginning in the early 1900s, a small number of Chinese men and women began to advocate women's independence and equality, showing strong feminist and anarchist tendencies.[62]

Jin Yunmei's concern for "feminine virtues" was soon echoed by Ida Kahn. A supporter of the republican revolution, Kahn nonetheless opposed the idea of women fighting in combat. Well-versed in English, Kahn wrote a short story in 1912 to express her disapproval of those women who had joined the "dare-to-die" bands in 1911–12. In this piece, "An Amazon in Cathay," Kahn sharply contrasted the experiences of two women: Pearl, a member of a "dare-to die" band, who was raped by her male colleague when fighting alongside men, and Hoying, a nurse in a missionary hospital, who rescued Pearl from her attempted suicide and helped the poor girl obtain a "vision of true service." Thereafter Pearl became a nurse herself, serving

China in a way that was "worthy," namely, to "help to ease the sufferings of women and children."[63]

The timing of Jin and Kahn's writings is important. This was a period when a small number of Chinese women were beginning to emerge as a visible social and political force, upsetting the old social order and challenging behavioral norms. Under these circumstances, both Jin and Kahn felt the need to reinforce traditional values. Given the sentiments they expressed, it seems certain that they would not have approved of their contemporary Qiu Jin, the iconoclastic Japanese-returned student who not only liked to dress in man's attire but was also involved in political and even terrorist activities against the Qing regime. Neither would they have been likely to support the women suffragists who seized the opportunity of the 1912 revolution to advocate female franchise and went as far as breaking into the parliament to press their demand. The "suddenness" of the changes affecting the lives of women after the 1911 revolution also worried some American missionaries, who expressed concern over changes in behavior in some Chinese women, whose usual "gentleness and modesty" were being replaced by "boldness and boisterousness."[64] One missionary woman felt particularly uncomfortable with the Chinese suffragist "Amazons," who, the Western woman charged, had "offended against the laws of the land and the humanitarian nature of womanhood."[65]

The Chinese doctors and the American observers appeared to have a similar understanding of femininity. To them, gender was not a matter of roles, but the essence of identity itself.[66] To a large extent, the doctors' perception of gender was influenced by the female missionary subculture in China, which was transfused into them through their early contacts with missionaries and reinforced by their missionary colleagues and friends in their later lives. Jane Hunter's study of missionary women in China at the turn of the century offers an insightful analysis of this distinct female subculture. Placing feminine qualities of empathy at the center, this subculture was characterized by a rhetoric of self-denial rather than personal satisfaction. Missionary women, the embodiment of this culture, perceived their work of teaching and caring for the sick as a service to humanity. Even when they tasted independence, status, and power while working in a foreign land, they expressed their satisfaction in the language of self-sacrifice. In this way, they maintained their sense of traditional femininity.[67]

The four Chinese doctors appear to have embraced this ideology, at once liberated and constrained by it. Although in their own lives they greatly broadened the conventional female sphere, they insisted on adhering to the "usual feminine virtues" and were critical of the radical, "unwomanly" behavior of the younger generation. Ideologically, they were closer to the missionary female subculture than to the indigenous radical women's movement that emerged after the turn of the century. However, the doctors' own "feminine virtues" were not expressed through the "usual" domesticity. Except for Jin Yunmei, the other three doctors never married. Their lifestyle reflected the influence of single missionary women, who composed an increasingly large proportion of the missionary personnel in the early twentieth century. Mary Stone once jokingly remarked of herself that she was "one of the products of Christianity, an old maid."[68] The doctors' decision to remain single may well have reflected their critical attitude toward the institution of marriage in China. At a conference on girl slavery held around 1900, Ida Kahn told the audience the story of a childhood friend who had been sold by her father as a concubine to a rich man.[69] Given her own background as an unwanted sixth daughter, Kahn must have felt fortunate that she was able to avoid a marriage that would probably have been unhappy. The doctors represented a new type of woman in China, one who chose to pursue a calling and a professional vocation, rather than to marry. Remaining single, however, did not mean that the doctors lived as lonely "old maids." On the contrary, rather than following the American female missionaries' rhetoric of sacrifice and self-denial, both Xu Jinhong and Mary Stone constructed alternative domestic lives.[70] In the better known case of Xu Jinhong, she adopted both a son and a daughter and lived a very comfortable life as a well-respected doctor in the local community. She was also not afraid of openly challenging patriarchal rules when opportunities arose. When it came time to give her granddaughter a formal "generational" name, she chose one that was usually reserved for males in the family, on the grounds that girls and boys were equal and should not be named differently.[71]

The four doctors composed the earliest group of Chinese women known to have received a higher education abroad. Coming back to China at a time of profound social change, their cultural marginality became an asset and their achievements as educated women were of highly symbolic value to the male reformers, who used the doctors' examples to argue for the feasibility of an indigenous female education. By becoming medical doctors, the doctors demonstrated the seriousness of educated women and inspired a younger generation of Chinese women to pursue a modern education. As it turned out in the following decades, the doctors partook in the professionalization of medicine in China[72] and helped make the medical profession one of the first acceptable and most venerable career options for Chinese women. They also acted as guardians of "feminine virtues" during the transitional period between the Qing and the republic, when the traditional gender ideas were being challenged. Missionary literature at this time presented the doctors as an embodiment of moral stability and disciplined social progress. Seeing gender as a primary identity of women, they believed that the suffragists and women militia violated the essence of femininity. For the younger generation of Chinese women who were increasingly concerned with women's political rights and the issue of gender equality, the doctors' position fell short of providing the guidance they were looking for.

MODERN-DAY GOOD MOTHERS AND VIRTUOUS WIVES

In the fall of 1907, an article in a New York newspaper reported the arrival of three Chinese women at Wellesley College.[73] Mistaking the women for "wards of the Emperor," the author anticipated a warm reception for the Chinese from the Wellesley community. Warning the Chinese women not to be shocked by the "freedom from restraint and the happy-go-lucky attitude" of the American girls, the author assured the Chinese that Wellesley did not "model its curriculum upon that of Harvard and Yale, but has kept prominently in the foreground the ideal of the womanly woman," which, the author assumed, "is presumably what China is searching for."[74] The three women were not only Wellesley's first students from China, but also the first officially sponsored Chinese female students in the United States. They came on Wellesley scholarships, offered by the college to Duan Fang, a powerful governor-general, during his visit to the Wellesley campus the previous year. After he came back from the trip, Duan Fang held an examination in Nanjing, the first of its kind, and three women were chosen from among fifty contenders.[75]

This was the same year in which formal education for women was finally sanctioned by the Qing government. Subsequently, schools for girls mushroomed. Within a few years, female education was transformed from a suspicious novelty to a welcome reality, taking root in China and underlining the general reform trend in the first decade of the twentieth century. Furthermore, this period witnessed the launching of a vigorous foreign-study movement. Japan attracted the largest number of Chinese students. Many women followed their husbands or brothers to the newly modernized neighboring country, where in Tokyo alone there were over a hundred women students in 1907.[76]

Some women took an even longer journey to come to America. In 1903, while traveling in the "new continent," Liang Qichao noted three Chinese women students in America.[77] In 1911, about fifty women were reportedly studying in America, most of whom were self-supporting. The majority came to America for a college education, which was largely unavailable to women in China at this time. Some women in this group, like the doctors before them, came from Christian families, such as the famous Soong sisters. Cao Yunfang, one of the first Wellesley girls, was the daughter of a well-known Protestant clergyman. Others were daughters of the new urban elite of business people and professionals. Still others were from gentry-official families. The other two Wellesley women both came from this background.

The differences in their family backgrounds notwithstanding, the women had received early education in mission girls' schools, whose goals had been broadened by the 1900s to provide a liberal education. Mission schools generally enjoyed higher academic reputations than the newly founded native schools and consequently attracted official and gentry families serious about their daughters' education. Some mission schools tried especially to appeal to the Chinese elite by lessening religious requirements and stressing English and music. One of the best known and most prestigious was the Southern Methodist McTeiyre School in Shanghai, represented prominently in the Chinese female student body in the United States.[78] Schools like McTeiyre not only taught the students Western subjects, but also a Western way of life. Soumay Tcheng, daughter of a ranking Qing official and a student in a missionary finishing school in Tianjin in 1908, remembered her school not only as a place where the students learned to speak the English language, but also to behave like an "English lady." She wore Western-style skirts and had her hair arranged in "European fashion," drank tea with sugar and milk, ate meals with a knife and fork, and did physical exercises.[79]

With female education officially endorsed and foreign study encouraged, the group I am discussing in this section of the chapter enjoyed a recognized place in the mainstream culture of China. Ironically, women in this group appeared to be more "traditional" than their doctor predecessors. If the belief in Christian "true womanhood" had led the doctors to serve in the wider world, the younger generation tended to insist on the domestic sphere as the central place in a woman's life, even though in reality some of them worked outside the home, mostly as teachers for the new schools. These women's proclamation of the domestic ideal, even if only rhetoric, resulted from their educational experience and intellectual nourishment, both of which compelled them to embrace the ideal of domesticity. Although it is true that the academic quality of mission girls' education steadily improved after the turn of the century, and an increasing number of mission school graduates took up teaching to meet the expanding demand for girls' education, the primary goal of girls' mission schools remained the training of "good homemakers." Critical of the way the Chinese conducted their home life, missionaries believed that the more receptive attitude toward Westerners in the early twentieth century offered them the opportunity to exert a far wider influence over Chinese home life than ever before. Foreseeing that many graduates of mission schools would eventually become wives of "businessmen, engineers, lawyers, physicians, teachers and ministers," occupying the "centers of homes of influence," mission educators laid great hope upon these women to reform the Chinese family.[80] Perhaps not incidentally, home economics (jiazheng), which covered such subjects as cooking, sewing, budget making, childrearing, house planning, and so forth, was introduced to the curriculum at about this time.[81]

The Chinese women arrived in America during an interesting phase in American higher education for women. With the idea of a college experience becoming widely accepted, the contemporary generation of American college women were generally less passionate about their studies than the serious-minded first generation of the late nineteenth century. The numerous "drifters," who tended to come from well-to-do families and were unlikely to seek employment after graduation, led some educators to suggest that there should be a female collegiate curriculum that would prepare women for their future as wives, mothers, and homemakers.[82] It was therefore not a coincidence that home economics, which was in essence the "education of housewifery," gained a solid place as an "academic" discipline in American colleges during the first two decades of the twentieth century.[83]

Ruby Sia, a highly visible Chinese female student in this period, wrote an article to explain the idea of home economics: if men were "specialists" as physicians, lawyers, and so forth, Sia argued, women should be prepared for their "profession" of homemaking. Their chemistry course should concentrate on nutrition and their physiology should teach them how to raise healthy children. Basically, women's curricula should be different from men's: modern education should prepare women to better play their traditional role.[84] Ruby Sia's line of reasoning echoed a contemporary American opinion that stressed different educational goals for women from those for men. Underlying Ruby Sia's article was an assumption that the domestic sphere was the rightful domain for women. This assumption was shared by other women students in this period. Margaret Wang, in her prize-winning speech at the 1909 Chinese students' summer conference, held that, "a Chinese woman does not seek a wider sphere in which to exert her power and influence, but realizing as never before her abilities and opportunities, her worth to the country, and to her home, does desire to be better fitted to fill the sphere allotted her by the Creator."[85] Wang's view was supported by another Chinese woman, Esther M. Bok. Critical of the "bad" influence of higher education on American women, especially the tendency of "depriv[ing] them of their love of home and children," Bok maintained that the purpose of female education in China "should be to make our girls better mothers and homemakers, as well as better social leaders and companions."[86] Note that Bok rejected career-oriented American collegiate women and identified with the home-oriented type.

In Margaret Wang's view, a "real home" should first of all be a "school for children," and the mother "the first teacher of that school." Wang was critical of the "traditional mother," who was ignorant of both the emotional and the physical needs of her children. Wang's criticism echoed the observations of some missionary women, who expressed dismay at the lack of proper methods in Chinese women's childrearing.[87] Wang saw a woman's role primarily as a mother rather than as a wife, a view shared by many other Chinese women at the time. Among the few articles written by female students that dealt with the husband-wife relationship, the description of this relationship bore little resemblance to the reality in China. In one article, the domestic portrait painted by the author resembled a companionate American white middle-class couple: "A good wife possesses firmness, decision, energy, economy, no condition is hopeless. Man is strong but his heart is not strong. To recover his ease of mind, home must be to him a place of repose, of comfort, of cheerfulness and of peace. With the strength renewed, he ventures out again with vigor to meet the toils and troubles of the world."[88] The wifely qualities and responsibilities described here were a far cry from those expected from a Chinese woman, who was supposed to be submissive not only to her husband but also to her in-laws.

Though women's traditional sphere was not questioned, the conventionally held view on women's inferior intelligence was challenged—as En Ming Ho contended, "The original endowments of women are as great as those of men"—and the differences between the sexes would "disappear if both sexes are subjected to the same training in politics, government and business." However, women's natural capacity did not justify their intrusion into men's world, since "it matters not what may be the original capacity of the sexes in intellectual and other capacities, but it is evident that nature has intended that they should have different spheres and duties. It is said that the mission of women is foreshown almost in the cradle, and it is a mission of humanity, tenderness, generosity and of love."[89] Obviously, En Ming Ho was torn between a new urge to assert herself and the habitual inclination to submit to the traditional womanly roles.

This new assertiveness, even though constrained, was manifested in the desire to seek more power in the domain of family. In the light of the new era, home should be a place where women ought to play a larger role. One woman charged that the backwardness of China was due to "the lack of real homes" because homes were usually dominated by "the old men." She further argued that the "success of new China depends very largely on the influence wielded by our educated women."[90] Patriarchal rule in the Chinese family system was thus questioned. In general, however, the students avoided taking a serious look at the basic inequality in the Chinese family structure and their approach was more technical than sociopolitical, with an emphasis on education and professionalization as the solution to solving China's domestic problems.

Although the students' notion of domesticity was clearly influenced by American ideals, particularly in the areas of childrearing and household management, their intellectual orientation had a definite Chinese origin. In fact, they were very much influenced intellectually by one Chinese man: Liang Qichao, who as mentioned earlier, was the most forceful advocate of female education at the turn of the century. Although Liang envisioned an enlarged role for women to play in order to strengthen the ailing nation, he did not feel it necessary for women to be educated for their own benefit. He foresaw the future role of women primarily as enlightened mothers, and by extension, as elementary school teachers.[91] As a modern scholar rightly points out, what Liang promoted here was an updated version of the traditional ideal of the "good mother and virtuous wife."[92] Nonetheless, Liang's view was progressive for its time. His earnest nationalistic concern struck a responsive chord in Chinese society at large. The generation of women coming of age at the turn of the century were deeply influenced by Liang's thinking, generally believing that the best way to serve their nation was to strengthen the "home front." The traditional domestic roles of mothers and wives thus acquired a nationalistic meaning in the new era.

If Liang Qichao was generally positive about the impact of education on women, the Qing government revealed a more ambivalent attitude toward female education and showed more concern for maintaining traditional feminine morality. The 1907 regulations issued by the Ministry of Education looked upon female education as a means to strengthen traditional feminine virtues, such as chastity, quietness, obedience, and thrift.[93] Both ethics and housework skills were emphasized in the curriculums of the government-sponsored schools, which included courses on moral education, housework, sewing, and needlework. One scholar in the republican period concluded that the educational structure under the Qing was a "two-track" system based on gender inequality.[94] After the republic was founded in 1912, the academic level of girls' education was raised to some extent, but the government's attitude toward the goals of female education remained largely unchanged. In 1914, Tang Hualong, the Minister of Education of the republican government, insisted, "The policy of the Board is to make women good wives and virtuous mothers."[95]

Yet the seeds of change were sown from the very beginning. The 1907 official provisions for girls' normal schools legitimized the existence of women teachers. Although confining women to teaching only in kinder-gartens and elementary schools, the provisions nonetheless acknowledged women's role outside the home. "To be womanly and useful" thus became an implicit double message to Chinese women. Although the rhetoric continued to focus on women's domestic roles, reality allowed certain leeway for talented and ambitious women to expand their lives beyond the home. The heavy demand for teachers in girls' schools and the relatively high pay attracted many women graduates to the occupation of teaching. This trend gained more momentum after the founding of the republic.

Information on women students' fields of studies in the entire period under study is meager. It appears that liberal arts, education, and music were more frequently chosen by women,[96] indicating that gender played a role in how they chose their fields of studies, as these subjects differed markedly from those favored by the Chinese male students, who tended to major in engineering and other technical subjects. What the women chose to study also reflected a new reality back in China: teaching was becoming an occupation newly opened to women. A study of twenty American-returned students conducted in 1911 found that five were married and presumably did not work outside the home, six were doctors (including our four doctors), and eight were teachers.[97] Teaching now surpassed medicine as a more popular career option for American-educated women.

Although making headway into the teaching profession, the women were eager to reassure the Chinese public of their essential identification with the domestic ideal. This contradictory posture was an adaptation to the anxiety of male-dominated society about women's education. The most frequently voiced fear was that education could blur the gender boundary. If women were given the opportunity to be educated, would some of them eventually demand an even further expansion of their freedom? If they were allowed to work outside home, what about their domestic responsibilities? By emphasizing the ideology of domesticity, government officials, reformers, and missionary educators all expressed the same desire, in varied languages, to see that the status quo of gender order was not disturbed.

To a large extent, the women students internalized this anxiety. Under the spotlight as the foremost beneficiaries of women's education in China, and possibly with a strong sense of their role as models for the Chinese female populace at home, they were careful about what they said, even if in reality some of them did not live out the domestic ideal they promoted. Ruby Sia, for one, is a case in point. Urging women to become "qualified" homemakers by studying home economics, Sia herself never married.[98] For the time being, the conventional justification for female education appeared to be convenient for women to accept while performing their gradually expanding roles. Tension certainly existed, both within and without, for the "modern-day good mothers and virtuous wives." It just had not quite come to the surface yet.

A closer look at the kind of domesticity promoted by the Chinese women students reveals that even this ideal contained dimensions that did not exist in traditional Chinese thinking. Concerns about nutrition, hygiene, "scientific" childrearing, and household management reflected a Western standard of domesticity that was quite different from that of the Chinese. The introduction of Western-style home life to China was significant in its own right. Linked with the idea of "modernity" that began to appeal to urban elite Chinese in the early twentieth century, it deserves careful examination. Although an in-depth discussion of this topic goes beyond the scope of this chapter, suffice it to say that American-educated women played an important role in introducing Western-style home life to China. Some individual women, particularly Hu Binxia, as we will see below, tried to spread the Western ideal to a large audience.

HU BINXIA: A WOMAN OF YESTERDAY AND TODAY

Among the women students who came to America at the beginning of the twentieth century, perhaps no one was in a better position to represent the emerging new Chinese woman than Hu Binxia. Born in the late 1880s to a wealthy official-gentry family in Suzhou, Hu began to live "under the new influence" when she was ten years old.[99] Always among the first to take advantage of the newly opened opportunities for Chinese women, Hu made her way through the missionary Laura Haygood School in Suzhou, to Tokyo in 1903, and eventually to America in 1907, as one of three girls sent by Governor-general Duan Fang. While a student in Tokyo, Hu Binxia had already distinguished herself. She was actively involved in the agitation movement against the Russian occupation of Northeast China and was the founder of *Gong ai hui* (Common Love Association), an association for patriotic Chinese female students in Tokyo.[100]

Hu Binxia stayed in America for seven years, spending the first two years in a preparatory school to learn English before she went to Wellesley College. In the spring of 1913, Hu graduated from Wellesley with high honors. By this time, she had become one of the best-known Chinese women students in America, standing out for her various leadership roles in the Chinese students' community, including at one time serving as the chief editor of *Nian bao*, an annual publication in Chinese for the Alliance, and another time as the president of the Chinese Academy of Arts and Sciences, an organization to promote professional association among the Chinese students. She was also the only female member in the exclusive fraternity J&D.

If Hu Binxia embodied the achievements of a modern woman, she also felt the anxiety of the new age. Like other members of her generation, Hu was caught between the clashing demands of traditional values and a modern education. In the fall of 1913, after her graduation from Wellesley, Hu went to Ithaca, New York, where her brother Hu Mingfu was a student at Cornell University. Hu delayed her return to China because of two assignments from Chinese government agencies: she was to conduct a study on the education of American women and to represent China in an international conference on children's welfare to be held in Washington, D.C., in 1914. One Ithaca newspaper interviewed Hu, describing her as an "attractive" woman who wore "a white Chinese jacket with fastenings of black, a black skirt and very American looking high tan boots."[101] Later in the year, Hu was invited to speak about Chinese women to the women students at Cornell University. Probably to the surprise of her audience, instead of celebrating the progress made in China regarding women's situation, Hu chose to talk about the conflicts of being a modern Chinese woman.

In her talk, Hu contrasted the modern woman with the traditional type, or in Hu's words, the woman of "yesterday." In a sympathetic and admiring tone, Hu presented the life of the woman from the past. This woman followed a clearly charted path from childhood through adolescence to adulthood. Home meant everything for her: it was her school and the center of her world. She always demonstrated "strength, patience and self-sacrifice" by serving other people. It was only later in her life, after she had become a mother and the head of the family, that she ascended to power and glory. She managed the large family and "commanded the respect of all the members of the community." A woman of such stature, Hu Binxia remarked, "must be a woman of power and ability," who achieved in her old age "the reward for her early sacrifice and care."[102] In contrast, Hu's account of the woman of "today" was less reassuring. Described as "self-centered," this woman valued her career and independence more than anything else. She considered being a good mother "hideous" and believed that "if marriage interferes with self-realization, then be done with it." However, she was also, Hu maintained, "the daughter or grand-daughter of the woman of yesterday." Therefore, "She can not help inheriting that spirit of self-sacrifice, that wholesome character, that sheer will power and ability to do good which had gloried the woman of the past." Although she might rebel against marriage and motherhood, she could not "change her nature." "In her good humor," Hu predicted, "she still can be a good wife and mother. Temporarily she may seem stormy and uncontrollable, but sooner or later she will be able to work out her principles of life."[103]

Compared with the forthrightly presented older woman, the portrait of the younger woman was ambivalent. Hu was especially concerned with the young woman's unwillingness to sacrifice for others and her general lack of moral strength. Hu Binxia's uneasiness with "the woman of today" reflected her confusion and uncertainty about the situation of her own generation. Torn between tradition, which demanded women's sacrifice while making their moral strength salient, and the new educational opportunities, which promised independence and self-realization, Hu could not make a simple choice. Thus she called herself "at once the girl of yesterday and the girl of today."[104] Ultimately, it seems, Hu considered a woman's ability to be a "good wife and mother" as the final test for her "principles of life."

In her speech, Hu made no references to her personal experiences in America. In her own life, however, Hu was a keen observer of the new influences and apparently absorbed a great deal of them herself. Before she went to Wellesley, Hu studied English at Walnut Hill Girls' School in Natick, Massachusetts, which was run by two female principals whom Hu remembered well and wrote about two years after she left the school.[105] The principals were different from the missionary type with whom Hu had been acquainted as a student at the Haygood School in Suzhou. Religion was still an important part of the school life at Walnut Hill, but it provided a basic moral tone rather than serving as the ultimate goal. On the other hand, the students were well informed about the political events of the day; hence Hu became familiar with women's suffrage and prohibition. Aiming at producing "well-rounded" individuals, the curriculum of the school was not confined to "women's subjects," but included both a strong academic program and athletics. Above everything else, it was the personalities and manners, speech and appearances of the two principals that fascinated Hu. The positive impression Hu had of the two American career women contradicted her critical view of "the self-centered women of today" expressed at Cornell. Obviously, Hu felt at once both the "pull" and the "push" of the modern ideals.

Hu Binxia returned to China in 1914 and married Zhu Tingqi, a Harvard graduate who was prominent in the American-returned-students' circle. The couple settled in Shanghai and eventually had two children. Contrary to what one would expect, Hu Binxia did not confine herself to the domestic sphere. Rather, she lived a highly visible public life, engaged in journalism, social reform, and the women's movement. From 1916 to 1919 Hu was the editor-in-chief of the influential *Funü zazhi* (Ladies' journal).[106] The quality of Chinese home life appeared to be the focus of her attention. Interestingly, Hu was now a great deal more critical of the traditional Chinese family structure, taking a stand directly opposite to the views she had expressed at Cornell. Notably, Hu's criticism of Chinese family life was not only technical, but also sociopolitical. In one article, Hu compared home life in America to that in China. While finding fault with many aspects of Chinese family life, Hu singled out the type of family where a matriarch dominated the entire household. In direct contrast with the glorifying portrait she had painted at Cornell, Hu described the old matron as an absolute autocrat, making servants and daughters-in-law surrender to her will. Hu even compared the woman to the "old Buddha," a reference to the hated Empress Dowager Cixi of the Qing dynasty.[107] Somehow this woman of "yesterday" had completely lost her moral appeal.

Hu's dramatic change of attitude after she returned to China could very well indicate the influence of the unfolding May Fourth New Culture Movement, which was relentlessly attacking the old Chinese family system. It could also result from her own reevaluation of the Chinese family after returning home. It is even arguable that, for psychological reasons, Chinese intellectuals tended to be defensive of the Chinese tradition while abroad and were more critical of the same tradition once back in China. Hu certainly showed this tendency in her writings. To be sure, Hu Binxia's criticism of Chinese home life also had a technical dimension. In *Ladies' Journal*, using American family life as the model, Hu wrote about hygiene, childrearing, table manners, house decoration, and related subjects. She even designed a plan for an "ideal" dinner party, with both Chinese and Western food served in buffet style and provided with public chop sticks, to meet "moral, economical, and hygienic" goals.[108]

The discussion of the "ideal" dinner party was a small part of a more serious article in which Hu argued that the foundation of a country was the family, yet the Chinese family had become rotten after thousands of years. The reform of the family would be the mission of Chinese women in the next fifty years, so that the Chinese men could devote themselves to building China into a strong and wealthy nation. To reform Chinese family life required "great abilities." Women therefore needed higher education to perform the enormous task of family reform.[109] Hu's message was immediately picked up by a young person named Li Ping, whose article appeared in the iconoclastic journal *New Youth*. Addressing Hu Binxia as "my teacher," Li Ping wholeheartedly embraced Hu's idea of family reform.[110] By advocating family reform in both sociopolitical and technical aspects, Hu had made her contribution to the New Cultural Movement.

In the early 1920s, Hu became a leader in the middle-class women's movement, which was concerned primarily with suffrage and women's general welfare.[111] She was also the chairperson of the national committee of the YWCA in China. Grace Thompson Seton, an American writer, met Hu Binxia in Shanghai around this time. Hu impressed Seton as an "executive," very much like an "American business woman." When Seton expressed her amazement at Hu's ability to maintain a busy working schedule on top of taking care of her family, Hu replied, "this work is not unlike keeping house, as one keeps a budget, has the management of servants, and the purchases in the same way."[112] The analogy of housekeeping is revealing, testifying as it does to the power of domesticity for Hu Binxia and her generation. Perhaps only through the "domestication" of her public life could Hu justify her busy life outside the home. Meanwhile, the updated version of the "good mother and virtuous wife" ideal no longer applied. Once calling herself a woman of both yesterday and today, by the 1920s Hu had firmly grounded herself in the camp of "today," drawing herself closer to the women in the next group I will discuss. It is worth adding here that, blessed with a "modern" marriage few Chinese women enjoyed at this time, Hu probably owed some of her success to the support of her Harvard-educated husband.

THE MAY FOURTH GENERATION

American-returned Chinese women attracted Grace Seton's attention during her visit to China around 1923. Prominent among a small number of career women Seton met in Beijing and Shanghai were a newspaper reporter educated at Smith College, a dentist trained at the University of Michigan, a Columbia University graduate working as a pharmacist, and the dean of a girls' school with a degree from Ohio Wesleyan University. These recent graduates from America joined the doctors and teachers in the earlier groups, adding new blood to the slowly growing rare species of Chinese career women.

Their career orientation distinguished these women from those that were still under the influence of the domestic ideal. Coming to America after 1914, a year that coincided with the launching of the women's Boxer Indemnity Scholarship Program,[113] this third cohort of American-educated women differed notably from their predecessors, at least in their rhetoric, in that they were less interested in proving the compatibility of modern education and womanly virtues and were more eager to pursue professional careers. By entering fields of study unrelated to the mother-wife role, this group sought to break the boundaries set by their male compatriots and took the initiative to define their own roles. In many ways, they were products of the May Fourth New Culture Movement, and therefore had their first taste of feminism in China. Upon arriving in America, their feminist convictions were greatly strengthened and even radicalized. Relying on new sources of justification for their actions, they pursued education and careers to seek personal fulfillment and economic independence. Their firmer commitment to women's independence exposed the narrowness of the male-defined nationalistic discourse. The tension between career and marriage was also intensified for this group. The story of Chen Hengzhe, told in a later section of this chapter, illustrates this dilemma.

In the fall of 1914, when the first group of female Indemnity students arrived in America, the writer of a *Monthly* editorial warmly welcomed them as women who would eventually become "physicians and teachers," two established professions for American-educated Chinese women. On the other hand, while showing no hostility toward women entering other professions, the author, presumably a man, predicted that "It will be a long time before China will have her women bankers and women commissioners of public works."[114] Most likely to his surprise, such changes came much sooner, even if they were only token changes at first. Only eight years later, in 1922, D. Y. Koo chose to major in banking at New York University, as "the only [Chinese] woman in the field."[115] In 1924, Grace Li, daughter of the former Chinese president Li Yuanhong, transferred from Wellesley College to Columbia University to study political science, possibly with an intention of becoming "a woman commissioner of public works."

Perhaps we can take a seemingly small event in the mid 1910s—the first Chinese woman, a Miss C. C. Wang, majoring in the "hard" science of chemistry—as the beginning of women's "intrusion" into this traditionally male domain. The following years witnessed a trend of diversity and "masculinity" in the academic majors chosen by women.[116] The rate of this change is indicated by the Alliance's essay competitions for female students. Sponsored by Madam Gu Weijun, wife of the Chinese minister to the United States,[117] the suggested essay topics in 1917 focused on home life. Only a year later, a different theme was posed: "Professional careers opened to girl students."[118] By the early 1920s, there were women studying banking, journalism, economics, political science, sociology, architecture, and dentistry. In 1921, Li Pinghua (Mabel Lee), a Columbia University graduate student of economics, became the first Chinese woman to receive a doctoral degree.[119] Admittedly these women represented only a minority of their cohort, as others in their group still chose more conventional fields of study, such as the liberal arts, education, and so forth. The real significance is not that some women were entering new professional fields; the doctors had done that decades earlier. The women in the early 1920s were distinguished from their predecessors primarily by the feminist argument that they used to justify their actions. Three articles, all written by women students in 1923, demonstrate this change of consciousness among the Chinese women students.

Gien Tsiu Liu, the author of "Chinese Women in Medicine," followed the line of thinking typical of an earlier generation. Praising Mary Stone and Ida Kahn's pioneer roles, Liu asked more women students to study medicine. Downplaying the financial benefit of being a doctor and critical of those who were "over-anxious to become economically independent," Liu emphasized the service nature of the profession and presented her opinion along the lines of the nationalistic argument of Liang Qichao.[120] In contrast to Liu's article, D. Y. Koo's "Women's Place in Business" suggests that pressuring a woman to study medicine essentially deprived her of free choice: "If physicians, nurses, or teachers are not what we wish to be and if we have any inclination toward business, we can soon take business as our profession."[121] Eva Chang, author of "Chinese Women's Place in Journalism," also felt the restricting effect of encouraging only teaching and medicine as professions for women. As a student of journalism, Chang wanted the "iron doors" of all professions to be open to women.[122] In a broad sense, Koo and Chang were challenging an ongoing sex segregation of the work force, a phenomenon that existed in many countries: certain fields of employment by which women first entered the work force eventually became defined as "women's work," with the effect of confining women to those professions.[123]

The desire for economic independence was an important reason for both Koo's and Chang's entering their chosen fields. As Chang declared, "Journalism is one of the professions that assure women economic independence. . . . I can not say that it is 'the' profession for women; but I have every confidence, that it is a possible, profitable and honorable profession for women."[124] Koo, on the other hand, contended that the main reasons why American women were "exceedingly free and happy in the good sense of the term" was because they were "economically independent."[125]

What Koo and Chang meant by economic independence was quite different from Liang Qichao's earlier advocacy of women's "economic self-support." For Liang Qichao and many men at the turn of the century, an economically productive role for women was justifiable only because of its usefulness to the nation. The May Fourth New Culture Movement challenged the whole framework of this discourse. Western individualism and the notion of *renge* (individual dignity and personhood) provided the basis for the leaders of the New Culture movement to attack oppressive Confucian ideology. In his speech at the Beijing Women's Normal School in 1918, Hu Shi advocated independence (*zili*) as the most precious thing in life for a human being. He coined the term *chao xianqi liangmu* ("above the 'good mother' and virtuous wife" ideal) to describe admiringly those American women who sought to fully develop their own individuality.[126] Women were emboldened by the new rhetoric. They began to assert their right to education and employment, even to the point of publicly rebelling against their parents, a trend that is best exemplified by a woman who used the power of the press to compel her conservative father to let her continue her education and to keep his promise to support her overseas studies.[127]

The issue of women's economic independence was raised as an indispensable part of women's emancipation in the context of valuing women as dignified individuals.[128] Reports on career progress made by Western women frequently appeared in the new journals that were published during this period. Western theories on the economic independence of women, such as that of the American feminist economist Charlotte Perkins Gilman, were also introduced to China around this time.[129]

The profound change in the intellectual atmosphere in China encouraged women like Koo and Chang to strive for their rights as individuals. Their first notions of individualism and feminism, in other words, were formed in their own cultural milieu. Chang, for example, admitted that she made the decision to study journalism, a "field for men," before she went to the United States in 1921.[130] If the decision to enter certain "men's" fields was made in China, America provided a favorable environment for those women to realize their goals and to further sharpen their feminist consciousness. As Koo observed, "One of my few everlasting impressions of America was formed when I saw many women in different lines of business. On entering any place . . . I found women working as clerks, cashiers, operators, waitresses, stenographers, secretaries, doctors, bankers and what not."[131] Eva Chang, on the other hand, was most impressed by American women reporters, correspondents, and editors-in-chief.

Koo and Chang also noticed the participation of American women in public life. Koo praised various women's organizations and clubs, through which "thousands of millions of American women, married and unmarried," participated in "civic affairs and in politics."[132] Chang described an effective investigation done by some women journalists on the poor working conditions of female department-store clerks, and went on to argue that only women reporters were able to represent the interests of their own sex. Evaluating Chinese society, Chang contended that if Chinese women wanted to champion their own cause, they would have to "rely everything on themselves" as the American women did: "If you want to make the women's pages and women's magazines true to their names and intention, you've got to let women themselves handle them."[133]

Both Koo's and Chang's arguments had a clear feminist tone, including a distrust of men in relation to women's struggle for economic independence and political organization. Perceiving women as a separate group with their own agenda, this position reflected the strong influence of the woman's movement in America in the 1910s, a decade of deep transformation for women. As women entered more and more areas of social, economic, and political power, their domestic role became increasingly obsolete. The historian Nancy Cott argues forcefully that the term "feminism" first came into frequent use in America in the 1910s, not just as a new catch phrase, but as a new way of defining the women's movement. While the previous "woman movement," which had based much of its ideology on nineteenth-century ways of life, stressed women's duties, the newly emerging "movement of consciousness" demanded women's rights, particularly women's suffrage. The intense advocacy for women's rights, in particular their political and economic rights, would eventually relax in the course of the 1920s, after women obtained the franchise and when the postwar generation turned their attention increasingly to personal matters.[134]

Sometimes, the eagerness of Chinese women of the May Fourth generation to champion feminist ideals made them think that American women were more emancipated than they really were. For instance, scholars point out that the achievements of American women in both journalism and business were nominal in the 1910s and 1920s: journalism remained predominantly a male profession with only a few glamorous female reporters, while there was no place for women at either the middle or the top ranges in the corporate world.[135] Yet to the keen and aspiring Chinese female students, the very presence of American women in the "masculine" professions, no matter how small it was, was in itself a strong enough testimony to women's capacity, which they cited to argue for the expansion of their own roles in

China. Two years after Koo wrote her article, she returned to China and, with another American-returned woman, cofounded a bank "for the women at Shanghai," possibly with the intention of realizing a goal set in America: to gather funds in order to help women organize themselves.[136]

The changing roles of Chinese female students in America paralleled similar developments in China, manifested in the growth of higher education of women in China after the mid 1910s as well as the rising expectations of women graduates.[137] By the time the third group of American-educated women began to return home in the early 1920s, a number of white-collar occupations were opening up to women in China. American-returned women featured prominently in the emerging career trend for women, slight as the trend may appear from our present perspective.[138] What they had acquired in America presumably strengthened their conviction to seek an independent life. The ideology behind the emergence of career women in China, best summarized in the belief in the emancipation of individuals and women's right to pursue economic independence, occupied an essential place in the new framework of thinking. The career progress made by women in this period should be looked at in this context and deserves a higher historical recognition than it has so far received.[139]

CHEN HENGZHE: TO CREATE ONE'S DESTINY

Chen Hengzhe (1890–1976), also known as Sophia Chen, arrived in the United States in 1914 as one of the first nine female students on a Boxer Indemnity scholarship. Six years later, with a B.A. from Vassar College and a master's degree from the University of Chicago, Chen was invited by Cai Yuanpei, president of Beijing University, to be the first female professor at Beida. In the next several decades, Chen continued to be active as an educator, writer, and social critic, establishing herself as one of the most prominent American-returned women in the republican era.[140] Although she left China a few years before the New Culture movement truly gained its momentum, Chen embodied the ideals that were representative of the third group of American-educated Chinese women. Her story provides us with a window into the complex inner world of career-aspiring Chinese women of this time, including the conflict they often felt between career and marriage.

Chen was born in 1890 to a gentry family in Jiangsu Province,[141] and she liked to point out that her family's tradition of educating its women was entirely independent of Western influence.[142] Brought up by her mother and grandmother, both accomplished poets and painters, Chen had been well aware of women's literary and artistic achievements since she was a little girl. On the other hand, as a young woman Chen also witnessed the deep frustration felt by these women, particularly a favorite aunt, an unusually talented and capable woman, who was trapped in an unhappy family situation. Chen could not forget her aunt's yearning for a more fulfilling life. Later, it was this aunt who pushed Chen to take the Boxer Indemnity scholarship examination.[143] Chen was also deeply influenced by an uncle, a Qing military official with progressive ideas. When she was still a little girl, this uncle taught Chen to believe in her own capacity to "create one's destiny" (*zao ming*) and told her stories about the independent Western missionary women he had seen in Guangdong Province.[144] Growing up in a family with a long tradition of educated women, and nurtured intellectually and spiritually by two unusual individuals, it is not surprising that Chen was discontent with being a wife in the traditional mold. When she reached marriageable age, she refused a family arrangement on the grounds that she wanted to continue her education, very much to the displeasure of her father.

Much as Chen Hengzhe wanted to live a useful life, there was little an unmarried young woman could do in those days. After graduating from a mission school, Chen tutored children of a wealthy family, a dead-end job with no real prospect for the future. When the Boxer Indemnity program was opened to women in 1914, it offered Chen a long-awaited opportunity. Both mentally and emotionally ready to break the traditional mold of womanhood, coming to America meant to Chen that she could finally "create her destiny."

Chen was twenty-four that year, far past the usual age of marriage for a Chinese woman. Having refused a marriage and observed the unhappy family life of her aunt, it is very likely that Chen had made up her mind to remain single even before she went to the United States. Once there, Chen must have been heartened to find that there was a place for single, career-oriented women. In Mary Lyon, the pioneer of female education and the founder of Mount Holyoke College, Chen found her model. One year after she came to America, Chen wrote a brief account of Lyon's life, admiringly describing Lyon's devotion to female education and specifically underscoring her decision to remain single.[145] Chen's determination to remain celibate was well known among her fellow Chinese students.[146]

Traditionally, celibacy was always an option for individual Chinese women who wished to escape undesirable marriages. Such women most often withdrew into Buddhist nunneries. Occasionally, celibacy took collective forms, as in certain rural Guangdong counties where a ritualized marriage-resistance custom was practiced by some women in the nineteenth and the early twentieth centuries.[147] However, celibacy was always thought of as the despondent last resort for a woman and was never regarded as socially and ethically desirable. During the May Fourth period, celibacy began to acquire a new meaning, becoming a politically progressive form of protest against the oppressive marriage system.[148] Chen Hengzhe's decision to remain single was apparently made before celibacy became a popular political issue during the May Fourth New Culture Movement.

Chen eventually disavowed celibacy and got married at the age of thirty. The man who made Chen change her mind was Ren Hongjun (Jen Hung-chün), a Cornell University graduate of 1916 who later became a prominent educator and an advocate of scientific learning in China. Even after her marriage, however, it appears that Chen continued to debate with herself about the pros and cons of married life. Her short story "Luoyisi de wenti" (Louise's problem), written in the mid 1920s, captures the intensity of the debate and offers us a rare glimpse of the inner world of a career-aspiring Chinese woman.

Louise, a young American woman in her twenties, is a philosophy student at the outset of the story. She is in love with her professor, Mr. Brown, but decides against marrying him lest the marriage interfere with her career goals. As she explains to Brown, "You said in the past that knowledge and career are the best company of one's life. You know I am extremely ambitious, though I am not a person of vanity. If I got married, there would be too many obstacles in front of me."[149] Twenty years later Louise is an accomplished scholar at a well-known women's college; Mr. Brown, meanwhile, is married and has many children. One day Louise has a strange dream. In the dream she is married, with two lovely children and a husband who is none other than Mr. Brown. Feeling satisfied both physically and emotionally, Louise wakes up to a reality she suddenly finds wanting. Her success has been indeed admirable, but it has failed to nourish her dry and bare soul. A career and family life, Louise contemplates at the end, are like the mountain and the lake in the neighborhood of her college. Located miles apart, each needs the other to complete a beautiful scene.[150]

It is not hard to detect that Louise's problem was indeed Chen Hengzhe's own. Chen indicates in her story that both family life and sexuality—not only career—are important to a woman; without them, her "soul," and perhaps also her body, are "dry and bare." Perhaps writing this story finally helped Chen come to terms with her own decision to marry. The fact that Chen used middle-class American characters in her story, a rare device in modern Chinese literature, indicates that she was probably aware of the elite nature of "Louise's problem," a problem with a foreign name and a luxury, however painful, available to only a few privileged Chinese women. The class distinctions of feminism in the early twentieth century are a well-known issue, discussed by Nancy Cott, among others.[151] Having recognized the class implications of the issue, however, we are still impressed by the degree of yearning for an independent professional career Chen expressed in her story. After all, she had gone a long way in her struggle to "create her destiny," an achievement her aunt, a frustrated woman unable to realize the promise of her talents, would both envy and be proud of. We are also struck, on the other hand, by the intensity of the conflict between career and family life that Chen (to judge by Louise's experience in the story) must have gone through.

Living in a rapidly changing world when the old notions of womanhood were constantly being challenged, Chinese women in the early twentieth century were faced with the unprecedented tasks of defining a new identity as modern Chinese women. *Nü liuxuesheng* (foreign-educated women students), and in our particular case, the women who came to America for an education, appeared to be under a special obligation to take up this challenge. Drawing on intellectual and moral resources from two cultures—Chinese and American—the women, roughly divided into three generational groups, cultivated a new women's consciousness in the first decades of the twentieth century.

Romantic love and sexuality did not play a significant role in developing a new consciousness for these women, as they usually did in the West and as they did after the May Fourth movement for some Chinese women who embraced "free love."[152] Known for their "serious-mindedness," these Chinese women, especially those in the first and the third groups, tended to regard sexuality with suspicion and to treat it as an obstacle to their pursuits of education and career.[153] Their way of declaring sexual emancipation was to demonstrate their ability not to be sexually exploited—to use their freedom and economic capacity, as part of a privileged group of Chinese women, to choose a single life.

They derived their sense of liberation mainly from their pursuit of a career. Professional life meant so much to the women in the first and third groups discussed in this chapter that it became the primary buttress of their identity and a major source of pride and meaning. Related to the issue of career was the issue of physical space, also crucial in the development of the new consciousness. The domestic sphere stopped being the defining and confining place to many women in the first and the third groups, who turned away from it to enter such public domains as hospitals, classrooms, and offices. Even to those in the domestic-oriented second group, "home" likely had implications different from its traditional meaning. For them, home was regarded not only as a "school" for the young, as Liang Qichao envisioned, but also as a "laboratory," in Hu Binxia's sense, a place where people could experiment with social reforms and test modern technological knowledge and devices. This emergence of "modern" Chinese domestic life deserves further study.

Interestingly, despite the tendency to minimize the importance of sexuality and to seek fulfillment mainly through a career, these women did not perceive themselves as "the third sex," that is, sexually "neutral" beings. If the first two groups were obviously very conscious about maintaining femininity as the essence of their identity, Chen Hengzhe and her group, although appearing to care more about being independent than being womanly, in some ways were more anxious about "feminine" issues, as Louise's story reveals, than the first two groups.

The three groups of women also related to nationalistic ideology, as defined by Liang Qichao and like-minded male thinkers since the turn of the last century, in different ways. The first group, the doctors, were drawn into the nationalistic discourse in the late 1890s that regarded women's education as necessary for the strengthening of the Chinese nation. Such an ideological framework apparently fit the doctors well, and they began to play a larger public role in the early twentieth century as testimony to women's capacity for education. For the women of the second group, who were asked by the male reformers and society at large to carry the responsibility of regenerating the ailing Chinese nation, nationalism was a convincing and convenient rhetoric. The women willingly played their designated role as intelligent mothers, while using the nationalistic argument to justify their entrance into the teaching profession. The relationship of the third group to nationalism was more problematic. May Fourth thinkers advocated the emancipation of women, which, they assumed, would in turn help produce a stronger Chinese nation. Nationalism helped justify the liberation of women, but it also had an inherent tendency to subordinate the interest of women to general nationalistic goals. Some women students, as we have shown, had specific women's issues in mind and began to set their own agendas that did not neatly fit the male-defined framework. It was also during this period that women's distrust of men's intentions and their ability to solve women's problems was openly voiced and a new feminist consciousness became manifest, which posed a potential challenge to the primacy of male-defined nationalism.

What role did American culture play in the development of the Chinese women's new consciousness? Obviously, the imprint of the missionaries was deep and lasting, especially in the lives of the first two groups, while for the third group, the American secular women's movement appeared to exert a stronger impact. The achievements of American women in various fields helped sharpen the Chinese women's feminist awareness and suggested both individual and collective solutions to the problems they brought with them from China. By viewing American career women and women activists as the exemplary "Other," the Chinese purposefully promoted their own cause.

The female American-educated students stood at the forefront of female education in China. Out of this group emerged the first generation of Chinese career women, who successfully established themselves in the medical and teaching professions within a relatively short period of time and began to enter other professional occupations as the 1920s unfolded. Some of these women chose to remain unmarried, introducing a lifestyle of single womanhood as independent career women. For those who eventually got married, the kind of "home" they created tended to differ from the traditional family, with new notions about the relationship between husband and wife, new concepts of childrearing, and new knowledge on how to "manage" a modern household. Some of the women were actively involved in various women's causes. They were more likely to be found in the Christian women's movement and the middle-class women's reform movement, two sometimes overlapping movements in the early decades of the twentieth century that dealt with such issues as temperance, footbinding, protection of motherhood, child education and welfare, and improvement of conditions for working-class women. Mary Stone and Hu Binxia, important figures in our study, were leaders of these movements.[154]

Thus far, scholars have not sufficiently examined or told the stories of American-educated Chinese women. It is time to look at them as important evidence of the evolving modern gender consciousness in late-nineteenth- and early-twentieth-century China, and as an integral and memorable part of the ongoing quest by women in modern China for the emancipation of women and gender equality.

FIGURE I. Boxer Indemnity students, 1910, in Beijing before leaving for America.

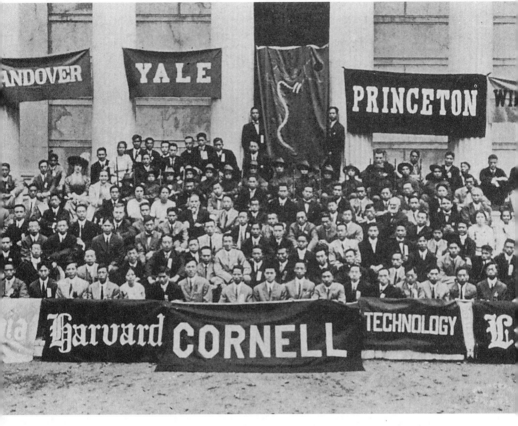

FIGURE 2. The 1911 Princeton Conference of the Chinese Students' Alliance
of the Eastern States.

FIGURE 3. The 1914 Boxer Indemnity students in Shanghai before leaving for America, including the nine women who were the first women students on the Indemnity program.

FIGURE 4. Dr. Xu Jinhong at the time of her graduation in 1894 from the Women's Medical College of Philadelphia.

FIGURE 5. Dr. Mary Stone, Dr. Ida Kahn, and five nurses in front
of the Elizabeth Skelton Danforth Memorial Hospital in Jiujiang,
Jiangxi. Kahn is standing, back row; Mary Stone is standing on the
far right.

FIGURE 6. Wellesley Chinese Students' Club. Sitting on the right is Hu Binxia.

FIGURE 7. Chen Hengzhe
as a student in America,
ca. 1914–18.

FIGURE 8. *Her Ideal*, a drawing that appeared in a 1911 *Chinese Students' Monthly* special issue about women students.

FIGURE 9. Wen Yiduo and his family before he left for America in 1922. Wen is standing on the far right.

FIGURE 10. Columbia University Chinese students' crew team, ca. 1918.

FIGURE II. A drawing that appeared in the January 1910 issue of the *Chinese Students' Monthly*, depicting the inauguration of the Boxer Indemnity Scholarship Program. Note that there is a ball at the foot of the boy with the words "Young China."

FIGURE 12. Li Jinghan in his
Beijing home in the 1980s.

FIGURE 13. Luo Longji in 1946.

FIGURE 14. Zhu Kezhen in Yangshuo, Guangxi, in 1963.

FIGURE 15. Wellington Koo (Gu Weijun), as a student at Columbia University, ca. 1910.

胡適 一九一四年照片，老友 Fred Robinson 題。

胡適

FIGURE 16. Hu Shi as a student at Cornell, 1914.

CHAPTER FIVE

Between Morality and Romance

In 1908, while on board a ship crossing the Pacific Ocean, Jiang Menglin found himself observing an event that was for him both embarrassing and fascinating: ballroom dancing by the Western passengers. Not used to the free mixing of men and women, let alone open display of intimacy between the sexes, Jiang described the scene as "the most striking thing."[1] Yet he soon managed to overcome this initial cultural shock; after watching the Westerners' dancing "several times," Jiang began to "appreciate the beauty of it."[2] Jiang's readiness to accept ballroom dancing, a distinctive Western pastime with sexual overtones, is itself "striking."

Jiang Menglin's open attitude would have been approved of by Yan Huiqing (W. W. Yen), then a middle-ranking official at the Chinese legation to America.[3] In 1908, the same year that Jiang made his trip to the United States, Yan was invited to speak at the Chinese students' summer conference held in Ashburnham, Masschusetts. Himself educated in America in the 1890s, Yan urged his audience to study "the way people in the West live, move and have their being" by "traveling," "meeting American friends," and "going to church or attending the theatre."[4] Challenging the young students with the question of "what are the best thoughts on the relation of marriage," Yan called their attention to the "American home," specifically "the position of women" and the "relations between man and wife." At the end of his speech, Yan contended, "There is much in every phase of American life that could be advantageously assimilated and adopted by our nation" and "it is our duty to study it as intensely as we do our books."[5]

Roughly three decades earlier, in the early 1880s, it was exactly the kind of experience Yan Huiqing was now encouraging that got the young men in the Yung Wing mission in trouble. The Chinese government supervisors were alarmed when they found that their charges become increasingly "Americanized"—that is, going to churches, dating American girls, and behaving in other "un-Chinese" ways. Regarding the students' acts as posing a serious threat to the preservation of the Chinese essence, the conservative officials frequently made negative reports to Beijing. On this matter, Yung Wing was a suspect himself, especially because of his marriage to the American woman Mary L. Kellogg. The accusations against the students helped the Chinese authorities to justify the sudden ending of the entire mission in 1881, when an outburst of anti-Chinese sentiment across America led to the backing off of the American government from its original agreement to let the Chinese students enroll in military academies.[6]

The social and cultural milieu changed profoundly between then and the turn of the century. When the second wave of Chinese students began to flow into America, educated Chinese, especially those residing in treaty ports, demonstrated increasing openness toward Western culture.[7] Meanwhile, a critical rethinking of China's own social customs, including marriage practices, was taking place. In major treaty ports, some young men began to challenge the age-old practice of arranged marriage by setting their own criteria for prospective spouses, which usually included natural feet and a modern education. Experiments with "modern" wedding ceremonies, often mixed with Chinese customs, were being conducted by some brave young couples in cities like Shanghai and Tianjin.[8] What was happening here was the crisis in the traditional Chinese social and cultural order; a process that began to reveal itself at the grassroots level during the Taiping Rebellion, deepened with the critiques from the gentry-reformers around

1898 and accelerated in the first decades of the twentieth century.[9] Challenges to Chinese marriage customs were voiced by people like Kang Youwei, Liang Qichao, and Tan Sitong in the late nineteenth century,[10] and were articulated with a radical slant by the woman revolutionary Qiu Jin and the anarchist couple Liu Shipei and He Zhen at the beginning of the twentieth century.

Perhaps not accidentally, the first wave in what is often dubbed mandarin-duck-and-butterfly fiction also arose in the early twentieth century.[11] Dwelling mostly on unfulfilled love between men and women, "butterfly" fiction reached the peak of its popularity right before the May Fourth New Culture Movement. While it might not be unparalleled in Chinese literary history, as its resemblance to the "sentimental-erotic" genre in Chinese literary tradition is rightly pointed out by C. T. Hsia,[12] the presence of romantic literature at this particular historical juncture, and the large quantity of its circulation thanks to the growth of a new publishing industry, makes it a unique phenomenon in Chinese cultural history. A complex occurrence, butterfly fiction might have provided a way of escape for some readers from the pressing national crisis caused by Western powers,[13] and perhaps also satisfied the psychological needs of some of its writers.[14] But most significantly, this genre expressed a heretofore largely suppressed yearning of the readers for emotionally more fulfilling relationships between men and women. Rarely did the Chinese display their emotional need and romantic longing in such an open and large-scale manner. The fact that it was an expression of need rather than a revelation of life experience explains why butterfly fiction tended to repeat itself.

Although the material, ideological, and psychological foundations of the old order were being undermined, Confucian morality was by no means about to back away. Butterfly fiction, oversentimental yet heavily didactic, noticeably embodied this paradox. The conservative undertone complicated the love theme in the literature, illustrating the contradictory character of the time. It was this peculiar cultural scene that people like Jiang Menglin left behind when they boarded ships to America, carrying with them a cracking yet still weighty Confucian baggage on the one hand, and a fairly open mind toward Western culture on the other.

If in 1908 Jiang Menglin only watched Westerners play the romantic game, then in 1923, two young Chinese, taking the same journey, were themselves characters in a romantic drama: on an America-bound ship, Xie Bingxin and Wu Wenzao first fell in love.[15] Baptized by the May Fourth New Culture Movement, people like Xie Bingxin and Wu Wenzao were generally more liberal in their thinking and more courageous in their behavior.[16] Meanwhile, American society itself was in flux. After World War I, roughly around the same time as China's iconoclastic May Fourth movement unfolded, America bade final farewell to the rigid Victorian morality. The Chinese youths coming to America in the postwar era encountered a quite different cultural milieu than their predecessors. The emotional need for a more fulfilling relationship came from the Chinese themselves. But, as several scholars contend, romantic love is a constructed experience and a product of learned expectations.[17] The West, and America in our particular context, served as important sources of reference and inspiration. Meanwhile, American society itself was undergoing profound changes to become "modern," which made the experience of the Chinese students culturally more complex and intriguing.

This chapter looks at a number of rather elusive issues in the lives of the Chinese students in America: gender relationships, divorce, marriage, love, interracial romance, and sexuality. Since most of the material here was produced by men, the following accounts necessarily reflect male perspectives. One-sided and insufficient as they are, the available information allows us to venture into the unfamiliar emotional world of Chinese students in the early twentieth century. This was a split world, still burdened with Confucian morality on the one hand, and beginning to be driven by longings for more fulfilling relationships with the opposite sex on the other. As members of the first generation given the opportunity to reconstruct their personal lives, the students' experiences were usually not characterized by a sense of joy and liberation, but by anxiety and tension. They not only had to learn how to interact with women in unfamiliar social settings in America, but also had to decide what to do about the women back at home chosen for them by their parents. They paid a great deal of attention to American women because it helped them to think about what they wanted "modern" Chinese women to be like. Interestingly, in their literary creations, the representations of Chinese women were ultimately conservative, disclosing a sense of uncertainty many Chinese men felt in this era of drastic social change.

The love affair Hu Shi had with an American woman, and his eventual marriage to a rural girl chosen by his mother illustrates the intense conflict between romance and morality experienced by this generation. As one of the most forceful advocates of individual liberty in the republican period, Hu Shi's modern identity as a free and independent individual was forged considerably through his experience of love, even though at the end his love appeared to be unfulfilled.

INTERESTED OBSERVERS

Jiang Menglin was not alone in his eagerness to observe Western social customs; other Chinese students, too, had their eyes open. Yet given the obvious obstacles of race and language, most of the students did not have easy access to American life and could only act as distant observers. A great deal of their attention was paid to the lives of American women.

Turn-of-the-century America was at the threshold of profound social and cultural changes, signified by a sharp increase in the number of women receiving higher education and finding employment, a fall in the birthrate among white middle-class women, and a rapidly rising divorce rate.[18] Meanwhile, Victorian morality still held some sway and the ideal of domesticity retained certain appeal. By the 1910s, defining women in purely domestic terms had become obsolete.[19] The "new women," embodying a "spirit of independence," began to ascend.

Women as a subject might be intrinsically fascinating to men, but the Chinese students seemed to be particularly interested in those women with higher education. By the early twentieth century many educated men in China had accepted the necessity of female education, but as noted in Chapter 4, they felt an intense sense of anxiety regarding the impact of such an education. What would become of the women if they were educated was what many Chinese males wanted to know. American women were a kind of model to which Chinese men could compare women in China, whose lives were just beginning to undergo deep changes. In an article written in 1914, Zhu Qizhe praised the American educational system for its success in implanting traditional feminine virtues in women.[20] Besides knowing how to cook, sew, dress neatly, and act properly, American women also embodied desirable qualities like diligence, frugality, and thoughtfulness. Zhu attributed the good behavior of American women to the education they received from women's colleges, where peer pressure helped "collective virtues" (*qun de*) to develop. As a result, Zhu maintained, American women were better prepared for their domestic responsibilities and more likely to create happy and harmonious family lives. By contrast, Zhu contended, most Chinese women, living in isolation, were unable to take advantage of *qun de*.

Unable or unwilling to see the potential challenge women's higher education posed to the traditional gender order, Zhu Qizhe projected his own perception of feminine virtues, which was rooted in the Chinese tradition, onto the American female college students. Kai F. Mok, a Chinese student at Yale, showed a better grasp of the conflict that higher education raised for American women. Mok's story of his American woman friend Lydia introduced to readers a "militant suffragette."[21] Lydia was so devoted to the suffrage cause that on one occasion she left her college work to attend a conference in London, where she met her future husband. After their marriage, Lydia became a different person. Not only did she find her "wifely duties" incompatible with politics, but she also realized that the "female sex of every living creature is invariably smaller than the male," and therefore "woman has been made only to be the help-mate and consort of man, while man is supposed to be her protector."[22] Mok was obviously pleased to see Lydia, after taking a detour in politics, settled contentedly in the domestic life.

In contrast to Mok's disapproval of Lydia's enthusiasm for gender politics, Yan Dixun was fascinated by similar traits in an American woman he met on a train. A graduate of the University of Michigan, she was interested in politics and journalism. "As zealous as a politician," she embodied everything opposite to the usual feminine ideals. Having visited Japan and Hong Kong, she was planning a round-the-world trip once the war was over. Listening to the woman talking about her adventures, Yan felt that his own manhood was being challenged even as he was also strongly attracted to her. When the two parted, Yan was left with a yearning for a Chinese woman with similar qualities.[23] This episode took place in 1918, a time when the "new woman" increasingly overshadowed the traditional domestic type in America and the New Culture movement was gaining momentum in China. Perhaps it was not accidental that Yan showed more appreciation for the independent spirit in a woman than the other two Chinese men, who had made their observations earlier.

Despite the different opinions about what education would hold for women, the Chinese men generally agreed that higher education would make women more interesting. F. L. Chang thus remarked, "The American girl is the most interesting person under the sun to talk to and about. She has been brought up in refined arts, and consequently she is well-versed in the subtle art of entertaining."[24] By contrast, the life of her "Oriental cousin," according to W. S. Ho, was "indeed wasted in a pitiful way,"[25] since the Chinese woman had no training either in "the high types of amusement such as music," or in "outdoor games" and "dancing."[26] One senses in these remarks both a readiness to utilize women's skills for the gratification of men's desires and a longing for some kind of companionship between the two sexes. A companionship based on a more equal partnership meant a changed relationship between men and women, and the change made some Chinese men uneasy. Weighing the pros and cons of American and Chinese women, F. L. Chang mused, "I am of the opinion that the American girl is the product of modern evolution, while her Chinese cousin is the survivor of the winning qualities of forty centuries. The former, the ideal of beauty and health, makes the most pleasant companion; but the latter, the expounder of patience and trust, makes the most faithful wife."[27]

The students' observations of American marriage customs, another focal point of their interest, betray similar ambivalence. Marriage as an institution was in flux in America in the early decades of the twentieth century, manifested particularly in the increase in divorce rates and the propensity of educated women to postpone marriage or even to remain single.

The American situation provided a reference point for Ma Yinchu and Zhang Chengyou to reflect upon the marriage system in China. A student at Columbia University, Ma Yinchu would become the president of Beijing University in the 1950s.[28] Ma Yinchu pointed out that in China the denial of individuals' participation in choosing a marriage partner made marriage like a gamble and often led to a lack of affection between husband and wife. On the other hand, Ma disagreed with the argument that *hunyin ziyou* (freedom of marriage) would be the solution. How many marriages in America, supposedly based on love, ended up in divorce? Ma asked. To avoid the pitfalls in both customs, and to uphold marriage as the basis for a stable society, Ma suggested that parents and the young people should work together in the selection of marriage partners.[29]

Zhang Chengyou was more positive in assessing the American situation, but he also showed a similar tendency to seek a middle ground between the Chinese and American customs.[30] Charging Chinese parents with having self-interest in mind when making marriage decisions for their children, Zhang observed that most marriages in China were unhappy. If young people had opportunities to get to know each other before marriage, Zhang argued, it would be more likely that they would enjoy each other's company afterwards. Zhang was impressed by the independent spirit of young Americans, who would only start families after they were able to support themselves and who seldom lived with their parents after marriage. By contrast, the Chinese tended to live together in large, extended families and the young, able-bodied men did not feel any shame if they continued to depend on their parents after marriage. Zhang also noted that in America there was no stigma attached to remarried women, which, Zhang maintained, was a much more sensible and humane attitude than the oppressive practice of demanding chastity of Chinese widows. Referring to Woodrow Wilson's second marriage to a widow, Zhang praised the generous reception from the American public. Yet there was another side of the coin. In America, a slight dispute between a couple could result in divorce and it was not unusual for people to seek financial benefit through separation. In Zhang's opinion, divorce was "the most uncivilized" occurrence in a civilized country and the problem had already become incurable. The high percentage of single people in the population also troubled Zhang, who blamed women's high level of education for causing so many to remain single. All these problems, Zhang concluded, were drawbacks of "equality" (*pingdeng*) and "freedom" (*ziyou*) in America.[31] To balance the complete lack of freedom in China with the individualistic orientation in America, Zhang suggested that free association between the sexes should be allowed in China and young people should have a certain degree of freedom in choosing their marriage partners, yet the opinions of the parents should also be respected. Also, divorce should absolutely be discouraged.

Through their rigorous rejection of divorce, both Ma Yinchu and Zhang Chengyou maintained that marriage was first and foremost the building block of a stable society. They also displayed a distrust of feelings, which, they believed, were apt to change over time and therefore should not be the sole justification for marriage. Consequently, neither wanted to see total freedom granted to young people, lest they would be misguided by their emotions. Around the mid 1910s when Ma and Zhang wrote their pieces, divorce had not yet posed a problem for the Chinese society. Soon, with the launching of the New Culture movement, many young people began to take a critical look at their loveless betrothals and marriages. Divorce became an issue with real-life implications and urgency.[32] What should one do with an arranged marriage? Was it immoral to divorce a woman chosen for you by other people? What made a marriage moral anyway? Increasingly, these questions confronted the Chinese youths, including the young men in America.

BREAKING AWAY FROM THE OLD BONDS

In 1904, when the sixteen-year-old Gu Weijun left China for America, the fact that he was already engaged to a young woman did not occupy much of his thought. The betrothal was an expression of gratitude from Gu's parents to the woman's father, a famous doctor. Although "new-style marriage" was beginning to appear in large coastal cities around this time, the dominant practice remained that parents arranged for their children's marriage, usually without asking for their consent. Betrothal was the crucial first step in the marriage rite, sealing the bond of affinity between two families. Breaking it would injure the reputation of both.

Available statistics of the period between 1900 and 1914 suggest that only a minority, less than one-third, of the Chinese male students were married at the time of their departure from China,[33] while the rest were likely to be already betrothed. Among those for whom we have information, the age of betrothal varied depending on local customs and individual circumstances. Jiang Tingfu (Chiang Ting-fu), who would later become a prominent diplomat for the Nationalist government, for instance, was betrothed at the age of five. Gu Weijun and Hu Shi were both engaged at twelve. Zhao Yuanren, whose parents died early, had his fiancee chosen for him by his relatives when he was fourteen. Engaged at a young age and presumably without ever meeting their fiancees, these men's emotional attachment to their prospective wives was understandably minimal at best. Yet before the May Fourth period, people tended to express their discontents privately. Influenced by advocates of progressive social change and having read some "modern fiction" (perhaps including "butterfly" stories?), Zhao Yuanren, while attending a modern school in Changzhou, lamented in his diary that he had no say in the decision of who he was going to marry.[34] Unable to openly disobey his widowed mother, Hu Shi managed to postpone his marriage by using various excuses to stay away from home. He finally left China for America without a farewell to his mother.

Another example of a more subdued protest is that of Gu Weijun when he was a junior at Columbia; having been away from China for three years, he received a letter from his father urging him to fulfill his marital obligation. "Greatly shocked," Gu wrote a letter home saying that he had to complete his studies first so that he would be able to support himself financially before he could think of marriage.[35] Failing to convince his father, Gu agreed to consider marriage only if the woman would unbind her feet and study English. Promised that both conditions should be met, Gu went back to Shanghai during the summer vacation of 1908. Once he was back in China, however, it was his father who had the final say. At the wedding ceremony, Gu Weijun felt he was like a puppet manipulated by his family. Gu discovered that the bride had neither unbound her feet nor gone to a modern school. When it was time for Gu to go back to America, his father made it clear that Gu must take his wife with him or he could not go. Once again, Gu had to bend to his father's will. When the newlyweds arrived in America, Gu first placed his wife with an American family in Philadelphia and then returned to New York by himself. Occasionally he paid his wife visits, treating her "like a sister."[36] It is hard to tell if Gu's friends in New York were aware of the existence of Gu's wife. Fortunately, her adjustment to America was quite smooth, thanks largely to the family she was staying with. Gu noticed that she was making "rapid progress both in comprehending American life and in comprehending personal life."[37] After about a year, Gu raised the issue of divorce and his wife agreed. The couple parted in a "friendly way."[38] Familiar with Chinese civil law and taking advantage of being in America, Gu achieved his goal by handling the case with skill and patience. Gu's divorce was one of the first among Western-educated Chinese men. After the divorce, Gu's ex-wife, who had "become interested in learn-ing,"[39] stayed in America for two more years to pursue her studies. Gu got married again soon after he returned to China in 1912. His new wife was the eldest daughter of Tang Shaoyi, a student on the Yung Wing mission and a powerful political figure in the early republican period.

Unlike Gu Weijun, Zhao Yuanren did not have a powerful father over him; with both parents dead, his marriage was arranged by his relatives. Resentful of the whole matter from the beginning, Zhao saw coming to America as an escape.[40] Once in America, Zhao had girlfriends, yet he did not dare to get too close to any one of them, not because he was not ready emotionally, but because his fiancee's shadow was always present. In his diary Zhao noted, "I weighed it [the betrothal] ethically and it weighed upon me ethically."[41] Zhao made several attempts to break the engagement, all to no avail. He stayed in America for ten years, longer than most of his friends, partly as a way of avoiding marriage. When Zhao finally went back to China in 1920, he met Yang Buwei, a Japanese-educated medical doctor, and the two fell in love. He managed to break his family-arranged betrothal. To com-pensate for his former fiancee, Zhao gave her a large amount of money as "tuition" for her education.[42] After the matter was settled, Zhao felt that "for the first time after almost twenty years, I was able to say 'my self is [was] my own.'"[43] His marriage to Yang Buwei was regarded as a celebration of love and their simple wedding ceremony became a model for young people.

By comparison, Jiang Tingfu's approach to his childhood betrothal was more straightforward. Having seen his elder brother suffer from an unhappy marriage, Jiang, a student at Oberlin College around 1915, wrote to his father asking to break his engagement. If his request was not granted, Jiang threat-ened, he would not go back to China. Meanwhile, he was dating American girls. After his father finally gave in,[44] Jiang fell in love with Tang Yuduan, a Chinese woman student in America. Their wedding ceremony took place in 1923 aboard the homebound ship, with the captain as their witness.[45]

The stories of Gu Weijun, Zhao Yuanren, and Jiang Tingfu suggest that before the May Fourth era, the American-educated Chinese men rearranged their personal lives in a variety of ways. Two of them, Zhao Yuanren and Jiang Tingfu, had the experience of dating women while in America. Learning how to "date" posed a new and bewildering challenge to the Chinese men, who had come from a society where gender segregation was strictly observed for the upper class. Some male students in America shunned romantic involvement partly because they did not know how to approach the opposite sex. Hu Shi, for one, was very critical of liberal dating in his early student days in America.[46] New ways to conduct one's behavior were needed to be learned as part of the modernity package, and America provided an inviting environment.

ADOPTING A DIFFERENT CODE OF BEHAVIOR

In the summer of 1906, two Chinese women students attended the annual conference of the Eastern Alliance held in Amherst, Masschusetts. One of the women was Song Ailing (Ailing Soong), of the Wesleyan Female College in Macon, Georgia, the eldest of the famous Soong sisters. At the summer gathering held two years later in Ashburnham, Massachusetts, nine women were present among more than one hundred men. The Chinese women attracted attention from the local people. One Ashburnham newspaper described them as "pretty" and dressed in "Yankee costumes," some wearing their hair "in a peculiar, but somewhat fantastic way."[47] The paper also noted that the women, taking up front seats and enjoying other privileges, received "due homage from the young men."[48]

The conference organizers made deliberate efforts to attract women students by providing them with free train fare and free room and board. The presence of women, in turn, was used by the organizers to lure more male students to come to the conference. From the very beginning, the Alliance's summer conferences had a special social function: to encourage socialization between men and women students from China. This function became increasingly prominent toward the second half of the 1910s and into the 1920s, eventually surpassing, as discussed in Chapter 1, the "serious" side of the annual gatherings. The social experiment conducted by the Alliance in the first decade of the twentieth century, a decade or so before the issue was raised by the May Fourth activists, was among the earliest attempts made by Chinese in modern times to achieve *nannü shejiao ziyou* (free socialization between the sexes). The decision to invite women students required deliberation on the part of the conference organizers. In doing so, they defied strict gender segregation in China. The courage demonstrated by the women participants was even more admirable, since they knew well that by mixing with a crowd of men they behaved outrageously by Chinese standards. As late as 1916, ten years after female education was officially endorsed in China, the Ministry of Education issued regulations forbidding girls to cut their hair short, to enter coed schools after the age of fourteen, and to enter "free marriage." Those who violated the rules were threatened with dismissal from school.[49] By mixing up at social gatherings, Chinese students, men and women alike, disregarded Chinese social norms and consciously took advantage of the American environment to taste freedom denied to them at home.

Women participants were often found either at the conference bazaar, where they "served as saleswomen," or on stage during evening entertainment, where they played musical instruments.[50] Their roles tended to be auxiliary and decorative, conforming to the "pleasant companion" ideal. Moreover, given the small number of women and the brevity of conference time, meaningful social mingling could hardly take place. It is no wonder that the outcome always fell short of expectations. A not uncommon complaint from the men was that conversations with women were "boring." The men's lack of knowledge about women students persisted, despite the annual conferences. As late as 1924, one woman student remarked, "What do the girls talk about when they are by themselves has become a very popular question. . . . When the Chinese boys know more of the Chinese girls through cultivation of sincere friendships and intercourse, the girls' conversation will not appear such a mystery."[51]

The unsatisfactory results of the Alliance's early social experiment underlined the difficulties many Chinese had in approaching people of the opposite sex. Ignorance in this respect could lead to misunderstanding of American social customs. A student thus observed, "In America, people do nice things for women. But it is usually not because they want to be intimate, but because to respect women has become habitual in the social custom. . . . Since in China men and women are socially separated, suspicion of intention can easily arise whenever the slightest courtesy is paid to a woman."[52] Having been subjected in their home country to strict gender segregation, many students found themselves socially handicapped upon arriving in America. To familiarize the Chinese with the basic code of behavior in America, guidance on etiquette was needed. In one piece written especially for the male students, more than one hundred different social situations were listed, many concerning dealings with women. The instructions included such items as "always let women go first," "stand up to show courtesy to women," and "carry things for women you accompany." Men were also told to pay attention to their appearance and to shave often, lest they would "disgust women."[53] The motivations of the students to adopt the Western gentlemanly behavior could be complex. While it might indicate a genuine concern for women, it also revealed a desire to gain respectability in American society. Living in a foreign culture and conscious of the inadequacy of their own country's social customs regarding gender-related etiquette, some students correctly sensed that they had to change the way they behaved. Showing courtesy to women, then, could be a proof of "being modern," and did not necessarily mean genuine respect for women.

While men were told to be thoughtful toward women, they were warned not to go too far. They were advised not to take the "kindness and niceness of American women" as "invitations of intimacy," since American women were "generally" kind and nice. On the other hand, they were told not to be startled when they saw "[American] men and women holding hands, kissing or walking together arm in arm in public."[54] Such cautions bespoke a belief that certain behavior, though permissible for Americans, should not be imitated by the Chinese, and revealed a sense of self-protection, crucial in a society where anti-Chinese prejudice was explicit. Almost all the instructions were concerned with social conduct in public situations. Only one item dealt with a vaguely romantic situation, and it was a piece of negative advice: a man should not buy expensive gifts for women to whom he has been recently introduced.[55] On the whole, the question of how to act in a more intimate relationship received little attention from the authors of the articles on etiquette. Advice on such matters, however, was increasingly needed.

LEARNING TO PLAY THE DATING GAME

If, for Gu Weijun and his peers, the primary concern was what to do with the women chosen by their families, for the May Fourth youths who sought and obtained more autonomy in their personal lives, how to conduct a romantic relationship became a more pressing issue. According to Meng Zhi (Paul Meng), an activist of the May Fourth movement who later would spend most of his adult life as the director of China Institute in New York, "practically" all his Qinghua classmates attempted to break their arranged betrothals and most of them succeeded before they came to America. Meng himself notified his parents that he would not marry the girl of their choice.[56] Even for those who did not sever their betrothal ties, some did things unthinkable to an earlier generation.

Before he left China, Fang Xianting asked to meet his fiancee and expressed a desire to see her receive a modern education while he was away. Both requests were agreed upon by his future in-laws, who treated Fang as a "honored guest" during his visit to their home.[57] Others began to tread on the unfamiliar ground of "free love." Liang Shiqiu, when studying at Qinghua College, was dating a woman graduate from a girls' normal school in Beijing.[58] Liang considered himself "exceptionally lucky" among his peers, since even with "free socialization between the sexes" (*nannü shejiao ziyou*) zealously promoted during the May Fourth period, few young people in China had a real taste of having a "friend" of the opposite sex.

The story of Wen Yiduo (Wen I-to), a good friend of Liang Shiqiu at Qinghua, illustrates that tradition still retained a considerable power over the people supposedly under the influence of new ideas. In 1922, Wen Yiduo was a senior at Qinghua and a leading member of an avant-garde literary society. One day, Wen received a letter from his parents urging him to return home to marry his fiancee. To Wen, the letter was like "a thunder cloud blowing suddenly overhead in a bright day."[59] Being an obedient son, Wen submitted to his parents' will. Wen Yiduo's marriage illustrates that the May Fourth movement, forceful as it was, did not root out once and for all the age-old practice of arranged marriage, even for the "new youth."[60] According to Liang Shiqiu, Wen's marriage was a rare case among Qinghua students, as the school usually frowned upon those who got married during their student days.[61]

On the whole, young Chinese men arriving in America after the late 1910s appeared to enjoy greater individual freedom and to be more adventurous in their personal conduct. They also came upon a society notably more relaxed towards social and sexual relations. The new trend was nowhere better exemplified than on college campuses, which as the 1920s unfolded increasingly became meeting places for young men and women. One Chinese student observed in 1921 that American male students had no interest in developing close friendships with other men, since they spent so much time after class with their girlfriends.[62] Although changes in American young people's sexual behavior did not escape the notice of Chinese students, the actual effect on them is hard to tell. Commenting on the differences between the American and the Chinese, however, Fang Xianting, then a student at Yale, observed, "While much of the time of an American student was spent on dating girls for dances and other pleasure, most of Chinese students, on account of racial difference, poor command of English, and anxiety over early completion and return home, did not fool around with American girls."[63] Despite his own remarks and the fact that he had a fiancee in China, Fang did date an American girl, a fellow worker at a YWCA cafeteria where Fang worked as a student employee. One evening, the two went to see a play at the Schubert Theater in New Haven. "Too green and shy for dealing with the fair sex," Fang neither held hands nor kissed the girl during the entire evening.[64] His recollections, however, suggest that he was aware that these were the things an American man would do in a similar situation.

A romantic relationship between two Chinese might be less sexually charged, at least at an early stage, though it could cause as much anxiety. The mutual attraction Xie Bingxin and Wu Wenzao felt for each other during their voyage to America continued to grow afterwards. When she arrived at her destination of Wellesley College, Xie wrote a letter to Wu, while to others she only sent postcards. The correspondence eventually led to a meeting in the summer of 1925, when they both went to Cornell University, ostensibly to attend the summer school there. Wu proposed to Xie while the two were boating on Beebe Lake, Xie replying that the final decision would have to be made by her parents, knowing well that if she agreed, her parents, both liberal-minded, would not object. When she returned to China in 1926, Xie Bingxin brought with her a letter containing a marriage proposal from Wu Wenzao. Better versed than her fiancé, Xie had made sure that it was properly written. Once home, too embarrassed to raise the issue openly, Xie quietly left the letter in her parents' bedroom. The ending, as expected, was a happy one. The couple married soon after Wu Wenzao finished his studies and returned to China in 1929.[65]

If the love story of Xie Bingxin and Wu Wenzao was filled with joy, the romantic encounter of Wen Yiduo resulted in pain. A poem in English, written when Wen was an art student in New York, expressed his feelings:

Let us part! Our meeting is through,
Though heart may hunger, heart may rue.
Your friendship's smile was undreamed of,
Still less hoped your signs of love.

Thus in after years if again we meet,
I famishing still, you replete,
Glad and unshamefaced I'll say:
"Once we met but did not stay."

"Once we met, our paths converged,
All currents of my being surged—
Once we met and parted soon."
In after years let my heart croon.

Sending this poem to his good friend Liang Shiqiu, Wen Yiduo added a line in Chinese: "Human beings are not made of wood and stone. How can one do without emotions?" Liang suspected that the poem was written for a Chinese female student in New York. Years later, Liang commented, "He [Wen Yiduo] was a passionate person, but was timid and scared whenever he encountered intimate man-woman relations. He would always nip the affection in the bud. That was why there was so much sadness in the poem."[66]

If for Wen Yiduo *li* (propriety) finally overcame *qing* (emotions), an ending conforming to the familiar traditional pattern, Meng Zhi's experience involved issues that were culturally more complex. A student at Columbia University in the early 1920s, Meng went to California during one summer vacation to work at a resort on Lake George. Among his coworkers, mostly American college students, one girl held special attraction for him. Identified by Meng as "R.O.," she had dark hair and fair skin, reminding Meng of his favorite sister. It is worth noting here that initially, Meng Zhi only saw "physical strangeness" in Western women. Only gradually did he begin to appreciate the beauty of Caucasian women and even start to think that "blondness could be good-looking."[67] A freshman at Mount Holyoke College, R.O. was planning to work in China as a missionary and often asked Meng about his native land. Eventually, the two began to do things together. "By the appearances and customs of the time," they "went steady."[68] Yet Meng carefully avoided physical contact with R.O., maintaining an almost rigid posture when he was with her. Everything remained under control until one "moonlit evening." After a quiet and private time together, before they were about to go inside, R.O. suddenly embraced Meng and kissed him. The magic feminine touch "electrified" Meng's "whole being," but it also disturbed him deeply.[69] For a person who was taught at an early age to "when young, restrain from sexual impulse," who remembered no physical intimacy even with his mother or sisters, R.O.'s behavior posed a serious question about her morality. Meanwhile, R.O.'s family, upon learning about their relationship, expressed strong opposition and the troubled romance came to an end. Meng Zhi and R.O.'s "cross-cultural" romance touched a nerve on two sensitive points: interracial relationships and sexuality. In the following pages, we will discuss these two issues separately.

INTERRACIAL MARRIAGE: A CASE STUDY

Meng Zhi was certainly not the first Western-educated Chinese man to be attracted to a white woman. In the 1870s, as mentioned earlier, Yung Wing set a precedent by marrying Mary Louise Kellogg. Later, a small number of Chinese men, studying in various Western countries, followed suit. For a while "international marriage" (*guoji hunyin*) became a fad among some foreign-educated Chinese men.[70] The Chinese government was not amused. In 1910, the Ministry of Education under the Qing, alarmed by the situation that "students going to the East [Japan] and the West tend to marry foreign women in the respective localities," issued an order to prohibit the practice.[71] In 1918, the Ministry of Education under the republican government decided to stop financial aid to those government-sponsored students who married foreigners, contending that "marrying foreigners can cause many problems and it is especially improper for government-supported students to do so."[72] The government's stance notwithstanding, the decrees were not effectively enforced.

Opposition to interracial marriage also existed among the Chinese students themselves. In 1914, Ma Yinchu translated a speech given by a professor of international law at Columbia. In the speech the American professor opposed interracial marriage between Chinese and Americans on the grounds that such marriages would dilute racial purity. In his footnote to the translation, Ma endorsed the professor's opinion, calling it "in agreement with the principles of sociology."[73] More than a decade later, Pan Guangdan also expressed disapproval of interracial marriage. Admitting that such marriages probably would not cause "biological" problems, Pan maintained that Chinese society was unable to cope with the "social" and "psychological" consequences of interracial marriages and therefore there was no need to "complicate" life in a country undergoing an already difficult enough transition.[74]

While racial prejudice existed on both sides, the Chinese found themselves in an unequal power relationship with the Americans as members of a race that was openly discriminated against. At this time, fourteen U.S. states had laws against marriages between whites and Chinese or "Mongolians."[75] In some cases, racial discrimination prevented even the most basic contact, let alone intimate relationships. As described at the beginning of Chapter 3, when Colorado College school administration in 1924 segregated Chinese male students from American female students at the school's commencement exercises, Wen Yiduo, who was then a student at the college, was deeply humiliated by the incident and subsequently left Colorado for New York City.[76]

Under the unfavorable racial circumstances, to make an interracial relationship work would require tremendous courage and commitment from both the Chinese and the American. The story of Tiam Hock Franking[77] of Xiamen (Amoy), China, and Mae Munro Watkins of Ann Arbor, Michigan, is a case in point. Their story is particularly intriguing because we have two versions of it at our disposal: one is told by the couple themselves, through their letters to each other and to the woman's family in America, and the other is a piece called "My Chinese Marriage," published in serial form in 1921 in the journal *Asia*, based on a manuscript of Mae Franking and ghostwritten by Katherine Anne Porter. Since no extant copy of Mae Franking's original manuscript has been found, the question of how much Porter interpolated herself into the piece remains unsolved.[78] A comparative reading of the two accounts, especially with regard to how love between the two young people initially took place, reveals an interesting contrast.

Mae Munro Watkins first met Tiam Hock Franking in 1907, when they both attended an Ann Arbor high school.[79] Mae was seventeen, daughter of a middle-class Scotch-Irish family, and Tiam was nineteen, son of a wealthy

Chinese merchant family from Fujian Province. Before long, mutual affection developed. Because they were still young, Mr. and Mrs. Watkins suggested that the two separate for a year to make sure about their feelings for each other. Tiam subsequently transferred to a high school in another town. It was during this year of separation that Tiam and Mae confirmed their love. In their frequent correspondence Tiam said that he believed "there is a perfect understanding and sympathy between us"[80] and declared, "Beyond any rational doubt, dearest, you have drawn my whole heart."[81] Mae replied with a simple affirmation, "Tiam, I love you."[82] Their relationship worried Mae's friends and some relatives. To one of her aunts who had expressed reservations, Mae stated that despite what others had said she could not change her feelings towards Tiam.[83] Fortunately, Mr. and Mrs. Watkins were understanding parents, and did not prohibit their daughter's love affair with the young Chinese man.

In her letters, Mae showed no sign of racial prejudice against Chinese. On the contrary, she expressed interest in Chinese culture. In "My Chinese Marriage," in contrast, Margaret (pseudonym for Mae) initially carried a great deal of racial bias. Having a hard time seeing Chan-king Liang (pseudonym for Tiam) "as a human being like the rest of us," Margaret had to remind herself constantly not to make any "thoughtless remarks" in front of Chan-king that "would reveal my true state of mind about China."[84] Eventually, Chan-king's intelligence and charm made Margaret lose the "sight of the race in the individual" and the two began to go out together. The overt hostility following them "awakened" in Margaret "brooding maternal tenderness." To defy the unfriendly environment, and after "Chan-king's eyes pleaded wistfully," Margaret finally gave Chan-king her "sacrificial offering," a kiss.[85]

In real life, Tiam began his studies at the University of Michigan Law School in the fall of 1910. A year later, Mae enrolled in the Department of Literature, Science, and Arts in the same university. It was at this time that Tiam received letters from his parents, urging him to break off his relationship with the American girl and reminding him of his obligation to his fiancee at home. When Tiam refused to listen to his parents, letters from home stopped, along with money. Tiam had to support himself in order to finish his law studies in America.

Tiam and Mae decided to marry after graduation, a plan that further isolated them from other people. In September 1912, the wedding took place, earlier than had been planned because of Mae's pregnancy. The day after their wedding, the newlyweds discovered that their private ceremony had become front-page news in the local papers, which gave a negative report of the wedding. To protest against the intrusion on their privacy and to straighten out the twisted information in the press, Tiam wrote a letter to a local paper, in which he asked, "[Is] the marriage confirmed with the laws of both holy gospel and the land, and with the consent of the parents, as well as the parties—after all a private matter?"[86] He also provided his address and telephone number for anyone who cared to discuss the matter with him directly. Tiam and Mae could not continue their studies at the University of Michigan. Tiam left for Detroit, where he enrolled at Detroit College of Law and supported himself by working as a waiter in a Chinese restaurant, Mae stayed at her parents' home, waiting for the birth of their baby.

Tiam received his degree in the summer of 1913 and returned to China the same winter. Soon Mae and their newborn child came to join him. In Shanghai, Tiam first taught English and later opened a law office. For a while Mae also found a job teaching English at a girl's high school, and this experience made her "feel quite intelligent again and as though I amounted to something."[87]

Eventually Tiam reconciled with his family. During their several visits to Tiam's hometown, Xiamen, Mae found that she liked both of his parents. Mae tried very hard to be a proper first daughter-in-law (Tiam was the eldest son of the family), even though she could only communicate with Tiam's family in "sign language."

In 1918, for reasons not clear, Tiam went to Beijing to seek a position in the foreign service. At the end of that year, the family came back to America, where Tiam was offered a job at the Chinese consulate-general's office in San Francisco. By then, the family had five members—two more children had been born. Soon after they were back in the States, however, Tiam fell ill and died in the spring of 1919 at the age of twenty-nine. After Tiam's death, Mae went back with her three children to Ann Arbor to live with her parents. It was presumably during the mourning period that Mae wrote the manuscript "My Chinese Marriage."

While in Beijing in 1918, Tiam had had a conversation with an acquaintance on the subject of interracial marriage. Asked whether his marriage was happy, Tiam replied, "I couldn't get a better and happier wife."[88] Earlier, in 1917, Mae reflected on the issue of interracial marriage in a letter to her parents: "I think I have experienced enough to be sure of one thing: There is such a thing in the world as racial intermarriage; but, like the art of poetry, people must be born for it. Such people could be content with no other kind of union. . . . Out of the thousands of Chinese students in America, a small percent—I do not know how small, but say one in two thousand—had the firm desire of bringing home a foreign wife,—and the moral courage and strength of purpose necessary to such an undertaking."[89]

The story of Tiam and Mae sheds light on why it was so difficult to pursue an interracial relationship. It is also interesting to note that Mae only referred to the "foreign wife," which indicates that if a "racial intermarriage" did occur, it was most likely between a Chinese man and an American woman.

SEXUALITY: A TOUCHY SUBJECT

Sexuality was another unsettling issue for Chinese men in America. As mentioned earlier, the 1920s was a turning point in American cultural history, with a definite change in manners and morals. Above all, this was an age of sexual revolution. At the heart of the revolution was the recognition and approval of female sexuality. "Dating," a new ritual of sexual interaction that involved heavy "petting and necking," had become common and acceptable. More than anywhere else, college campuses, especially coeducational campuses, provided a fertile social environment for the new mores to emerge.[90]

Meng Zhi's confused reaction to R.O.'s "necking" should be placed in this larger context. Meng admitted that he had a hard time accepting the sexual conduct of contemporary American youths: "The hardest hurdle for me to negotiate was the social behavior between American boys and girls. I did not approve of their free and wild carryings-on."[91] More specifically, he could not bring himself to accept the open expression of female sexuality, which was regarded as "evil" in Chinese culture. Meng was caught between the pursuit of modern ideals and the discipline of an old patriarchal morality. Meng Zhi's attitude makes us wonder about the general attitude of male Chinese students toward sexuality in the 1920s.

Back at home, a "sexual revolution" was also going on, conducted primarily on an abstract intellectual level. An examination of contemporary magazines and newspapers shows that sexuality was an earnest concern of the day, discussed in the context of love, marriage, and family reform.[92] Zhou Zuoren's translation of the Japanese writer Yosano Akiko's article "Zhencao lun" (On chastity), published in the May 1918 issue of *New Youth*, touched off a debate that consumed people's attention throughout the May Fourth period. Some writings further explored the sexual dimension of chastity. One article asked if *zhencao* (chastity) was still necessary in a love relationship. Contending that love should be based on the attraction of both spirit and flesh, the author argued that there was no need to discipline lovers with *zhencao*.[93] The dual nature of love, with both physical and spiritual components, appears to have been generally accepted by the contemporaries. The frank discussion of sexual attraction was a distinctive phenomenon in the May Fourth period, reflecting an amazing openness on the part of the Chinese on this issue. Such an openness was partially due to the influence of a number of Western thinkers, among whom the impact of the Swedish writer Ellen Key was especially significant. Her writings praised the moral value of sex for its contribution to the continuation of the human race and its uplifting effect on human society. The legitimacy of sexuality was also affirmed by evolutionary theory, which linked humankind with animal species, both driven by basic sexual desires. Meanwhile, Margaret Sanger's visit to China in the spring of 1922 further demystified sex and helped bring the topic of birth control out into the open.[94] Female sexuality was widely acknowledged at this time, though many writers held that "by nature" the female sex (both among human beings and animals) tended to be the passive partner in a sexual relationship.

In contrast with the open attitude toward sexuality in China during the May Fourth period, little on the issue is found in the students' publications in America.[95] One article appeared in the *Monthly* in 1915, written by an American and advocating a "sensible" sex education for adolescents in schools to counterbalance the bad impact of "harmful information."[96] It was not until 1924 that another article on sexuality appeared in the same journal, overtly celebrating sexual love. The article boldly stated that since "our love instinct is a gift of nature," it should not be "suppressed, killed, or destroyed."[97] The irony is that the article was translated from the *Ladies' Journal* published in China. Living in the midst of a "sexual revolution" in

America in the 1920s, the Chinese students there were curiously silent on the subject of sexuality.

The lack of open discussion did not mean that the students' behavior remained unchanged. Some of the people, as already noted, were learning to play the dating game. Ballroom dancing quickly became a favored form of social event for some people. One student described what he saw at the 1916 summer gathering: "In the evening those who can, enjoy themselves in dancing, while others who have not acquired the art stand around and watch with intense interest. It is surprising to find the rapid increase in the number of dancers among us to notice the high degree of proficiency that many have attained."[98] Yet not everybody approved of dancing. Some believed that it was amoral, or even immoral, because of the "unwholesome stimulation" it could provoke in the dancers.[99] Despite the disapproval, ballroom dancing became even more in vogue among the students as the 1920s unfolded. The "queen" of the 1921 conference, for instance, was Hilda Yan, the niece of Yan Huiqing. Two male students competed for her favor, and even challenged each other to a duel.[100]

Back in China, the cultural influence of the American-returned students could also be felt. Grace T. Seton, who visited China in the early 1920s, noted that she met an American-educated young Chinese woman in Beijing who represented to her "the best example of the flapper type," with bobbed and waved hair and chic French gowns. She was often found at dances in big hotels, and was seen riding and skating in company with young men.[101] While conservative-minded Chinese undoubtedly frowned at her behavior, Rosamunde Soong (Song Qingling), the wife of Sun Yet-sen, probably thought of her differently. In an interview with Seton in the early 1920s, Madam Sun observed, "I think the foreign trained student is valuable at present. For instance, the social life of China has been much changed by the returned student. A lady and a gentleman may walk and talk together now! Even dancing is in vogue in the port cities."[102]

NOT ABOUT LOVE

Lu Xun once lamented that in China love was so attenuated that most Chinese couples did not know what it was.[103] During the May Fourth period, it was widely accepted by the progressive-thinking youths that "love must be the basis of marriage and that only love is sufficient to make marriage moral."[104] The equation of love and morality, however, did little to simplify a very complex reality, where new values intertwined with the old and the resulting confusion and anxiety made the concern for love secondary. An examination of the students' literary creations in America indicates that even though they enjoyed a greater degree of personal freedom, they were unable to completely escape from the moral burden of their culture. In what follows, I examine two short stories and two plays by Chinese students in America, all with the same subject matter: love affairs between male and female Chinese students in America. If literary creations have the function of helping their writers and readers work out problems and contradictions in real life, then a close look at these works will shed light on how the students thought about romantic relationships, what problems and obstacles they perceived as the most taxing, and how they wished to see them solved. Since there are noticeable differences between the works written before the May Fourth era and those after, I will examine them separately.

Woon Yung Chun's short story "East Is East and West Is West" was published in April 1914.[105] At the beginning of the story, a young Chinese man bids farewell to a young woman. The couple has only been engaged recently and now the man is on his way to America. Once in the new country, the man's adjustment to the American environment goes smoothly; he quickly learns to wear fashionable clothes, to smoke, to use slang, and to play sports, enjoying the "frolic and gaiety" of American undergraduate life. A deeper change is happening inside him: the "fresh values of life" he is experiencing lead him to question the "old teachings" in China. In the summer of his last year in America, he meets a Chinese woman from Shanghai. The woman, a recent graduate from Wellesley College, is a "new type," "ambitious and progressive." Amidst Wellesley's "beautiful surroundings and happy influences," she has grown into "perfect womanhood." Finding each other "compatible in nature, in intellect and in aims," the two fall in love.

The man seldom thinks of his fiancee at home, and when he does, she is always seen in an unfavorable light. How could he, the man asks himself, be happy with a woman who possesses no "personal charm," entertains "no high ideals of life," and is so much his "intellectual inferior?" Finally he decides to dissolve the engagement in China to marry the Wellesley girl.

When the news reaches the woman at home, she appears to take it calmly. During the long separation from her fiance, she has won respect from her neighbors for her high moral conduct. Now she swallows her humiliation in a classical manner, leaving home to become a nun and retreating into "silence, deathless and eternal."

If "East Is East and West Is West" sees no solution to the conflict between "East" and "West" other than sacrificing the former, the play *The New Order Cometh*, written in 1915, ends on a more heartening note.[106] In it, the "new order" is represented by two American-returned students who have fallen in love in the United States. The "old order," on the other hand, is symbolized by the father of the young man's fiancee in China. Upon learning that his future son-in-law wants to sever the betrothal tie, the old man replies that since the engagement has been jointly decided by the two families before the death of the young man's father, it should stand as it is unless the young man can bring his father back to life again. In the end, it is the daughter of the old man, demonstrating a strange sympathy for her fiance and his lover, who helps to break the impasse. She is rewarded in turn with the devotion of another man, hence herself becoming a happy participant in a modern romance. This play, written by Zhang Pengchun (P. C. Chang), was performed in New Haven by a group of Chinese students from Yale and Columbia. Described as "exceedingly successful," it was warmly received by the American audience.[107]

On the surface, both "East Is East and West Is West" and *The New Order Cometh* affirm love as the basis for marriage, sympathetically depicting the romances between the American-educated young people. Yet it is not hard to discern that the real focus of these stories is the women left behind in China. The same question is implied by both: What happens to such women when the men to whom they're engaged find the girls of their own choice in America? In *The New Order Cometh*, the woman is surprisingly adaptable to a grave humiliation and unusually fortunate to be immediately rescued from her predicament. In comparison, the author of "East Is East and West Is West" lets his abandoned heroine act in a way that is more consistent with the traditional behavioral pattern. By letting the woman spend the rest of her life in a monastery, a stark contrast to the happy union of the modern couple, the author reveals his doubtfulness about the cost of modern romance. Thus, while *The New Order Cometh* releases its hero from moral responsibilities, "East Is East and West Is West" ends ambivalently.

A few years later, this moral dilemma was worked out in a different manner, in the story "The Comedy of Ignorance" and the play *For Romeo and Juliet*, written respectively in 1919 and 1920.[108] In both works, the abandoned fiancees become modern educated women. Instead of depending on fate or luck to determine their lives, they are capable of taking initiative and come to America to pursue modern learning themselves. A closer look at these "modern women," however, reveals that underneath the surface they are not that much different from the women in the works discussed above.

In "The Comedy of Ignorance," Ah-tsu, having learned that her fiance in America has terminated their engagement, decides to come to the Western country herself. Her family supports her action on the grounds that a girl ought to be educated "for her husband and her children." Changing her name to Sophia, the woman conceals her true identity. She manages to find her fiance in the United States, although she has never met him before, and the two fall in love. The man is pleasantly surprised when he discovers that his lover is the same woman he was betrothed to years ago. The story ends with a happy reunion of the two. As in *The New Order Cometh*, there is no moral burden to be shouldered by the characters of "The Comedy of Ignorance." Ah-tsu rescues herself by becoming the modern woman Sophia. The value of her education, it seems, lies in her calculated success in gaining her fiance back. Apparently appealing to a large number of people, this story won the second prize in the short-story contest conducted by the *Monthly*.

The play *For Romeo and Juliet*, written by Hong Shen (Shen Hung), conveys a different message, although its plot is similar to the Ah-tsu/Sophia formula. Miss Chang, the heroine of the play, is deserted by her fiance. Several years later, the two meet in America. The man, without realizing that Miss Chang was once his fiancee, falls in love with her and proposes marriage. Knowing who he is but not intending to reveal her own identity, Miss Chang seizes the opportunity to pour out her bitterness that has been accumulated for years: "From the day of my childhood, I kept a mirror which witnessed my sorrow and my happiness. In a moment of despair [when she learned that the man severed the betrothal tie], I broke my mirror and sent half to him, . . . to show him that a woman's heart, like a mirror, is pure and clean. Once broken, it can not be repaired."[109] Unlike Ah-tsu in "The Comedy of Ignorance," Miss Chang refuses to make up with the man. Instead of using her modern education as leverage to reclaim her once lost fiance, she uses it to secure herself a position equal to his so that she can launch her revenge. Miss Chang is more dignified than Ah-tsu in the way she handles the humiliation of being abandoned by her fiance, but she is not really that different from Ah-tsu in her attitude toward marriage: by honoring a nonexistent love, Miss Chang legitimizes arranged marriage; empowered by her Western education, she is able to defend the rightfulness of an old custom; like Ah-tsu, she clings to the values of the past. Despite their modern education, both characters uphold the same basic values of womanhood as their older sisters, adhering to the cult of chastity as the highest principle in life.

The representation of women as ultimately conservative discloses a sense of ambivalence many Chinese men felt in this era of rapid social change. In an earlier section, I mentioned that some Chinese male students perceived highly educated American women as essentially traditional. By holding onto tradition, women appeared to be capable of providing men with a sense of security needed in an uncertain world, where, ironically, men themselves pursued progressive ideas.

No easy solution could be found to the moral dilemmas embedded in this period of transition. If, by inventing wish-fulfilling characters, the authors of *The New Order Cometh* and "The Comedy of Ignorance" managed to escape a complex reality, "East Is East and West Is West" and *For Romeo and Juliet*, by presenting more plausible characters, posed a serious question that no sensible people could lightly dismiss. Both Gu Weijun and Zhao Yuanren, just to mention two individuals we have discussed in this chapter, had to deal with the moral responsibilities in their personal lives. Even Meng Zhi, a "May Fourth" youth, admitted that he felt a deep sense of guilt about renouncing the betrothal arranged by his parents.[110] Before turning to cultivate their feelings, the students had to come to terms with issues that were more urgent and troubling to them: how to dissolve the past. For many of them, the past was embodied by their previously betrothed spouses. The literary works of the students indicate that Chinese men perceived Chinese women more as personifications of morality than as partners in a romantic relationship.

The statement that Lu Xun made, "Love, I don't know what you are," remained valid.[111] In stories and plays, love was left in the background while concern with morality took center stage. When the question of love was raised, it tended to be treated as a social and political issue rather than a personal and emotional matter. In the play *For Romeo and Juliet*, when the man proposes his marriage to Miss Chang, he justifies his action on the grounds that their union would set an example in "this period of reconstruction" for "the social reform of China."[112] This apparent uneasiness about love echoed the writings of Luo Jialun, who used high-minded "humanism" to vindicate love during the May Fourth period.[113]

The students' literary works raise still another interesting subject: the romantic affairs between the male and female students in America. In the present study, we have met a few couples in this category: Hu Binxia and Zhu Tingqi, Chen Hengzhe and Ren Hongjun. Starting in 1911, the *Monthly* began to record marriages and engagements among the Chinese students. By the end of 1924, a total of ten marriages and twelve engagements were reported. Even allowing for cases that escaped the notice of the *Monthly* editors, the number is insignificant. A Chinese woman student named Rosalind Me-tsung Li offered her explanation of the situation in an article that provides us with a rare glimpse of a woman's perspective. Writing in 1922, Me-tsung Li first asks: "Is it not abnormal that with so many Chinese young men and women studying together in the colleges and universities of America, all in the supposedly romantic age, no scandal has ever occurred?"[114] She then proceeds to blame her fellow female students for the dearth of romantic affairs: "How geometrically correct is our conversation with men, in so far as we can be credited with conversations. How chillily correct is our dress! How mechanically correct are our ways of walking, of holding our eyes rigidly in their sockets!"[115] In her opinion, the Chinese women students were dominated by two ideals: correctness and usefulness, which they learned mostly from their missionary schools in China, where "our own Puritanism is made doubly, nay triply, 'grundyish' by the old Testament and the American frontier tradition."[116] If the "uniform yellow of Chinese social etiquette and morals" was very much like "frost in April," then the missionary education further "killed, cured, and ossified" the vitality of the Chinese women.[117] Rosalind Me-tsung Li's resentment against missionary influence reflects a widespread sentimentality in China in the 1920s, and mirrors the rapid decline of moral authority in American society at this time. While critical of the "missionary" type, Me-tsung Li also expresses disapproval of the "flappers of the Broadways." Not satisfied by either of the two American models, she turns her eyes back toward China: "If the Chinese revolution is to be something which our descendants shall be proud of, it must mean a renewal of life. Of course, it cannot renew life in China if it does not touch the broad and populous realm of the womanhood of China."[118]

THE STORY OF HU SHI

Ever since Hu Shi returned to China in 1917 to marry the woman he had been betrothed to since the age of twelve, his personal life has been a fascinating puzzle. It has not been easy for people, scholars and laymen alike, to reconcile Hu Shi, the quintessential American-returned Chinese and one of the most prominent leaders of the May Fourth New Culture Movement, with his marriage to Jiang Dongxiu, a "semiliterate" country woman with bound feet.[119] In recent years, several studies have come out, both in Chinese and English, exploring the personal life of Hu Shi.[120] These studies have featured a number of women that had close relationships with Hu Shi, revealing Hu's complex, and at times tension-ridden emotional life.

In America, Hu Shi had an unusual friendship with an unusual American woman, Edith Clifford Williams. Scholars have generally agreed that it was a love relationship, but they tend not to fully recognize the impact of this relationship on the process of Hu Shi's "self-becoming": his transition from a man oriented toward family and society into an independent-thinking modern intellectual.

Edith Clifford Williams, daughter of a geography professor at Cornell University, studied modern art and lived by herself in New York. Wearing short hair and plain, casual clothes, she embodied every trait of a "Bohemian" avant-garde artist. When she walked in the streets of New York, she often drew disapproving stares. Not only did she look iconoclastic, she was also in fact unusually independent in her thinking. An extraordinarily intelligent person with broad interests, E. C. Williams stood out even among the "new women" in America.

Hu Shi first met her in the summer of 1914, when E. C. Williams was still a student at Cornell. Because of Williams, Hu paid a visit to the girls' dorm for the first time of his almost four years at the college. It is worth noting here that Hu Shi justified this visit as something beneficial for his character development, since he believed that women had the capacity to mold and temper men's character.[121] The fact that Hu Shi had to explain the meeting in such lofty terms revealed his apprehension about relationships with women. Convincing himself that he was only looking for "pure and high" friendship between the sexes,[122] Hu Shi soon realized that his relationship with E. C. Williams was going to be emotionally intimate and would change him profoundly.

Some scholars attribute Hu Shi's eventual association with the female sex to "the American influence," which was "too great for Hu to resist,"[123] implying that the environment made the outcome inevitable. Recent studies, however, show that campus culture in this period at Cornell and other coeducational schools did not generally favor male students' association with coeds. Rather, the student body tended to be separated by gender and other hierarchical barriers.[124] Furthermore, when a young woman was with a young man, she was usually accompanied by a "chaperon." This Victorian etiquette, though already in decline, was still being observed by the properly bred upper- and middle-class students, as Hu Shi noted in his diary.[125]

After E. C. Williams moved to New York, Hu Shi visited her there several times and eventually transferred to Columbia University, partly to be close to Williams. Once they were both in the city, they spent many long hours together, in Williams' apartment overlooking the Hudson River, in museums and art galleries, in the woods and under the moonlight. Imagine Hu Shi, a young Chinese man, and E. C. Williams, an eccentric-looking young American woman, walking together in New York. It is not surprising that they looked conspicuous to people in the streets. They had much to talk about: literature, art, Eastern and Western philosophies, ethics, current affairs, war and peace. Hu Shi enjoyed their conversations enormously and filled his diary with admiring words for Williams, such as the following: "The lady's extraordinary vision is head and shoulders above that of an ordinary woman. I know many, many women, but there is only one who has such intellect, vision, decisiveness and compassion."[126] On another occasion, Hu frankly admitted to Williams her influence on him: "I have long needed a steersman who can set me on the right course. Yet so far no one, except you, has been able to give me what I am sorely in need of."[127]

There was certainly not just intellectual exchange going on between the two. In the first part of 1915, Hu wrote several love poems, all in Chinese, which have been rightly interpreted by scholars as expressions of his feelings toward Williams.[128] Williams, for her part and in her "high-minded way," also admitted in her letter to Hu Shi that there was "sex attraction" in their relationship. Yet Williams believed that the real meaning of life among people of "the highest type" was "spiritual and not physical." Thus she asked Hu Shi and herself to "value" the sex attraction "for just so much as it is good for," and go beyond it to concentrate on the "closest and most stimulating interaction of thought."[129] A cultural rebel in every other sense, Williams was obviously not ready to embrace sexuality as so many young people would do in the 1920s. Defining their relationship as primarily "spiritual" and between two persons of the "highest type," Williams contended in a letter that theirs should not be subjected to the judgment of conventional propriety, and should be comprehended only by "propriety of thought." This letter, an important document in the relationship between Hu and Williams, not only demonstrates how highly Williams valued Hu's friendship, but also shows Williams's awareness of the unconventional nature of their relationship.

Around this time, in the first half of 1915, a period that clearly witnessed the height of Hu and Williams's mutual attraction, Hu Shi began to criticize the restrictiveness of American etiquette regulating the behavior of young people.[130] In one diary entry, Hu Shi commented, "In this so-called 'free' country, social and religious customs are nonetheless extremely conservative."[131] On another occasion, Hu Shi compared America with Russia, contending that young people in Russia enjoyed greater freedom than their counterparts in America. Culling his information from Russian novels, Hu Shi wrote that young men and women in Russia did all kinds of things together, including participating in the revolutionary cause, and they treated each other equally without entertaining any indecent thoughts. This was true freedom, Hu maintained, that went beyond the comprehension of "the conservative old ladies in America."[132] Writing this diary entry, Hu Shi may have had one particular "old lady" in mind: a letter from Hu in early 1916 suggests that she might well be Mrs. Williams, mother of E. C. Williams. Emotionally charged and somewhat covertly antagonistic, this long and rather uncharacteristic letter of Hu Shi was a reply to a previous letter from Mrs. Williams:

You wondered "What an Oriental must really and honestly think in his innermost heart—of some American young ladies" (with regard to their unconventionalities)? . . .

It seems to me the whole matter is a question of consistency. One must choose either absolutism or liberalism, either treating woman as a puppet or as a free human being. One must either lock her up in a beautiful chamber, or one must set her really free.

Now, the American treatment of woman as I understand it, is supposed to be based on the principle that woman is a free and rational being. Can you trust her? Have you confidence in her ability to act freely and rationally, though at times unconventionally, when the logical and proper thing will be to lock her up in her own chamber and never to allow her to go out of your sight. That is consistency. But if you have such confidence in her, then let her be really free. Let her do what she herself considers proper and reasonable to do. That's also consistency.

There is no middle ground between freedom and slavery. . . .

And why should we care about what "the other people" think of us? Are we not just as good (if not better) judges of ourselves as they? And is not conventionality after all a man-made thing? Is not an intelligent man or woman greater than conventionality? The sabbath was made for man, and not man for the sabbath! How very true![133]

Judging from Hu's reply, Mrs. Williams's letter must have been written in an apparently anxious and possibly offensive manner. One wonders if she had sensed the unusual relationship between her daughter and Hu Shi and felt uncomfortable about it. By criticizing the "unconventionalities" of "American young ladies," possibly with her own daughter in mind, Mrs. Williams indirectly voiced her disapproval of her daughter's friendship with "an Oriental." The racial factor, never openly brought up either by Hu Shi or by E. C. Williams, may well have been an important part of what Mrs. Williams meant by "unconventionality."[134]

Hu Shi did not touch upon the question of race in his reply. One can only assume that, given the patent prejudice against Chinese in American society, the racial barrier was a hard hurdle to cross even for Williams and Hu. Hu directed his attention in the letter mostly to the defense of "young American ladies." Here, he upheld the right of an individual human being, inherently "free and rational," to conduct her own life as she saw fit. Conventionality, society's standard of propriety, should not be imposed on the individual. This was what Hu Shi meant by "freedom." Measured against this high standard of "freedom," the social conventions of American society betrayed inconsistency and hypocrisy. Hu Shi sounds like a "cultural rebel" in the letter, defying the opinion of American society in the name of individuals' inherent right to freedom. This radical position, expressed by a Chinese to an American, may have seemed quite strange. It contrasted markedly with many of his compatriots who tended to view American social customs as anything but conservative. What made Hu Shi's perspective so different from that of other Chinese? Among the factors contributing to Hu Shi's rather unique outlook, E. C. Williams's influence was a decisive one. The year 1914 was crucial in Hu Shi's transformation from a cultural conservative ardently defending traditional Chinese social convention to an earnest believer in women's independence and individual liberty. This was the year when Hu met E. C. Williams.

When scholars evaluate Williams's influence on Hu Shi's intellectual development, they tend to dwell on the issues of family and women,[135] issues that were fully acknowledged by Hu Shi himself. Hu Shi's change of perspective on these issues was a sign of a deeper transformation, one which has not been fully explored. By upholding women as "free and independent" human beings, Hu Shi recognized the primary attributes of all human beings, men and woman alike. Seeing individuals as such, Hu Shi entrusted them with the responsibility to decide on how they should live their own lives. In his study on Hu Shi, Jerome Grieder maintains that the mark of Hu Shi's American experience was perhaps nowhere more evident than in his attempt to define his role as an independent and critical scholar.[136] Among the sources of influence that helped make Hu Shi see his role, however, Grieder does not mention E. C. Williams. Williams's inquiring and critical mind and devotion to the pursuit of art, defiance of "conventionality," and unorthodox lifestyle, personified for Hu Shi what it meant to be a free and independent human being. More important, Hu did not observe Williams from afar. Together, they did things to express their individual freedom and to challenge "conventionality." The experience itself must have been an invaluable lesson for Hu Shi on "self-becoming."[137]

There was also real love between the two. The lovers wandered in a world of their own creation, weaving art, literature, and poetry into their romance. Falling in love for Hu and Williams, two persons of the "highest type," must have touched the deep layers of the "self." Hu himself stated that his true self came forth through his letters to Williams. Going through these letters while visiting Williams in Ithaca just before he returned to China, Hu Shi reflected, "My *intellectual* and *emotional* change in the past two years has been recorded in the over a hundred letters here. Nowhere else can the *true me* be found."[138] No words can better summarize the nature of the friendship between Hu and Williams. Suffice it to say that largely due to his relationship with Williams, Hu Shi went through a more thorough transformation to become a modern individual than most of his contemporaries.

A year or so before Hu wrote the above words, somewhere in the course of 1916, his relationship with Williams appeared to become less intense. Mrs. Williams's letter to Hu might have been one reason for the cooling down of the friendship. E. C. Williams's own unreadiness to turn the relationship from a supposedly "spiritual" one into an explicitly romantic/sexual one, indicated as early as her letter to Hu Shi in February 1915, was presumably even more crucial.[139] Hu Shi apparently accepted the line drawn by E. C. Williams. In his diary entries in late May 1915, Hu wrote that he and Williams had both agreed to concentrate on their studies, implying that they would thereafter stay away from the dangerous romantic course they had let themselves wander along for a while.[140]

The reasons for Hu Shi's restraining his feelings towards Williams and eventually fulfilling his marital obligation in China were complex. The most important factor, as several scholars have pointed out, was his sense of filial piety toward his mother, who was widowed at twenty-three and single-handedly raised Hu Shi. During his student days in America, the thought of his mother surfaced frequently, always accompanied with love, reverence, and a deep sense of guilt. Acutely aware that if he broke the betrothal, it would be too heavy a blow for his mother, Hu Shi finally decided that he had no choice but to go along with the arranged marriage. Like Lu Xun, Hu Shi also married "for the mother."[141] Both men lost their fathers at an early age, and grew up in a "uterine family" that was centered around a loving, self-sacrificing, and innately manipulative mother.[142] It turned out that to rebel against an authoritarian father or a group of relatives, as in the cases, respectively, of Gu Weijun and Zhao Yuanren, was much easier both emotionally and morally than to rebel against a sacrificing mother.

Hu Shi became an ardent champion of individual autonomy and women's liberation after he returned to China in 1917, playing a preeminent role in promoting women's causes. In his discussions on marriage, love, and morality, he introduced the idea of *renge de aiqing*, endorsing a love relationship between a man and woman that was based on a mutual respect for each person's individual dignity. With this kind of love relationship, Hu Shi maintained, conventional concern with "chastity" and "morality" was beside the point.[143] When he made this argument, Hu Shi presumably did not have in mind his own "marriage of compromise," but an ideal state of marriage he had occasionally observed in America, and perhaps more important, his own love experience with E. C. Williams. The type of American woman Hu Shi portrayed for the Chinese was based on Williams and other women like her. In his 1918 speech to a group of girl students in Beijing, Hu Shi discussed the concept of *chaoyue xianqi liangmu renshengguan* (beyond good mother–and–virtuous wife outlook).[144] He described a number of educated American women who, not content about being somebody's good mother and virtuous wife, insisted on living a life of their own choice and pursuing their own careers. Without mentioning her name, Hu Shi talked about E. C. Williams. Calling her a personification of *zili* (independence), Hu Shi admiringly spoke of her unconventional lifestyle and her persistent pursuit of art. "Independence" became an ideal Hu Shi valued most highly in a woman and this ideal was most tellingly illustrated by his good friend E. C. Williams.

On the issues of love in marriage and women's independence, Hu Shi appeared to be more liberal than many of his fellow male students, notwithstanding the way he handled his marriage. Hu Shi's advocacy of women's causes and individual independence inspired young people to strive for a less burdened and brighter future. In this sense, Hu Shi transcended the limitations of his own personal life. Unable to realize his own ideal of marriage, Hu Shi showed unusual understanding and gave persistent support for his less burdened and more fortunate friends in their pursuit of personal happiness. When Zhao Yuanren and Yang Buwei decided to marry, they asked Hu Shi to be their witness. In his diary, Hu describes his friends' unconventional wedding ceremony as "the most simple and the most sensible—not only in China, but in the world."[145] When the poet Xu Zhimo died, Hu Shi noted, "His failure was the failure of a pure idealist. His quest makes us ashamed of ourselves, for we are too cowardly to dream his dreams."[146] Xu Zhimo, as was well known by his contemporaries, had pursued love relentlessly.[147] In mourning his friend, Hu Shi reflected critically upon his own personal life.

The gap between ideal and reality inevitably caused tension in Hu's personal life and led him to pursue occasional extramarital affairs, as recent studies have brought to light.[148] While the exploration of such affairs goes beyond the scope of this study, it is fair to suggest that the feelings he had for E. C. Williams were the most profound Hu Shi ever experienced for any woman, for it was the closest to the ideal love Hu Shi himself espoused, namely, a loving relationship between two individuals who were highly compatible spiritually (*jingshen de qihe*).[149]

In 1936, Hu Shi came to America to attend a conference and afterwards stayed for a few months, during which, apparently, he saw E. C. Williams for the first time after almost twenty years. The following year, Hu visited America again, and Williams, still single, accompanied him on his trip across the country. This reunion was recorded by Hu in two poems written in Chinese. Seldom was Hu Shi so frank about his youthful love.[150] One poem describes how Hu valued the precious time they spent together:

It is hard to let go your hands,
after not seeing you for another year!
I have come back from afar,
to meet you by the big river.
Together we ride the northward train,
crossing thousands of miles.
Leisurely we reminisce.
Such a moment is so enjoyable,
that we forget about sleep.
No mentioning of either historical or current affairs.
Who cares about the people passing through our eyes.
What matters
is this heart-sharing friend by the Hudson River,
who looks unchanged.
After we finish talking,
the moon is high up in the sky.[151]

The nature of love and the importance a society attaches to it can tell us a great deal about that society. As Charles Taylor convincingly argues, it is not that affections did not exist before the modern age. The difference between our time and the past is that we make much more of these emotions. In Western Europe and North America, a culture began to emerge in the latter half of the eighteenth century that has placed a high value on love and the family. The "affirmation of ordinary life" and the importance given to romantic love confirm and nurture the development of the modern "self" and constitute a major manifestation of the "modern identity."[152]

As one scholar correctly contends, Hu Shi's generation faced a two-front challenge, intellectual and personal, whereas the pioneer thinkers of the previous generation, though bold and open on intellectual matters, remained comfortable within the old culture in terms of their personal lives.[153] Liang Qichao, for one, shunned the advances of a westernized American-Chinese woman during his visit to Hawaii, and lived contentedly with his old-fashioned wife and a young concubine. Being the first to begin the quest for personal happiness, Hu's generation still had one foot caught in the traditional morality, yet another moving, perhaps tentatively, toward a new way of life. The experiences of the Chinese students in America demonstrate the uncertainty, the tension, and the unfailing yearning that were characteristic of this generation's pursuit of personal freedom.

CHAPTER SIX

The Serious Business of Recreation

An article published in the Shanghai-based *World Chinese Students' Journal* in 1907, most likely written by a student returned from abroad, defined tasks facing the young Chinese in the modern world as follows: "we must learn, we must teach, we must serve, but just as important, we must enjoy."[1] To be able to "enjoy" life hence acquired a modern meaning, as opposed to the lifestyle of an old-fashioned Chinese scholar who had to "repress his natural inclinations to play and to enjoy life."[2] Chinese students in the United States, taking advantage of the American environment, pursued a wide variety of recreational activities, including ballroom dancing, picnics, movies, and travel. In this chapter, the focus will be on two especially important and popular forms of recreation for the Chinese: sports and the theater, activities that were infused with nationalist ideals and by no means taken lightly. In the words of the same article cited above: "the duty of enjoyment should be taught as a matter of morals."[3] In other words, recreation should be "enjoyed" for reasons larger than pure enjoyment itself.

Nationalism alone, however, did not adequately explain the attraction of recreational activities for the students. Through participation in sports, the students, especially the males, developed an appreciation for physical fitness and nurtured a more rounded personality ideal than that of the intellectual elite of the past. They also acquired new notions of masculinity that emphasized action, competitiveness, and physical prowess. By performing on stage, on the other hand, the Chinese students, men and women alike, discovered both a new forum in which to explore issues of common concern and a new mode of self-expression. Both athletics and theater enlivened the students' experience in a foreign country and added dimensions to the meaning of modernity. When the students returned to China, they brought with them new concepts and new practices that would enrich the quality of everyday life for the urban Chinese. From these people there came China's first systematically trained physical educators, who contributed to the development of sports in modern China. There were also a number of individuals who, having had a taste of amateur theater in America, went back to China to become professional directors and heads of newly founded drama schools, pioneering China's infant modern theater. The questions some of them raised about how to integrate China's own dramatic heritage with Western theatrical art are still relevant today.

AN HISTORICAL OVERVIEW OF MODERN ATHLETICS IN CHINA

For the Chinese students arriving in America in the first decades of the twentieth century, athletics were not just a means of assimilating into American life, nor were they valued simply because they brought enjoyment to the participants. From the late nineteenth century on, the promotion of physical fitness in China served the higher purpose of nationalism. Initially, it was the awareness of China's vulnerability in the modern world that led to the introduction of Western-style physical exercises to China. The early history of modern athletics in China paralleled China's early efforts to modernize. The need to introduce Western-style physical training arose in the 1860s, during the Self-Strengthening Movement, in order to revitalize the military forces of a decaying dynasty. Mainly in the forms of German- and Japanese-style military drills, the new physical training only affected the military personnel in the emerging "new army" and the students in the recently opened military schools.[4]

The reformers of the late 1890s, in contrast, sought to broaden the application of physical fitness to the society at large. Both Kang Youwei and Liang Qichao included physical exercises in the curriculums of their respective schools, partially to resume a long-lost Confucian tradition, and partially to adapt to a more competitive modern world. In his famous utopian treatise *Datong shu* (The book of universal commonwealth), Kang Youwei proposed that gymnasiums and playgrounds should be built in schools of all levels.[5] Liang Qichao praised the ancient Spartans for their military spirit and applauded modern Western schools' emphasis on physical fitness.[6] Influenced by the Western notion of harmony between physical, mental, and moral powers, Liang placed physical education along with academic and moral learning as the three indispensable areas of education.[7] His friend Tan Sitong, another notable leader in the 1890s reform movement, blamed the long-revered notion of "tranquillity" (*jing*) for the deterioration of the Chinese nation, and upheld the ideal of "action" (*dong*) for a regeneration of a new China.[8] Tan himself was a practitioner of physical exercises, and was particularly good at the Chinese martial art of swordplay. By teaching and practising physical fitness, these early reformers espoused physical competence as a new personal virtue for the modern Chinese male. By the early twentieth century, physical education had become a regular subject in the curriculums of many newly opened schools. The introduction of social Darwinism to China at this time led people to perceive the relationship between body and nation in a new way.[9] Under the heavy influence of military nationalism, however, physical education in the majority of Chinese schools consisted of little more than monotonous and simplified military drills.[10] The kind of physical education that stressed competition, teamwork, and individual initiative, such as track and field and ball games, hardly existed in the public schools. This situation prompted the young Mao Zedong to write "Tiyu zhi yanjiu" (The study of athletics), published in 1917, an early article in which Mao reproached military-style physical education for its failure to produce mentally sound people: "The teacher gives an order, and the pupil has to obey; the body follows but the heart rebels, and the spirit suffers enormously; the frustrated spirit turns to torment the body. At the end of the class, few people don't look physically exhausted and spiritually wounded."[11] It was not until after World War I, with the influence of military nationalism dwindling, that military drills were formally eliminated from public elementary and middle school curriculums.

Competitive sports were more likely to be found in missionary schools. One of the first modern athletic events was held at St. John's School in Shanghai in 1890;[12] and a baseball game was played in 1895 between two missionary schools in Beijing. The YMCA, which began its activities in China in 1885, was prominent in promoting modern sports in China. Basketball, first introduced to the Chinese in Tianjin in 1896 by the American YMCA staff, rapidly gained popularity among missionary school students in the north.[13] After 1900, an increasing number of inter-school sports meets were held, some of which even included girl students. In 1910, the first Chinese national sports meet, which the YMCA helped to organize, was held in Nanjing.

ATHLETICS IN THE LIVES OF THE CHINESE STUDENTS IN AMERICA

Since a large number of the Chinese students in America had been educated either in missionary schools or Western-style Chinese schools, they already had exposure to modern sports before leaving China. Meng Zhi, who graduated from the famous Nankai Middle School in Tianjin in 1916, recalled that "extracurricular activities were required" at Nankai, including competitive sports such as basketball and soccer.[14] The Qinghua College was especially demanding in its athletics requirements; students were not able to graduate if they failed to pass physical education tests.[15]

From the very beginning, the Alliance made a conscious effort to promote sports among the Chinese students.[16] Athletic contests were a major attraction of the Alliance's summer gatherings, occupying a considerable amount of the conference time. During the 1907 Andover conference of the Eastern Alliance, for instance, five afternoons out of a total of six were devoted to sport events, which included a tennis tournament, a track meet, a football game, and two baseball games. One of the two baseball games and the football game were played with the local people in Andover, Massachusetts, and these games were regarded by some conference participants as "perhaps the most interesting events during the conference."[17] After the Andover confer-

ence, it became customary for the Chinese to play a ball game, usually baseball, with a local American team during the summer gathering. Sports such
as baseball symbolized the "American spirit," and were used by their promoters in the early twentieth century to "acculturate" recent immigrants
from Eastern and Southern Europe.[18] The cultural implications of sports
were not missed by the Chinese observers. One returned student from
America remarked, in 1907, "that our students fully enter into the spirit of
American life . . . is proved by the fact that part of the time was devoted to
athletics—that branch of training has been so woefully neglected in our old
system of education."[19] In this light, the baseball games with local American
teams were not simply played for fun. By displaying their skills in the
American "national pastime," the students were making the statement that
they were "competent" in modern (and Western) terms.

The student athletes took their competitions very seriously.[20] It was
reported that at least "eight track records were broken" at the 1910 conference.[21] (The records that were broken, of course, were those set by the students themselves in previous years.) To encourage athletics, the Alliance
awarded gold, silver, and bronze medals to the winners of various contests.
Winning a contest at the summer conference would be proudly remembered
by some individuals for the rest of their lives. In his old age, Zhao Yuanren
still knew by heart the precise time it took him to win the one-mile walk at
the 1913 conference.[22]

Athletic competitions also enhanced school identity among the students,
as team sports were often played between students representing different
schools at the summer conferences. School identity, as pointed out in
Chapter 1, was a new identity being cultivated by the Chinese at this time.
Chinese students from Yale, Harvard, and Princeton often traveled long distances to watch Yale-Harvard or Yale-Princeton games, and they reacted no
less strongly to the outcome of the games than their American schoolmates.

A commentator on the 1910 conference attributed the successful athletic
performance of the students to "the greater attention paid by our students
during the college year" to sports[23]—a remark that reflected some reality. The
students at Cornell University, for instance, had to walk or jog two to three
miles twice a week to meet the requirements of the school, and they were
also expected to swim at least sixty feet in order to graduate. The daily walk
up to the campus was in itself a strenuous exercise, especially in wintertime

when people had to trudge through foot-deep snow. Since Beebe Lake was right on the edge of the campus, many Chinese students learned to skate. Zhao Yuanren was among the people who benefited from the physical challenges at Cornell. Coming from a region in China with a much milder climate, Zhao had fewer colds in the severe winter weather in upstate New York.[24] Zhao's good friend Hu Shi, though less apt to engage in physical activities than some of his fellow students, learned to swim and play tennis during his Cornell years. At a sports meet organized by the Cornell Chinese students' club, Hu ran in the 100-meter dash, the first athletic race he had ever taken part in.[25] Columbia University was another place where sports were enthusiastically pursued by the Chinese. During the winter vacation of 1915, a student proudly reported that the "dormant" campus was "awakened" by the Chinese who played a "full game of football" against the team from Yale.[26] A few years later, the first Chinese crew was organized at Columbia with the help of the university's physical education department.

In the 1920s, sports continued to have a firm place in the lives of some Chinese students. At Cornell, four teams were organized (soccer, basketball, volleyball, and baseball) in 1923 by the Chinese and they did very well in a number of contests against other Cornell teams. The club's secretary boasted to the *Monthly* that the Chinese athletes were "but a step from getting [the Cornell championship]" in one of the games.[27] Students at Ohio State University claimed that they were "traditionally" interested in athletics, and the club there captured the university's "soccer crown" for the 1924–25 academic year.[28] The Chinese students' club at Stanford University was prominent on the West Coast, and helped organize the students to play team basketball and participate in the university's tennis tournament. Proudly, they announced that "athletically speaking, we are just as well active."[29]

The Chinese students' interest and achievements in sports amazed some American observers. Covering a baseball game between a local American team and a Chinese team at the Alliance 1911 conference, a reporter remarked, obviously unaware of previous contests between the Chinese and American teams,[30] that "the Chinese play good baseball. . . . So far as known it is the first time an all-Chinese team has met an all-American team in the American national game, but the contest Thursday showed that the Chinese students had mastered the technique and rules of the game surprisingly well."[31] In 1918, a soccer team composed of Chinese students from New York and Boston played a game against the Bridgeport all-star team, the champion team of Connecticut. The result, a 2-2 tie, impressed the United States Football Association, which decided to recognize the Chinese team as a member.[32]

Participation in sports events gave the students a sense of enjoyment and accomplishment. Jin Shixuan, a student at University of Pennsylvania from 1923 to 1927, liked to watch baseball and tennis games and often found himself part of the cheering and shouting crowds. Jin also loved to swim and to play tennis. Years later, he credited his American experience with these benefits: "My spirit was happy and high, my body was strengthened. The improvement of my health was an important outcome of my four-year stay in America."[33] Those who excelled in athletics were rewarded with the honor of having their names printed in the pages of the *Monthly*. For example, E. M. Ho and Kuo Tso Tsai, who played on Harvard's football team and the Cornell soccer team, respectively, were mentioned in the journal's "Personal News" section. Yet the people who enjoyed such honors were few, and it was believed that the majority of the Chinese students were not "strong or big enough to join the American teams."[34] Nevertheless, athletic excellence became a new ideal to aspire to for the Chinese students.

New Notions of Masculinity

Yang Quan, a student at Harvard who would later become a well-known scholar and educator, observed in 1914 that "comparing Americans with Chinese, is like comparing tree trunks with weeds."[35] Yang argued that a country made up of "handicapped" people was a handicapped country. Without "fit and brave" men, the country could not become strong even with modern weaponry.[36] Yang Quan's perception of the Chinese people's physical "inferiority" appeared to be confirmed by "a bit of very interesting statistics" published in the *Monthly* in 1915 on the physical conditions of both the Ya-li students in Changsha (a middle school in Changsha, Hunan, that was affiliated with Yale University) and the students at Yale. Using the average measurements of the American students as the basis of comparison, the statistics revealed "striking differences, with the Chinese students proving physically smaller."[37]

In Hao Gengsheng's case, the idea that the Chinese had an "inferior" physique came in a painful personal way, and eventually led him to change his major from engineering to physical education. Hao was from a well-to-do family and had been well nourished by Chinese standards. Yet when he was looking for a part-time job, the American foreman refused to hire him on the grounds that he was too short and thin. This incident led Hao to conclude that if the Chinese people did not become "physically healthy and strong," China as a nation would be wiped out and the Chinese race would become extinct. Consequently, Hao decided to switch his major to physical education, after discussing the matter with his good friend, the future poet Xu Zhimo. Hao transferred to a college in Springfield, Massachusetts, where there was one of the best physical-education programs in the country. Hao had three "very happy and exciting years" there, taking full advantage of the school's rich athletic opportunities by joining the tennis, football, and swimming teams. With a much stronger body, Hao graduated in 1923 as one of the first Chinese students with a degree in physical education from an American university, ready to promote physical education in China.[38]

While nationalism typically underlay students' argument for physical fitness, ideas such as "individual responsibility" and "the totality of [a] person" were also important in the students' thinking. A 1908 *Monthly* article maintained that modern education "must train character as well as cultivate intelligence; it must develop the body as well as enlighten the mind," in order to nurture a sense of "individual responsibility" and a devotion to "social service."[39] The concepts of "utility" and "action" were also upheld, as the article states, quoting Woodrow Wilson, then president of Princeton University: "We are put into this world not to sit still and know; we are . . . to act."[40] The primary object of a university, the article maintained, was "to make men useful." It was only through practical actions, athletic activities included, that "sound health, strong character, and broad principles of self-sacrifice and public devotion" could be realized. Only when equipped with these qualities, the article concluded, quoting John Milton, could men become "steadfast pillars of the state" when called upon to sit "in the nation's council to direct the destiny" of the country.[41] Physical fitness hence became a necessary aspect in the new personality ideal for the Chinese male social elite. Physical perfection, along with moral and intellectual perfection, would compose a totality of qualities desirable for the "future leaders" of China. Meanwhile, some students acquired an aesthetic appreciation for the Western ideal of the development of the human body. One person suggested that his fellow students should often go to visit "art galleries, especially those containing Greek statues."[42]

Physical perfection alone, however, was insufficient as an ideal in itself. It is not surprising that one student who named individuals who personified his athletic ideal did not mention sports celebrities, adored by the American public. Instead, he cited Theodore Roosevelt as a "robust specimen of American manhood," and praised Woodrow Wilson and William Taft for their vigorous involvement in sports. The only Chinese exemplar mentioned by the writer was Sun Yat-sen, who "always led an active life."[43] Similar sentiments were expressed in another article, which held that being fit was one aspect of "character-building," and the ultimate purpose was to "make men" and to produce "a class of students who will be wise leaders in whatever department of work they might be engaged in."[44]

The idea of "making men" deserves special attention. From Liang Qichao's tribute to ancient Spartans to Tan Sitong's repudiation of the notion of "tranquillity," and from Yang Quan's metaphors of "weeds" and "trunks" in his comparison of the Chinese physique with that of the Americans to Hao Gengsheng's determination to make himself "physically healthy and strong," we observe a cultural, male-Chinese reconstruction of masculinity, based upon a Western, especially an American, model of "manhood." The new notions of masculinity upheld the ideas of action, competitiveness, and physical prowess, as opposed to the ideas of "refinement," "bookishness," and even "femininity" that were usually associated with a well-educated Chinese scholar in the past. The reconstruction of masculinity took place in the larger political context of China's encounter with Western powers since the nineteenth century and China's struggle to survive in a world determined by might.

This was not the first time the Chinese men were made to readjust their notions of masculinity. Earlier, during the period of the Song dynasty (960–1279), the Chinese experienced a major shift in cultural orientation as well as gender construction. To differentiate themselves from the "barbarian" rivals from the northern steppes such as the Jurchens and Mongols, there was a need for Chinese men, especially those in the upper class, to become subdued and refined. Physical prowess was looked upon with contempt and dismissed as being associated with the "less civilized" nomads.[45] The irony is, another encounter with another ethnic "Other," this time the Western rivals, in another historical context, brought about entirely different results. Instead of scolding the physical ideals of the Western "barbarians," the modern Chinese intellectual elite at the turn of the twentieth century accepted the Westerners' espousal of physical strength, along with their notions of masculinity. Their acquisition of a new ideal of masculinity was an important aspect in the Chinese male's quest to become modern. This shift in Chinese construction of the male gender marked a significant cultural event in modern times that warrants further study.

What is even more ironic, as well as culturally intriguing, is that the Chinese students came to America at a time when the Western country itself was undergoing a modern transformation of its attitudes toward masculinity. A powerful upsurge of interest in male physicality and a cult of muscularity in turn-of-the-century America were partly derived from America's interest in overseas expansion, hence were underlaid with both imperialistic and racial overtones.[46] Playing sports was believed to be the best way to "build character," to foster combativeness in a violent and competitive world, and to acquire manliness. Sports and sporting ideologies were widely embraced by members of respectable society, and college campuses became the places where athletics were most enthusiastically pursued.[47] The Chinese students' arguments for physical fitness echoed the sporting ideologies of the Americans, even though their sense of crisis regarding masculine identity had different historical sources from that of the Americans.

Despite the aspiration to a new masculine ideal that included athletic fitness, however, not many Chinese male students participated in athletics on a regular basis. Articles appeared from time to time in the *Monthly* to complain about the insufficient attention given to athletics by the Chinese students. At one point, the establishment of a permanent Alliance athletic committee was proposed, in order to ensure that sports would constitute a constant part in students' daily lives, but the plan never materialized.

Women and Athletics

Even fewer women students were active in sports. At the Alliance summer athletic contests, men competed and women only watched. The absence of women in athletics did not pass unnoticed by the women themselves. In the early twentieth century, sports like basketball, tennis, field hockey, and bicycling were popular among American college girls. Ying Mei Chun, a Chinese woman at Wellesley College, was very much impressed by this open attitude toward physical fitness for women. Chun believed that Chinese women were "inferior to the European women in strength and vigor" and blamed the "evil customs" in China that confined women to "the four walls of their homes" and deprived them of "the stimulus resulting from a wide social intercourse with men and women." She called for a "no restriction" approach to women's education, so that women would be able to "take whatever sensible exercises [that] seem necessary to build up their constitution and improve their health." Realizing that this proposal was hardly feasible in China, Chun urged her fellow female students to take advantage of the facilities and opportunities in America.[48]

Chun's liberal approach to women's physical education was countered by Bertha Hosang, the winner of the 1918 Alliance's girls' essay competition. Seeing women primarily as "mothers and guardians of the Chinese race," Hosang justified some forms of physical education for women on the grounds of nationalism, praising certain kinds of "team play" that could nurture "a new spirit of friendliness and good fellowship" and help the development of "thoughtfulness and courtesy and all true social graces."[49] However, she did not approve of intensely competitive sports for women.

The few women who did embrace athletic opportunities in America and excelled in sports naturally attracted attention. Alice Huie of Barnard College, captain of her class swimming team in 1914, was hailed by the *Monthly* as a manifestation of "what a Chinese girl can do."[50] A few years later, Gao Zi, a student at the University of Wisconsin, caught people's attention by being selected to play on the university's basketball team. Gao's interest in sports was first nourished in China, when she attended a YWCA school in Shanghai in the late 1910s. Gao attracted quite a few male admirers when she returned to China to teach physical education at the Women's Normal University in Beijing.[51]

EARLY HISTORY OF MODERN THEATER IN CHINA

Like athletics, the theater was another form of recreation that attracted a noticeable number of Chinese students in America. It turned some of them, men and women alike, into "amateur" playwrights and directors, actors and actresses. Prepared by their theatrical experiences in America, a number of individuals went on to play prominent roles in modern theater when they returned to China. Like athletic activity, participation in modern-style theater required a change of attitude on the part of the Chinese students. In traditional Chinese culture, the social status of an actor was extremely low, regardless of how talented and accomplished he was. People of the gentry class were strictly prohibited from participating in the performance arts. Some early Chinese visitors to the West were struck by the absence of prejudice against people of high social standing who were involved in theater. Wang Tao, for instance, observed in the late 1860s that school pupils in European countries were encouraged to perform on stage, whereas in China, Wang remarked, "no individuals with self-respect and from respectable families would dare to do the same thing."[52]

Barriers to theatrical participation first crumbled in missionary schools, where students' dramatic activities became part of the extracurricular programs. From the very beginning, "new theater," as opposed to traditional Chinese operas, was associated with modern education and, as the titles of the students' plays indicate, was concerned with political and social issues of the day.[53] One of the earliest school plays, *The Ugly Scene in the Official Circle* (*Guanchang choushi*; a political satire mocking corrupt officials), was put on by students at St. John's School in Shanghai in 1899. In the following year students at Nanyang School depicted onstage the story of the "six martyrs" who had recently been executed by the Qing court after the abortive One Hundred Days Reform. At this early phase, the performance of the actors was rather rudimentary and, as in traditional Chinese theater, men played the female roles. The significance of the early school drama in China lay in its defiance of the social taboo and its sensitivity to contemporary issues.

THEATRICAL EXPERIMENT IN AMERICA

Theater enabled Chinese students in America to explore and express their feelings and concerns, and to communicate with the American audience. Plays had a well-established place in the Alliance summer conferences. From 1908 until well into the 1920s, it was customary for at least one local club to present a play on "interclub night," an event that was often regarded as the most enjoyable at the summer gathering. The students were able to satisfy their dramatic interests on other occasions as well. On many college campuses, a "Chinese night," usually sponsored by cosmopolitan clubs or similar organizations, gave the students an opportunity to introduce Chinese culture to the American audience. Theater often became a favored medium on these occasions.

One notable aspect of the students' dramatic activity in America was that women students acted alongside men. This was, of course, a well-established norm in Western theatrical practice. But considering that women were excluded from the Chinese drama societies in Japan in the early twentieth century, and that men played women's roles in the "new theater" movement in China well into the 1920s, this phenomenon was quite remarkable. It was therefore not surprising, then, that the first person to break the taboo and introduce mixed-gender acting to the Chinese stage was an American-returned student, Hong Shen, whose story will be told in more detail later in this chapter.[54]

The plays put on by students in America fell into three broad categories: (1) illustrations of China's social customs and political changes; (2) contemplation and exploration of political and social issues, including ones regarding personal lives; and (3) famous Chinese historical legends. The plays and tableaux in the first category were almost always performed for American audiences on occasions like "Chinese night." The old educational system and traditional marriage practices were two favorite themes. A play called *The Chinese Old-Time Marriage* treated its subject so humorously that "the audience was kept in a continuous fit of laughter."[55] The traditional education system was also depicted mockingly, in a play produced by the students at Yale called *Chinese School Life*, which satirized a "typical old-fashioned Chinese teacher."[56] Political subjects were also touched upon, as in the six tableaux given by the students at Columbia University in May 1912 for the benefit of the famine fund in China. This performance illustrated political changes taking place in China during the 1911–12 republican revolution, with scenes of the confrontation between revolutionary soldiers and the old empire, the abdication of the young emperor, and the inauguration of the president of the new republic.[57] These plays all conveyed a similar message:

China was shedding its old traditions and changing into a new nation. This theme was especially evident in the play *Outline of the Chinese History*, presented by students in New York in 1923. The two main characters are a young woman, representing "new China," and an old man, "dressed in leaves" symbolizing ancient Chinese civilization. The man and woman converse about Chinese history, paying special tributes to its glorious moments. At the end, they hold hands and sing the republican national anthem together.[58]

If the plays in the first category served a propaganda purpose, promoting an image of China the students hoped the American public would accept, the plays in the second category dealt with problems of various kinds that were related more closely to the daily lives of the students themselves. In 1910, for example, the students at the University of Pennsylvania put on a play called *When the East and the West Meet*. The first act focuses on a Confucian scholar who is strongly opposed to Western culture. When a student of his comes to the United States, he meets an Irishman who is portrayed as "narrow-minded." Both the Confucian schoolmaster and the Irishman are ridiculed for their intolerance toward other cultures. The play was positively received by the university community at the "Chinese night," praised by the university newspaper for showing "a keen appreciation of local life in the West as contrasted with the doctrine of Confucius."[59]

The subjects of love and marriage had a wide appeal for the students, many of whom, as discussed in Chapter 5, were facing difficult choices in their own personal lives.[60] The role of returned students in China's future also received attention. In 1919, a five-act play entitled *The New Soul of the Nation* was staged, exploring the theme of the regeneration of China "through the persistent patriotic efforts of the returned students."[61] A few years later, the subject of returned students was again dealt with, this time in a less optimistic light: a Harvard-educated man returns to China only to find that the country is in the throes of a civil war. The only cheerful note in the play is the man's marriage to the woman he has always loved in secret.[62]

Occasionally, political crises in China also found their way into the students' plays. In *The Nation's Wound*, a play presented at the 1925 Eastern Alliance summer conference, the May Thirtieth Incident in Shanghai is the subject matter. The play depicts two young men, deeply disturbed by the deaths of their fellow students on May Thirtieth, deciding to make sacrifices, one with his life, the other with his love, in order to awake their fellow countrymen. The producers intended to make the play convey a "true message" instead of being mere entertainment.[63]

The representations of Chinese historical legends made up the plays of the third category. Interestingly, some plays in this category were laden with traditional Chinese values. The play *Shao jeh yee* (*xiao jie yi*), for instance, as indicated by its title, praised the ideals of filial piety, chastity, and personal loyalty. Performed by students in Pittsburgh on "Chinese night," the story is about a man seeking revenge on behalf of a deceased friend whose wife and mother have both committed suicide after being humiliated by a man to whom they owed money. *The Virtue's Victim*, a play about the legendary woman Meng Jiangnü, celebrates the traditional feminine virtues of patience, devotion, and self-sacrifice.[64]

In the spring of 1925, students in the greater Boston area put on the play *Piba ji* (The story of *piba*; *piba* is a traditional Chinese musical instrument with plucked strings and a fretted fingerboard), which was based on a Ming-dynasty drama about a famous love story that took place during the Han dynasty. Two students, Liang Shiqiu and Gu Yuxiu, both graduates of Qinghua College, rewrote the ancient drama into a modern play in English.[65] Among the cast were Liang Shiqiu and Xie Bingxin, who played, respectively, the scholar-lover and the heroine's maid. Liang's friend Wen Yiduo and drama student Zhao Taimou came all the way from New York to help with costumes and set designs. On the night of the show, more than one thousand people packed the theater. The costumes glittered beautifully on stage, lending an air of elegance to the performance. The play was so well received that, in the words of Liang Shiqiu, "the roof was almost shaken off by the stormy applause."[66]

The idea of staging *Piba ji* in Boston was inspired by an earlier theatrical performance that took place in New York, *The Imperial Concubine Yang*, a play about the famous love story between a Tang-dynasty emperor and his favorite consort. The core members in this project were a group of Chinese students studying drama and art in New York: Yu Shangyuan, Wen Yiduo, Xiong Foxi, Zhao Taimou, and Zhang Jiazhu. The staging of the play in 1924 turned out to be an event that should be remembered in the history of modern Chinese theater, for it led to the births of both the Chinese Drama Reform Society, and more significantly, the Chinese national theater movement.[67]

THE NATIONAL THEATER MOVEMENT

The idea of launching the Chinese national theater movement was first suggested in Yu Shangyuan's kitchen, during the celebration of the success of *The Imperial Concubine Yang*. Subsequently, the Chinese Drama Reform Society was founded. The academic majors of Yu Shangyuan, Zhao Taimou, and Xiong Foxi were all related to drama. Through them, Wen Yiduo, who had left Colorado to come to New York, was introduced to drama, which soon became his new passion. Wen was particularly absorbed in set design and costume creation.

Wearing long hair and casual clothes and following no regular daily schedule, these people lived the lifestyle of Bohemian artists. Wen Yiduo stopped studying studio art and dropped out of school completely. These young aspiring Chinese artists found New York to be a tolerant and inspiring place. To prepare for the production of *The Imperial Concubine Yang*, they spent months investigating the plays currently performed on and off Broadway, seeking advice from managers of theater companies, and meeting actors wherever they could find them.[68]

What they were aiming to do was not just to put a Chinese play on the American stage, but also to search for a new form of theater that would be modern and yet still rooted in China's own artistic tradition. Wen Yiduo, as was already mentioned in Chapter 3, had come to America to create a modern Chinese culture. In Yu Shangyuan and the others, Wen found comrades in the same cause. To achieve their goal, they took as their model and inspiration the Irish national theater movement of the late nineteenth and early twentieth centuries, which concerned itself primarily with the preservation of the Irish artistic heritage and was an integral part in the overall struggle for Irish cultural and political independence.[69] The promoters of the Chinese national theater movement recognized the unique aesthetic value of Chinese theater, which they believed was different from but not inferior to other forms of theatrical expression and deserved recognition amongst the world's theatrical achievements. In the words of Yu Shangyuan, Chinese theater was characterized by "impressionism" (*xieyi*), while Western theater was known for its "realism" (*xieshi*), each a high artistic achievement. The purpose of the Chinese national theater movement was to "build a bridge" linking the two achievements.[70]

Yu Shangyuan defined Chinese "national theater" as an art form in which Chinese practitioners used Chinese material to produce Chinese dramatic work for a Chinese audience.[71] Yu and his comrades were products of the May Fourth New Culture Movement, yet rather than blindly rejecting China's theatrical tradition, they endeavored to protect and preserve the Chinese cultural heritage in the face of strong Western cultural influences. Yu's pronouncement explicitly challenged the position of a number of influential new cultural advocates during the May Fourth movement, who had denounced Chinese traditional theater as primitive, vulgar, and rigidly formalistic. Some extreme antitraditionalists in China even called for the closure of all traditional opera theaters.[72]

Yu Shangyuan emerged as the leader of the national theater movement.[73] Coming to the United States in 1923, Yu was required by his financial sponsor to major in political science,[74] but, always fascinated by theater arts, Yu ignored this request and entered Carnegie University in Pittsburgh to study theater. Although not the first Chinese ever receiving a formal education in theater in America, Yu was most likely the first to take theater as his academic major immediately upon arriving in the United States. Yu left Pittsburgh to go to Columbia University in 1924. Both in Pittsburgh and in New York, he managed to see numerous performances of both classical and modern plays, often by standing at the back of the theater. New York is where, to his great delight, he met with the other Chinese who shared his passion in drama and his desire to create China's own modern theater.

Imagining themselves as China's Synge and Yeats, the leaders of the Irish national theater movement, Yu Shangyuan, Wen Yiduo, and Zhao Taimou went back to China in the summer of 1925, driven by the urge to start a national theater movement in China. With the Irish model in mind, they drafted a grand proposal for the founding of a "Beijing art theater."[75] What came out of their ambitious plan was the establishment of a drama department in Beijing Art School, an unprecedented event in Chinese cultural history, by which the study of drama became a respectable academic subject.[76] Moreover, a drama column appeared in the influential Beijing-based newspaper *Chenbao* (Morning news), creating a public forum for the discussion of theatrical reform. The existence of a newspaper column devoted to drama was itself a new thing in the history of China's modern journalism.[77]

Though the subsequent development of the national theater movement fell below expectations, the advocates of the movement breathed fresh air into Chinese modern theatrical circles. Their idea of a national theater movement became widely known and was endorsed enthusiastically by a number of prominent intellectuals of the day. Except for Wen Yiduo, who eventually turned his attention to Chinese literature, the other members of the original New York group, Yu Shangyuan, Zhao Taimou, and Xiong Foxi, continued to work for the cause of modern theater in republican China. Eventually, the three all became leading figures in their profession.[78] In the history books on modern Chinese theater, the assessment of the national theater movement is mixed and the place allocated to it is marginal.[79] Further study is necessary to restore it to its deserved place in history. As Tian Benxiang, a historian of modern Chinese theater argues, advocates of the Chinese national theater movement touched upon an issue central to the May Fourth New Culture Movement, namely, how to integrate Western influence with China's own cultural heritage,[80] an issue that is still at the heart of China's search for its cultural identity in the modern world.

ZHANG PENGCHUN AND HONG SHEN

When Yu Shangyuan and his friends came back to China in the mid 1920s to promote drama reform, two American-returned students, Zhang Pengchun (Chang Peng-chun, P. C. Chang) and Hong Shen (Shen Hung), had been working for some time to introduce modern theater to China. Arriving in America in 1910, Zhang Pengchun studied education and philosophy and received a doctoral degree from Columbia University in 1916. He was, however, better known among his friends as a man of literature and theater.[81] When in America, he produced two plays: *The New Order Cometh*, already discussed in Chapter 5, and *The Intruder*.

Written in 1915, *The Intruder* appears on the surface to be a conventional family tale but actually alludes to Japan's aggressive demands on China's territory—demands that were made public in early 1915 and aroused strong opposition among the Chinese students in America. The play was performed at Barnard College in the spring of 1915. Reviewing the play for the *New York*

Times, an American drama critic remarked that it "has dramatic interest, and departs radically from the old-time conventional style of Chinese plays."[82] The play was also praised for its effective employment of "the technique and conventions of the contemporary stage" by another American, who apparently understood the "double entendre" of the play, though a "rigid neutrality" forbade him from pointing it out.[83]

Zhang Pengchun returned to China in 1916 and worked under his older brother Zhang Boling, the principal of the prestigious Nankai School in Tianjin. By this time, the dramatic activity, begun at Nankai as early as 1909, had already become well established, and the New Theater Troupe, one of the first modern theater troupes in northern China, had already been in existence for some time. Under Zhang Pengchun's capable leadership, the New Theater Troupe soon became the best troupe nationwide, in the opinion of Hu Shi.[84] In the 1920s and 1930s, it represented the highest level of student acting in China. A new auditorium, built on the campus of Nankai Middle School in 1934 and described by contemporaries as the "best theater for modern drama in entire China,"[85] further enhanced the prestige of the Nankai Troupe.

Zhou Enlai and Wan Jiabao were among the people whose theatrical talents were discovered and encouraged by Zhang Pengchun. Zhou was an active member of the New Theater Troupe, often playing female roles on stage. Wan Jiabao, better known for his pen name, Cao Yu, would become the most distinguished playwright in twentieth-century China. Cao Yu had his first theatrical experience at Nankai Middle School, where he learned "why to act and how to act" under the "strict supervision of the learned capable director Prof. P. C. Chang."[86] Some people believe that Zhang was the first person to establish the director system in China.[87]

Throughout his life, Zhang retained his love of theater, but he always remained an amateur and his dramatic activities were confined mostly to Nankai. This might explain why he has been largely neglected by scholars of modern Chinese theater. Only twice did Zhang Pengchun become involved in theatrical activities outside of Nankai, and these two occasions were memorable both in Zhang's personal life and in China's history of cultural exchange with foreign countries. In 1930 Zhang accompanied the troupe of Mei Lanfang, the famous Beijing opera actor, to the United States, and in

1935 they visited the Soviet Union. Invited by Mei Lanfang as his artistic advisor, Zhang worked diligently to introduce Beijing opera, the highly refined and formalistic form of traditional Chinese drama, to the Western audience. His familiarity with Western audiences' taste and his knowledge of Beijing opera helped make Mei Lanfang's performance a major success in both countries.[88]

By contrast, Hong Shen, who worked mostly in Shanghai, another center of China's modern theater movement, has been widely considered one of the foremost figures in modern Chinese theater. Hong Shen had his first exposure to modern drama while he was a student at Qinghua College from 1912 to 1916. Upon arriving in America in 1916, Hong first studied engineering at Ohio State University. In 1919, Hong transferred to Harvard to pursue his real interest, drama, becoming the first Chinese student abroad ever to major in theater art. At Harvard, Hong studied under a leading authority in dramatic studies, Professor Baker. Hong Shen learned all the dramatic techniques, onstage and backstage, from the master.

Five plays are known to have been written by Hong Shen when he was in America. The first was *The Wedded Husband*, written before Hong went to Harvard and staged by the Chinese students at Ohio State University, where it drew favorable comments from the theater critics for the "extraordinary beauty of the lines and delightful bits of comedy."[89] The other four plays were all written after Hong Shen went to Harvard; these include *Rainbow*, a political satire; *For Romeo and Juliet*; *Pingmin canju* (The plight of the poor), whose theme is clear enough from the title; and *The Cowherd and the Weaving Maid*, a play based on a well-known Chinese folk tale.[90] Yu Shangyuan, Wen Yiduo, Xiong Fuoxi, and Zhao Taimou all participated in the production of this last play and proceeded from there to work on their own play *The Imperial Concubine Yang*.

In the spring of 1922, Hong Shen returned to China as the first person with a systematic Western training in modern theater art. Pursuing theater as a career, Hong Shen brought professionalism to China's modern drama, greatly elevating the social status of performance art in the Chinese society. Against tremendous prejudice from conservative circles, he introduced various modern theatrical concepts and techniques to China, including, as mentioned earlier, mixed-gender acting. Few people can match his stature in the modern theater of twentieth-century China.

CHINESE MODERN THEATER AND AMERICAN-EDUCATED INNOVATORS: AN ASSESSMENT

It is worth pausing here for a moment to raise a question regarding the place of the America-bound Chinese students' dramatic ventures in history. Possibly because of the use of English in most of the plays performed by the students, scholars have generally ignored the theatrical activities of the students in America. By contrast, they give ample credit to the dramatic experiments of Chinese students in Japan, who performed in Chinese.

There were differences besides the choice of language in the student dramatic activities in the two countries. One obvious one was the content: the majority of the plays performed by the students in America were not as concerned with sensitive and controversial political issues as those by the students in Japan. For example, the only indication of the content of the play performed by the Ithaca Chinese Students' Club in 1908 was that it belonged to the category of "entertainment." By contrast, the Spring Willow Society, a dramatic group founded by Chinese students in Tokyo, staged in 1907 such works as *The Black Slaves' Cry to Heaven*, a play based on Lin Shu's translation of Harriet Beecher Stowe's novel *Uncle Tom's Cabin* that clearly commented on the contemporary political situation in China. In 1909, another Chinese drama society in Tokyo, the Shen You Society, put on the play *Hot Blood*, based on a story by the French romantic writer Vitorien Sardou. Overtly advocating freedom and liberty, the play was enthusiastically received by the revolutionary-minded students in Japan, so much so that afterward the Chinese consul in Tokyo threatened to take government scholarships away from those involved in the play. By comparison, the plays performed by the students in America never caused any political controversy.

Besides exerting certain political impact, the plays put on by the Chinese drama societies in Tokyo also appeared to be artistically more sophisticated and innovative. The Chinese there were influenced by Japan's new theater movement. The Spring Willow Society even received professional instructions from the famous Japanese actor Fujisawa Asajiro.[91] The dramatic activities of the students in America, on the other hand, were primarily extracurricular. Yet precisely because of their extracurricular nature, the theater had a secured place in the lives of the students in America, whereas the "golden period" of drama for the Chinese in Japan was short-lived.[92]

The Chinese students' theatrical activity in America in the first decades of the twentieth century should be regarded as an integral part of the early history of modern Chinese theater. It was a broad-based phenomenon, involving a sizable number of student drama activists. A number of talented and committed individuals, having been nurtured by the generous theatrical atmosphere and equipped with new concepts and new techniques, eventually emerged from the rank and file. Prepared by their practices in America, they went on to become China's leading figures in modern theater, bringing profound, and in some cases even revolutionary, changes to the Chinese theater. In turn, a young generation of theatrical professionals grew up under their influence. Twentieth-century Chinese theater would have been something considerably different without the influence of these American-educated individuals.

Epilogue

In early 1918, four months after returning to the China he had left seven years before, Hu Shi summarized his impressions of home, using the Grand Theater of Shanghai (*Shanghai dawutai*) as a metaphor:

> The Grand Theater stands as a miniature of today's China. Doesn't the name "Grand Theater" sound very new? Isn't the architecture of Western style? Aren't the seats and stage setting all modern-looking? But the actors are all old antiques. They were there when I first arrived in Shanghai at the age of thirteen. Another thirteen years have passed, yet it is still the same people who occupy the stage. Where are the new actors?[1]

Hu Shi went back to China determined to displace the "old antiques" and to make things truly new.[2] Twentieth-century China, frequently shaken by internal dissension and foreign assault, inevitably created frustration and disappointment for many recently returned students. Operating under formidable circumstances, Hu Shi and his cohorts brought new and revolutionary changes to the ancient land, giving multifaceted meaning to the modernity that they had sought in China's name.

With a few exceptions, most of the returned intellectuals studied in this book have died,[3] and not a few left the world still labeled negatively in terms of politics. Hu Shi, of course, was one of them.[4] With a relatively stable and reform-oriented society emerging in China since the late 1970s after decades of mass political campaigns, and the "modernization paradigm" replacing or supplementing the "revolution paradigm" in Chinese historiography,[5] many individuals and events that have been obscured and negated since 1949 are now being rediscovered and reevaluated. The many American-returned students in our study are cases in point. The recent rehabilitation of Western-educated intellectuals is indicative of how the Chinese are rethinking their recent past as well as their future.

While my focus in this study has been mostly on the students' process of becoming modern through their experiences in the United States, and to a lesser extent their influence on China's modernization, now I would like to turn my attention to what the return and readaptation to China were like for three individuals who have appeared only briefly in the book so far: Zhu Kezhen, a natural scientist specializing in meteorology; Li Jinghan, a sociologist; and Luo Longji, an activist trained in political science. I will aim in this epilogue to trace these individuals' lives before and after 1949 and to weave their compatible stories together into a coherent piece. While it is important to keep in mind that the people studied in this book might differ from each other in their approaches to life, work, politics, and the question of modernization of China, there are nonetheless some general patterns. The lives of the three men here are representative, in my view, of the experiences for similar people in their fields and emblematic of their entire generation. By introducing three largely new biographies, I hope to further illustrate the dilemmas and difficulties confronting Western-educated Chinese intellectuals in the course of the twentieth century. Their experiences help us reflect upon the meaning of Chinese modernity, and the tumultuous process of modernization in twentieth-century China. Because the information is scarce in other areas, I will focus mostly on their political experiences and professional activities.

YOUTH AND TRAINING IN AMERICA

Born in 1890, Zhu Kezhen (Chu K'o-chen, also known in the West as Coching Chu) was the oldest of the three men under discussion in this epilogue. Zhu's father made a modest fortune as a rice merchant in a small town near Shaoxing, Zhejiang. From a very early age, Zhu was interested in the changes of seasons, taking note of the dates when swallows came back to their nests and peach flowers were in blossom. After a few years of classical education at home, in 1899 Zhu went to a newly opened modern elementary school. The intervention of foreign troops in the wake of the Boxer Incident, angrily discussed by his teacher in class, was possibly the first nationalistic lesson the young Zhu Kezhen received. In 1906 he left his hometown to attend a modern high school in Shanghai, where he was strongly influenced by the notion of "saving China through science" (*kexue jiuguo*).[6]

In 1910, Zhu came to the United States as a member of the second cohort of the Boxer Indemnity scholarship program. After receiving a B.S. degree in 1913 at the University of Illinois, Zhu went to Harvard University for graduate studies. Five years at Harvard gave Zhu ample opportunity to observe how a world-class university was run. Zhu was particularly impressed by how, in a period of forty years, President Charles Eliot had transformed Harvard College into an advanced modern research institution. While in Cambridge, Zhu joined the Science Society, originally founded by a group of Chinese students at Cornell.[7] In 1918 Zhu earned his doctoral degree from Harvard and returned to China the same year.[8]

A year before, in 1917, Li Jinghan (Franklin C. H. Lee) had arrived on the West Coast of the United States. Born in 1895 into a poor peasant family near Beijing, Li was able to receive a modern education through the connections of his carpenter uncle, who did work for the missionaries in the local community.[9] When the president of Li's alma mater, the missionary Luhe School in Tongzhou, came back to the United States on a vacation, he brought Li with him. Li enrolled at Pomona College, California, where the Luhe president had a relative. Having hardly any money left after the journey to America, Li had to work part-time to support himself.[10] At the end of his study at Pomona, Li received a half scholarship from the Boxer Indemnity fund program,[11] which enabled him to continue his academic work at the University of California, where he earned a master's degree. After this, Li headed east and enrolled at Columbia University.[12]

While at Pomona, Li had taken a seminar on social research, in the course of which Li was often asked various things about China by his American professor and classmates, such as China's population figures, land distribution, wages, and so on. Unable to provide precise information, Li felt embarrassed, even as he was impressed by studies about Chinese society conducted by Western scholars.[13] Then and there, Li made up his mind that when he returned to China he would devote himself to social research. Li went back to China in 1924 after two years' study at Columbia.[14]

Luo Longji (Lo Lung-chi), the youngest of the three men examined here, came to America in 1921 as a graduate of Qinghua College. Born in 1898 into a scholar's family in Jiangxi Province, Luo went to Beijing in 1913 to attend Qinghua.[15] Luo's interest in politics and his leadership quality were already evident at Qinghua, where he was once the president of the Qinghua Student Union and the chief editor of the student magazine, the *Tsinghua Weekly*. When the May Fourth movement broke out in 1919, Luo emerged as a student leader.[16] Yet some of the abilities Luo was known for in his later life, such as his eloquent oratorical skill, did not come to him naturally. Before each speech contest at Qinghua, which he never missed, Luo always practiced intensely.[17] He made a conscious effort to groom himself for a future career in politics, and Qinghua appeared to be just the right place to help prepare him.

Luo majored in political science. After receiving both his B.A. and M.A. from the University of Wisconsin and being enrolled in a doctoral program at Columbia University, Luo went to England for two years, where he studied at the London School of Economics under the renowned Fabian scholar Harold Laski and became a convert to Laski's liberal socialism.[18] Luo returned to the United States in 1927 and in the following year received a Ph.D. from Columbia with a dissertation entitled "Parliamentary Elections in England." While in America, Luo was active in Chinese students' activities, serving once as the president of Chinese Students' Alliance and the editor of the *Quarterly*. He was also a member of the nationalistic Big River Society.

Nationalism underlay the lives of all three of these men, leading Zhu Kezhen to embrace "science" as the solution to "save China," Li Jinghan to study the social conditions of his own country, and Luo Longji to aspire to a career in politics. It is also significant that they were all connected in one way or another to the Boxer Indemnity scholarship program.

EARLY YEARS OF RETURN TO CHINA DURING THE NATIONALIST ERA

By 1928, Zhu Kezhen had been back in China for ten years, a period mostly spent on teaching. In 1921, he founded the first department of physical geology in China at the National Southeastern University, Nanjing, and he also started to teach courses on meteorology. The founding of China's Meteorological Society in 1924 was largely due to the efforts of Zhu and his colleagues.[19] When the Academia Sinica was established in Nanjing in 1927, Zhu became the head of the Institute of Meteorology.[20]

The next ten years were an important period for the establishing of meteorology in China, and Zhu played a leading role in this endeavor. One of the first tasks facing Zhu and his colleagues was to launch China's own weather-forecasting program—since the late nineteenth century, China's meteorological stations had been operated by Westerners. Through the efforts of Zhu and his staff, the foreign monopoly was finally brought to an end in 1930. Meanwhile, the Chinese scientists also started doing research and gathering data on climate and other matters in various localities in China, often under extremely arduous conditions.

In 1936, Zhu Kezhen left his beloved meteorological research and the Institute of Meteorology to take up the presidency of the National Zhejiang University, or Zheda, thus beginning a new, and equally successful, career as an administrator in higher education.[21] Originally agreeing to work only for one year at Zheda, Zhu ended up spending the next fourteen years there. From 1940 to 1946, due to the Sino-Japanese War, the university was relocated in the remote town of Zunyi in Guizhou Province, where the students found relative peace from wartime disturbances and were able to concentrate on their studies. To find a suitable location for the university after the war started, Zhu had taken long journeys to various places to investigate the local conditions, at a time when both his wife and a child were seriously ill; both soon died.[22] Despite the Japanese invasion and the subsequent civil war between the Nationalists and the Communists, Zheda was transformed, under the leadership of Zhu Kezhen, from the internally divided and academically inadequate provincial school of 1936 into one of China's best institutions of higher learning, regarded by Joseph Needham, then a British diplomat in wartime China and later a highly acclaimed scholar on the history of science in China, as comparable to Oxford, Cambridge, and Harvard.[23]

Zhu had two models in mind for Zheda: the classical academies in traditional China, and the modern universities in the West. To make Zheda both *modern* and *Chinese*, Zhu consciously and skillfully blended the neo-Confucianist ideal of *qiushi* (seeking the truth) with the scientific spirit of the West.[24] Following the example of Charles Eliot, Zhu made great efforts to attract high-quality professors to Zheda. His unassuming personal style, his liberal and democratic way of running the university,[25] and his total dedication to his job won him deep respect from faculty and students alike.

When Li Jinghan returned to China in 1924, he knew that he did not want to become an "official" (*bu zuoguan*) and he also knew what he wanted to do: study his native society. Li eventually made himself one of the most respected scholars on rural China and a highly acclaimed expert in statistical studies. Numbers were very important to his work. A *duilian* (antithetical couplet, traditionally written on two vertical scrolls) given to him by some friends made fun of this fact: the left scroll simply said "one, two, three, four, five"; the right said "six, seven, eight, nine, ten"; and the *hengpi* (a horizontal scroll usually placed above the two vertical scrolls) said "add, subtract, multiply, and divide."[26]

Li Jinghan would be more capable than most people to provide precise statistical data related to China, but he was not just interested in numbers. He cared about people, particularly those at the lower end of society, an empathy partly explained by his own humble family background.[27] The subject of his first study after returning to China was rickshaw men in Beijing,[28] a study carried out under the auspices of the Beiping Social Research Society, founded by, among others, the American social scientist Sidney Gamble.[29] It was Gamble who had invited Li Jinghan to come back to China from America to join him in this newly founded institute. The rickshaw was the "most numerous, or at least the most conspicuous thing" in Beijing, holding a central place both in the city's scenery and in popular imagination.[30] Li started his investigation with enthusiasm, mixing with rickshaw men in the streets rain or shine, and paying no heed to ridicule from "respectable" society. Li's pioneering study helped draw attention to the plight of the rickshaw men. It is believed that Lao She, one of the finest novelists in twentieth-century China, was inspired by Li's study to write his famous "Camel Xiangxi," a story about a wretched rickshaw man in Beijing.[31] Li learned through this kind of study how to relate to the common people and how to get them to tell the truth about their lives—experiences that would be invaluable to Li's future research and that would enable him to become an authority on the methodology of doing social research in China.[32]

Li started researching peasant life in the suburbs of Beijing around 1926,[33] when he was teaching in the sociology department at Yanjing University. Li was also active in the expanding community of Chinese sociologists, being an important member in the Chinese Society of Sociology founded in Beijing.[34] Both Zhu Kezhen and Li Jinghan, as it turned out, helped the professionalization of their respective fields in China.

In 1928, Li's name began to be linked with the rural reconstruction experiment in Dingxian County, under the leadership of Yan Yangchu (known in the West as James Yen).[35] Li spent the next seven years in Dingxian, living very simply among the peasants. The result of Li's Dingxian stay was a huge volume entitled *Dingxian shehui gaikuang diaocha* (Dingxian: A social survey), which was regarded as the most detailed and authoritative study ever conducted on a Chinese rural community.[36] A side project of this period was a collection of peasants' drama.[37] In his later life, Li always fondly and nostalgically remembered his Dingxian years.[38]

In the preface to *Dingxian shehui gaikuang diaocha*, Li summarized four basic problems he saw in the Chinese society: ignorance (*yu*), poverty (*qiong*), weakness (*ruo*) and selfishness (*si*).[39] This analysis, shared by Yan Yangchu, represented an ideological understanding of China's internal situation. The purpose of Li Jinghan's social research, it should be emphasized, was not just academic. Like Yan Yangchu, Li wanted to play a part in changing China, and the approach he espoused was a carefully planned reform rather than revolution. Li's numerical studies were meant to provide reliable and systematic data, which would be the basis of practical and effective plans for bringing gradual change to Chinese society. Like Yan, Li realized the importance of rural China for bringing about change in the general society. He once urged some college students to "go to the masses" and start doing "small and practical" things for the peasants.[40]

The Dingxian program was interrupted by the Japanese invasion of northern China in 1937. By then, Li had been teaching for a couple of years in the sociology department of Qinghua University. After the war broke out, Li moved with Qinghua (now part of the National Southwest United University) to western China, where, despite wartime privations, Li and his colleagues produced one of the largest population surveys ever conducted in modern China.[41]

In 1944, Li came to the United States to acquire the most up-to-date techniques in census gathering. When the United Nations was founded, Li worked as a senior advisor for the UN's Food and Agriculture Agency. Li returned to China at the end of 1948. A month later, in January 1949, the Communist People's Liberation Army peacefully took over Beijing (then called Beiping). The United Nations was providing transportation for its employees and their families to evacuate China. Li decided not to leave, telling his children, "We are Chinese and we should stay in China." Li's wife, an American woman, willingly agreed with this decision.[42]

A similar decision of whether to stay on or leave the mainland awaited Zhu Kezhen, and Zhu also opted to stay. Toward the end of the Nationalist regime he had become increasingly disillusioned by the autocratic and corrupt government. As the president of Zheda, he had tried to protect those "leftist" students who were on the blacklists of the Guomindang secret police. When it came to the critical moment of deciding whether to stay or to leave the mainland, Zhu chose to stay, very much to the displeasure of the high-ranking Guomindang officials who had repeatedly urged him to go to Taiwan.

In the spring of 1949, Luo Longji was in danger of being taken by force to Taiwan by the Nationalists. Politically the most active of the three men discussed in this epilogue, Luo had become a prominent figure in the 1940s as a leader of the Democratic League, which he had helped to found in 1941 and which had been denounced as illegal by the Nationalist government in the fall of 1947.[43]

The period after the end of the Sino-Japanese War in August 1945 was the golden time for Chinese liberals. The Democratic League, the liberals' major representative organization, was a mediator between the Nationalist and Communist parties, trying to bring peace and a coalition government to a country that had long suffered foreign invasion and internal strife. When the civil war finally broke out between the two parties in 1947, it became virtually impossible for the Chinese liberals, without the backing of any military power, to seek a "third" path and to continue to maintain neutrality. Thereafter the Democratic League leaned increasingly toward the Communists, and the heyday of Chinese liberalism was over.[44]

Luo Longji was one of the most prominent spokesmen as well as one of the most articulate thinkers of Chinese liberalism in the republican era.[45] He persistently promoted the ideas of civil liberty, the rule of law, and government by a well-qualified professional bureaucracy.[46] Although not a supporter of communism,[47] Luo directed his sharpest attack toward the Nationalist regime and was particularly critical of the government's autocratic ruling style and its tendency to place their party above the nation. Never hesitant to voice his opinion, Luo became a thorn in the side of the Nationalist government. Within the first several years of his return to China, Luo experienced arrest, imprisonment, dismissal from his teaching positions, and even one attempted murder. He refused to be silenced, though. Soon after his release from one arrest, Luo published an article describing in detail his experience, openly protesting against the absence of due legal process and the lack of basic civil protection for the citizens of China.[48]

The most brilliant period in Luo's political career began in 1941, with the formation of the League of Chinese Democratic Groups (later reorganized as the Chinese Democratic League). The platform of the Democratic League bore a clear imprint of Luo's thinking: to adopt a politically democratic system from the West and an economically democratic system from the Soviet Union.[49] In 1946, Luo represented the Democratic League at the Political Consultative Conference and served on the conference's constitution drafting committee. He worked closely with the delegation of the Communist Party to try to curtail the power of the ruling Nationalist government. The murder of Luo's good friend Wen Yiduo in the summer of 1946 by Nationalist agents significantly estranged liberal intellectuals from the Nationalist regime and greatly strengthened Luo's opposition to the Guomindang government.

Meanwhile, Luo tried to maintain a friendly relationship with both

George Marshall, the then American envoy to China, and John Leighton Stuart, the United States ambassador.[50] After full-scale civil war broke out in early 1947, and when it became clear that the Communist troops had the upper hand in the battlefield, Luo and some of his colleagues in the Democratic League hoped that the United States could help strengthen the liberal forces in China to counterbalance the power of the ascending Communists.[51] This hope vanished with the United States' firm alliance with the Nationalist government and the subsequent rupture of its relationship with the Communists.[52]

During the last stage of Nationalist control in China in the spring of 1949, Luo virtually lost his freedom in Shanghai. He barely escaped a second attempted murder by Chiang Kai-shek's secret police.[53] After being rescued by Communist agents and safely escorted to Beiping, Luo received a hero's welcome from the top leaders of the Communist Party.

AFTER THE FOUNDING OF THE PRC

The founding of the Communist government gave Zhu Kezhen hope for a new China. Writing in his diary three days after the Liberation Army entered Shanghai, Zhu observed,

> People welcome the arrival of the Liberation Army as if they brought timely rain after a long drought. [I] hope the Communists will keep their diligent spirit and never fall into the trap of corruption like the Nationalists. Science is extremely important to the construction of a country. [I] hope the Communists will pay serious attention to it.[54]

The new government did not disappoint Zhu Kezhen. Soon after the People's Republic was founded, Zhu was appointed vice president of the newly founded Chinese Academy of Sciences, responsible for the planning of natural science research, becoming in effect the highest-ranking scientist in China. As the top administrator in charge of scientific work, Zhu was given full responsibility at the academy, playing a leading role in laying the groundwork for scientific research in the People's Republic. One thing Zhu and his colleagues did in the early 1950s that proved to have far-reaching consequences was to attract a sizeable number of well-trained Chinese scientists, then abroad (many in America), to return to China.[55] In addition to being a busy administrator, Zhu was able to continue his own research, mostly in meteorology.

Li Jinghan's experience in the early 1950s was much less heartening, and largely mirrored the fate of sociology in the new China. Like many intellectuals of his background (educated in the "old society"), Li underwent a period of intense "thought reform."[56] In one of the self-criticisms Li made in 1951, he denounced the training he had received in America, and wrote: "the social research methodology I used in the past was bourgeois in nature, reformist in its approach (*gailiang zhuyi*), and for the sake of pure research. . . . It helped the reactionary government, anaesthetized the revolutionary consciousness, and led to the delay of the success of the revolution."[57] After the "thought reform," Li was assigned to teach statistics in Beijing Institute of Finance and Economics (Beijing Caijing Xueyuan). The year was 1952, when a reorganization of institutes of higher learning was taking place, based on the Soviet Union's model, and when the discipline of sociology, now regarded as "pseudoscience," was almost completely eliminated from the newly reorganized universities.[58] Many famous sociologists, some of whom we have come across in this study, had to relocate professionally.[59] One thing worth mentioning is that Li joined the Democratic League around this time, when the league was one of the several "democratic parties" that participated in the new PRC government and when it was vigorously recruiting members from the intellectual elite.

As an anti-Nationalist hero in the civil-war period and a vice chairman of the Democratic League, Luo Longji was rewarded with high posts in the new government.[60] Although a single man, he lived in a huge residence that used to belong to a Qing-dynasty prince. Luo's personal life was the least stable of the three individuals, and the most colorful. After two failed marriages, the first to a Chinese woman in England and the second to an American-educated woman, Luo began in 1946 to date Pu Xixiu, a very capable newspaper correspondent.[61] Because of the opposition from Pu's children, the two did not marry, but they maintained an intimate relationship.[62]

In general, information is scarce about the personal lives of the men under discussion here. Zhu Kezhen remarried after the death of his first wife—apparently his second wife was well educated and the marriage was a happy one. Li Jinghan, meanwhile, as mentioned earlier, had an American wife whom he divorced in the 1950s.[63] Nor do we know much about the details of their daily lives. Devoted to work, Li Jinghan probably found little time for recreation. The trophy he won for a tennis tournament at an Alliance summer conference, however, always occupied a conspicuous place in the family's home,[64] reminding Li of a happy moment he had in a remote land.

THE ANTIRIGHTIST CAMPAIGN AND THE CULTURAL REVOLUTION

Nineteen fifty-seven, the year of the antirightist campaign, was a watershed in the history of the People's Republic, a year that changed, to a greater or lesser degree, the lives of Zhu, Luo, and Li, as it did those of so many other Chinese intellectuals. Luo Longji's life was the most profoundly altered of the three men's: he was accused of being the head of an alleged anti-Party alliance, along with Zhang Bojun, another vice chairman of the Democratic League. The exposure of the "Zhang-Luo anti-party clique" was regarded as one of the major victories of the antirightist campaign.[65]

During the brief period of politically open and free "Hundred Flowers" that preceded the antirightist campaign, Luo Longji suggested that since many people had been wrongly accused in various mass campaigns after 1949, it would be appropriate to set up a "rehabilitation committee" to correct previous mistakes, so that people would no longer fear to express their opinions in the Hundred Flowers. Moreover, instead of having it handled solely by the Communist Party, the rehabilitation work should be jointly conducted with the participation of the democratic parties. Luo also raised the issues of freedom of speech, and the CCP's relationship with intellectuals. Later, when the political climate suddenly changed, this suggestion was used as major evidence of Luo's anti-Party thinking.[66] Luo strongly resisted the verdict, insisting that he had harbored no anti-Party thoughts, and also dismissed the accusation that he had formed any alliance with Zhang Bojun, with whom he had never gotten along. To show that there was nothing between him and Zhang Bojun, he went to Zhang's home one day with a walking stick, and angrily broke it in front of Zhang.[67] This kind of act had no effect on those who were determined to make Luo Longji an "enemy of the people." By the end of 1958 Luo had been stripped of all his important posts. Thereafter Zhou Enlai met with Luo and suggested that he leave China to go to the United States and that the government would pay for his trip. Luo's reply was, "I would rather die in China."[68] The antirightist campaign forcefully silenced any outcry for political democracy that might be voiced by Western-educated intellectuals, and dealt a heavy blow to the democratic parties, particularly the Democratic League, labeling one-sixth of its members as "rightists."[69]

Li Jinghan also became a "rightist," along with almost all the other sociologists we have come across in this study, many of whom were members of the Democratic League.[70] Li Jinghan said during the Hundred Flowers period that when a decision was made, it should be based not only on correct political viewpoints, but also on reliable statistics and data[71]—a notion that would later be interpreted as "rightist talk." Having been labeled rightist, Li was no longer able to do field work. Being confined to working at home caused a great deal of agony to a person who had always been socially active.[72]

Unlike Luo Longji and Li Jinghan, Zhu Kezhen was not directly touched by the antirightist campaign, although his elder son was, dying later in a labor camp of illness and malnutrition—an experience that, for a loving father, weighed heavily on Zhu. Zhu Kezhen's feelings were recorded in a poem titled "Crying for Xiwen" (Xiwen was his son's name), which he showed to few people.[73]

The Western-educated Chinese intellectuals were discredited as a group after 1957. Continuing to be the vice president of the Chinese Academy of Sciences, Zhu nonetheless found himself unable to lead as before. Thereafter, Zhu spent much of his time investigating natural resources across China. Through such investigations, Zhu realized the seriousness of the country's ecological problems; therefore, he repeatedly urged the government to protect the environment—an appeal that was largely ignored.

When the Cultural Revolution swept over China in 1966, Luo Longji was the only man among the three under discussion here who was spared that catastrophic event. One day in December 1965, Luo was found dead alone in his home,[74] apparently as a result of a sudden heart attack.[75] His long-time companion, Pu Xixiu, had been estranged from him since 1957.[76] Although he was younger than either Zhu or Li, it is not surprising that Luo died the earliest, given the severity of political persecution he had been subjected to.

Zhu Kezhen was among the few top scientists in China who were placed under special protection from the Cultural Revolution's mass-struggle meetings and violence. This did not mean, however, that he was not criticized by the "big character posters." In 1972, the year when Deng Xiaoping was brought back to power from political exile, Zhu also resumed his vice presidency at the Chinese Academy of Sciences. By then, his health had deteriorated badly. Throughout the Cultural Revolution years Zhu had never stopped observing and recording changes in nature, a habit he had formed in childhood. When he swept his own courtyard, he noticed that the amount of dust falling onto the Beijing area had increased substantially since the beginning of the Cultural Revolution, a worrisome indicator of air pollution. His last diary entry, on the day before his death in early February 1974, records only that day's temperature.[77]

Li Jinghan managed to survive the Cultural Revolution and was able to see not only his own political rehabilitation but the revival of sociology in China.[78] Since his death in 1986 at the age of ninety-two, he has been recognized as one of the most accomplished scholars in his field. In the preface to one of his books, recently reprinted, the then eighty-seven-year-old Li expressed a wish to go back to field work. Knowing that he was too old to do so, he placed his hope on the emerging young generation of Chinese sociologists.[79]

LOOKING BACKWARD AND FORWARD

These three individuals, all born in the last decade of the nineteenth century, belonged to a "transitional" generation that was caught in a time when Chinese society was undergoing drastic changes. Taking advantage of the modern educational opportunities that were just becoming available, they came to the United States to study. After they returned to China in the early decades of the twentieth century, they taught for varied lengths of time at universities. Emerging institutions of higher learning in the Nationalist period provided them with job opportunities, and as the first generation of

Chinese professionals, they contributed to the building of academic disciplines and, in the case of Zhu Kezhen, the making of a modern Chinese university. All this was accomplished under difficult and at times formidable conditions. As academicians, they had a certain degree of autonomy, which they managed to guard and make good use of.

Politically, they all leaned toward a liberal, gradualist approach to solving the problems confronting China in modern times. Luo Longji, in particular, persistently and bravely promoted Fabian-style socialist democratic ideals in Guomindang-dominated China. All three of these men also upheld the notion of "scientific" rationalism and believed in the importance of professional experts in managing the affairs of the country. Overall, they pointed to a different route to modernity from that of a mass social revolution, represented by the Chinese Communist Party.

Like most Western-educated Chinese intellectuals, the three men stayed on the mainland after the founding of the People's Republic. Sciences and technology now had the social stability and state sponsorship they needed to flourish. On the other hand, sociology and other social sciences were subjected to tight ideological control. The contrasting experience of Zhu Kezhen and Li Jinghan in the early 1950s tellingly illustrates the different fates of the natural sciences and some social sciences in the first decades of the PRC.

Luo Longji's Democratic League and other democratic parties were incorporated into the governing body of the new state, where they played a visible yet clearly subordinate role. But 1957 marked the end of any political and cultural influences Western-educated Chinese intellectuals had been able to exert after 1949. Thereafter, Western-educated intellectuals were valued, if at all, mostly for "technical" knowledge.

Western-educated Chinese intellectuals, including the generation of American-educated students who have been the subject of this study, have been the focus of interest again since the end of the Cultural Revolution. Now that the eventful twentieth century has concluded, people in China are pondering the paths they have taken in their arduous "search for modern China,"[80] and their endeavors to become modern Chinese. The stories of the Western-educated Chinese intellectuals discussed in this book, long forgotten, have reemerged, and stand as a rich, important, and indispensable legacy for the people of China.

Notes

Introduction

1. The change of hairstyle and clothing was required of the America-bound students. "Youmei lüeshuo," by Xu Xianjia, discusses in detail what clothing was needed and how much it cost.

2. This journal was originally called *The Chinese Students' Bulletin*, which was started in 1905 by the Chinese Students' Alliance of the Eastern States. The later name was adopted in the summer of 1907 at the organization's Andover conference. It became the official organ of the Chinese Students' Alliance of the United States after the nationwide association came into existence in the fall of 1911. The journal lasted until April 1931. The places of publication varied according to the locations of the editorial boards.

The earliest Chinese student publication in the United States, an annual called *The Dragon Students*, was issued in 1904 in the Chinese language by the students at Cornell University. For information on student publications and directories, see "Liumei Zhongguo xuesheng chubanwu zhi jinbu," 25–26.

3. See F. L. Chang, "Innocents Abroad."

4. The experiences of the Chinese students as a group in the United States in the early twentieth century have never been studied in America or in China as a separate subject. Studies published in America have either surveyed China's foreign-study movement in general or focused on well-known individuals. Among the books on famous individuals published in America, see Grieder, *Hu Shih and the Chinese Renaissance*, and Chou, *Hu Shih and Intellectual Choice in Modern China*; on Hong Ye, see Egan, *A Latterday Confucian*; on Shen Zonghan, see Stross, *The Stubborn Earth*; and on Yan Yangchu, see Hayford, *To the People: James Yen and Village China*.

5. On their roles in these respects, see E-Tu Zen Sun, "The Growth of the Academic Community," esp. pp. 363–68, "Personnel: An Elite Trained Abroad."

6. On the roles played by American-educated Chinese in industry, see Hu Guangbiao, *Bozhu liushinian*. Also see Zhong Shaohua, "Zhongguo gongchengshi xuehui."

7. Hu Shi's final post, in which he was serving at the time of his death in 1962, was president of the Academia Sinica in Taiwan.

8. Hu Shi scored fifty-fifth among the seventy people at the selection examination taking place in the summer of 1910.

9. Both Nankai University and Nankai Middle School were founded by Zhang Boling, Zhang Pengchun's elder brother. Nankai Middle School was well known for its theatrical activities in northern China in the first half of the twentieth century.

10. See Dong Shouyi, *Qingdai liuxue yundong*; Li Xisuo, *Jindai Zhongguo de liuxuesheng*; Wang Qisheng, *Zhongguo liuxuesheng de lishi guiji*; Ding Xiaohe, ed., *Zhongguo bainian liuxue quanjilu*; and Sun Shiyue, *Zhongguo jindai nüzi liuxueshi*. Taiwan has also published a number of books on the foreign-study movement; see Lin Zixun, *Zhongguo liuxue jiaoyushi*, and Liu Zhen and Wang Huanchen, eds., *Liuxue jiaoyu*.

11. The white-haired palace maid is a figure from a well-known Tang dynasty poem by Bai Juyi (772–846), entitled "Xinggong." The teachers Fei writes about include Wu Zelin, Wu Jingchao, Pan Guangdan, and Wu Wenzao.

12. Furth, *Ting Wen-chiang*.

13. Furth, "Intellectual Change," pp. 322–23.

14. Y. C. Wang, *Chinese Intellectuals and the West*, and Jerome Chen, *China and the West*.

15. Sarri, *Legacies of Childhood*, p. ix.

16. Hao Chang, *Chinese Intellectuals in Crisis*, p. 1. About this generation, also see Lin Yü-sheng, pp. 30–37, "The First Generation of the Chinese Intelligentsia"; and Schwartz, "Limits of 'Tradition vs. Modernity,'" pp. 80–81.

17. See Leo Ou-fan Lee, "In Search of Modernity," pp. 110–11.

18. Hao Chang uses this term in his study of Liang Qichao; see Chang, *Liang Ch'i-ch'ao and Intellectual Transition*, p. 166. Among a number of books on Liang Qichao, the other one that is most relevant to this study is Tang Xiaobing's *Global Space and the National Discourse of Modernity*.

19. On Yan Fu, among other studies, see Schwartz, *In Search of Wealth and Power*. In his recent study of Yan Fu, Wang Hui challenges some of Schwartz's interpretations of Yan Fu's thinking. Wang in particular emphasizes the tension in Yan Fu's thought on the question of "modernity." See Wang Hui, "Yan Fu de sange shijie."

20. Benjamin Schwartz makes this argument in "The Limits of 'Tradition vs. Modernity,'" p. 80.

21. See Schwartz, "Themes in Intellectual History."

22. Several of Liang Qichao's children received professional training in various fields in the United States and became well-accomplished members in their professions. Liang Sicheng, the eldest son of Liang Qichao, for instance, was a prominent architect trained in the States. On Liang Sicheng, see Fairbank, *Liang and Lin*. On Liang Qichao's children, see Wu Liming, *Liang Qicho he tade ernümen*.

23. In Gong, ed., *Jindai Zhongguo yu jindai wenhua*, there are a number of articles on changes of lifestyle in the early twentieth century.

24. Myron L. Cohen, p. 118.

25. Giddens, p. 81. In his discussion on Shanghai modernity in the 1930s and 1940s, Leo Ou-fan Lee also argues that modernity was about the material transformation of everyday life. See Lee, "The Cultural Construction of Modernity in Urban Shanghai."

26. I am grateful to the second reader of the book manuscript for this nice turn of phrase.

27. See Schwartz, "The Limits of 'Tradition vs. Modernity.'" In "Culture, Modernity, and Nationalism," Schwartz further discusses his ideas on modernity.

28. In *Keywords: A Vocabulary of Culture and Society*, Raymond Williams indicates that modern is viewed as "the Other" to tradition and is embedded with the notions of "improvement" and "progress" (to underscore a linear understanding about time) (see Williams, pp. 208–9, 160–61, 243–45, and 318–20). The literature on modernity is vast and multifaceted. In a very general way and for purposes of convenience for the present discussion, "modernization" refers to processes of development in economic, political, legal, military, and other terms, and "modernity" refers to certain modes of thoughts and modes of sensibility. On the evolution of these terms, see Calinescu, *Five Faces of Modernity*.

29. Schwartz, "Culture, Modernity and Nationalism."

30. Wang Hui, *Wang Hui zixuan ji*, pp. 1–35.

31. In his study on Yan Fu, Wang Hui makes a convincing case on how Yan Fu both rejected and reconnected to the Chinese intellectual heritage in his endeavor to construct a Chinese modern identity. See Wang, "Yan Fu de sange shijie."

32. Levenson, *Confucian China and Its Modern Fate*.

33. Chang Hao makes this argument in *Chinese Intellectuals in Crisis*, p. 3. Wang Hui's recent study further reveals a complex relationship some leading Chinese intellectuals had with Chinese cultural heritage. See Wang, "Yan Fu de sange shijie."

34. In a letter to me, dated May 13, 1985, E-tu Zen-Sun makes a similar point.

35. Leo Ou-fan Lee, in his recent book, *Shanghai Modern*, discusses similar issues regarding modernist writers in Shanghai in the 1930s and 1940s. See, in particular, chap. 9, pp. 307–23.

36. *Liumei xuesheng jibao* (The Chinese students' quarterly) was published in Chinese by the Chinese Students' Alliance. It was printed in Shanghai, and was a continuation of *Liumei xuesheng nianbao* (The Chinese students' annual), which is believed to have started in 1907 and which ceased to exist around 1914. It is difficult to locate the first several issues of the *Nianbao*. The social-sciences branch of the library of the Chinese Academy of Sciences has 1911 and 1912 issues. *Liumei xuesheng jibao* first appeared in March 1914; in mid 1922 the publication was terminated temporarily; the resumed publication began in March 1926 and lasted till June 1928.

37. Pan Guangdan, "Jinhou zhi jibao yu liumei xuesheng"; page number not available.

38. The students in this generation did not have the option of staying in America after completing their education, since the United States had extremely restrictive immigration laws regarding Chinese nationals. Therefore, "to stay or not to stay" never became an issue for the students in this study.

39. Wang Hui argues convincingly that modernity for the Chinese is a cross-cultural enterprise (*Wang Hui zixuan ji*, pp. 32–33).

40. The estimated number of foreign-study students from China since the late 1970s is 250,000. See *Shijie ribao*, 26 July 1996, p. A10, "Dalu liumei xuesheng zongshu gaoju geguo bangshou" (The number of students from mainland China has topped that of any other country in the world). In his recent book on the current generation of Chinese students in America, Qian Ning argues that it is impossible to get precise figures of Chinese studying abroad since the late 1970s (*Liuxue meiguo*, pp. 76–81).

There is a very important distinction between the foreign-study movement in the late twentieth century and that of the early twentieth century. Many students of the current generation settled in the foreign, mostly Western, countries after they finished their studies. They comprise a large percentage of Chinese immigrant population in recent decades, which has given the current foreign-study movement a strong "immigration flavor."

41. On the contemporary generation, see Orleans, *Chinese Students in America*; Lampton, Madancy, and Williams, *A Relationship Restored*; Kallgren and Simon, eds., *Educational Exchanges*; Hayhoe and Bastid, eds., *China's Education and the Industrialized World*; Zweig and Chen, *China's Brain Drain to the United States*; and Bullock, "Promoting the American Way." Also see Qian, *Liuxue Meiguo*.

42. The Qing government sent students to both America and Europe. See Lin Zixun, pp. 86–118.

43. On this educational mission, see Yung, *My Life in China and America*; LaFargue, *China's First Hundred*; and Gao, *Zhongguo liumei youtong shuxinji*.

44. See LaFargue, chaps. 2, 3, and 4.

45. In a recent article, Xiao Gongqin reassesses the impact of the abolition of the civil service examination system, seeing it as the most critical occurrence in the abrupt cultural rupture in modern Chinese history ("Cong kejiu zhidu de feichu kan jindai yilai de wenhua duanlie," pp. 11–17).

46. On a discussion of Zhang Zhidong's formula, see Y. C. Wang, pp. 52–54. On Zhang Zhidong, see Bays, *China Enters the Twentieth Century*, and Ayers, *Chang Chih-tung and Educational Reform in China*.

47. Hao Chang discusses the crisis of "orientational symbolism" in *Chinese Intellectuals in Crisis*, p. 7.

48. The Qing government expected the students on the mission to study military technology and other related subjects.

49. See Huang Fu-ch'ing, *Chinese Students in Japan in the Late Ch'ing Period*, and Saneto Keishu, *Zhongguoren liuxue riben shi*.

50. Levine, *The Found Generation*.

51. On the Chinese students in other European countries, see Lin Zixun, pp. 86–106 and 381–92.

52. I decided to adopt the figure of 1,600 for 1925 rather than 2,500–2,600, suggested both by Y. C. Wang (p. 147) and Wang Qisheng (p. 45). This decision is based on my reading of the students' statistical information around this period and my belief that there wasn't any reason for a sudden increase of number of students in 1925, which was the year, in Wang Qisheng's table 2, that the number of students jumped from 1,673 to 2,500. "Liumei Zhongguo xuesheng zhi diaocha," an anonymous article in the journal *Jiaoyu zazhi*, also gives the number 1,600 (p. 13). Generally speaking, statistics regarding the students in America of this period are not very reliable, and the figures presented here are only estimates.

53. On the localities of Chinese students in America, see "Liumei Zhongguo xuesheng zhi diaocha," and Su Yunfeng, p. 382.

54. Standard stipends paid by the Chinese government to students in the United States were $960 in 1909 and $1,080 in 1924. See Y. C. Wang, p. 153, n32.

55. Types of government programs included, besides the Boxer Indemnity program, provincial government scholarships and scholarships by certain central government ministries. An example of a missionary sponsored student was Dong Xianguang; see his *Dong Xianguang zizhuan*, chap. 1.

56. Su Yunfeng discusses the Qinghua students' family backgrounds and concludes that they generally came from fairly well-off families (pp. 234–41).

57. Between 1921 and 1934 the percentages of students from Jiangsu, Zhejiang, and Guangdong were, respectively, 24.9, 12.8, and 12.8 (Y. C. Wang, p. 157). This factor also applied to the student body in Japan, but it did not apply to the student body in France (see ibid., p. 160).

58. Ren Hongjun was critical of this phenomenon; see Ren, "Jiaohui jiaoyu yu liuxuesheng." Shu Xincheng also expressed his concern over the large proportion of missionary school graduates in America; see Shu, *Jindai Zhongguo liuxueshi*, pp. 236–48. According to Shu, from 1921 to 1925 missionary school graduates composed 30.68 percent of the total population of self-supporting students in various countries and 89.4 percent of them went to America. America had a much higher percentage of missionary school graduates (ibid., p. 247).

59. In 1905, approximately 61 percent of the Chinese students in America held government scholarships; in 1910, about 32 percent; in 1925, 20 percent (see Y. C. Wang, p. 151).

60. It was called Qinghua Xuetang in 1911. The name was changed to Qinghua Xuexiao in 1912. Its English name was Tsinghua College. Primarily a high school, it offered a total of eight years' education. In 1925, the junior high school section was eliminated and a four-year college was added. On the history of Qinghua, see Su

Yunfeng; Qinghua Daxue University History Project Office, ed., *Qinghua Daxue xiaoshi gao*; and Qinghua University History Project Office, ed., *Qinghua Daxue shiliao bianxuan*, vol. 1.

61. For an exact number, see Su Yunfeng, p. 382. In 1929, Qinghua College, whose graduates had been the only people receiving full Indemnity scholarship since 1911, became a national university, ending Qinghua's history as a preparatory school for sending Chinese students to America. Thereafter, competition for Indemnity scholarships was open to all aspiring candidates.

62. See Su Yunfeng, pp. 387–98. Also see Qinghua University History Project Office, eds., *Qinghua renwu zhi*.

63. Hunt, "The American Remission of the Boxer Indemnity," and *The Making of a Special Relationship*, pp. 266–70. At the end of the former reference, an informative and well-written article, Hunt quotes the following lines from the *Daily Consular and Trade Report* (15 November 1909) to demonstrate that the Americans did not hide the benefits they hoped to derive from a corps of American-educated Chinese leaders: "They will be studying American institutions, making American friends, and coming back here to favor America for China in its foreign relations. Talk about a Chinese alliance! The return of the indemnity was the most profitable work Uncle Sam ever did. . . . They will form a force in our favor so strong that no other government or trade element of Europe can compete with it."

64. Hunt, "The American Remission of the Boxer Indemnity," p. 549, and Su Yunfeng, p. 8.

65. Liang Shiqiu, a graduate of Qinghua College in 1923, always had an ambivalent feeling toward his alma mater because its origin was intimately connected to the shameful experience of China with the West. See Liang, "Qinghua banian," in *Liang Shiqiu sanwen*, p. 204.

66. Liang Cheng, a native of Guangdong Province, came to America in 1875 (when he was twelve years old) as a member in the fourth group of the Yung Wing mission. He received his education first at Philip's Academy in Andover, Massachusetts, and then at Amherst College.

The American government realized that there was a huge surplus indemnity to China even at the time of the indemnity negotiation, but it took Liang over two years of persistent effort (from early 1905 to June 1907) before the Roosevelt administration finally made its intention of returning the excessive money a matter of formal record. At one point, when his efforts did not seem to get anywhere, Liang tried to influence public opinion: "He obliged newsmen with off-the-record interviews, gave speeches on China's claim, and sought out friendly Congressmen to support the cause." See Hunt, "The America Remission of the Boxer Indemnity," pp. 543–47. Once America decided to return the money, Liang Cheng, declaring that the money was China's and therefore that no strings should be attached to the return of it, nonetheless realized that a suitable compromise had to be made to "give the Americans their educational program but without making explicit assurances linking the remitted funds irrevocably to this specific project" (ibid., pp. 547–548). On Liang Cheng's mission in the United States, also see Luo, *Liang Cheng de chushi meiguo.*

67. Once the return of the money was settled and the idea of using it for educating the Chinese students in the United States was agreed upon by the Chinese government, Liang Tunyan, who became the minister of foreign affairs (*waiwu pu*) in 1909, recommended that the majority of the students on the educational program should study technical and practical subjects such as engineering and related fields, so that they could help China's industrialization and economic construction. His recommendation was accepted by the Ministry of Education and became the official policy (see Su Yunfeng, pp. 16–17). See further discussion of this subject in Chapter 2.

A third person on the Wing Yung mission who was involved in the return of the Indemnity money was Tang Shaoyi. Tang agreed with Yuan Shikai that it was utterly important to develop a Chinese-controlled system of transport, to encourage migration, to develop natural resources, and to reform and extend the Chinese political administration in Manchuria to offset the increasing influences of both Japan and Russia in that region. With the Indemnity money, a bank under official control could be organized to achieve the above outlined goals. Tang, therefore, opposed the idea of using the money for education. He even made a trip to the United States (late November 1908–January 1909) to solicit support for the establishment of the bank. His visit turned out to be fruitless. See Hunt, "The American Remission of the Boxer Indemnity," pp. 551–56.

68. While Thomas E. LaFargue's book *China's First Hundred* studies the Yung Wing mission, which contained only male students, there has been no systematic study of Chinese female students in the United States in the nineteenth century. This is why I decided to cover a span from the 1880s to the 1920s in this chapter, in order to give a fuller historical overview of the history of the female students.

69. *The Chinese Students' Monthly*, for example, a major source for my study, becomes less informative and interesting toward the late 1920s.

70. Among those I interviewed that winter were Zhang Yuanshan (Djan Yuanshan), who received a B.A. from Cornell University in 1915 and was a founder of the Science Society; Chen Hansheng, who came to America and received a M.A. from University of Chicago in 1922. In his book *Sige shidai de wo*, Chen discusses his experiences in America (pp. 14–27). I also interviewed Chen Daisun and Zhou Peiyuan. Chen Daisun came to America in 1920 and studied at the University of Wisconsin. Two years later he received a bachelor's degree from Wisconsin and went on to do graduate work at Harvard University, where he received his Ph.D. in economics in 1926. He was a professor of economics at Beijing University until his death in 1997. Zhou Peiyuan was born in 1902. After graduating from Qinghua College in 1924 he went first to University of Chicago, where he received his master's degree; he was at California State Polytechnic University from 1927 to 1928,

where he received his Ph.D. in physics. He was vice president of the Chinese Academy of Sciences from 1978 to 1981. All these interviewees were men. The only woman I managed to locate broke her hip and had to be hospitalized just a few days before our scheduled interview.

71. Li Weige, Li Jinghan's son, remembers that when he was small, the two prizes always hung on the wall of their house (Li Weige, interview by Weili Ye, 19 June 1993).

72. Not just his neighbors, but people in his department did not know who he was either. In the summer of 1993, I was in the office of the Statistics Department of the People's University, the official "work unit" of Li Jinghan's before his retirement. The staff there had no idea who Li Jinghan was. By then, of course, Li had been dead for a number of years.

Chapter 1: Associational Life and Nationalism

1. My figures primarily come from the *Monthly*. In 1908, the total number of Chinese students was reported to be 217, two-thirds of whom joined the Alliance. In 1911, out of the total number of 650 students, 385 were members. In 1914, 644 out of the roughly 1,000 students joined the Alliance.

2. Among the people who served in some capacity as officers of the Alliance were Gu Weijun (Wellington Koo), Guo Bingwen (Kuo Ping-wen), Song Ziwen (T. V. Soong), Wang Zhengting (C. T. Wang, Wang Cheng-ting), Wang Jingchun (C. C. Wang, Wang Ching-chun), and Hu Shi.

3. Yan Fu translated Herbert Spencer's book *The Study of Sociology* as *Qunxue yiyan*. The term *qun* was taken from Xun Zi's saying "ren zhi suoyi yiyu qinshou zhe, yi qi neng qun ye." (Human beings differ from beasts because of their ability to group.) On Yan Fu's ideas on *qun*, see Wang Hui, "Yan Fu de sange shijie."

4. Liang Qichao, "Shuo qun xu," pp. 3–7. See Hao Chang's discussion of Liang's notion of *qun*, in *Liang Ch'i-ch'ao and Intellectual Transition*, pp. 95–112.

5. On study societies during One Hundred Days Reform period, see, among other works, Li Wenhai, "Wuxu weixin shiqi de xuehui zuzhi," pp. 403–26. Besides study societies in the late 1890s, Li also briefly discusses the elite associations during the "new policies" period. See also, Sang Bing, *Qingmo xin zhishijie de shetuan yu huodong*, pp. 273–75. Sang argues that the number of voluntary associations established between 1901 and 1904 is much higher than previously estimated.

6. Hao Chang discusses eloquently the crisis of "orientational symbolism" in *The Chinese Intellectuals in Crisis*; see the introduction, p. 7. Benedict Anderson discusses the "quasi-religious" center of meaning of nationalism in *Imagined Communities*, chap. 3.

7. "Chung-Hwa Sing" (A plea for true patriotism), *CSM* (November 1915): pp. 39–43.

8. Tang Xiaobing's book *Global Space and the National Discourse of Modernity* is a recent study on the relationship between nationalism and modernity.

9. The 1895 divide is proposed by Chang Hao; see Chang, "Intellectual Change and the Reform Movement," p. 335. Benjamin Schwartz, meanwhile, questions Prasenjit Duara's argument that nationalist themes could be found in premodern China. See "Culture, Modernity, and Nationalism," pp. 219–22.

10. James Townsend discusses the relationship between "culturalism" and nationalism, and argues that the protean qualities of the long-existing "culturalism" in China made the transition to modern nationalism easier than some scholars have believed. And the transition among the intellectuals was accomplished in roughly a generation. See Townsend, "Chinese Nationalism," p. 114. I believe the transition was started by the generation of the 1890s and was completed by the generation who began to arrive on the scene in the early twentieth century.

11. In his book *Chinese Intellectuals in Crisis* (p. 2), Hao Chang argues that for the "transitional generation" of the 1890s (represented by four figures in Chang's book), there existed a polarity between nationalism and "universalism."

12. Hao Chang uses this phrase in his study of Liang Qichao (*Liang Ch'i-ch'ao and Intellectual Transition in China*, p. 166).

13. Tang Xiaobing uses this term in his book *Global Space and the National Discourse of Modernity*.

14. Tang Xiaobing's study is one recent book that looks at the spatial change for the Chinese in modern times. However, Tang only focuses on the change in the international setting (see his book's introduction).

15. Young, "Politics in the Aftermath of Revolution," p. 208. On this issue, also see Prasenjit Duara, *Rescuing History from the Nation*, chap. 6, "Provincial Narratives of the Nation: Federalism and Centralism in Modern China."

16. Lucian Pye asserts that the Chinese have been generally spared the crisis of identity common to most other transitional systems, and that "the more they have been exposed to the outside world the more self-consciously Chinese they have become." My study of the students appears to confirm the second half of Pye's argument. Pye, *The Spirit of Chinese Politics*, pp. 5–6.

17. Wang Qisheng, *Zhongguo liuxuesheng de lishi guiji*, p. 22.

18. Ibid.

19. Here, I use the date provided by Gu Weijun in his article "A Short History of the CSA in the U.S.," *CSM* (March 1912): 420–31. According to "Liumei zhongguo xueshenghui xiaoshi" (A brief history of Chinese Students' Alliance), in *The Eastern Miscellany*, the date was December 17, 1902.

20. Founded in 1895 in Tianjin, the Beiyang School was one of the first modern polytechnic schools in China. According to Xu Yuzhai, the eight people were Wang Chonghui, Chen Jintao, Wang Chongyu, Zhang Yujuan, Tan Tianchi, Wu Guiling, Pu Dengqing, and Yen Jirong. See *Xu Yuzhai zishu nianpu*. According to Liang

Qichao's "Xindalu youji jielu," Theodore C. Hu and Lu Yaoting replaced Tan Tianchi and Pu Dengqing (pp. 127–31).

21. See Harrell, pp. 98–100; also Dong Shouyi, pp. 228–33.

22. The question of loyalty was raised in the context that the Chinese, if not born in the United States, could not become naturalized citizens and would remain Chinese nationals. This policy was changed after 1943.

23. "Xindalu youji jielu," pp. 127–31. Liang's account is possibly the earliest record available about the organization.

24. On American campus life in late nineteenth century and the beginning of the twentieth century, see Horowitz, pp. 273–75.

25. On Max Weber's definitions of "rational-legal authority" and "traditional authority," see Weber, pp. 57–60.

26. The concepts of "civil society" and "public sphere" are discussed by Jürgen Habermas in *The Structural Transformation of Public Sphere*.

27. C. Y. Chin, "The Proper Meaning of the Chinese Students' Alliance," *CSM* (June 1913): 527.

28. Wan L. Hsu, "A Lesson in Co-operation," *CSM* (February 1925): 37.

29. Koo, memoirs, Columbia University Archives and Columbiana Library.

30. The organization finally became inactive or "paralysed," in 1931–32, due to "political opinion divergence." See "Historical Sketch of Chinese Students' Alliance," p. 24.

31. In 1905, the CSA of the Eastern States began to publish the *Chinese Students' Bulletin*. In 1907, it became the *Chinese Students' Monthly*. The journal lasted until April 1931.

32. "Chinese Students in Conference at Andover," newspaper clipping on the conference held by the Eastern Alliance in Andover, Massachusetts, in the summer of 1907, from H. D. Fearing's scrapbooks on Chinese students' Alliance Conference, 1908–14, in the Meng Chih Collections at Wesleyan University.

33. President's message, *CSM* (November 1907): 26.

34. President's message, *CSM* (November 1908): 22.

35. I borrow the term from the title of Benedict Anderson's book, *Imagined Communities*.

36. H. D. Fearing's two scrapbooks contain many newspaper clippings from the local newspapers in various towns where the conferences were held from 1908 to 1914. The reports show a great deal of interest in the Chinese students. After Fearing's death, the scrapbooks were collected by Meng Zhi (Chih Meng), along with photographs of the students on the Yung Wing mission and two guest books of photographs and writings of the students, 1907–9. H. D. Fearing befriended a number of Chinese boys on the Yung Wing mission. When the second wave of Chinese students arrived in the early twentieth century, Fearing showed great interest in helping the Chinese and managed to attend all the early conferences of the

Eastern Alliance, which probably explains why he had clippings from the local newspapers, 1908–14.

37. Almost all the Chinese ministers to America were invited to the conferences and spoke to the students. The relationship with the Chinese legation in Washington was friendly. The fact that the Chinese ministers to America tended to be Western-educated people themselves might very well have been an important factor in explaining this friendly relationship. Among the American officials, there were John W. Foster, the former secretary of state, Frank B. Weeks, the governor of Connecticut, and David I. Walsh, the former governor of Massachusetts.

38. Y. S. Tsao, "A Brief History of the 1910 Conference," *CSM* (November 1910): 36. Tsao did not give the detail of Yung Wing's speech.

39. "The First Government Student Conference," *World Chinese Students' Journal* (hereafter abbreviated as *WCSJ*) (November 1911): 607–8. The first summer camp was held in the West Hill of Beijing in 1911.

40. Conference notes, *CSM* (November 1908): 44.

41. Editorial, *CSM* (August 1908): 269.

42. Wellington Koo, "Brief History of 1909 Conference," *CSM* (November 1909): 44.

43. Ibid.

44. Hu Shi, for instance, clearly had frequent correspondence with relatives and friends at home. See Hu Shi, *Hu Shi liuxue riji*.

45. On the constitutional movement, see Fincher, *Chinese Democracy*; Rhoads, *China's Republican Revolution*; Schoppa, *Chinese Elites and Political Change*.

46. On the social and educational backgrounds of the elected assembly members, see Zhang Pengyuan, pp. 26–30. Also see Harrell, p. 215.

47. Min Tu-ki summarizes the achievements in the following words: "Although one may not agree that this was a 'bloodless revolution,' the traditional gentry did take over new functions, and leadership within the gentry class shifted from the conservative gentry with high degrees and high rank to the enlightened intellectuals. Clearly, a new era arrived" (Min Tu-ki, p. 171).

48. Rankin, *Elite Activism and Political Transformation in China*.

49. Min Tu-ki, p. 207.

50. Chin Chun Wang, "The Coming Struggle in the Far East," *CSM* (January 1910): 174–83.

51. S. T. Lok, "Why Join the Alliance?" *CSM* (January 1909): 170.

52. "New Provincial Assemblies Formed and Convened," *CSM* (December 1909): 83–84.

53. Editorial, "The National Assembly," *CSM* (January 1911): 242.

54. "Prize Awarded by Minister," 1906 conference newspaper clipping.

55. The importance of *jinguan* to traditional Chinese literati has been well recognized and studied. See Ho Ping-ti, "The Geographical Distribution of Hui-Kuan."

A recent study by Bryna Goodman discusses the transformation of older *huiguan* to new forms of native-place associations (*tongxianghui*) in Shanghai in the early republican period. See "New Culture, Old Habits: Native Place Organization and the May Fourth Movement," in Frederic Wakeman, Jr., and Wen-Hsin Yeh, eds., *Shanghai Sojourners*, pp. 76–107.

56. See Harrell, pp. 100–101. Also see Huang Fu-ching, *Chinese Students in Japan in Late Qing Period*, pp. 136, 139, and 145.

57. Huang, p. 95.

58. Horowitz, p. 91.

59. Ibid. p. 11.

60. Ibid., p. 91.

61. Liang Qichao, "Xinmin shuo."

62. Hao Chang has a whole chapter devoted to the analysis of Liang Qichao's "Xinmin shuo." See *Liang Ch'i-ch'ao and Intellectual Transition in China*, chap. 6, "The New Citizen," pp. 149–219.

63. Chinese Oral History Project, East Asian Institute, Columbia University; Wellington Koo Memoir (Glen Rock, N.J.: Microfilming Corporation of America, 1978), vol. 1, page number unmarked.

64. Ibid.

65. Ibid.

66. Ibid.

67. In early 1915, when they learned about Japan's "Twenty-one Demands" on China, many students in America were so outraged that they demanded war against Japan, for which a resolution was passed in the *Chinese Students' Quarterly*. Hu Shi, on the other hand, was opposed to the idea, and wrote a letter to the *Monthly* to call for cool-headedness. The letter was criticized by many students. See Hu Shi, "A Plea for Patriotic Sanity: An Open Letter to All Chinese Students," *CSM* (April 1915): 425–26.

68. The movement originated in Italy in 1898, with the founding of the Federation Internationale des Etudiants, "Corda Fratres" (FIDE). After the turn of the century, as the number of foreign students studying in American universities increased, the movement began to attract a following in the United States. An International Club was established at the University of Wisconsin in 1903. The Cornell Cosmopolitan Club was founded the following year, the first of many similarly constituted organizations that by 1912 numbered close to thirty. In 1907 the Association of Cosmopolitan Clubs was formed, and four years later it was recognized as the American affiliate of the FIDE.

69. Hu Shi, *Hu Shi liuxue riji*, vol. 1, p. 142.

70. Tang Degang, trans., "Hu Shi de zizhuan," p. 188.

71. Hu Shi, *Hu Shi liuxue riji*, p. 1053.

72. Ibid., p. 180.

73. Mei noted, "It is a rare chance to see an American professor actively engaged

in public affairs; he considers it quite beneath his academic dignity to rally with the hero of the mob and to be in the limelight." K. T. May, "Our Need of Interest in National Affairs," *CSM*, (February 1917): 210.

74. Ibid.: 211.

75. Ibid.

76. Ibid.

77. These people founded a journal called *Xueheng* (Critical Review) in 1922, which lasted, on and off, until 1933. The *xueheng* school was deeply influenced by Irving Babbit, a Harvard scholar of classics and a cultural conservative. On the *xueheng* school, see "Statement by the Critical Review"; Sun Shangyang, "Zai qimeng yu xueshu zhijian"; and Kuang Xinnian, "Xuehengpai dui xiandaixing de fansi."

78. C. Y. Chin, "The Proper Meaning of the Chinese Students' Alliance."

79. Horowitz, p. 7. Horowitz argues that campus life was structured as a hierarchy, ranking people according to class, race, religion, and gender.

80. Sun Longji, "Liangge geming de duihua 1789 & 1911," and Li Liangyu, "Cong xinhai dao wusi." There has not yet been any careful and focused examination of this significant political transformation. Some recent scholarship even fails to recognize that there was a change. See Michael H. Hunt, "Chinese National Identity and Strong State," pp. 62–79, and Samuel S. Kim and Lowell Dittmer, "Whither China's Quest for National Identity?" pp. 237–90. The argument in both cases is that the tendency in both the late Qing and early republic was consistent for a strong and centralized state. Kim and Dittmer's article further maintains (p. 252) that this tendency originated from "the state's pivotal role in both historical fact and historical myth" in the past three thousand years of Chinese history. Another recent book on the subject, Jonathan Unger, ed., *Chinese Nationalism*, also does not address the issue.

81. Wellington Koo memoir, page number unmarked. This memoir, available also in microfilm, has been translated into Chinese by the Institute of Modern History, Chinese Academy of Social Sciences, entitled *Gu Weijun huiyilu* (The memoir of Gu Weijun). See the Bibliography.

82. Ibid. Gu was introduced to Sun in the fall of 1909, by W. F. Chen, a student from Guangdong Province. The three had a "pleasant chat" and the conversation lasted until after midnight, during which Sun talked about organizing a political party to overthrow the Manchus. However, nothing appeared to come out of this meeting as far as Gu was concerned. Gu pointed out that Sun's support came mostly from the overseas Chinese community in Chinatown and, although he believed that there were some students who belonged to the Revolutionary League, they did not make their membership known. On the other hand, according to Gu, "a public debate [on revolution versus constitutionalism] was purposefully avoided at Chinese students' conferences."

83. One of the few articles regarding the radical students in Japan had this to say: "Our students in Japan have, many a time, been misrepresented and unjustly

accused. It is hoped that this secret official investigation will remove the suspicions from the mind of the government officials and re-establish good feelings and mutual confidence between them." See "Students in Japan Under Close Watch," *CSM* (November 1907): 6.

84. There has been some rethinking going on about the debate between the revolutionaries and the reformers both among the scholars in China and in the West. See, for instance, Tang Xiaobing, pp. 137–64.

85. This argument is made, most implicitly, by Rankin, p. 280, and Min Tu-ki, p. 216.

86. T. C. Chu, "Current News from China," *CSM* (November 1911): 11–15. This is also the view held by a number of historians, including Min Tu-ki, who contends, "The anti-governmental stance of the provincial assembly was related to its inherent tendency to oppose centralized power, which eventually led to revolution (p. 171).

87. "The Ai-kwoh-hwei (The Chinese National Union)," *CSM* (January 1912): 221–28.

88. Editorial, "A Republic is Inevitable," *CSM* (February 1912): 283.

89. Ibid.

90. T. C. Chu, "Review of Home News: China's Revolution," *CSM* (December 1911): 140.

91. Yun-slang Tsao, "Letter to the President of the United States of America," *CSM* (February 1913): 243–44.

92. Editorial, "A Strong Central Government," *CSM* (March 1912): 396.

93. Editorial, *CSM* (January 1911): 242.

94. Yoeh Liang Tong, "Over-Progressiveness," *CSM* (November 1913): 46–49.

95. Ibid.

96. Duara, *Rescuing History from the Nation*, chap. 6, "Centralism and Federalism in Republican Period."

97. See Duara, "Minguo de zhongyang jiquan zhuyi he lianbang zhuyi," p. 30. The article is translated into Chinese by Lin Liwei. Also see Zhang Xueji, pp. 43–49.

98. Editorial, "The Supreme Task," *CSM* (November 1913): 3–4.

99. Kim and Dittmer, p. 252.

100. Many students were puzzled and some were angered by the attitude of the American government, which appeared to the students to be hesitating about recognizing the new republic in the first year of its existence. For instance, the *Monthly* editorial "The Chinese Republic and Its Recognition" urged the American government to recognize the Chinese republic, saying that "the Chinese Republic expects more sympathy and earlier recognition from America than from any other country," because the Americans supposedly had "disinterested friendship for China" and "sympathy for a Republican cause." Given these reasons, the editorial continued, "we can not well understand why America has not yet complied with the request for recognition." *CSM* (March 1912): 397.

101. In "Liangge geming de duihua," Sun Longji discusses in particular how the French Revolution was viewed as a model by the Chinese in the early twentieth century.

102. Editorial, "Government and Constitution," *CSM* (January 1914): 175.

103. In "Cong xinhai dao wusi," Li Liangyu discusses the political positions of Cai E and Li Yuanhong regarding centralized nationalism in the early republic (pp. 75–79). Sun Longji in "Liangge geming de duihua" discusses Li Dazhao's attitude in the early republic.

104. Liang's view on this issue was expressed in "Xinzhongguo jianshe wenti."

105. Liang's idea on a strong central government had a long history, dating back to 1905 when he wrote "Kaiming junzhu lun." Liang remained essentially committed to Yuan Shikai until he learned about the latter's scheme to revive monarchy.

106. Jerome Chen argues that at the beginning of 1912 there was no one else who had the slightest chance of holding the country together. See Chen, *Yuan Shih-k'ai*, p. 254.

107. "Revolution and the Supreme Cause," *CSM* (January 1912): 203–4.

108. "Yuan Shikai—a Traitor," *CSM* (February 1912): 345. Hu Shi and Zhao Yuanren were among the people who signed the letter.

109. Reply of Y. S. Tsao, editor-in-chief of the *Monthly*, *CSM* (February 1912): 347.

110. See Editorials, "Republic or Monarchy?" *CSM* (November 1915): 1–5; "Republic or Monarchy?" on p. 7 of the same issue; and Suh Hu (Hu Shi), "A Philosopher of Chinese Reactionism," on pp. 16–19 of the same issue.

111. "Republic or Monarchy?" p. 5.

112. President's message, *CSM* (January 1917): 26.

113. Editorial, "Success of Our Women Students," *CSM* (November 1909): p. 4.

114. "Student World," *CSM* (November 1924): 71.

115. Editorial, *CSM* (November 1924): 2.

116. *CSM* closely followed the development of the Shangdong question, devoting a number of editorials during this period to it.

117. Chih Meng, *Chinese American Understanding*, p. 109.

118. "Student World," *CSM* (November 1925): 73.

119. The adoption of the "Peking dialect" at the summer conference in Syracuse, New York, provoked a heated debate among the students, since to some of them the northern dialect was almost like a "foreign language." It was also blamed as a major reason for the small attendance of that year's conference. See Sinley Chang, "The Syracuse Conference, Part III: Miscellaneous," *CSM* (November 1925): 74.

120. Thomas Ming-heng Chao, "At the Eastern Conference," *CSM* (November 1926): 66.

121. Ibid.: 67. Without actually seeing the play, we cannot not be certain whether or not some students were experimenting with gay sexuality in it.

122. "He Knows His Onions," *CSM* (February 1927): 76.

123. "Personal and Otherwise," *CSM* (February 1927): 76.

124. For instance, Wang Chonghui, a founding member of the Alliance, became the foreign minister of Sun Yat-sen's provisional government in 1912; Wang Zhengting, a one-time president of the Alliance, served as the vice president of the Board of Commerce and Industry. The most conspicuous success story was Gu Weijun's, who left Columbia University in 1912 to serve as Yuan Shikai's private secretary and went from there to pursue a successful career.

125. Dr. V. K. Wellington Koo, "Address Made at the Platform Meeting of the Chinese Students' Conference at Brown University, Providence, R.I., on Sept. 6, 1917," *CSM* (November 1917): 20–28.

126. On American youth culture of the 1920s, see Fass, *The Damned and the Beautiful*; on the political attitude of American college students, pp. 326–55.

127. E. K. Moy "Thirteen Years of Chinese Students," *CSM* (December 1923): 9.

128. Hao Chang, *Liang Ch'i-ch'ao and Intellectual Transition in China*, pp. 154–67.

129. In his article, Wang Hui convincingly argues that in the political discourse of the late Qing, the concepts of *jun* or *shehui* (society) were closely related to China's historical task of creating a modern nation-state. The making of modern China not only involved the building of a modern nation-state, it also implied the creation of a modern "society." The relationship between state and society in late Qing China differed significantly from that in modern Europe. The historical challenge facing China was first and foremost national survival in a Western-dominated world. The logic of the state-society dichotomy in a liberal Western country did not apply to the situation of China. See Wang, "Yan Fu de sange shije."

130. Yü, "Zhongguo zhishi fenzi de bianyuanhua."

131. Ibid., 19–20.

132. The New Haven Club rented a house on Whalley Avenue for many years as their meeting place.

133. CSCA published an English quarterly. The name of this journal varied over the years. It was called *Liu Mei Tsing Nien* from 1914 to May 1917, *Chinese Students' Christian Journal* from November 1917 to May 1919, and *Christian China* from October 1919 on.

134. Editorials, *Liu Mei Tsing Nien* (October 1915): 5.

135. On fraternities, see Fass, pp. 139–67, and Alfred McClung Lee regarding the problem of racial discrimination by fraternities, in *Fraternities Without Brotherhood*.

136. On the history of CCH, see Wu Xiangxiang, pp. 143–59. On Cands, see the account of Hong Ye (Hung Yeh, English name William Hung), a founder of Cands and later a professor at Yanjing University. Hong once stole a deceased member's diary, which was believed to contain information about the fraternity (see Egan, p. 60).

137. See Fong, p. 25. Fong (Fang Xianting) remembered his first meeting with CCH, through the introduction of He Lian (Franklin Ho), a graduate student of economics at Yale. It was a week-long fraternity convention filled with nationalistic

rhetoric. Later "Brother Franklin" helped Fang to transfer to Yale and eventually also helped him find a job at the Economics Research Institute at Nankai University. Looking back years later, Fang believed that his experience with CCH had changed the course of his life.

138. Wu Xiangxiang believes that the reason Kong Xiangxi (H. H. Kung) recommended Jiang Tingfu to Chiang Kai-shek had something to do with the fact that both were CCH members (pp. 152–53).

139. In government service, there were, among others, Wang Chonghui, once the minister of foreign affairs; Kong Xiangxi, the minister of commerce; Wang Zhengting, acting prime minister and ambassador to the Soviet Union; Jiang Tingfu, ambassador to the Soviet Union; and Dong Xiankuang, ambassador to Japan and ambassador to the United States. In education, among others, there were Zhang Boling, the president of Nankai University; Zhou Yichun, the president of Qinghua University; Guo Bingwen, the president of the National Southeast University; Meng Zhi, the director of China Institute (based in New York); Lu Zhiwei, the president of Yanjing University; and Yan Yangchu (James Yen), the founder of the rural reconstruction movement in Dingxian County. In banking, there were Chen Guangfu, founder of the Shanghai Commercial Saving's Bank; Li Daonan, the general manager of the Communication Bank; and Bei Zuyi, the general manager of the China Bank and the president of the Central Bank. In business, there were Liu Hongsheng, one of the best-known industrialists in republican China; and Kears S. Chu and C. C. Lin. See ibid., pp. 154–58.

140. Among the people who did discuss their experiences with CCH were Fang Xianting and Hong Ye. See Fong, *Reminiscences of a Chinese Economist at 70*, and Egan, *A Latterday Confucian* (on Hong Ye).

141. Sinley Chang, "Is Fraternity Desirable among the Chinese Students?" *CSM* (January 1925): 26.

142. Pan Guangdan, "Evaluation of Chinese Student Fraternities in America," *CSM* (June 1925): 26–37.

143. Sources on *Dajiang hui*: Liang Shijiu, "Tan Wen Yiduo," pp. 359–435; Wen Liming, "Dajiang hui yanjiu"; and the journal *Dajiang jikan*.

144. Wen Liming, "Dajiang hui yanjiu" (unpublished article, page number unmarked).

145. *Guojia zhuji* was defined by these goals: free political development, free economic choice, and free cultural progress of the Chinese people. *Dajiang jikan* 1 (1924).

Chapter 2: The Professionals

1. Zhan Tianyou was a member of the Yung Wing educational mission and a Yale-trained engineer. On Zhan Tianyou (Jeme Tien Yau), see LaFargue, pp. 60, 108,

110, 111–13; and Mao Yisheng, "Zhongguo jiechu de aiguo gongchengshi Zhan Tianyou," pp. 638–44.

2. The majority of Zhan's fellow students did not stay in the United States long enough to either receive or complete a college education. Nor did the members on another major educational mission, sent to Europe by the Qing government in the 1880s and 1890s, obtain sufficient training. Only eight people in the Yung Wing mission completed their college education. On these people's occupations after they returned to China, see LaFargue, pp. 173–76. Among the eighty-four students sent to England, France, and Germany between 1876 and 1897, most of them studied military technology related subjects. Their overall performance after they returned home was rather unsatisfactory. On these students, see Y. C. Wang, pp. 45–49, 80, 85.

3. Tung-li Yuan, *A Guide to Doctoral Dissertations by Chinese Students in America*, pp. 1–239.

4. Y. C. Wang has discussions on the professional performance of both Japanese- and European-trained students (pp. 164–66).

5. Vera Schwarcz argues that the key to the emergence of a "modern intelligentsia" in China was their liberation from the civil service examination system. See Schwarcz, *The Chinese Enlightenment*, p. 292. The civil service examination system was formally abolished in 1905. After that the Qing government sponsored an annual examination for the students returned from foreign studies. On this examination, see Shang Yanliu, *Qingdai keju kaoshi shulu*; and "The Recent Imperial Metropolitan Examinations for Returned Students," by W. W. Yen.

6. On professionalization and professionalism, see Larson, *The Rise of Professionalism*; Vollmer and Mills, eds., *Professionalization*; and Terence J. Johnson, *Professions and Power*.

7. Liang Qichao, "Xindalu youji jielu," vol. 5, p. 130.

8. The imperial decree was recommended by Liang Dunyan, previously a student on the Yung Wing mission and currently the minister of foreign affairs. For more information on the role played by Liang Dunyan, see Yan Huiqing, *Yan Huiqing zizhuan*, pp. 54–56. Also see Su Yunfeng, pp. 16–17. Y. C. Wang mentions that the idea of having the majority of the students studying practical subjects came from a "censor" (p. 57).

9. Liu and Wang, p. 145.

10. Y. C. Wang, p. 58.

11. Not everybody who studied certain subjects in America would eventually work in the same field, of course. Hu Shi was a case in point; he originally majored in agriculture when he came to the United States.

12. Lin Zixun, pp. 56–65.

13. Hao Chang, *Chinese Intellectuals in Crisis*, p. 9.

14. See Elman, pp. 76–85.

15. See deBary, ed., *The Unfolding of Neo-Confucianism*, and deBary and Bloom, *Principle and Practicality*, introduction.

16. Beiyang University was founded in Tianjin in the 1890s. After 1949, the school's name was changed to Tianjin Daxue (Tianjin University).

17. Chinese Oral History Project, interview with Liu Chingshan (Liu Jingshan).

18. Y. C. Wang, p. 104.

19. A steady diversification can be discerned in the fields of study of the Qinghua students from 1909 to 1929 (data are taken from Y. C. Wang, p. 111):

FIELD OF STUDY	PERCENTAGE OF STUDENTS
Engineering	32.33%
Social sciences	23.84
Business	11.25
Science	10.99
Humanities	5.54
Medicine	5.19
Education	5.04
Agriculture	3.63
Military science	1.94
Music	0.25

20. Ibid.

21. Li Xisuo, *Jindai Zhongguo de liuxuesheng*, p. 225.

22. See Feuerwerker, "Economic Trends in the Late Ch'ing Empire" and "Economic Trends, 1912–49"; and Wellington K. K. Chan, "Government, Merchants, and Industry to 1911."

23. Ruby Sia, "China's Need of Industrial Education," *CSM* (March 1910): 300.

24. Y. S. Tsao, "The First Chinese National Exposition of Industry," *CSM* (April 1911): 536.

25. Editorial, "Indicia of China's Progress," *CSM* (April 1911): 533.

26. Ibid.

27. For an account of the "White City," see Trachtenberg, pp. 208–34.

28. *CSM* (January 1912): 246. A large number of articles published in the *Monthly* in the wake of the republican revolution were of a technical nature, bearing such titles as "Future Work for Geological Engineers in China," "Scientific Agriculture and Its Prospective in China," and so forth.

29. Y. Tsenshan Wang, "Our Hope and Our Task," *CSM* (June 1910): 535.

30. M. H. Li, "Industrial Development of China," *CSM* (April 1913): 406.

31. T. L. Li, "What Chinese Students Should Do When They Return," *CSM* (January 1919): 163.

32. M. H. Li, "The Social and Economic Significance of Technical Development," *CSM* (January 1914): 219.

33. T. L. Li, "What Chinese Students Should Do When They Return."

34. "The Prospects of Foresters in China," *CSM* (May 1912): 618–19.

35. John Wang, "China's Industries," *CSM* (May 1914): 540.

36. C. L. Wu, "The Importance of Chemical Engineering to China at Present," *CSM* (May 1918): 382.

37. Levenson, p. 43.

38. Loy Chang, "The Need of Experts," *CSM* (May 1916): 467.

39. K. T. May, "The New Chinese Scholar," *CSM* (May 1917): 342.

40. Ruby Sia, "Education for Efficiency," *CSM* (June 1910): 549.

41. T. L. Li, "Production, Profession, and Specialization," *CSM* (February 1917): 194.

42. "Vocational Education Narrows," *CSM* (June 1912): 642.

43. "Engineers Should Have Self-Respect," *CSM* (September 1914).

44. W. Way Tam, "Students' Problem of the Hour," *CSM* (January 1908): 113.

45. Thomas T. Read, "Future Work for Geological Engineers in China," *CSM* (March 1914): 383.

46. Terence J. Johnson, p. 17.

47. Bledstein, preface and p. 123.

48. Introduction to Furth, *Ting Wen-chiang*.

49. *Who's Who: American Returned Students*. The 340 people whose names appear in the directory included those from the late nineteenth century as well as those who studied in the twentieth century.

50. Y. C. Wang, p. 169.

51. *Who's Who*, p. ii.

52. Y. C. Wang, p. 172; see table 3. The American-trained in China in 1925: suitability of their preparation as measured by their occupations.

53. Interview with Wellington Koo, Widener Library Microforms, Harvard University, Cambridge, Mass., vol. 1, page unmarked.

54. Furth, *Ting Wen-ching*, p. 2.

55. "The Recent Examination in Nanking" (page number not available).

56. Ibid.

57. Chinese Oral History Project, interview with Liu Chingshan (Liu Jingshan).

58. Ibid.

59. On the examinations for returned students, see Y. C. Wang, pp. 68–71, and Liu and Wang, vol. 2, pp. 848–986.

60. In 1905, all fourteen were subsequently awarded titles and positions in the government.

61. Yen, pp. 34–39.

62. Larson, Introduction.

63. Tyau, "Educational Comments."

64. "The Returned Students and the Peking Examination," p. 388.

65. From 1914 to 1926, about 358 government scholarships were awarded to students in America and Europe. Chinese government fellowships abroad were subject to one great inconvenience: the failure of stipends to arrive on time. The delay first occurred during the 1911 republican revolutionary period. Financial difficulties

appeared again after 1917 as political chaos spread in China. In 1924, some government students petitioned to the people at home for help, after appealing in vain to their respective provincial governments and the Chinese Educational Bureau in Washington for financial assistance. Consequently, the director of the bureau resigned from his post and his agency was closed in 1925.

66. For details on how the Chinese government supervised Chinese students in America, see Y. C. Wang, p. 103.

67. On the relationship between the academic community and the Nationalist government, see E-Tu Zen Sun, "The Growth of the Academic Community."

68. Ren, "Jianli xuejie lun," 43–50.

69. Ibid.

70. T. L. Li, "Production, Profession, and Specialization," CSM (February 1917): 194.

71. T. L. Li, "What Chinese Students Should Do When They Return," CSM (January 1918): 163–67.

72. Nathaniel Peffer, "The Returned Students," CSM (April 1922): 498.

73. "The Returned Students," CSM (April 1922): 493.

74. Furth, Ting Wen-chiang, p. 55.

75. Kexue jishu tuanti shiliao; also see Yi Gongcheng, pp. 47–56.

76. Carr-Saunders and Wilson, p. 154.

77. Larson, Introduction.

78. See Kang, "Qiangxuehui xu," and Liang Qichao, "Lun xuehui."

79. Liang Qichao, "Lun xuehui."

80. Pingsa Hu, "Chinese Academy of Arts and Science," CSM (December 1910): 185–89.

81. See ibid., and "Constitution of the Academy," CSM (December 1910): 189–193.

82. "The Organization and Work of the 'Arts and Science Groups,'" CSM (March 1914): 436–41.

83. On the Science Society, see Li Xisuo, pp. 238–43; Buck, chap. 4; Daniel W. Y. Kwok, Scientism in Chinese Thought; and Huang Zhizheng, "Wusi shiqi liumei xuesheng dui kexue de chuanbo."

84. See Daniel W. Y. Kwok, chaps. 6 and 7.

85. Ibid., chap. 1.

86. Ibid., p. 199.

87. Ibid.

88. Ren Hongjun and Hu Shi are two examples.

89. A recent example of a well-argued article on the issue is by Wang Hui, "'Kexue zhuyi' yu shehui lilun de jige wenti."

90. The Chinese Chemical Society was founded in 1932. On the history of Western chemistry in China, see Reardon-Anderson, The Study of Change.

91. On the history of the society, see Zhong Shaohua, "Zhongguo gongcheng-

shi xuehui"; *Kexue jishu tuanti shiliao*, pp. 213–35; Mao Yisheng, "Zhongguo gongchengshi xuehui jianshi"; and Hu Guangbiao, *Bozhu liushinian*, pp. 163–64.

92. China's Engineers' Society was founded in 1912 by Zhan Tianyou and other established people in the engineering profession. The two societies' names are extremely similar in both English and Chinese. In Chinese, the one founded in China was called *Zhonghua gongchengshi xuehui*, whereas the one founded in America was *Zhongguo gongchengshi xuehui*.

93. Mao Yisheng, "Zhongguo gongchengshi xuehui jianshi," p. 427.

94. "Zhongguo gongchengshi xintiao," (Rules for Chinese engineers), in *Kexue jishu tuanti shiliao*, p. 235.

95. Chen Lifu, Xu Enzeng, and Zeng Yangfu, all ranking Nationalist officials, were involved in the activities of the society.

96. Both Chen Lifu and Zeng Yangfu were elected as presidents during the wartime period, Zeng in both 1937 and 1938 and Chen in 1939. Chen was the general secretary of the Nationalist Party and Zeng was at one point the minister of transportation.

97. E-tu Ren Sun, "The Growth of the Academic Community," p. 388.

98. See "Zhongguo gongcheng xuehui zongzhang" (The general regulations of China's Engineers' Society), in *Kexue jishu tuanti shiliao*, chap. 8, "Finance." A member was supposed to pay a membership fee of three dollars at the time of joining the society and an annual fee of two dollars every year. It is hard to tell if this policy was effectively enforced. No available information indicates that the Society had other sources of income, either from the government or from international foundations. The Rockefeller Foundation helped the Chinese Chemical Society financially in 1938, but no record indicates that the foundation helped China's Engineers' Society. See the Rockefeller Foundation Archives, Record Group, 1.1 Projects, Inventory, ser. 601, China, no. 18.

99. William Kirby addresses the issue of the roles of engineers and their relationship with the state in the Nationalist period in his article "Engineering China," pp. 149–50.

100. See Larson, Introduction.

101. Philip C. C. Huang, "Public Sphere/Civil Society in China?"

102. Y. C. Wang, pp. 173–74.

103. D. Hoe Lee, "The Chinese Students of American Agriculture," *CSM* (April 1918): 333.

104. Although Hu Shi was always interested in history and philosophy, what finally made him decide to leave agriculture was a course he took on pomology. This course taught, among other things, how to categorize apples. One week, the students were asked to label thirty apples. Without much difficulty, the American students quickly finished the assignment, leaving the three Chinese students, Hu Shi included, to struggle with the fruits. After this episode, Hu Shi began to wonder: what was the point of remembering "four hundred different kinds of apples," most

of which did not even exist in China? This episode ended Hu Shi's training in agriculture. See Tang Degang, trans., pp. 180–81.

105. Stross, p. 195. In Shen's case, some of the most important crops in China—rice, sorghum, millet, and sugar beets, were rarely grown in the United States and hence were little studied. On Shen, also see Shen Tsung-han, *Autobiography of a Chinese Farmer's Servant*.

106. On the history of sociology in China, see Sun Benwen, *Dangdai zhongguo shehuixue*; Xu Shilian, "Zhongguo shehuixue yundong de mubiao jingguo he fanwei"; Leonard Shi-lien Hsu (Xu Shilian), "The Sociological Movement in China"; Cai Yucong, "Zhongguo shehuixue fazhanshi shang de sige shiqi"; Han Mingmo, *Zhongguo shehui xueshi*; Siu-lun Wong, *Sociology and Socialism in Contemporary China*.

107. Sun Benwen, *Dangdai zhongguo shehuixue*, p. 300.

108. Arkush, p. 26.

109. In 1901, Yan Fu translated Herbert Spencer's book *Study of Sociology* and gave it a Chinese title, *Qunxue*. The concept of *qun* came from Xun Zi, a Confucianist thinker of more than two thousand years ago.

110. In 1902, Zhang Binglin, a provocative thinker and a radical anti-Manchu activist, translated a sociological work from Japanese. He adopted the Japanese translation of "sociology," *shehuixue*.

111. On the influence of Japanese translations of Western terms, see Lydia Liu, *Translingual Practice*.

112. The first Chinese person to join the ranks of missionary teachers was Zhu Youyu (Y. Y. Tsu), who earned a Ph.D. in sociology from Columbia University in 1912 (Zhu later became an Episcopal bishop). The teaching of sociology at the Christian colleges was often connected with social work and served evangelical ends.

113. The first sociological work written by a Chinese author was *Chinese Village and City Life*, coauthored by the British-trained Tao Menhe and Liang Yukao, published in 1915 in English.

114. Two representative works are Yi Jiayue and Luo Dunwei, *Zhongguo jiating wenti* (1922), and Chen Dongyuan, *Zhongguo funü shenghuoshi* (1928).

115. Han, pp. 51–52.

116. Siu-lun Wong, "Zhongguo jiefangqian shehuixue de chengzhang," p. 189.

117. "Wu Wenzao zizhuan," p. 44: "All the May Fourth ideas, such as nationalism, democracy, science, made me interested in social and political theories, and later became important factors in my decision to study sociology."

118. Pan Guangdan (1899–1967) studied eugenics, among other subjects, while in America. He was an authority on eugenics in China and was very active in the sociology circle after returning to China. Wu Zelin was interested in the study of Chinese ethnic minorities after returning to China and was a pioneer in setting up museums of minority cultures. Wu Jingchao was also a well-known sociologist.

119. The society was named *dongnan shehui xueshe* (the Southeast Sociology

Society). A professional journal, *Dongnan shehui xuekan*, was published the following year.

120. Besides *Shehuixue kan* (The journal of sociology), there were other professional journals, such as *Shehuixue jie* (Sociology world), published by the sociology department of Yanjing University.

121. By 1930, there were eleven universities that had independent sociology departments. In another five universities, sociology was taught along with other academic subjects. Altogether, sixteen universities either had sociology departments or offered courses on sociology. The number remained unchanged in the next decade. Another period of growth was in the 1940s.

122. Siu-lun Wong, "Zhongguo jiefangqian shehuixue de chengzhang," p. 191.

123. Fei and Chang, *Earthbound China*, p. ix.

124. At the end of the period, in 1948, of the 119 instructors (professors, associate professors, and lecturers), all but five were Chinese.

125. Sun Benwen, *Shehuixue yuanli*.

126. Han Mingmo, p. 130.

127. Ibid., p. 144.

128. Chen Da, *Xiandai Zhongguo rengou*.

129. Li Jinghan, *Shidi shehui diaocha fangfa*, preface.

130. On Fei Xiaotong, see Arkush, *Fei Xiaotong and Sociology in Revolutionary China*; the introduction to McGough, *Fei Hsiao-tung: The Dilemma of a Chinese Intellectual*; Fei Xiaotong and Chih-i Chang, *From the Soil: The Foundations of Chinese Society* (see the translators' introduction); and Fei Xiaotong, "The Study of Man in China—Personal Experience," pp. 9–20.

131. Wu Wenzao, "zizhuan."

132. Ibid., p. 45.

133. Wu's teaching at Yanjing ended in 1938, after the Sino-Japanese War began.

134. On Yanjing, see West, *Yenching University and Sino-Western Relations*.

135. Chiang Yung-chen, "Social Engineering and Social Sciences in China."

136. Ibid., p. 100.

137. Xie Bingxin, "Wode laoban Wu Wenzao," p. 8.

138. As a sociology major at Yanjing in the early 1930s, Fei was not pleased with the way sociology was taught. He writes: "A number of our teachers understood and sympathized with our [Fei and his fellow students] dissatisfaction. Together we proposed the establishment of a Chinese sociology." See Fei, "Chongjian shehuixue de youyi jieduan," pp. 42–43.

139. Wu Wenzao, "zizhuan," p. 48.

140. Park and Radcliffe-Brown, both from University of Chicago, came to lecture in China in 1932 and 1935, respectively. In a recent article, Fei Xiaotong describes the influence of Park on him (Fei, "Wo you zhao daole paike laoshi").

141. Quoted by Chiang Yung-chen, p. 100.

142. Among these people were Li Anchai (Li An-che), Hsu Yung-shun (class of

1932, Ph.D. at the University of Minnesota in 1943), Yang Qingkun (Yang Ching-kun, class of 1933, Ph.D. at the University of Michigan in 1940, professor emeritus at the University of Pittsburgh), Lin Yaohua (class of 1932, Ph.D. at Harvard in 1940). See Wu Wenzao, "zizhuan," p. 47; Chiang Yung-chen, p. 100.

143. In his Ph.D. thesis, "Social Engineering and Social Sciences in China," Chiang Yung-chen argues that American philanthropic foundations, particularly the Rockefeller Foundation, largely dictated the research agenda and methodology for the Chinese social scientists in the republican period, by encouraging them to study rural China and by pressing them to adopt an empirical approach. The two case studies Chiang conducted are the "social service wing" of the Yanjing University's sociology department and the Naikai Institute of Economics. Chiang has made a convincing argument on the two cases, but a general conclusion can not be drawn regarding the roles played by American philanthropic foundations on the research agenda and methodology of China's social sciences in the republican period. The China Program of the Rockefeller Foundation did not help Wu until after the war broke out. Their aid had been focused on the "social service wing" in the sociology department at Yanjing. See Chiang Yung-chen, p. 126.

144. Fei Xiaotong, "The Study of Man in China—Personal Experience."

145. On Yanyang Chu and the rural reconstruction movement, see Hayford, *To the People.*

146. Chiang Yung-chen, p. 281.

147. Han Mingmo, p. 4, quoting Sun Benwen's *Dangdai zhongguo shehuixue.*

148. Wu Wenzao, for instance, was familiar with Marxism but, as he wrote in his autobiography, he "did not have a correct understanding of the historical material-ism from the very beginning" and did not use Marxism in his research. See Wu Wenzao, "zizhuan," p. 45.

149. Feuerwerker, "Economic Trends," p. 63.

150. For instance, sociology basically disappeared as an academic discipline in China after 1952. In 1957, many famous sociologists, including almost everyone dis-cussed in my text, were labeled as "rightists." Sociology as a discipline was revived only in the early 1980s. In the Epilogue, I will discuss the predicament of sociology in the 1950s.

151. During the "antirightist" campaign in 1957, for instance, those people who advocated *waihang buneng lingdao neihang* ("people without professional knowledge can not supervise the professional know-how") were severely criticized.

Chapter 3: The Question of Race

1. See Liang Shiqiu, "Tan Wen Yiduo."

2. On this issue, and the role played by science, see, for instance, Gossett, *Race: The History of an Idea in America*; Banton and Harwood, eds., *The Race Concept*;

Banton, *Racial Consciousness*; Stepan, *The Idea of Race in Science: Great Britain*; and Leo Kuper, ed., *Race, Science, and Society*. Michael Banton points out, for instance, that though physical differences have existed among groups of humans since time immemorial, "it is only within the last two centuries that these differences have been conceptualized as racial" (*Racial Consciousness*, p. 16).

3. See, for instance, Gossett's assessment of Darwin's contribution to modern race theory: "Darwin changed the basis of race theory, but he did not change the argument that some races are superior to others" (p. 67). Banton and Harwood's, and Stepan's books also have sections on Darwin and about how Darwinism affected people's thinking on race. See Stepan, chap. 3, "Evolution and Race: An Incomplete Revolution," pp. 47–82; and Banton and Harwood, eds., p. 31.

4. Seen in the light of the Western origin of "race" in modern times, the recent work by Frank Dikötter on the "discourse of race" in modern China errs precisely because it fails to recognize this key element in the evolution of the modern notion of "race." See Dikötter, *The Discourse of Race in Modern China*. The problems notwithstanding, Dikötter's book is an important pioneering study on the issue of race in modern China. Also see Dikötter, *The Construction of Race in China and Japan*.

5. Ten exempt classes of Chinese, who were not considered a threat to the employment of white Americans, were given admission to the United States. These included: (1) teachers, ministers, missionaries of religious denominations, newspaper editors, and other public instructors; (2) students; (3) people traveling for curiosity or pleasure; (4) merchants and their lawful wives and minor children; (5) government officials, their families, attendants, servants, and employees; (6) Chinese previously lawfully and permanently admitted to the United States returning from temporary visits abroad; (7) Chinese in continuous transit; (8) Chinese born in this country and their children; (9) Chinese citizens lawfully admitted to the United States who later went in transit from one part of the United States to another through foreign contiguous territory; (10) bona fide seamen. See Shih-Shan Henry Tsai, *The Chinese Experience in America*, p. 66.

6. "A Problem," *CSM* (November 1909): 5.

7. Tan Sitong, "Views on the Management of World Affairs" (1889), cited by Dikotter, in *The Discourse of Race*, p. 50; and Liang Qichao, "Xin Shixue" (New historiography), also mentioned by Dikotter, p. 76. Hao Chang discusses at length Liang's thinking on race; see Chang, *Liang Ch'i-ch'ao and Intellectual Transition in China*, pp. 159–62.

8. Dikötter, *The Discourse of Race*, p. 55.

9. Ibid., chap. 1.

10. See Wang Fuzhi, "Huang Shu," written in 1656. This is what Wang said about the differences between the Chinese and the "barbarians": "Chinese and barbarians are born in different places, which brings about the differences in their

atmosphere, which in turn are responsible for the differences in their customs, when their customs are different, their understanding and behavior are all different." Dikötter's translation in *The Discourse of Race*, p. 27.

11. Hao Chang discusses the influences on Chinese intellectuals of both the sinocentric view of world order and the Confucian idea of universal harmony. See Chang, *Liang Ch'i-ch'ao and Intellectual Transition in China*, pp. 157–58.

12. Dikötter, *The Discourse of Race*; see "Race and Cultural—Historical Background," pp. 1–17. I am not convinced by Dikötter's argument. The classical works he refers to, such as *Zuozhuan*, *Shanhaijing* and *Shijing*, contain passages that demand more careful reading. For instance, Dikötter translates the line "fei wo zulei, qi xin bi yi" (*Zhozhuan*) into the following sentence: "If he is not of our race, he is sure to have a different mind" (p. 3). "Race," a modern concept, is not appropriately used in a fourth-century-B.C. Chinese text.

13. Dikötter's argument that "the development of a racial consciousness during the nineteenth century was due largely to internal development [in China]" (Dikötter, *The Discourse of Race*, p. 34) evidently minimizes the impact of an aggressive West in China.

14. Leo Kuper argues for the importance of "the right to define" in a racial relationship: "the person who defines the issues, thereby assumes the initiative, driving the opponent into a defensive position; power consists in originating definitions, and in making them socially effective." Kuper, ed., p. 14.

15. Dikötter argues that the Chinese largely misunderstood both Darwinism and social Darwinism. Dikötter is right in saying that "Chinese intellectuals received the theory of evolution in a social-political context very different from that of the West. They operated within a symbolic universe that led them to reinforce different aspects of the evolutionary paradigm." Dikötter, *The Discourse of Race*, pp. 100–101.

16. On anti-Chinese acts and practices, see Tsai, *China and the Overseas Chinese in the United States*, p. 60, and *The Chinese Experience in America*, pp. 67–72; Jack Chen, *The Chinese of America*; Sung, *The Story of the Chinese in America*; and Sucheng Chan, *Entry Denied*. On the role of organized labor on anti-Chinese agitation and activity, see Saxton, *The Indispensable Enemy*.

17. See Miller, *The Unwelcome Immigrant*.

18. See, for instance, Banton, *Racial Consciousness*, pp. 16–21, and Daniels and Kitano, pp. 35–45. The 1850s have been identified as the decade in which theories of "scientific racism" were first advanced, and a new concept of race as type popularized. See Banton, *Racial Consciousness*, p. 19.

19. Jones, pp. 31–36.

20. On Fu Manchu and Chinese image in American popular culture, see Cheng-tsu Wu, ed., p. 136; and especially Dorothy B. Jones's well-researched study, *The Portrayal of China and India on the American Screen*, pp. 18–19, 30–31.

21. William Wu, pp. 164–206.

22. "The Chinaman's Queue," *CSM* (April 1915): 409.

23. Cai Zheng, "Lümei Wenjian," p. 126.

24. "Going Through College," *CSM* (December 1925): 45.

25. LaFargue, pp. 36–52.

26. McKee, *Chinese Exclusion Versus the Open Door Policy*, chap. 3.

27. Chinese Oral History Project, interview with Chen Kuang-fu (Chen Guangfu) (December 1960–June 1961).

28. Tsai, *The Chinese Experience in America*, p. 78.

29. On the 1905 boycott, see McKee, pp. 67 and 216–17; and Tsai, *The Chinese Experience in America*, pp. 77–79.

30. See Miner, pp. 984–88; also see McKee, pp. 69–71. Recently, Kong's experience has attracted the attention in both mainland China and Taiwan. See Zhang Jianhua, "Cong aobolin dao mingxian"; Zhang Ruohua, "Rujia zidi yangjiaotu"; and Zhou Gu, "Kong Xiangxi Fei Qihe fumei liuxue beiju rujing jingguo."

31. McKee, p. 94.

32. F. C. Yen, "The Alliance and the Students Coming to America," *CSM* (November 1907): 77–79.

33. McKee, p. 94.

34. Ibid. p. 43.

35. Ibid. p. 104.

36. Ibid.

37. Hunt, *The Making of a Special Relationship*, pp. 5–40, 116–43, and 185–298.

38. On Roosevelt's attitude toward Chinese exclusion, see ibid., pp. 241–249, and Tsai, *The Chinese Experience in America*, p. 79.

39. Rose Hum Lee, *The Chinese in the United States of America*, chap. 5.

40. The new regulations required students to be over fifteen years of age and to have credentials of acceptance by an American institution of higher learning at the time of landing (ibid., chap. 6). The exclusion legislation in 1924 not only specified a student's age and level of education upon arriving in the country, but also required the student's institution, which had to be an accredited college, to keep the government informed of the student's academic progress. The students were also forbidden to have practical training in industrial plants upon graduation. The Chinese Ministry of Education quickly reacted to these provisions by issuing a memorandum instructing provinces to send their scholarship students to countries other than America, although the memorandum was not vigorously enforced and had little practical effect. See Y. C. Wang, p. 115. On the Chinese students' reaction to the restriction on practical training in industrial plants, see Chao Ying Shill, "The Effect of the Immigration Bill of 1924 on Chinese Students," *CSM* (December 1924): 16–19.

41. Lin Zixuan, p. 279.

42. Chen Da, p. 188.

43. Chinese Oral History Project, interview with Chen Kuang-fu.

44. Ibid.

45. Li and Chang, eds., *Jindai Zhongguo nüguan yundong shiliao*, p. 1253.

46. Cai Zheng, p. 129.

47. Cao Ting, "Nanmei liuxue yutan," p. 91.

48. *Foreign Students in America*; see "Introduction and Summary."

49. Alfred E. Stearns, "Chinese Students and the American People," *CSM* (November 1907): 15.

50. "American Conception of the Chinese," *CSM* (April 1912): 531. Note that in the students' opinion, even the "intelligent class" could not get the basic facts right, like the names of important political figures such as Yuan Shikai and Sun Yat-sen.

51. Editorial, *CSM* (February 1925): 1.

52. Ibid.

53. Hsiao Chuan Chang, "Why I Left the University of Michigan," *CSM* (February 1925): 31.

54. Tsai, *The Chinese Experience in America*, p. xi.

55. See Chinese Oral History Project, interview with Kuang Hsian-hsi (Kong Xiangxi), 1958. In this interview, Kong did not mention the mistreatment he received when he first arrived in the United States in 1901.

56. Cai Zheng, pp. 124–32.

57. Cao Ting, p. 95.

58. Loewen, *The Mississippi Chinese*.

59. Chen Hengzhe, "Zhi mounüshi shu."

60. John Yiubong Lee, "Can We Help Our Countrymen in the United States?" *CSM* (March 1910): 292–99.

61. Hu Shi's diary has no account of his contact with the resident Chinese, nor his observations of their situation.

62. Yuen Ren Chao, *Life with Chaos*.

63. Chiang Monlin, *Tides from the West*, p. 86.

64. Bingxin, *Ji xiaoduzhe*, pp. 88–89.

65. Liang Shiqiu, "Tanren zi he chu lai," pp. 79–81.

66. Cao Ting, p. 95.

67. Chinese Oral History Project, interview with Chen Guangfu.

68. "Do Chinatown[s] Deserve Attack?" *CSM* (December 1910): 162–64.

69. Chiang Monlin, p. 70.

70. "On Chinese Immigration," *CSM* (January 1910): 149.

71. See, for instance, Y. C. Ma, "The Problem of Chinese Immigration into the United States and Its Possible Solution," *CSM* (February 1912): 333–43.

72. S. H. Kee, "The Chinese: A Social Entity in America," *CSM* (May 1912): 602–11.

73. In *Hu Shih and the Chinese Renaissance*, Jerome B. Grieder discusses the cosmopolitan movement and Hu Shi's involvement in the movement (pp. 52–61).

74. Hu Shi, *Hu Shi liuxue riji*, vol. 2, pp. 501–2.

75. On the two female students, see ibid., pp. 425–26.

76. See Patterson's scrapbooks, Cornell University Archives.

77. Editorial, "A Problem," *CSM* (November 1909): 5.

78. Ibid.

79. John Yiubong Lee, "Can We Help Our Countrymen in the United States?" *CSM* (March 1910): 292.

80. Kung Chao Chu, "To the Editor-in-Chief of the *Monthly*," CSM (December 1909): 131–32.

81. Mrs. Harry E. Mitchell, "What Can We Do for Our Working Class?" *CSM* (February 1910): 221–23.

82. Crunden, *Ministers of Reform*, prologue and pp. 23–25. Crunden argues that one important legacy of progressivism was its essentially religious character. People like Jane Addams, the famous Chicago Hull House settlement leader, were impelled by an ethical and religious drive to seek a moral and secular democracy in this world.

83. Lui-ngau Chang, "Working for China's Welfare Abroad," *CSM* (June 1910): 544–48.

84. "Boston Tech" was then a commonly used name for the Massachusetts Institute of Technology.

85. Benedict Anderson, in his book *Imagined Communities*, discusses the importance of a common language in binding people together. See p. 154.

86. "Report of the General Welfare Association of Boston," *CSM* (May 1910): 419–29.

87. On the study of Chinese political activities in Chinese communities in America, see L. Eve Armentrout Ma, *Revolutionaries, Monarchists and Chinatown: Chinese Politics in the Americas and the 1911 Revolution*; Tsai, "Chinese Political Activities in America," in *The Chinese Experience in America*, pp. 90–94; and Tsai, *China and the Overseas Chinese in the United States*.

88. During Sun Yat-sen's visit to America (1909–11), a chapter of the Tongmenghui was established in Boston, among other cities. See Tsai, *The Chinese Experience in America*, p. 95. According to Liang Qichao's travel journal in 1903, a Reform Party branch had already been founded before Liang's visit. See Tsai, *China and the Overseas Chinese in the United States*, p. 132. Tsai argues in *The Chinese Experience in America* that after the death of Emperor Guangxu, the influence of the Reform Party began to decline even among the reform leaders in Chinese communities.

89. "Report of the General Welfare Association of Boston."

90. Ibid.

91. Ibid.

92. See, for instance, the *Monthly* editorial "Objections Against the Coming of Chinese Laborers": "The Chinese laborers have also been accused of indifference to the laws of hygiene and of living in ways to defy sanitation. Much of this we believe to be true." *CSM* (March 1910): p. 254.

93. He Maoqing, "Boshidun gongyishe baogao."

94. Ibid.

95. "A Report of the General Welfare School in New York," *CSM* (January 1911): 287–91.

96. I have not been able to locate any information about the political association of the students with the people in New York's Chinatown. The only information published in the *CSM* about the Philadelphia school was that it was in need of funding. See "The Philadelphia General Welfare School," *CSM* (January 1911): 304.

97. "The Chinese Laborers in America," pp. 111–14.

98. Be Di Lee, "Social Work Among Chinese Women in Pittsburgh," *CSM* (February 1919): 263–64. Besides interviewing people, Lee did not mention what else she had done, though she claimed that she had gained respect from the local Chinese women in Pittsburgh.

99. Y. C. Yang, "The Boy Scouts of America," *CSM* (March 1916): 337–42.

100. H. C. Chen, "The Chinese Boy Scouts in New York," *CSM* (March 1918): 269–72. Also see Chen Heqin, *Wo de bansheng*, p. 189.

101. I have not been able to locate records of these welfare associations from other sources.

102. In his article written in spring 1921, Zhong Beiying suggested a number of ways to help the immigrants, including establishing public entertainment places, savings banks, publishing vernacular language newspapers, and setting up schools. There is no evidence that any of these projects was pursued. See Zhong Beiying, "Liumei xuesheng ying ruhe fuzhu huaqiao."

103. Hsu Kai-yu, *Wen-I-to*, p. 61.

104. Dikötter, *The Discourse of Race*, p. 157.

105. See Wen and Hou, eds., *Wen Yiduo nianpu changbian*, pp. 203–4. The writers discuss Wen's effort to combine the best from Chinese tradition and Western culture to create the new Chinese poetry.

106. Ibid., p. 193.

107. Ibid., p. 242. What Wen Yiduo said, allegedly, was the following: "I don't know how much America has changed now. But things were like that then! I, knowing how to avoid unpleasantness, always shut myself up inside to read and paint, seldom going out. I would rather eat cold bread and wear long hair than be bullied."

108. Ibid., pp. 167–69. The article was published in *Qinghua Weekly* 248 (19 May 1922).

109. Ibid., p. 183.

110. Hsu Kai-yu, p. 64. The translation is Hsu's.

111. Liang Shiqiu, who recorded the incident, held that Wen was not among the six people. However, he was there to observe the humiliating scene and was greatly enraged by it. See Liang, "Tan Wen Yiduo." In *Wen Yiduo nianpu changbian*, the authors insist that Wen was a member of the graduating class that year and presumably should be marching in the parade (Wen and Hou, eds., p. 241). There is no account by Wen himself on this event.

112. Liang Shiqiu, "Tan Wen Yiduo," pp. 386, 391.

113. The poem is translated by Hsu Kai-yu. See Hsu, pp. 78–79.

114. Wen and Hou, eds., p. 273.

115. Liang Shiqiu, "Gongli," and Hu Yi, "Beimei paihua liüshi," are among the articles on the subject.

116. Charles Ling Wu (Wu Zelin), "Attitude Toward Negroes, Jews, and Orientals in the United States."

117. Ibid.

118. Ibid.

119. Editorial, "Objections Against the Coming of Chinese Laborers," *CSM* (March 1910): 253.

120. Wu Zelin, *Xiandai zhongzu.*

121. Ibid., pp. 1–3.

122. Ibid., p. 55. Boas pointed out the importance of environment on the shape of the heads of the American-born immigrant children from Southern and Eastern Europe.

123. Ibid., pp. 45–71.

124. Ibid., pp. 137–45.

125. Ibid., p. 153.

126. On Franz Boas's contribution, see Banton and Harwood, eds., p. 44, and Gossett, p. 429.

127. For a discussion of the shift in the academic disciplines in America, see Gossett, pp. 409–18. Gossett mentions that Franz Boas, an authority in several academic fields, was a key figure in challenging racist theories (p. 418). Among the twelve "important" books cited by Wu Zelin, all by Western scholars, however, none was written by Boas.

128. Pan Guangdan, "Jieshao Wu Zelin xiansheng de *xiandai zhongzu*," (Introducing Mr. Wu Zelin's *Modern Races*), in Wu, *Xiandai zhongzu.* Two articles published in 1932 appear in Pan Guangdan, *Minzu yanjiu wenji*, pp. 16–21.

129. Pan's interest in the study of sexuality can be traced back to his student days at Qinghua, when he read Havelock Ellis's *Studies in the Psychology of Sex.*

130. In chapter 1 of Yuehtsen Juliette Chung's dissertation, she discusses eugenics and its variations in Britain, America, Germany, and France. See Chung, "Struggle for National Survival," pp. 1–4.

131. For a discussion of eugenics, see Dikötter, *Imperfect Conceptions*, pp. 164–65; Gossett, pp. 155–60; and Banton and Harwood, eds., p. 39.

132. Chung, p. 1.

133. Dikötter points out that in the West, eugenics drew little criticism until the mid 1930s. It was the cruelty of Nazi policies that eventually led to a strong reaction, supported by a long-standing and influential anti-eugenics coalition among people both of secular and religious backgrounds; see Dikötter, *Imperfect Conceptions*, p. 187. Also see Kevles, *In the Name of Eugenics.*

134. Chung, pp. 7–15 and chap. 4.

135. Before the term *yousheng xue* was settled on, it was also translated as *shanzhong xue* and *shuzhong xue*.

136. *Yousheng xue* can be translated as "the improvement of birth." See Chung, pp. 89–90. On how *yousheng xue* is understood in contemporary China, see Qiu Renzong, "Cultural and Ethical Dimensions of Genetic Practices in China."

137. See Dikötter, *Imperfect Conceptions*, chap. 6, "Race as Seed (1915–1949)," pp. 164–90.

138. Chung contends that "the May Fourth intellectuals tended to present the Chinese civilization and physique as overripe and declining." Both Chen Duxiu and Lu Xun, among others, helped to construct a "degeneration discourse." In this context, eugenics ideas became a possible source of inspiration for national salvation. Zhou Jianren, Lu Xun's younger brother and a Japanese-returned student, was particularly prominent on this subject; he translated a series of biology-and-eugenics-related topics and urged that basic eugenic knowledge of inheritance of genetic defectiveness and the danger of kin marriage be disseminated through sexual education among young people (Chung, pp. 94 and 172). Also see Dikötter, *Imperfect Conceptions*.

139. According to Dikötter, Pan became interested in eugenics as a student at Qinghua. However, I have found no evidence to support this assertion. See Dikötter, *Imperfect Conceptions*, p. 174.

140. Wen and Hou, eds., p. 246.

141. One of Pan's earliest articles on eugenics is called "Yousheng gailun" (On eugenics), originally published in the *Quarterly*, in which Pan divided the eugenic movement into three schools. The first and second schools were described by him as closely related to social reform (see Pan Naimu, ed., p. 256). The article was published in the *Quarterly* 11, no. 4 (May 1927): 51–70. Dikötter analyzes Pan's thinking on the subject; see *The Discourse of Race*, p. 176. Yuehtsen Juliette Chung also analyzes Pan's ideas; see Chung, chap. 4.

142. Although Pan generally regarded the intellectual class as superior, he did state in one article that the inherited quality of the Chinese peasants was not bad. See "Xihua dongjian ji Zhongguo zhi yousheng wenti," in Pan Naimu, ed., vol. 1, p. 279. The article was originally published in the *Eastern Miscellany* 21, no. 22.

143. Pan Guangdan, "Jindai zhongzu zhuyi shilüe." This article is collected in Pan Naimu, ed., pp. 367–89.

144. Ibid., p. 385.

145. Ibid., pp. 384–88.

146. Their friend Wu Wenzao was also interested in issues of race and ethnicity. Wu examined the issues in his first scholarly paper, titled "Minzu yu guojia" (Ethnicity and nation), published in the *Quarterly*. It is collected in Wu Wenzao, *Renleixue shehuixue yanjiu wenji*.

147. Fei Xiaotong, "Zai rensheng de tianping shang."

148. See Chung, p. 102.

149. For an analysis of Pan's ideas, see ibid., pp. 96–97 and chaps. 4, 5, 6.

150. Ibid., pp. 97 and 355.

151. On Pan's ideas on race and ethnicity, see Pan Guangdan, *Pan Guangdan minzu yanjiu wenji*. Recently, more works of Pan Guangdan have been reprinted that contain relevant information. See Pan Naihe and Pan Naigu, eds., *Pan Guangdan xuanji*.

152. Another work Pan embarked upon in the 1950s was the translation of Charles Darwin's *The Descent of Man* into Chinese, which he completed in early 1966. It was only published in the early 1980s because of the ensuing Cultural Revolution. When the Cultural Revolution broke out, Pan at first was able to maintain a stable spirit. He told a friend that his philosophy was three Ss: submit, sustain, and survive. But things continued to get worse and his suffering became unbearable (handicapped with only one leg, he nonetheless had to do very hard menial labor). The last time his friend saw him, he was lying unattended in a hospital bed. The friend tried to use his own words to cheer him up, but he only replied, with just one S: succumb. He died a few days later.

153. After 1952, a number of American-educated sociologists, including Wu Zelin, Pan Guangdan, and Wu Wenzao, were all assigned to work in the Central Institute of Chinese Minority Nationalities in Beijing. Wu Zelin first worked at the Institute of Chinese Minority Nationalities in Chengdu, and then in Wuhan.

Chapter 4: The Women's Story

1. There has been some confusion regarding the spelling of Jin Yunmei's English name and the writing of her Chinese name. I take her Chinese name from K. Chimin Wong and Wu Lien-teh's book *History of Chinese Medicine*, p. 889.

2. Information on Jin Yunmei is scattered. I have drawn information mainly from the following sources: Sia, p. 85; Loy Chang, "Dr. Yamei King, the Story of a Chinese Woman Doctor," *CSM* (March 1911): 479; F. Y. Tsao, "A Brief History of Chinese Women Students in America," *CSM* (May 1911): 619; Kin, p. 101; Zhu Jineng, pp. 11–15; Li and Chang, eds., pp. 1386–88; Wong and Wu, p. 347; Latourette, p. 459; Choa, *Heal the Sick*, pp. 81 and 129.

3. Li Bi Cu, a graduate of the Philadelphia Woman's Medical College, could also have studied medicine in America during this early period. She was practicing medicine in Woocheng, Fujian, around 1911. However, little is known about her. See Tsao, pp. 219–20.

4. The figure of around two hundred is gathered from statistics in contemporary Chinese students' publications. This figure suggests that Y. C. Wang's figure of over six hundred in 1925 is much exaggerated. See Y. C. Wang, p. 73.

5. In her recent book, *Women and the Chinese Enlightenment*, Wang Zheng discusses the emergence of career women in the wake of the May Fourth Movement.

6. I am indebted to Ryan Dunch for the correct Chinese name of Xu Jinhong.

7. In the book *Heal the Sick* (p. 82), G. Choa provides a different Chinese name, Gan Jiehou, for Ida Kahn. In missionary writings, there is an indication that her last name is Kong; see *Encyclopedia of World Methodism*, vol. 1, p. 1305. Not being able to verify which name is correct, I still use Kang Aide as her Chinese name in this text.

8. On the history of medical education for American women, see, among other books, Walsh, chaps. 5 and 6.

9. On female higher education in this period, see Solomon, p. 95.

10. Information on Xu Jinhong is sketchy. I gathered my material from Burton, *Notable Women of Modern China*, pp. 15–57; Sia, "Chinese Women Educated Abroad;" Tsao, "Brief History of Chinese Women Students"; and Zhu Jineng, "Jiawu zhanqian siwei nüliuxuesheng." I have also been helped a great deal by Ryan Dunch, who, in his letter to me dated July 18, 1995, provided some very interesting and useful information on Xu Jinhong, her family (especially her father), and the Fuzhou Methodist Church. Ryan was writing his dissertation at Yale University on Chinese Protestants in the Fuzhou area from 1850 to 1927. Mary Stone's (Shi Meiyu) papers can be found at the General Commission on Archives and History, the United Methodist Church, Madison, N.J. Also, in Margaret Burton's book *Notable Women*, there is a chapter on Stone. Ida Kahn's (Kang Aide) papers are kept at the same archives in Madison. In Burton's book, there is also a chapter on Kang.

11. Missionary publications commonly described Ida Kahn's adoption as follows: when little Ida was born to a family in which there were already five daughters, a fortune teller told her parents that she must be killed or given to another family. Hearing about this, Gertrude Howe went to Ida's parents and offered to adopt her. Gertrude Howe eventually adopted three other Chinese girls. See Burton, *Notable Women*, pp. 115–16, and Amy Gifford Lewis, "Dr. Ida Kahn—Nanchang, China."

12. Jane Hunter discusses the subject of the relationship between missionaries and their adopted Chinese children in *The Gospel of Gentility*, p. 194. It was not uncommon around this time for missionaries to adopt Chinese children but not to raise them themselves. Presumably, they hired others to take care of the children.

13. Jin spent several years of her childhood in Japan with her foster parents and came to the United States for her education at sixteen.

14. On this subject, see Paul Varg, *Missionaries, Chinese, and Diplomats*, and Nathan Hatch, *The Democratization of American Christianity*.

15. Generally speaking, prior to the growth of an indigenous antifootbinding movement among Chinese reformers in the 1890s, most missionaries tolerated what they could not change. See Hunter, p. 22. For a general discussion on missionaries' role in the antifootbinding movement in the late Qing, see Drucker, pp. 179–99.

16. Burton, *Notable Women*, p. 162.

17. Ibid., p. 21.

18. Ibid. pp. 15–19, 161–63. Also, On Xu's father, Xu Yangmei (Hu Yong Mi), see *Xu Yangmei mushi xinxiaolu* (The way of faith illustrated: Autobiography of Hu Yong Mi) (Yale Divinity School "Day Missions" Collection).

19. On the early Chinese gentry converts, see Bennett and Liu, pp. 159–96. Paul A. Cohen's article "Littoral and Hinterland in Nineteenth Century China" (pp. 197–225 of the same volume as the Bennett and Liu article) also helps us understand the early Chinese Christians.

20. Bennett and Liu, p. 188. For a discussion of Yuan Mei, Yu Zhengxie, and Li Ruzhen on women's issues, see Beahan, pp. 14–32.

21. Stone, "Miss Gerturde Howe," p. 7.

22. See Lutz, p. 22.

23. See Robert, 173–89.

24. On the discussion of female missionary physicians, see Beaver, pp. 129–36.

25. On missionary education of Chinese women in this period see Burton, *The Education of Women in China*, pp. 52–99, and Lutz, pp. 15–17.

26. See newspaper clipping, 6 June 1920, in Ida Kahn's papers. I suspect that the Shanghai gentleman's son was a young man on Yung Wing's educational mission, and returned to China with others in 1881. The alleged marriage proposal was made around 1885.

27. The other three women all married Chinese Christians and apparently raised families instead of pursuing professional careers as Ida Kahn did.

28. Paul W. Cohen discusses the state of English instruction in this period in "Christian Missions and Their Impact to 1900," p. 577. Whether or not to teach English to the Chinese was heatedly debated among the Methodist missionaries in Fuzhou. While the majority of them were against the idea throughout the 1870s and 1880s, Chinese pastors were strongly for it. See Robert, pp. 173–89.

29. Mary Stone, "Miss Gertrude Howe."

30. Ibid.

31. Ibid.

32. In Dana Robert's "The Methodist Struggle over Higher Education in Fuzhou, China" (p. 183), there is a section on how the Chinese pastors in Fuzhou pressed the mission to improve the quality of education for women and asked the mission to sponsor Xu Jinhong to study medicine in America.

33. The woman's boards of the Methodist Episcopal Church were among many Protestant woman's mission boards that emerged after the Civil War. They played an important role in recruiting female missionaries to foreign countries and in pushing education for women in those countries. See Beaver, 85–175.

34. Burton, *Notable Women*, p. 29.

35. Because of her father's illness and her own ill health, Xu took two years' leave of absence from medical school, went back to China around 1890, and returned to America in 1892. After her graduation in 1894, she stayed in the United States for one more year to do an internship.

36. Jin returned to China in 1888, and practiced medicine in Xiamen and Chengdu. Later she left China to go to Japan, which is where she got married. Her husband is believed to have been an English man. On her marriage, see, "Nüyishi Jin Yunmei jilüe," in Li and Chang, eds, pp. 1386–88.

37. Burton, *Notable Women*, p. 42.

38. Liang Qichao, "Ji Jiangxi Kang nüshi," pp. 119–20.

39. Fletcher Brockman, "A Daughter of Confucius," in Kahn's papers.

40. Lutz, pp. 82–96.

41. Burton, *Notable Women*, p. 130. Howe apparently let the Chinese male visitors take away with them the diploma of one of the doctors and bring it to the people in the reformist circle.

42. Due to bad health, Xu did not go.

43. Burton, *Notable Women*, p. 131.

44. See ibid., p. 55.

45. Ibid., p. 211.

46. See Walsh, pp. 2–3, 24–25.

47. Ahern, pp. 193–214.

48. Burton, *Notable Women*, p. 130.

49. Paul A. Cohen, "Littoral and Hinterland in Nineteenth Century China," p. 198.

50. Stone's departure in 1920 from the Danforth Hospital apparently had a lot to do with Hughes's doctrinal dispute with the Methodist hierarchy. The Bethel Mission consisted of a nurse training school and a high school, among other facilities.

51. In 1916 Kahn went to Tianjin to work at a government hospital. Her reason for leaving the mission hospital in Nanchang appears to have been primarily financial: her salary from the mission hospital was not enough, because at this time she also had to support the aging Gertrude Howe. Some arrangement was soon made by the missionary hierarchy to bring Kahn back to Nanchang. See Ida Kahn's papers, letter from Bishop Lewis to Miss Sinclair, Kuling, 8 June 1917.

52. It is believed, for instance, that Mary Stone, as the head of the Elizabeth Danforth Hospital, personally trained five hundred women as nurses. See the *Encyclopedia of World Methodism*, vol. 2, p. 2259.

53. Stone, "Miss Gertrude Howe."

54. For instance, some missionaries were concerned that Xu Jinhong might not be able to readjust to the conditions in China after her long stay in America. They were relieved that "all the attention she had received in America had left her unspoiled." Burton, *Notable Women*, p. 129.

55. *Chinese Medical Missionary Journal* (December 1896), quoted in Burton, *Notable Women*, p. 129.

56. Amy Gifford Lewis, "Dr. Ida Kahn—Nanchang, China."

57. Most of the Protestant missions working in China did not accept Chinese as missionaries. The Methodists were more ready than most missions to give authority

to the Chinese, and to give authority to women. I was made of this fact by Ryan Dunch, in his letter to me dated July 18, 1995.

58. Xu Jinhong, quoted in Burton, *Notable Women*, p. 66.

59. Sherwood Eddy, "Days with a Chinese Lady Doctor," in Mary Stone's papers.

60. Bishop Lewis to Miss Sinclair, regarding Dr. Ida Kahn, June 8, 1917. Kahn's papers.

61. King, "As We See Ourselves."

62. See Ono, *Chinese Women in a Century of Revolution 1850–1950*.

63. Ida Kahn, "An Amazon in Cathay," in Kahn's papers.

64. Garrett, p. 28.

65. Hunter, p. 265.

66. Jane Hunter discusses ways in which gender roles have functioned in Chinese women's lives (p. 259).

67. Hunter, chaps. 2 and 3.

68. Burton, *Notable Women*, p. 166.

69. Ibid., p. 137.

70. Mary Stone lived with a close female friend, Jennie Hughes, an American missionary. Stone met Jennie Hughes while her own sister was dying in 1906, and they remained inseparable for the rest of their lives. This relationship was possibly homosexual. On their relationship, see Jane Hunter, p. 74. In Ida Kahn's case, she lived with and supported Gertrude Howe when the latter became old, acting like a good daughter.

71. I am indebted to Ryan Dunch for this information (letter to the author, 18 July 1995).

72. For instance, Mary Stone and Ida Kahn participated in the activities of the Chinese National Medical Association, founded in 1914 by a group of Chinese physicians, and they attended the association's first conference in Shanghai in the following year. The doctors also wrote for Chinese professional medical journals.

73. "College Wards of an Empress," *Evening Post*, New York, 3 October 1907.

74. Ibid.

75. Duan Fang was widely hailed in the 1900s as a promoter of women's education.

76. Huang Fu-ch'ing, pp. 41–48. The number could be higher than this, given the large number of Chinese males in Japan at this time.

77. Liang Qichao, "Xin dalu youji," pp. 205–6.

78. Beaver, p. 125.

79. Tcheng, pp. 77–79.

80. Burton, *The Education of Women in China*, p. 201.

81. Hunter, p. 16.

82. Solomon, p. 84.

83. Ibid., pp. 84–86.

84. Ruby Sia, "The College Curriculum in Relation to Home Making," *CSM* (January 1910): 172.

85. Margaret Wang, "What Does an Education Mean to a Chinese Woman?" *CSM* (December 1909): 107–9.

86. Bok, "The Education of China's Daughters."

87. Burton, *The Education of Women in China*, pp. 93–94.

88. En Ming Ho, "The Influence and Duties of a Woman," *CSM* (April 1910): 361.

89. Ibid.

90. Huang Chen-ch, pp. 215–16.

91. Liang Qichao, "Lun nüxue," pp. 37–44.

92. Beahan, "The Women's Movement and Nationalism in Late Ch'ing China."

93. Chen Dongyuan, p. 343.

94. Cheng, p. 96.

95. Ida B. Lewis, p. 34.

96. My information on the fields of study by female students is taken from data provided by the *CSM* and other sources, including *A Survey of Chinese Students in American Universities and Colleges in the Past One Hundred Years* and *Qinghua tongxue lu*.

97. Tsao, "A Brief History of Chinese Women Students in America," 616–21.

98. I am indebted to Ryan Dunch for this information, in a letter to me (July 1995), about Sia's personal life.

99. Pingsa Hu (Hu Binxia), "The Women of China," *CSM* (January 1914): 200. There is no information available about the precise dates of Hu's birth and death. According to Zhang Yuanshan (Djang Yuan-shan), a graduate of Cornell University in 1915 and a friend of Hu and her brothers, Hu died of illness sometime in the 1920s. I had several interviews with Zhang in Beijing in the winter of 1985.

100. Hu's patriotic activities in Japan are well documented. See *Zhejiang chao*, vol. 4; also see Feng, p. 35; and Li and Chang, pp. 911, 916.

101. "Chinese Woman Is Here to Study Women of the U.S.," Patterson's scrapbooks.

102. Pingsa Hu, "The Women of China."

103. Ibid.

104. Ibid.

105. Hu Binxia, "Hutaoshan nüxiaozhang."

106. Jacqueline Nivard argues that Hu's job at the journal was mostly symbolic, and that the many articles published under her name were actually written by others. My research tells a different story. I believe the articles signed by Hu were written by her, given the facts that Hu was capable of writing essays in good Chinese, that the content of the articles reveals the author's familiarity with American life, and perhaps most important, that Hu was an independent-thinking person. See Nivard, "Women and Women's Press," pp. 37–55. In her recent book, *Women and*

the Chinese Enlightenment, Wang Zheng has a chapter on the *Lady's Journal* (pp. 67–116). She also accepts that the editors were all males.

107. Hu Binxia, "Meiguo jiating," pp. 1–8.

108. Hu Binxia, "Jichu zhi jichu," pp. 1–12.

109. Ibid.

110. Li Ping, pp. 191–192.

111. Quanguo fulian, ed., p. 130; Pui-lan Kwok, pp. 130, 152.

112. Seton, p. 231.

113. The Boxer Indemnity Scholarship Program was opened to women in 1914. Every two years thereafter about ten women were sent to America under the auspices of the program. Forty-four women were sponsored by this program in the next decade. After 1923, this program was abruptly interrupted due to Qinghua College's financial problems.

114. Editorial, "Welcome," *CSM* (October 1914): 6.

115. "Personal News," *CSM* (November 1922): 69.

116. The diversity and "masculinity" of the subjects of study is suggested by a comparison of the majors of the female Indemnity students in the years of 1916 and 1921 respectively:

SUBJECT	1916	1921
Education	4	4
Medicine	3	1
General arts	3	0
Science	0	2
Agriculture	0	1
Journalism	0	1
Unidentified	0	1
TOTAL	10	10

On the 1916 figures, see *CSM* (December 1916): 55. On the 1921 figures, see Lin Zixun, *Zhongguo liuxue jiaoyushi,* p. 270. Generally speaking, there is a paucity of data on Chinese women's fields of studies for this period.

117. Her name was Tang Mei. She was the daughter of Tang Shaoyi, a student on the Yung Wing Educational Mission and a powerful political figure in the early republican period.

118. "Subjects for the Essay Competition," *CSM* (November 1917): 8.

119. Yuan Tung-li, *A Guide to Doctoral Dissertations by Chinese Students in America,* p. 35. The title of Li Pinghua's Ph.D. dissertation is "The Economic History of China, with Special Reference to Agriculture" (Columbia University, 1921).

120. Gien Tsiu Liu, "Chinese Women in Medicine," *CSM* (January 1923): 38–40.

121. D. Y. Koo, "Women's Place in Business," *CSM* (November 1922): 34–36.

122. Eva Chang, "Chinese Women's Place in Journalism," *CSM* (March 1923): 50–55.

123. In *The Grounding of Modern Feminism*, Nancy Cott discusses the ongoing sex segregation in the United States in the early decades of the twentieth century (p. 132).

124. Eva Chang, "Chinese Women's Place in Journalism."

125. D. Y. Koo, "Women's Place in Business."

126. Cheng Zhefan, p. 91.

127. Croll, pp. 89–90.

128. On the impact of May Fourth movement on women, see Croll, chap. 4; Witke, "Transformation of Attitudes Toward Women During the May Fourth Era of Modern China"; and Collins, chap. 6.

129. Gilman's ideas on women's economic independence were quite attractive to intellectual women during the May Fourth period. Although her ideas were being introduced at this time, her book *Women and Economy* was not translated into Chinese until 1929. See *Zhongguo funü yundongshi*, p. 99.

130. Eva Chang, "Chinese Women's Place in Journalism," p. 50.

131. D. Y. Koo, "Women's Place in Business," p. 34.

132. Ibid., p. 36.

133. Eva Chang, "Chinese Women's Place in Journalism," p. 53.

134. Cott, pp. 7–39.

135. Solomon, p. 109.

136. "Personal News," *CSM* (April 1924): 68. We do not know what happened to the bank Koo helped found in Shanghai. Neither do we know what happened to Koo later in her life. We do know that around the same time when Koo returned to China, a women's bank was established in Shanghai, in 1925. It was called *Shanghai nüzi shangye chuxu yinhang* (The Shanghai women's commercial savings bank). Koo's name was not among the founders. See Tan, pp. 22–23, for more information about the bank. People like Koo might not be able to realize what they had aspired to due to circumstantial reasons, but their aspiration itself deserves to be taken seriously for our understanding of this May Fourth generation.

137. In her study conducted in the mid 1910s among 992 female mission school students in China, Ida B. Lewis found that when asked "After you have finished school, what work do you expect to do," 661 people wanted to become students in higher institutions, teachers, evangelists, physicians, musicians, social workers, business women, and nurses; 296 people were not certain; and only one said that she wanted to be a full-time housewife. See Ida B. Lewis, p. 34.

138. According to the *Qinghua Alumni Register* of 1937, of the fifty-three female students on Indemnity scholarships between 1914 and 1929, one-fifth were college professors, one-fifth medical doctors, one-fifths workers in various fields such as the YWCA, and two-fifth housewives.

139. Few scholarly works have addressed the subject at length. For instance, Ono Kazuko, in her book *Chinese Women in a Century of Revolution*, only mentions coeducational schools and women's suffrage as two "tangible results" of women's struggles during the May Fourth period (p. 109). Elisabeth Croll does discuss women in

business in the 1920s, but her discussion is too brief (p. 93). Roxane H. Witke, while correctly pointing out that women's struggles for economic independence during the May Fourth period was tied with the women's rights movement, does not provide any details on the "struggles" themselves, probably because they were part of a "middle class movement" that "affirmed the political order and did not seek to overthrow it" (p. 276). *Zhongguo funü yundongshi*, compiled by the All Women's Federation of China, contains a great deal more information on career progress made by women in the May Fourth era, but concludes that women's career demands were "bourgeois" in nature and only represented the interest of a small number of "intellectual women" (p. 119). Even Chen Dongyuan's pathbreaking book *Zhonguo funü shenghuoshi*, which is amazingly liberal in many aspects, shows reservations in its appraisal of career women. Chen held economic "necessity" rather than desire for economic independence as the key factor in women's decisions to seek employment (pp. 396–99). Recently, Wang Zheng addressed the issue of career women in *Women and Chinese Enlightenment*.

140. E-tu Zen Sun, Chen Hengzhe's daughter, was interviewed in March 1992 by the researchers at the Institute of Modern History, Academia Sinica: Taipei. The interview contains valuable information on Chen Hengzhe. See *Ren Yidu jiaoshou fangwen jilu*. I met with E-tu Zen Sun in spring 1985. She followed up with a letter to me, dated May 13, 1985, regarding my interest in her parents.

141. Ibid., pp. 8–10.

142. Sophia H. Chen, "A Non-Christian Estimate of Missionary Activities." Some recent studies take a look at educated women in late imperial China. Among them, see Susan Mann, *Precious Records*, and Dorothy Ko, *Teachers of the Inner Chambers*.

143. Chen Hengzhe, "Jinian yiwei laogumu," pp. 67–70.

144. Chen Hengzhe, "Woyoushi qiuxue de jingguo," pp. 84–88.

145. Chen Hengzhe, "Laiyin nüshi xiaozhuan."

146. In the 1930s, Hu Shi wrote in a letter, "my friends and I all knew at the time that Miss Chen believed in celibacy, therefore nobody dared to approach her" (*Zhuanji wenxue*, February 1983, p. 21).

147. Topley, pp. 67–88.

148. Celibacy became a subject of discussion and debate during the May Fourth. See Chen Dongyuan, p. 106. Roxane Witke discusses the issue of celibacy in her dissertation. Witke especially quotes people who opposed the idea of celibacy and argues that celibacy during the May Fourth, though it expressed a new assertion of female independence, was also a denial of women's sexuality (pp. 203–10).

149. Chen Hengzhe, "Luoyisi de wenti."

150. Ibid.

151. Cott, p. 192.

152. Ding Ling was a case in point. On Ding, see Barlow, ed., particularly Ding's story "Miss Sophia's Diary," pp. 49–81.

153. It appears that the tendency among these women to shun sexual love could

be a result of both their missionary education and the neo-Confucianist tradition in Chinese society. This is a question worth exploring.

154. Mary Stone was the president of WCTU (Women's Christian Temperance Union) in 1922, and Hu Binxia was the first chairperson of the national committee of YWCA in 1923. Pui-lan Kwok discusses the movements and the roles of these two women. On Mary Stone, see pp. 120, 132, 162; on Hu Binxia, see pp. 130 and 152. On the improvement of conditions for working class women, Cheng Wanzhen, who had studied in Greensborough, North Carolina, stood out as forceful spokesperson. Representing China's YWCA, Cheng attended an international conference on working women held in 1921 in Geneva, and later published a detailed report on the conference in *Funü zazhi* (Ladies' journal) 8, no. 3 (1922). Cheng's essay greatly helped draw people's attention to the plight of working class women in China. See *Zhongguo funü yundongshi*, p. 134.

Chapter 5: Between Morality and Romance

1. Chiang Monglin, p. 67.
2. Ibid.
3. On Yan Huiqing, see Yan Huiqing, *Yan Huiqing zizhuan.*
4. "Speech Delivered by Dr. W. W. Yen at Ashburnham, Mass., August 1908," *CSM* (December 1908): 111–18.
5. Ibid.
6. LaFargue, chap. 3.
7. Some recent Chinese scholarship addresses the change of attitude toward Western social customs and Western culture in general in treaty ports of China at the turn of the century. See Xu Jiansheng, "Jindai Zhongguo hunyin jiating biange sichao shulun"; Xing, "Qingmo minchu hunyin shenghuozhong de xinchao"; Gong Shuduo, "Jindai shehui xisu bianhua manhua"; and Hu Shengwu and Cheng Weikun, "Minchu shehui fengshang de yanbian."
8. On the emergence of modern-style weddings in this early period, see Xing, "Qingmo minchu hunyin shenghuozhong de xinchao"; and Li Yu-ning and Chang Yü-fa, eds., p. 1314. According to Xing Long, the earliest recorded new style wedding ceremony took place in Tianjin in 1902. See Xing, p. 176. Also see Min Jie, "Jindai Zhongguo zuizao de zhenghun guanggao he xinshi hunli."
9. Among a good number of books on the subject, see Lamson, *Social Pathology in China*; Stacey, *Patriarchy and Socialist Revolution in China*; Kay Ann Johnson, *Women, the Family and Peasant Revolution in China*; Goode, *World Revolution and Family Patterns*; Freedman, *Family and Kinship in Chinese Society*; Levy, *The Family Revolution in Modern China*; Lang, *Chinese Family and Society*; Witke, "Transformation of Attitudes Towards Women During the May Fourth Era"; and Collins, "The New Women."

10. One article specifically addressing the ideas by these people is by Xu Jiansheng, "Wuxu nüzi jiefang xintan."

11. According to Perry Link, there were several waves in the mandarin-duck-and-butterfly fiction. The first major wave was the love stories in the early teens; the second wave, arising in the later teens, consisted of satirical "social novels"; and the third wave consisted of novels that were generally antiwarlord in sentiment. See Link, p. 54. Wei Shaochang, in his book *Wo kan yuanyang hudiepai*, also discusses the different waves.

12. This is a major argument that C. T. Hsia makes in "Hsü Chen-ya's Yü-li hun."

13. See Rey Chow, p. 75.

14. Leo Lee argues in his *The Romantic Generation in Modern Chinese World* that an important reason for Lin Shu to translate "La Dame Aux Camellias" was due to his own emotional need as somebody who had just lost his wife, among other family members (p. 46).

15. Xie Bingxin, pp. 81–84.

16. A number of studies have examined the impact of the May Fourth New Culture Movement on the thinking of the contemporary young men and women, particularly their attitude toward family and marriage. See Chow Tse-tsung, *The May 4th Movement*; Croll, *Feminism and Socialism in China*; Schwarcz, *The Chinese Enlightenment* and *Time for Telling the Truth is Running Out*; Witke, "Transformation of Attitudes Towards Women During the May Fourth Era of Modern China"; and Collins, "The New Women."

17. Lawrence Stone, p. 191; Skolnick, p. 204.

18. Steven Mintz and Susan Kellogg argue in *Domestic Revolutions: A Social History of American Family Life* that for turn-of-the-century America, the family was an institution in crisis (pp. 107–8). On the "new woman" and the reconstruction of family life in the early twentieth century in America, also see Woloch, *Women and the American Experience*.

19. Cott, p. 7.

20. Zhu Qizhe, "Meiguo nüzi zhi jiaoyu."

21. Kai F. Mok, "Lydia and Her Experience," *CSM* (December 1913): 140.

22. Ibid.

23. Yan Dixun, "Shujia lüxing ji."

24. F. L. Chang, "Innocents Abroad," *CSM* (February 1914): 300.

25. W. S. Ho, "Old Fashioned Girls in China," *CSM* (February 1924): 53.

26. Ibid.

27. Chang, "Innocents Abroad."

28. Ma Yinchu is known for his opinions on population control in China. His ideas were criticized in the 1950s as "anti-Marxist." He subsequently lost his position as the president of Beijing University.

29. Ma Yinchu, pp. 84–85.

30. Zhang Chengyou, "Hunyin," 117–24.

31. Ibid.

32. For instance, in April 1922, *Funü zazhi* (Ladies' journal) had a special issue on divorce, which contained sharply divided opinions on the subject.

33. The statistics are gathered from *Who's Who: American Returned Students*, published in 1917 in Beijing by Tsing Hua College (Qinghua College) and reprinted by Chinese Material Center, San Francisco, 1978.

34. Yuen Ren Chao, p. 59.

35. Interview with Wellington Koo; no page number available.

36. Ibid.

37. Ibid.

38. Ibid.

39. Ibid.

40. Buwei Yang Chao, p. 180.

41. Yuen Ren Chao, p. 88.

42. Ibid., p. 105.

43. Ibid., p. 109.

44. Jiang Tingfu, p. 101.

45. Zhao Jiaming, p. 21.

46. Hu Shi, *Hu Shi liuxue riji*, vol. 1, p. 154.

47. "Nine Young Women in Attendance at the Conference of Chinese Students at Ashburnham," in H. D. Fearing, scrapbooks on Chinese Alliance Conference, 1908–14.

48. Ibid.

49. *Jiaoyu zazhi* 8 (October–December 1916): 61.

50. "Bazaar a Success," Fearing, scrapbook on Chinese Alliance conferences, 1908–1914.

51. Dorothy Tsienyi Wong, "Among Us Girls," *CSM* (June 1924): 49.

52. Cai Zheng, p. 129.

53. Cao Boquan, "Liumei riyong lijie shuolüe."

54. Ibid., p. 208.

55. Ibid.

56. Chih Meng, *Chinese American Understanding*, p. 76.

57. Fong, p. 15.

58. Liang Shiqiu, "Qinghua banian," p. 233.

59. Liang Shiqiu, "Tan Wen Yiduo," p. 368.

60. Chen Heqin, "Xuesheng hunyin wenti zhi yanjiu." According to Chen, out of a sample of 630 male high school and college students in Jiangsu and Zhejiang, two of the most "progressive" provinces, more than half (57.7 percent) were either married or engaged, and almost all these marriages and engagements were decided by the parents.

61. Liang Shiqiu, "Tan Wen Yiduo," p. 367.

62. Shen Shouze, p. 53.
63. Fong, p. 29.
64. Ibid.
65. Xie Bingxin, "Wode laoban Wu Wenzao."
66. Liang Shiqiu, "Tan Wen Yiduo."
67. Chih Meng, *Chinese American Understanding*, p. 116.
68. Ibid., p. 117.
69. Ibid.
70. Xing Long, "Qingmo minchu hunyin shenghuozhong de xinchao."
71. Li Yu-ning and Chang Yü-fa, eds., p. 1315.
72. See *Jiaoyu zazhi* 10 (September–December 1918): 67.
73. Ma Yinchu, p. 83.
74. Pan Guangdan, *Zhongguo zhi jiating wenti*, pp. 200–201.
75. Lyman, p. 91.
76. Liang Shiqiu, "Tan Wen Yiduo," p. 391.
77. It is hard to figure out why this Chinese man had an English-sounding family name. His father's last name was Ng (Wu in Mandarin).
78. According to Holly Franking, the granddaughter of Tiam Hock and Mae Watkins Franking, in 1920 the magazine *Asia* hired Katherine Anne Porter, then a still unknown journalist, to rewrite the autobiography of the marriage of Tiam Hock and Mae Franking. The magazine published "My Chinese Marriage" in serial form in its June, July, August and September issues of 1921. The story drew attention and stirred some controversy. Duffield and Company subsequently published the articles in book form, and the book went through several printings. As for the authorship, from 1921 to 1952, the cards in the Library of Congress listed M.T.F. and/or Mae Franking as the author. Cross-references to Porter did not appear until 1953. Porter herself was quoted as saying that this book "is a mere setting down of someone else's story, nothing of my own." In 1991, University of Texas Press published an annotated edition of the book *My Chinese Marriage*, edited by Holly Franking, with foreword by Joan Givner. The new edition contains a long introduction by Holly Franking and over fifty pages of appendix, including correspondence between Tiam Hock Franking and Mae Watkins before and after their marriage, Mae's letters to her parents from China, and contemporary newspaper clippings on their marriage. While Joan Givner's foreword focuses on Katherine Anne Porter, arguing that *My Chinese Marriage* is an important and inseparable part of Porter's literary career, it is Holly Franking's introduction and the appendix that provide rich and original material on the interracial marriage itself, offering an interesting contrast to the story presented in *My Chinese Marriage*.
79. In *My Chinese Marriage*, it is said that they met at the University of Michigan.
80. *My Chinese Marriage: Annotated*; letter dated 15 April 1910. See app., p. 62.
81. Letter dated 27 July 1910. *My Chinese Marriage: Annotated*; app., p. 63.

82. Ibid.; app., p. 63.

83. Ibid.

84. M.T.F. (Mae M. Franking), *My Chinese Marriage*, p. 6.

85. Ibid., p. 19.

86. *My Chinese Marriage: Annotated*, letter to the editor (*Ann Arbor Times*), p. 75.

87. Ibid., p. 92.

88. Ibid., p. 108.

89. Ibid., p. 103.

90. On the sexual revolution and campus life in the 1920s, see Allen, *Only Yesterday*; Mintz and Kellogg, *Domestic Revolution*; Fass, *The Damned and the Beautiful*; and Horowitz, *Campus Life*.

91. Chih Meng, *Chinese American Understanding*, p. 116.

92. See, for example, articles published in *Funü pinglun* (Shanghai) from August 1921 to September 1922.

93. Peiwei, "Lianai yu zhencao de guanxi."

94. Chen Dongyuan, p. 399.

95. Students in America appeared to adopt a generally more conservative attitude toward the New Culture Movement at home. Among a number of articles on the movement, see Yu-tang Lin, "The Literary Revolution and What Is Literature," *CSM* (February 1920): 24–29; Yueh-lin Chin, "Radicalism in China," *CSM* (June 1921): 575–78; Wu Mi, "Lun Xinwenhua yundong"; and Meng Chengxian, "Liumei xuesheng yu guonei wenhua yundong." In the last article (page numbers not available), Meng quotes Chen Duxue as saying that except for Hu Shi and a few others, the majority of the foreign-educated students had little to do with the New Culture Movement.

96. M. J. Exner, "Sex Education," *CSM* (May 1915): 478–80. Exner was the student secretary of the International Committee of the YMCA.

97. Anonymous, "Husband, Wife, and Family," *CSM* (January 1924): 45.

98. T. Chen, "The Twelfth Annual Conference of the Eastern Section," *CSM* (November 1916): 46.

99. "Dancing in Chinese Society," p. 7.

100. Chih Meng, *Chinese American Understanding*, p. 107.

101. Seton, p. 215.

102. Ibid., p. 182.

103. Lu Xun, "Suiganlu No. 40," p. 26.

104. Witke, p. 141.

105. Woon Yung Chun, "East Is East and West Is West," *CSM* (April 1914): 491–93.

106. K. F. Mok, "Chinese Play Charms New Haven Audience," *CSM* (March 1915): 399.

107. Ibid.

108. Lin Pu-chi, "The Comedy of Ignorance," *CSM* (June 1919): 488–94; Shen Hung, *For Romeo and Juliet, CSM* (April 1920): 50–53; (May 1920): 46–53.

109. Shen Hung, *For Romeo and Juliet.*

110. Chih Meng, *Chinese American Understanding*, p. 76.

111. Lu Xun, "Suiganlu No. 40," p. 26.

112. Shen Hung, *For Romeo and Juliet.*

113. Witke, p. 139.

114. Rosalind Me-tsung Li, "The Chinese Revolution and the Chinese Woman," *CSM* (June 1922): 673.

115. Ibid.

116. Ibid.

117. Ibid.

118. Ibid.

119. Many studies on the marriage between Hu and Jiang like to describe Jiang as "semiliterate." In fact, Jiang could read and write. Her letter to Hu Shi on display at the Hu Shi memorial room in Nangang, Taipei, shows that she wrote adequately and her handwriting was clear. I was there in the summer of 1993. Also see *Hu Shi Jiang Dongxue*, which includes Hu's letters to Jiang from 1911 to 1946.

120. Chou, chap. 5; Shen Weiwei, "Hu Shi hunyin lüelun"; Yun Zhi, "Hu Shi de liangshou qingshi"; Zhou Zhiping, "Chui pu san de xin dou ren ying"; Li Yun-ing, ed., *Hu Shi yu ta de pengyou*; Yan Zhengwu, ed., *Hu Shi yanjiu conglu*; Yi Zhuxian, *Hu Shi zhuan*, pp. 114–25; and Shen Weiwei, *Hu Shi zhuan*, pp. 85–95. An earlier article by Chow Tse-tsung, entitled "Hu Shizhi xiansheng de kangyi yu rongren," is reprinted in *Zhuanji wenxue*. This article, written in 1962, is one of the earliest exploring the relationship between Hu Shi and E. C. Williams. Recently, Zhou Zhiping published a book in Chinese on the relationship between Hu and Williams, in which he examines the fifty-year-long correspondence between them that became available only recently. See Zhou, *Hu Shi yu Weiliansi*.

121. From his own childhood experience, Hu Shi seems to have developed a belief about women's capacity to mold and temper men's character. Raised single-handedly by his widowed mother, Hu Shi lived in a women's world and had little contact with men till he left home at the age of thirteen. Looking back at this childhood experience after he became a young man, Hu Shi realized that he was different from and better than other village boys from an early age. He attributed the difference to the good influence of his mother and other women relatives. See *Hu Shi liuxue riji*, vol. 1, p. 252.

122. Ibid., p. 146.

123. Chou, p. 63.

124. Horowitz, pp. 11–13, 39–51, 64. Also see Conable, *Women at Cornell.*

125. Hu Shi, *Hu Shi liuxue riji*, vol. 3, p. 659.

126. Ibid., p. 524. Chou Min-chih's translation.

127. Hu Shi, *Hu Shi liuxue riji*, vol. 3, p. 654.

128. Chou Min-chih, pp. 63–64.

129. Hu Shi, *Hu Shi liuxue riji*, vol. 2, p. 536.

130. Ibid., p. 537; vol. 3, pp. 650, 659.

131. Ibid., vol. 2, p. 537.

132. Ibid., vol. 3, p. 650.

133. Ibid., pp. 835–37.

134. Apparently, Hu Shi's relationship with Mrs. Williams was overall very good. See Zhou Zhiping, *Hu Shi yu Weiliansi*, pp. 80–89. But at least at some point, Mrs. Williams felt uneasy about the close relationship between Hu and her daughter and did not want them to spend time by themselves without other people's presence (ibid., pp. 23–27). There is no way to tell under what circumstances Hu wrote the long letter to Mrs. Williams.

135. Chou Min-chih, pp. 64–65.

136. Grieder, *Hu Shih and the Chinese Renaissance*, p. 201.

137. I borrow the phrase from Vera Schwarcz. See Schwarcz, *The Chinese Enlightenment*, p. 116.

138. Hu Shi, *Hu Shi liuxue riji*, vol. 4, p. 1137.

139. Ibid., vol. 2, pp. 535–37.

140. Ibid., vol. 3, pp. 653–55.

141. On Lu Xun, see *Lun Xun quanji*, vol. 11, p. 422.

142. The concept of "uterine family" was first introduced by Margery Wolf in her book *Women and the Family in Rural Taiwan*, chap. 3, "Uterine Families and the Women's Community," pp. 32–52.

143. Hu Shi, "Lun zhencao wenti—da Lan Zhixian," pp. 676–83.

144. Hu Shi, "Meiguo de funü," pp. 39–61.

145. Zhou Zhiping, "Chuibusan de xindou renying," p. 140.

146. Hu Shi, "Zhuidao Zhimo," p. 363.

147. On Xu's love affairs, see Spence, *The Gate of Heavenly Peace*, pp. 201–4, 212–19, 231–32.

148. See Zhou Zhiping and Shen Weiwei. In the early 1920s, Hu fell in love with Cao Chengying. Eleven years her senior, Hu was for Cao, in my opinion, a combination of a lover, big brother, and teacher. See Zhou Zhiping, "Chuibusan de xindou renying."

149. In Zhou Zhiping's recent book, *Hu Shi yu Weiliansi*, the letters between Hu and Williams, most of which are made public for the first time, clearly reveal the nature of their relationship.

150. Both in his autobiography, written at forty, and in the interviews conducted in the 1950s with Tang Degang, Hu Shi avoided talking about his emotional life.

151. The poem is quoted in Yun Zhi, "Hu Shi de liangshou qingshi." I want to thank Zhu Hong for helping me translate the poem into English.

152. Taylor, preface and pp. 292–94.

153. See Chou, chap. 11, "The May Fourth Generation in Historical Perspective."

Chapter 6: The Serious Business of Recreation

1. The article was entitled "To Learn, to Teach, to Serve, and to Enjoy."
2. Ibid.
3. Ibid.
4. On the early history of athletics in modern China, see, among other books, *Zhongguo jindai tiyushi jianbian*; Wu Wenzhong, *Zhongguo tiyu fazhanshi*; and Huang Wenzhong, *Zhongguo jinbainian tiyushi*. Also see Brownell, chaps. 2 and 8.
5. On Kang Youwei's ideas on physical education, see *Wuxu bianfa*, vol. 4, pp. 12–13.
6. Liang Qichao, *Yinbingshi quanji*, vol. 9, pp. 5–6.
7. Ibid., vol. 12, p. 48.
8. *Tan Sitong Quanji*, p. 37.
9. Brownell, p. 44.
10. Shu, *Zhongguo jindai jiaoyushi ziliao*, pp. 223–24.
11. Mao Zedong, "Tiyu zhi yanjiu."
12. Wu Wenzhong, pp. 69–70. Also, *Zhongguo jindai tiyushi jianbian*, p. 39.
13. Wu Wenzhong, p. 76. According to Wu, Dr. R. R. Gailey was the first person to introduce basketball to China, yet it was Dr. C. Saler, a student of Dr. James Naismith, inventor of basketball, who made a memorable contribution by bringing basketball to school pupils. Sent by the international YMCA in 1912, Saler taught basketball at Tianjin's YMCA and often visited local schools to teach basketball. Also see *Zhongguo jindai tiyushi jianbian*, pp. 39, 47.
14. Chih Meng, *Chinese American Understanding*, p. 57.
15. Liang Shiqiu, "Qinghua banian," pp. 218–21.
16. There was a variety of sports at the conferences. For instance, the 1909 conference included the following events: 100-yard dash, 220-yard dash, 440-yard dash, 880-yard dash, one-mile relay (interclub or interschool), high jump, broad jump, shot-put, and tug-of-war (interclub or interschool).
17. "Conference Notes," *CSM* (November 1907): 29.
18. Riess, chap. 2.
19. Ting, "Chinese Students in America."
20. It is hard to determine the percentage of students taking part in the sports events. At the 1907 conference, the track meet alone drew twenty participants out of a total number of ninety-one male students registered for that year's conference.
21. "A Brief History of the 1910 Conference," *CSM* (November 1910): 37.
22. Yuen Ren Chao, *Life with Chaos*, p. 80.
23. "A Brief History of the 1910 Conference," p. 37.
24. Yuen Ren Chao, *Life with Chaos*, p. 80.
25. Hu Shi, *Hu Shi liuxue riji*, p. 20.
26. "Physical Development of Chinese Students," *CSM* (January 1915): 246.
27. "Student World: Cornell Club," *CSM* (March 1923): 65.

28. "Chinese Girls Like Sports," *CSM* (March 1923): 65.

29. "Student World: Stanford Club," *CSM* (March 1924): 74.

30. One of the most memorable games between a Chinese team and an American team took place in 1882 in San Francisco, just before the boys on the Yung Wing educational mission left America to go back to China. The Chinese boys played against the Oakland baseball team and the Chinese won, to the great surprise of the Americans. See LaFargue, p. 53.

31. "Chinese Play Good Baseball," *CSM* (November 1911): 35.

32. K. F. Mok, "Chinese Soccer Teams," *CSM* (December 1918): 130.

33. Jin, "Liumei sinian de huiyi."

34. Yuen Ren Chao, *Life with Chaos*, p. 80.

35. Yang, "Tiyu pian."

36. Ibid.

37. "Physical Development of Chinese Students," *CSM* (January 1915): 245.

38. Hao, "Xinsuan hua liumei," pp. 28–30.

39. "An Appeal to Chinese Students," *CSM* (April 1908): 216.

40. Ibid.

41. Ibid.

42. *Liu Mei Tsing Nien* (March 1917): 136.

43. "All Work and No Play Makes Jack a Dull Boy," *CSM* (April 1913): 368.

44. Chinson Young, "Is It Worthwhile to Be Grinds?" *CSM* (January 1910): 169.

45. In her article "Women, Marriage, and the Family in Chinese History," Patricia Ebrey discusses the shifts in Chinese construction of gender during the Song. She makes the interesting argument that new notions of masculinity invited and required new notions of femininity: "if the ideal man among the upper class was relatively subdued and refined, he might seem too effeminate unless women came to be even more delicate, reticent, and stationary." Footbinding became widespread in this context (pp. 220–21).

46. Scholars of American culture argue that masculine anxiety was very high at the turn of the century and was expressed in the accentuation of the physical and assertive side of the male ideal. Shifts were made from emphasizing piety, thrift, and industry, to emphasizing vigor, forcefulness, and mastery. Complex economic and social changes caused the shifts. See Gorn, *The Manly Art*; and Pleck and Pleck, *The American Man*, particularly chap. 10 ("The Boy Scouts and the Validation of Masculinity") and chap. 11 ("Progressivism and the Masculinity Crisis"). On racial and imperial impulses, see Gorn, pp. 189–91.

47. Gorn, pp. 185–86.

48. Ying Mei Chun, "Physical Education for Chinese Women," *CSM* (February 1912): 329.

49. Bertha Hosang, "Physical Education for Chinese Women," *CSM* (May 1918): 373–81.

50. "Personal Notes: Chinese Girls Do Sports," *CSM* (January 1915): 254.

51. Gao was the head of the Department of Physical Education at the Beijing Women's Normal University for seven years before she went to Shenyang with her husband, Hao Gengsheng, where Hao was to head the Department of Physical Education at the Dongbei (Northeast) University. Hao Gengsheng, "Sishinian hunyin shenghuo zhi huiyi," pp. 23–28.

52. Quoted from Tian, p. 21; and Wang Tao, p. 141. Paul Cohen's book *Between Tradition and Modernity* has a section on Wang's visit to Europe (pp. 67–73).

53. On the early history of modern Chinese theater, see, among other books, Chen Baichen and Dong Jian, pp. 34–39; Tian, pp. 3–5; Wu Ruo and Jia Yili, pp. 5–6; Deng, pp. 137–41; *Zhongguo huaju yundong wushinian shiliaoji*; and Dolby, *A History of Chinese Drama*.

54. Hong Shen is often given the credit for breaking the taboo on mixed-gender acting in China after he returned to China in 1923. See Tian, p. 133.

55. "Club News: Pennsylvania," *CSM* (February 1917): 224.

56. "Club Activities: Yale Club," *CSM* (March 1913): 357.

57. "Chinese Tableaux for Famine Fund," May 1912. Columbia University Archives.

58. "Student World: Chinese National Night," *CSM* (April 1923): 67.

59. "Echoes from the Local Clubs: Pennsylvania," *CSM* (April 1910): 346.

60. Plays like *The New Order Cometh* and *For Romeo and Juliet*, already discussed in the last chapter, addressed such personal issues.

61. "Student World: Entertainment," *CSM* (March 1919): 341.

62. "Student World: Double Ten Celebration in Boston," *CSM* (December 1924): 70.

63. "The Syracuse Conference," *CSM* (November 1925): 74.

64. "Student World: Illinois Chinese Students' Club," *CSM* (January 1926): 69.

65. Liang Shiqiu, "Tan Wen Yiduo," pp. 396–400; Gu Yixiu, p. 20.

66. Liang Shiqiu, "Qiushi zayi," in *Liang Shiqiu sanwen*, p. 62.

67. The members include: Yu Shangyuan, Wen Yiduo, Liang Shiqiu, Liang Sicheng, Lin Huiyin, Gu Yuxiu, Chai Shiying, Zhang Jiazhu, Xiong Foxi, Xiong Chengjin, and Zhao Taimou. See Wen and Hou, p. 251.

68. Yu Shangyuan discussed their life in New York in his letter to Zhang Jiazhu. See Yu, ed., pp. 271–79.

69. Led by William Butler Yeats and John M. Synge, these Irish artists consciously promoted the revival of the indigenous Irish theater. The Irish national theater movement was an integral part of a larger national cultural campaign that included Irish folk music, dancing, and ancient Irish language in an overall quest for Irish cultural and political independence. On the introduction of the Irish national theater movement to China, see Tian, pp. 261, 269–70.

70. Quoted from Wu Ruo and Jia Yili, p. 103. The authors claim that the quotation is taken from Yu Shangyuan's article "Jiuju pingjia" (Assessing traditional the-

ater), in *Guojiu yundong*. However, the quotation cited is not found in that partic-ular article.

71. Yu, preface, p. 1.

72. Tian, pp. 112–15.

73. Yu had eight years of missionary education in Hubei Province and a degree in English from Beijing University before he went to work at Qinghua College. Most major works on modern Chinese theater have sections on Yu, though always very brief. Liang Shiqiu, an old friend of Yu, wrote a piece entitled "Daonian Yu Shangyuan" (Commemorating Yu Shangyuan), collected in Liang Shiqiu, *Liang Shiqiu huairen conglu*, pp. 306–13. Liang mentioned in the essay that Yu's wife Chen Hengcui had written a brief biography of Yu, who died in 1970 in Shanghai.

74. Yu was on a partial Boxer Indemnity scholarship. The other half of the money came from a friend of Yu's father, who gave the money under the condition that Yu had to study political science.

75. Wen and Hou, pp. 277–83.

76. Wen and Hou quote Hong Shen: "This was the first time that the study of drama, traditionally regarded with deep contempt in China, began to be a part of the official educational system" (p. 286).

77. One concrete outcome was a volume entitled *Guoju yundong*, published in 1927. Edited by Yu Shangyuan, this was a collection of articles originally appearing in the drama column of the Beijing-based *Chenbao*. To have a special column devoted to drama was itself a bold innovation in the history of modern Chinese journalism. Leading intellectuals such as Xu Zhimo, Yang Zhensheng, Liang Shijiu, and Chen Xiying all wrote for the column and their articles were also included in the volume *Guojiu yundong*.

78. Yu Shangyuan, Zhao Taimou, and Xiong Foxi all began their career with the Beijing Art School. Later, Yu went to Shanghai and became the principal of the National Drama School, founded in 1935, and remained in the post until late 1948. In 1935, Yu accompanied Mei Lanfang, one of the best-known Beijing opera actors of any period, to visit the Soviet Union. The visit turned out to be a huge success. Yu did a lot of work to introduce Beijing opera to the Western audience during the visit. Zhao Taimou went to Shandong and started the Shandong Experimental Theater. Jiang Qing (then Li Yunhe), who was later to marry Mao Zedong, was involved in the theater as a young actress before she went to Shanghai. Xiong Foxi returned to China in 1926, a year later than his friends. He eventually became the chairman of the drama department of the Beijing Art School (which was renamed the Art Institute attached to the National Beijing University in 1928). Xiong left Beijing to go to Dingxian County in 1932 to help with James Yen's rural reconstruc-tion experiment. From 1932 until 1937 when the Sino-Japanese War broke out, Xiong studied folk theater and worked on promoting the modern theatre among the local people.

79. Two recently published authoritative books on the history of modern theater in China, one by Chen Baichen and Dong Jian, published in 1989, the other by Tian Benxiang, published in 1993, clearly differ in their assessments of the national theater movement. Chen and Dong see the movement as "detached from the times and reality" and therefore having no positive impact, whereas Tian believes that the movement touched upon some important issues about the role of art, Western influence, and Chinese tradition that are still relevant today. Chen and Dong, pp. 107–8; Tian, pp. 264–84.

80. Tian, p. 134.

81. Boorman, ed., vol. 1, p. 104.

82. *New York Times*, 24 April 1915.

83. Elmer L. Reizenstein, "The Intruder," *CSM* (May 1915): 489.

84. Xia Jiashan, Cui Guoliang, and Li Lizhong, eds., p. 15.

85. Long and Kong, p. 118.

86. Cao Yu, preface to the *Nankai huaju yundong shiliao*.

87. Tian, p. 236.

88. Long and Kong, pp. 118–27. Zhang's role was not adequately acknowledged by Qi Rushan, another artistic advisor to Mei Lanfang during the two trips.

89. "Club News: Columbus," *CSM* (June 1919): 503.

90. "Student World: Ames," *CSM* (April 1924): 65.

91. Most of the books on early Chinese modern theater have sections on Spring Willow Society and Shen You Society. In particular, see Oyang Yuqian, "Huiyi chunliu" (Reminiscences of Spring Willow). Also see Dolby, chap. 10.

92. The dramatic activities of Chinese students in Japan lasted from 1907 to 1909.

Epilogue

1. Hu Shi, "Guiguo zagan," pp. 621–22.

2. In his diary entry of March 8, 1917, Hu Shi quoted a line from John Henry Newman, the leader of the Oxford Movement, a religious reform movement in nineteenth-century England: "Now that we are coming back, see what changes we will bring about." Hu Shi then remarked, "This can be an inspiration for us foreign-educated Chinese" (*Hu Shi liuxue riji*, vol. 4, p. 1106).

3. The only person that is still alive among all the people I interviewed in the mid 1980s is Chen Hansheng, a renowned economist.

4. Hu Shi died in 1962. From the 1950s to the 1970s, he was regarded in mainland China as a collaborator of the Guomindang government and a "running dog" of American imperialism.

5. See Dirlik, "Reversals, Ironies, Hegemonies," which discusses the changing paradigms in modern Chinese studies.

6. See *Zhu Kezhen zhuan*, chap. 1, pp. 3–12.

7. The Science Society moved at this time from Ithaca to Cambridge after a number of its key members went to study at Harvard.

8. The title of Zhu's dissertation is "A New Classification of the Typhoons of the Far East."

9. Author's interview with Li Jinghan's son, Li Weige, 19 June 1993.

10. Author's interview with Li Jinghan, November 1985. Li talked about how he started looking for jobs one month after he was enrolled at Pomona. The first job he found was cleaning windows for an elderly woman. When the woman asked Li how much he would charge for his work, he told her to decide herself. She was impressed by the honesty of this young Chinese man.

11. A half Indemnity scholarship at this time was forty dollars per month. According to Li Jinghan, a self-supporting student had to have recommendation from his or her professors in order to receive the half scholarship.

12. Li explained that in those days a degree from an eastern university was regarded by the Chinese as more prestigious than that from a university on the West Coast. Interview with Li Jinghan.

13. After many years, Li still remembered the two books that impressed him the most. Both were written by Arthur H. Smith, *Chinese Characteristics* (London: K. Paul, Trench, Trübner, 1894) and *Village Life in China: A Study in Sociology* (New York: Fleming H. Revell, 1899). Smith was a missionary working in China for twenty-two years and one of the first Western scholars conducting social research on China. Interview with Li Jinghan.

14. After a year at Columbia, the half scholarship was terminated. By then, Li had become very experienced in finding profitable part-time jobs—teaching Chinese language to Americans, for instance, an experience he recalled with a great deal of pride. Interview with Li Jinghan.

15. Both Boorman, ed., p. 435, and Grieder, *Intellectuals and the State in Modern China*, pp. 341–42, say the year was 1912, which is incorrect.

16. Among other things he did during the May Fourth period, Luo was one of the two people from Qinghua who volunteered to go to downtown Beijing, the day after May Fourth, to find out about the situation. Later he was arrested and imprisoned briefly for his participation in one demonstration.

17. Chen Xingui, "Ji Luo Longji de sanci yanshuo."

18. Both Ye Duyi and Jin Ruonian stressed Laski's influence on Luo's political thinking. Author's interviews with Ye Duyi and Jin Ruonian in Beijing, August 1994. According to Ye Duyi, Luo sometimes used "Laski's student" as his pen name in his writings before 1949.

19. Zhu remained an active member and a leader of the society until the breakup of the Sino-Japanese War in 1937.

20. Zhu's involvement with the Academia Sinica had a lot to do with Cai Yuanpei, whom Zhu respected greatly. See *Zhu Kezhen zhuan*, p. 23.

21. Guo Renyuan, Zhu's predecessor at Zheda, worked closely with the

Nationalist Party's office in Zhejiang and ran the university in a military way, which alienated many faculty and students and led to a students' protest movement.

22. Both Zhu's wife and his child died of illness in the summer of 1938. Zheda by this time had been moved to Jiangxi Province due to the Sino-Japanese War. With the continuous marching of the Japanese, Jiangxi was no longer considered safe. To look for a relocation site, Zhu went to Hunan and Guangxi. Because of his wife and child's illnesses, he was called back to Jiangxi by a telegram. When he got back home, his child had already died. His wife, who was suffering from dysentery, died soon after. Zhu remarried in 1940. His new wife, Chen Ji, was the sister of the famous writer Chen Yuan.

23. In 1944, after visiting many universities in China, Needham concluded that Zheda was one of the four best universities in China. He also said that both Zheda and the National Southwest United University were comparable to the best universities in the West, such Cambridge, Oxford, and Harvard. Zhu Kezhen, p. 84.

24. Zhu was an admirer of Wang Yangming. He once quoted Wang to explain the spirit of *qiushi*. Ibid., p. 75.

25. In many ways, Zheda was run by members of the faculty who took care of the day-to-day business of the university in various committees. This method was adopted by Zhu from Western schools like Harvard.

26. *Qinghua renwu zhi*, vol. 3; see the section on Li Jinghan, p. 95.

27. This is how his son Li Weige explains it. Author's interview with Li Weige.

28. Li Jinghan, "Beijing renli chefu xianzhuang de diaocha."

29. Gamble is regarded by David Strand as "the premier Western student of Beijing society during the Republican period." His works include: *Peking: A Social Survey* (New York: George H. Doran, 1921) and *How Chinese Families Live in Peiping* (New York: Funk and Wagnalls, 1933). See Strand, p. 72.

30. Ibid., p. 21.

31. *Qinghua renwu zhi*, vol. 3, p. 93.

32. In the preface to his book *Shidi shehui diaocha fangfa* Li discusses this experience.

33. The result of this research is *Beiping jiaowai zhi xiangcun jiating* (1929).

34. The head of the society was Yu Tianxiu. The society was founded in 1922 and was the first professional sociology society ever established in China.

35. On Yan Yangchu, see Hayford, *To the People*.

36. Li Jinghan, *Dingxian shehui gaikuang diaocha*.

37. Li Jinghan and Zhang Shiwen, *Dingxian yangke*.

38. Interview with Li Weige.

39. Li Jinghan, preface to *Dingxian shehui gaikuang diaocha*.

40. *Qinghua renwu zhi*, vol. 3, p. 96.

41. *Yunnan chenggongxian kunyangxian huji ji renshi dengji chubu baogao* (A preliminary report on census and other affairs in Chenggong County and Kunyang County in Yunnan Province). *Qinghua renwu zhi*, vol. 3, p. 97.

.42. Interview with Li Weige. According to Li Weige, his mother said at the time, "I am also a Chinese and my life is in China." After 1949, she taught English at the Foreign Language Institute in Beijing.

43. On the history of the Democratic League, see History Committee of the Democratic League, comp., *Zhongguo minzhu tongmeng jianshi* and *Zhongguo minzhu tongmeng lishi wenxian.*

44. On this subject, see Grieder, *Intellectuals and the State in Modern China*, chap. 8; Ma Qianli, "Sishi niandai zhengzhi ziyou zhuyi zai Zhongguo"; Xie Yong, "Xinan Lianda zhishi fenziqun de xingcheng yu shuailuo"; and Xu Jilin, "Zhongguo ziyou zhuyi zhishi fenzi de canzheng, 1945–1949."

45. On Luo Longji, see Grieder, *Intellectuals and the State in Modern China*, pp. 341–45.

46. These ideas are clearly suggested by the titles of the articles he published in the *Crescent (Xinyue)*, such as "Meiguo de lizhifa yu lizhiyuan" (The Civil Service Act and civil service in America), "Lun renquan" (On human rights), "Zhuanjia zhengzhi" (Governing by experts), "Wo dui dangwushang de jinqing piping" (My unreserved criticism on party affairs), "Gao yabo yanlun ziyouzhe" (A warning to those who suppress the freedom of speech), and "Shenmo shi fazhi?" (What is the rule of law?). Some of these articles are collected in *Renquan lunji* (Essays on human rights). This collection of essays also includes articles by Hu Shi and Liang Shiqiu.

47. In the *Crescent*, he published the following articles to criticize communist ideology: "Lun Gongchan zhuyi" (On communism) and "Lun Zhongguo de gongchan" (On China's communism).

48. "Wo de beipu de jingguo yu fangan" (My arrest experience and my resentment), in the *Crescent*.

49. Both Ye Duyi and Jin Rongnian emphasized this point in their interviews.

50. See "Luo Longji 1946 nian riji zhaichao" (Excerpts from Luo Longji's 1946 diary), in *Zhonghua minguoshi ziliao cungao* (The documentation material on the history of republican China), suppl. ed., vol. 6.

51. Ye Duyi, "Wo he situleideng" and "Wo he Luo Longji." On the liberals' relationship with the United States, also see Ma Qianli.

52. In the early 1950s, Luo was criticized for his "pro-America" stand. See Ye Duyi, *Wo he Luo Longji.*

53. Ye Yonglie, pp. 53–54.

54. Zhu Kezhen, vol. 4, p. 1256.

55. Among the scientists that eventually came back to China were Tong Dizhou, Bei Shizhang, Dai Fanglan, Tang Peisong, Pei Wenzhong, Wang Dezhao, and Wang Ganchang. These people later became leaders in various branches of science research in the PRC.

56. Li Jinghan was enrolled in a "revolutionary college," the Huabei University, during this period. On these colleges and their function, see Spence, *The Search for Modern China*, pp. 564–65.

57. During my 1993 visit in Beijing, when I was looking for materials on Li Jinghan at the People's University, Li's official work unit before his death, I was eventually directed to the office where all the files (*dang'an*) of deceased faculty were kept. I asked to see Li's file; a staff member brought it out for me and I was able to read through some of it, and even to take some notes.

58. After the reorganization of Chinese universities in 1952, the only places that still had sociology departments were Zhongshan University in Guangzhou and Yunnan University. However, a year later, these two departments were also eliminated. Both the reorganization of universities and the elimination of sociology were results of the Soviet Union's influence. See *Zhongguo da baike quanshu*, the vol. on sociology, p. 495.

59. After 1952, Chen Da also taught for a while at the *Caijing xueyuan* (the Institute of Finance and Economics). Both Wu Wenzao and Pan Guangdan worked at *Zhongyang minzu xueyuan* (the Central Institute of Ethnology). Wu Zelin worked at the Southwest Institute of Ethnology; Wu Jingchao worked in the economics department of People's University; and Sun Benwen worked in the geography department of Nanjing University.

60. Luo was a member of the Zhengwuyuan (Government Administration Council) in the early 1950s and became the minister of timber industry in 1956.

61. Pu Xixiu was one of the most famous female newspaper correspondents in the Nationalist period. She was known for her report in late 1941 on how Soong Ailing, the wife of Kong Xiangxi and the sister-in-law of Chiang Kai-shek, was able to leave Hong Kong by airplane with her dogs after the Japanese bombed Hong Kong in the wake of Pearl Harbor, while many other people could not get their family members out because of the shortage of airplane seats. Pu Xixiu's sister Pu Anxiu was the wife of Marshal Peng Dehuai.

62. The information on Luo's personal life is taken from Ye Yonglie's article, pp. 57–63.

63. Interview with Li Weige. After her divorce, the American woman stayed in China and continued to teach at Beijing Foreign Language Institute. Li later remarried.

64. Interview with Li Weige.

65. The accusation of "Zhang-Luo fandang lianmeng" (Zhang-Luo antiparty clique) first appeared in the July 1, 1957, *People's Daily*'s editorial "Wenhuibao de zizhanjieji fangxiang yinggai pipan" (The Wenhui Daily's bourgeois orientation should be criticized). The editorial was written by Mao Zedong himself. Zhang and Luo's names have remained uncleared after the majority of the "rightists" were rehabilitated in the late 1970s. In 1986, however, the Central Committee of the Democratic League held a meeting to commemorate Luo's ninetieth birthday. Yan Mingfu, then the head of the United Front Ministry under the Communist Party, attended the event.

66. Ye Yonglie, pp. 17–19. Also see Luo Longji, "Wo de chubu jiaodai."

67. This account was provided by Li Jiansheng, Zhang Bojun's wife. See Shang Ding, "Luo Longji de shouzhang."

68. Ye Duyi, "Wo de youpai zuizhuang," p. 24.

69. Ibid.

70. Pan Guangdan, Wu Wenzhao, Wu Zelin, Wu Jingchao, and Fei Xiaotong all became "rightists." In the case of Pan Guangdan, he did not say a word critical of the Party during the Hundred Flowers period, but was still labeled as a rightist later in the antirightist campaign. See Ye Duyi, "Wo de youpai zuizhuang," p. 24.

71. Interview with Li Weige.

72. Ibid.

73. Zhu Kezhen, vol. 4, pp. 509–10, 20 February 1961.

74. Luo still lived in the grand house assigned to him in the early 1950s.

75. Ye Yonglie, p. 2.

76. As head of the Beijing office for the Shanghai-based *Wenhui bao*, which was a major target during the antirightist campaign, Pu Xixiu also became a "rightist" and was forced to denounce Luo Longji, which hurt Luo deeply. The two became estranged thereafter.

77. Zhu Kezhen, vol. 5, p. 637. The day was February 6, 1974.

78. On the revival of sociology, see *Zhongguo da baike quanshu*, the volume on sociology; Han Mingmo, pp. 174–81; and Zhang Zhuo, pp. 1–6.

79. Preface to *Beijing jiaoqu xiangcun jiating shenghuo diaocha zaji* (The account of the survey on the peasant families in the suburbs of Beijing) (Beijing, 1981). This survey was previously published in the *People's Daily* in early 1957. The survey came out of the idea of somebody from the *People's Daily*, who suggested that Li go back to the same villages in the suburbs of Beijing to do a second round of research. Li went back in the fall of 1956, after a lapse of thirty years. The survey was very positive on the changes brought about by collectivization to the lives of peasants. The few problems pointed out by Li were mostly minor. However, during the antirightist campaign, it was used by some people to attack Li.

80. Here I borrow the title of the book by Jonathan D. Spence.

Bibliography

Ahern, E. M. "The Power and Pollution of Chinese Women." In Margery Wolf and Roxane Witke, eds., *Women in Chinese Society* (Stanford, Calif.: Stanford University Press, 1975).

Allen, Frederick Lewis. *Only Yesterday*. New York: Harper and Row, 1931.

Anderson, Benedict. *Imagined Communities: Reflections on the Origin and Spread of Nationalism*. London and New York: Verso, 1991.

Arkush, David. *Fei Xiaotong and Sociology in Revolutionary China*. Cambridge: Harvard University Press, 1981.

Ayers, William. *Chang Chih-tung and Educational Reform in China*. Cambridge: Harvard University Press, 1971.

Banton, Michael. *The Racial Consciousness*. London and New York: Longman, 1988.

———. *Racial Theories*. Cambridge and New York: Cambridge University Press, 1987.

Banton, Michael, and Jonathan Harwood. *The Race Concept*. New York: Praeger, 1975.

Barlow, Tani E., ed., with Gary J. Bjorge. *I Myself Am a Woman*. Boston: Beacon Press, 1989.

Bays, Daniel. *China Enters the Twentieth Century: Chang Chih-tung and the Issues of a New Age, 1895–1909*. Ann Arbor: University of Michigan Press, 1978.

———. *Christianity in China*. Stanford, Calif.: Stanford University Press, 1996.

Beahan, Charlotte. "The Women's Movement and Nationalism in Late Ch'ing China." Ph.D. diss., Columbia University, 1976.

Beaver, Pierce. *All Loves Excelling*. Grand Rapids, Mich.: William B. Eerdmans, 1968.

Bennett, Adrian A., and Kwang-ching Liu. "Christianity in the Chinese Idiom: Young J. Allen and the Early Chiao-hui Hsin-pao, 1868–1870." In John K. Fairbank, ed., *The Missionary Enterprise in China and America* (Cambridge: Harvard University Press, 1974).

Bingxin. *Ji xiaoduzhe* (To young readers). Hong Kong: Hong Kong Wanli shudian, 1959.

Bledstein, Burton J. *The Culture of Professionalism: The Middle Class and the Development of Higher Education in America.* New York: Norton, 1976.

Bok, Esther. "The Education of China's Daughters." *Chinese Students' Bulletin* (February 1907).

Boorman, Howard, ed. *Biographical Dictionary of Republican China.* 5 vols. New York: Columbia University Press, 1971.

Brownell, Susan. *Training the Body for China.* Chicago: University of Chicago Press, 1995.

Buck, Peter. *American Science and Modern China, 1876–1936.* New York: Cambridge University Press, 1980.

Bullock, Mary Brown. "Promoting the American Way: Exchanges with China, Revisited." Paper presented at the Conference on Sino-American Educational and Cultural Exchange, East-West Center, Honolulu, 18–22 February 1985.

Burton, Margaret E. *The Education of Women in China.* New York: Fleming H. Revell, 1911.

———. *Notable Women of Modern China.* New York: Fleming H. Revell, 1912.

Cai Yucong. "Zhongguo shehuixue fazhanshi shang de sige shiqi" (The four phases in the development of sociology in China). *Shehui xuekan* 2, no. 3 (April 1931): 1–33.

Cai Zheng. "Lümei wenjian" (Impressions of traveling in America). *Chinese Students' Quarterly* (Fall 1919): 124–32.

Calinescu, Matei. *Five Faces of Modernity.* Durham, N.C.: Duke University Press, 1987.

Cancian, Francesca M. *Love in America: Gender and Self-Development.* Cambridge and New York: Cambridge University Press, 1987.

Cao Boquan. "Liumei riyong lijie shuolüe" (Brief introduction on daily etiquette in America). *Chinese Students' Quarterly*, no. 1 (Spring 1919): 201–10.

Cao Ting. "Nanmei liuxue yutan" (Studying in the South of the United States). *Chinese Students' Quarterly*, no. 2 (Summer 1920): 87–96.

Carr-Saunders, A. M., and P. A. Wilson. "Professional Associations and Colleague Relations." In Howard M. Vollmer and Donald Mills, eds., *Professionalization* (Englewood Cliffs, N.J.: Prentice-Hall, 1966).

Chan, Sucheng. *Entry Denied: Exclusion and the Chinese Community in America, 1882–1943.* Philadelphia: Temple University Press, 1991.

Chan, Wellington K. K. "Government, Merchants, and Industry to 1911." In John K. Fairbank and Kwang-Ching Liu, eds., *The Cambridge History of China* (Cambridge: Cambridge University Press, 1980), vol. 11, pp. 416–62.

Chang, F. L. "Innocents Abroad." *Chinese Students' Monthly* (February 1914): 300–301.

Chang, Hao. *Chinese Intellectuals in Crisis: Search for Order and Meaning, 1890–1911.* Berkeley: University of California Press, 1987.

———. "Intellectual Change and the Reform Movement, 1890–98." In John K.

Fairbank and Kwang-Ching Liu, eds., *The Cambridge History of China* (Cambridge: Cambridge University Press, 1980), vol. 11.

——. *Liang Ch'i-ch'ao and Intellectual Transition in China, 1890–1907*. Cambridge: Harvard University Press, 1971.

Chao, Buwei Yang. *Autobiography of a Chinese Woman*. Westport, Conn.: Greenwood Press, 1970.

Chao, Yuen Ren. *Life with Chaos*. Vol. 2. Ithaca, N.Y.: Spoken Language Service, 1984.

Chen Baichen, and Dong Jian. *Zhongguo xiandai xijiu shigao* (The draft history of Chinese modern theater). Beijing: Zhongguo xijiu chubanshe, 1989.

Chen Da. "Ting wo suku" (Listen to me pouring my bitterness) *Chinese Students' Quarterly*, no. 2 (Summer 1920): 188–89.

——. *Xiandai Zhongguo renkou* (Chinese population in modern times). Trans. Liao Baoyun. Tianjin: Tianjin renmin chubanshe, 1983

Chen Dongyuan. *Zhongguo funü shenghuoshi* (The history of women's lives in China). Shanghai: Shangwu yinshuguan, 1928.

Chen Hansheng. *Sige shidai de wo* (My life in four periods). Beijing: Zhongguo wenshi chubanshe, 1988.

Chen Hengzhe. *Chen Hengzhe sanwen xuanji* (Selected essays of Chen hengzhe). Ed. Zhu Weizhi. Tianjin: Baihua wenyi chubanshe, 1991.

——. "Jinian yiwei lao gumu" (In memory of an old aunt). In *Chen Hengzhe sanwen xuanji*, pp. 67–70.

——. "Laiyin nüshi xiaozhuan" (A brief biography of Miss Lyon). *Chinese Students' Quarterly* (Fall 1915).

——. "Luoyisi de wenti" (The problem of Louise). In Chen Hengzhe, *Xiao yudianer* (Little rain drops) (Shanghai, 1928).

——. "Woyoushi qiuxue de jingguo" (My pursuit of learning when I was young). In *Chen Hengzhe sanwen xuanji*, pp. 71–81.

——. "Zhi mounüshi shu" (A letter to a female friend). *Chinese Students' Quarterly* (Spring 1915). Collected in *Chen Hengzhe sanwen xuanji*.

Chen Heqin. *Wo de bansheng* (The first half of my life). Shanghai: Shijie shuju, 1941.

——. "Xuesheng huyin wenti zhi yanjiu" (A study on students' marriages). *The Eastern Miscellany* 18, no. 4 (February 1921): 101–12.

Chen, Jack. *The Chinese of America*. San Francisco: Harper and Row, 1980.

Chen, Jerome. *China and the West: Society and Culture, 1815–1937*. Bloomington: Indiana University Press, 1979.

——. *Yuan Shih-k'ai*. Stanford, Calif.: Stanford University Press, 1961.

Chen, Sophia H. (Chen Hengzhe). "A Non-Christian Estimate of Missionary Activities." *Chinese Recorder* 65, no. 2 (February 1934): 110–19.

Chen Xingui. "Ji Luo Longji de sanci yanshuo" (An account of the three speeches given by Luo Longji). *Tuanjie bao* (29 November 1986).

Cheng, Zhefan. *Zhongguo xiandai nüzi jiaoyushi* (History of women's education in modern China). Shanghai: Zhonghua shuju, 1936.

Chiang Monlin (Jiang Menglin). *Tides from the West*. New Haven, Conn.: Yale University Press, 1947.

Chiang Yung-chen. "Social Engineering and Social Sciences in China." Ph.D. diss., Harvard University, 1986.

"The Chinese Laborers in America." *Liu Mei Tsing Nien* (March 1916).

Chinese Oral History Project. Interviews with Liu Chingshan (Liu Jingshan), Chen Guangfu, Kong Xiangxi, and Gu Weijun (Wellington Koo). East Asian Institute, Columbia University, New York.

Chinese Students' Christian Journal. 1917–19.

Chinese Students' Monthly (*CSM*). 1907–31.

Choa, G. *Heal the Sick*. Hong Kong: Chinese University Press, 1990.

Chou Min-chih. *Hu Shih and Intellectual Choice in Modern China*. Ann Arbor: University of Michigan Press, 1984.

Chow, Rey. *Women and Chinese Modernity: The Politics of Reading Between West and East*. Minneapolis: University of Minneapolis Press, 1991.

Chow Tse-tsung. "Hu Shizhi xiansheng de kangyi yu rongren" (Two aspects of Mr. Hu Shi: Protest and tolerance). Reprint, *Zhuanji wenxue* 55, no. 3 (September 1989): 41–48.

———. *The May 4th Movement: Intellectual Revolution in Modern China*. Cambridge: Harvard University Press, 1960.

Chu Xun. *Hu Shi Jiang Dongxue*. Beijing: Zhongguo Qingnian chubanshe, 1995.

Chung, Yuehtsen Juliette. "Struggle for National Survival: Chinese Eugenics in a Transnational Context, 1896-1945." Ph.D. diss., University of Chicago, 1999.

Cohen, Myron L. "Being Chinese: The Peripheralization of Traditional Identities." *Daedalus* (Spring 1991): 113–34.

Cohen, Paul A. "Christian Missions and Their Impact to 1900." In Denis Twitchett and John K. Fairbank, eds., *The Cambridge History of China* (Cambridge: Cambridge University Press, 1978), vol. 10.

———. "Littoral and Hinterland in Nineteenth-Century China: The 'Christian' Reformers." In John K. Fairbank, ed., *The Missionary Enterprise in China and America* (Cambridge: Harvard University Press, 1974).

———. *Between Tradition and Modernity: Wang T'ao and Reform in Late Ch'ing China*. Cambridge: Harvard University Press, 1974.

"College Wards of an Empress." *Evening Post* (New York), 3 October 1907. Wellesley College Archives, Wellesley, Mass.

Collins, Eugene Leslie. "The New Women: A Psychohistorical Study of the Chinese Feminist Movement from 1900 to the Present." Ph.D. diss., Yale University, 1976.

Conable, Charlotte Williams. *Women at Cornell: The Myth of Equal Education*. Ithaca, N.Y.: Cornell University Press, 1977.

Cott, Nancy. *The Grounding of Modern Feminism*. New Haven, Conn.: Yale University Press, 1987.

Crescent (xinyue). 1928–33.

Croll, Elisabeth. *Feminism and Socialism in China*. London: Routledge and Kegan Paul, 1978.

Crunden, Robert. *Ministers of Reform: The Progressives' Achievement in American Civilization*. New York: Basic Books, 1982.

Dajiang jikan (The Big River Quarterly). 1925.

"Dancing in Chinese Society." *Christian China* (October 1919).

Daniels, Roger, and Harry H. L. Kitano. *American Racism*. Englewood Cliffs, N.J.: Prentice-Hall, 1970.

deBary, William Theodore, ed. *The Unfolding of Neo-Confucianism*. New York: Columbia University Press, 1973.

deBary, William Theodore, and Irene Bloom. *Principle and Practicality*. New York: Columbia University Press, 1979.

Deng Suining. *Zhongguo xijiu shi* (History of Chinese drama). Taipei: Zhonghua wenhua chuban shiye weiyuanhui, 1956.

Ding Wenjiang. *Liang Qichao nianpu changbian* (Biographical materials of Liang Qichao). Shanghai: Shanghai renminchubanshe, 1983.

Ding Xiaohe, ed. *Zhongguo bainian liuxue quanjilu* (Chronicle of one hundred years of the foreign-study movement in China). Guangdong: Zhuhai chubanshe, 1998.

Dikötter, Frank. *The Construction of Racial Identities in China and Japan*. Honolulu: University of Hawaii Press, 1997.

———. *The Discourse of Race in Modern China*. Stanford, Calif.: Stanford University Press, 1992.

———. *Imperfect Conceptions: Medical Knowledge, Birth Defects, and Eugenics in China*. New York: Columbia University Press, 1998.

Dirlik, Arif. "Reversals, Ironies, Hegemonies: Notes on the Contemporary Historiography of Modern China." *Modern China* 22, no. 3 (July 1996): 243–84.

Dittmer, Lowell, and Samuel S. Kim. "Whither China's Quest for National Identity?" In Lowell Dittmer and Samuel S. Kim, eds., *China's Quest for National Identity* (Ithaca, N.Y.: Cornell University Press, 1993).

Dolby, William. *A History of Chinese Drama*. London: P. Elek, 1976.

Dong Shouyi. *Qingdai liuxue yundong* (The foreign-study movement in the Qing dynasty). Shenyang: Liaoning renmin chubanshe, 1985.

Dong Xianguang. *Dong Xianguang zizhuan* (Autobiography of a Chinese farmer). Taipei: Taiwan xinsheng baoshe, 1973.

Drucker, Alison. "The Influence of Western Women in the Anti-footbinding Movement, 1840–1911." In Richard W. Guisso and Stanley Johannesen, eds., *Women in China* (Youngstown, N.Y.: Philo Press, 1981).

Duara, Prasenjit. "Minguo de zhongyang jiquan zhuyi he lianbang zhuyi"

(Centralism and federalism in the republican period). *Twenty-first Century* 25 (October 1994): 27–42.

———. *Rescuing History from the Nation.* Chicago: University of Chicago Press, 1995.

The Eastern Miscellany (Dongfang zazhi). 1904–48.

Ebrey, Patricia. "Women, Marriage, and the Family in Chinese History." In Paul Ropp, ed., *Heritage of China: Contemporary Perspectives on Chinese Civilization* (Berkeley and Los Angeles: University of California Press, 1990).

Egan, Susan Chan. *A Latterday Confucian.* Cambridge: Harvard University Press, 1987.

Elman, Benjamin A. *Classicism, Politics, and Kinship: The Chang Chou School.* Berkeley: University of California Press, 1990.

The Encyclopedia of World Methodism. Vols. 1 and 2. Prep. and ed. under supervision of World Methodist Council and the Commission on Archives and History. Nashville, Tenn.: United Methodist Publishing, 1974.

Fairbank, John K., ed. *The Missionary Enterprise in China and America.* Cambridge: Harvard University Press, 1974.

Fairbank, Wilma. *Liang and Lin: Partners in Exploring China's Architectural Past.* Philadelphia: University of Pennsylvania Press, 1994.

Fass, Paula. *The Damned and the Beautiful.* New York: Oxford University Press, 1977.

Fearing, H. D. Scrapbooks on Chinese Students' Alliance Conferences, 1908–14. Chih Meng papers. Mansfield Freeman Center for East Asian Studies, Wesleyan University, Middletown, Conn.

Fei, Hsiao-tung, and Chih-i Chang. *Earthbound China: A Study of Rural Economy in Yunnan.* London: Routledge and Kegan Paul, 1948.

Fei Xiaotong. "Congjian shehuixue de youyi jieduan" (To reestablish sociology). In Fei Xiaotong. *Fei Xiaotong xuanji* (Selected works of Fei Xiaotong) (Tianjin: Tianjin renmin chubanshe, 1988).

———. *From the Soil: The Foundation of Chinese Society.* Trans. Gary G. Hamilton and Wang Zheng. Berkeley: University of California Press, 1992.

———. *Shizhe rusi* (Reminiscing those who have passed). Suzhou: Suzhou University Press, 1993.

———. "The Study of Man in China—Personal Experience." In Chie Nakane and Chien Chiao, eds., *Home Bound Studies in East Asian Society* (Hong Kong: The Center for East Asian Cultural Studies, 1992).

———. "Wo you zhao daole Paike laoshi." (I found Professor Park again). *Bainian chao* (January 1999): 14–17.

———. Zai rensheng de tianping shang (On the scales of life). In *Shizhe rusi*, pp. 110–17.

Feng Ziyou. *Geming yishi* (An anecdotal history of the revolution). Shanghai: Shangwu yinshuguan, 1947.

Feuerwerker, Albert. "Economic Trends, 1912–49." In John K. Fairbank, ed., *The*

Cambridge History of China (Cambridge: Cambridge University Press, 1983), vol. 12, pp. 28–127.

———. "Economic Trends in the Late Ch'ing Empire, 1870–1911." In John K. Fairbank and Kwang-ching Liu, eds., *The Cambridge History of China* (Cambridge: Cambridge University Press, 1980), vol. 11, pp. 2–69.

Fincher, John H. *Chinese Democracy: The Self-Government in Local, Provincial, and National Politics, 1905–1914.* Canberra: Australian National University Press, 1981.

"The First Government Student Conference." *World Chinese Students' Journal* 1, no. 1 (November 1911): 607–8.

Fong, H. D. (Fang Xianting). *Reminiscences of a Chinese Economist at 70.* Singapore: South Seas Society, 1975.

Foreign Students in America. A study by the Commission on Survey of Foreign Students in the U.S., under the auspices of the Friendly Relations Committees of the YMCA and YWCA (1925).

Franking, Mae M./M.T.F. "My Chinese Marriage." *Asia* (June–September 1921). Later published in book form by Duffield and Company (New York, 1922).

Franking, Mae M./M.T.F., and Katherine Anne Porter. *My Chinese Marriage: An Annotated Edition.* Ed. Holly Franking. Austin: University of Texas Press, 1991.

Freedman, Maurice. *Family and Kinship in Chinese Society.* Stanford, Calif.: Stanford University Press, 1970.

Furth, Charlotte. "Intellectual Change from the Reform Movement to the May Fourth Movement, 1895–1920." In John K. Fairbank, ed., *The Cambridge History of China* (Cambridge: Cambridge University Press, 1983), vol. 12, pp. 322–405.

———. *Ting Wen-chiang: Science and China's New Culture.* Cambridge: Harvard University Press, 1970.

Gao Zunlu. *Zhongguo liumei youtong shuxinji* (A collection of letters from young Chinese students in America). Taipei: Zhuanji wenxue chubanshe, 1986.

Garrett, Shirley S. "Image of Chinese Women." In John C. B. and Ellen Low Webster, eds. *The Church and Women in the Third World* (Philadelphia: Westminster, 1985).

Giddens, Anthony. *Modernity and Self-Identity.* Stanford, Calif.: Stanford University Press, 1991.

Gong Shuduo. "Jindai shehui xisu bianhua manhua" (Changes in social customs in modern times). In Gong Shuduo, ed., *Jindai Zhongguo yu jindai wenhua.*

Gong Shuduo, ed. *Jindai Zhongguo yu jindai wenhua* (Modern China and modern culture). Changsha: Hunan renmin chubanshe, 1988.

Goode, William J. *World Revolution and Family Patterns.* New York: Free Press, 1970.

Goodman, Bryna. "New Culture, Old Habits: Native Place Organization and the May Fourth Movement." In Frederic Wakeman, Jr., and Wen-Hsin Yeh, eds., *Shanghai Sojourners* (Berkeley: University of California Press, 1992), pp. 76–107.

Gorn, Elliott J. *The Manly Art: Bare-Knuckle Prize Fighting in America.* Ithaca, N.Y.: Cornell University Press, 1989.

Gossett, Thomas. *Race: The History of an Idea in America.* New York: Schocken, 1963.
Grieder, Jerome B. *Hu Shi and the Chinese Renaissance.* Cambridge: Harvard University Press, 1970.
———. *Intellectuals and the State in Modern China.* New York: Free Press, 1981.
Gu Weijun huiyilu (The memoir of Gu Weijun). 13 vols. Trans. Institute of Modern History, Chinese Academy of Social Sciences. Beijing: Zhonghua shuju, 1983.
Gu Yuxiu. "Gu Yuxiu zishu" (About myself). *Zhuanji wenxue* 68, no. 2 (February 1996): 15–22.
Habermas, Jürgen. *The Structural Transformation of the Public Sphere: An Inquiry into a Category of Bourgeois Society.* Trans. Thomas Burger and Frederick Lawrence. Cambridge: MIT Press, 1992.
Han Mingmo. *Zhongguo shehui xueshi* (The history of sociology in China). Tianjin: Tianjin renmin chubanshe, 1987.
Hao Gengsheng. "Sishinian hunyin shenghuo zhi huiyi" (Reminiscence of my forty years' marriage). *Zhuanji wenxue* 13, no. 4.
———. "Xinsuan hua liumei" (Talking about my student life in America with bitterness in the heart). *Zhuanji wenxue* 12, no. 3 (October 1968): 23–28.
Harrell, Paula. *Sowing the Seeds of Change: Chinese Students, Japanese Teachers, 1895–1905.* Stanford, Calif.: Stanford University Press, 1992.
Hatch, Nathan. *The Democratization of American Christianity.* New Haven, Conn.: Yale University Press, 1989.
Hayford, Charles W. *To the People: James Yen and Village China.* New York: Columbia University Press, 1990.
Hayhoe, Ruth, and Marianne Bastid, eds. *China's Education and the Industrialized World: Students in Cultural Transfer.* New York: M. E. Sharpe, 1987.
He Maoqing. "Boshidun gongyishe baogao" (Report of the Boston General Welfare Association). *Liumei xuesheng nianbao* (1912).
"Historical Sketch of Chinese Students' Alliance." In *The Handbook of the Chinese Students in the U.S.A.* (New York, 1934).
History Committee of the Democratic League, comp. *Zhongguo minzhu tongmeng jianshi* (The brief history of the Democratic League of China). Beijing: Qunyan chubanshe, 1991.
———. *Zhongguo minzhu tongmeng lishi wenxian* (Historical documents of the Chinese Democratic League). Beijing: Wenshi ziliao chubanshe, 1983.
Ho Ping-ti. "The Geographical Distribution of Hui-Kuan [*landsmanschaften*] in Central and Upper Yangtze Provinces." *Journal of Chinese Studies* (December 1966): 120–52.
———. *A Historical Survey of* Landsmanschaften *in China.* Taipei, 1966.
Horowitz, Helen L. *Campus Life: Undergraduate Cultures from the End of the Eighteenth Century to the Present.* New York: Alfred A. Knopf, 1987.
Hsia, C. T. "Hsü Chen-ya's Yü-li hun: An Essay in Literary History and Criticism." *Renditions*, nos. 17–18 (Spring–Fall 1982): 199–253.

Hsu Kai-yu. *Wen I-to*. Boston: Twayne Publishers, 1980.

Hsu, Leonard Shi-lien (Xu Shilian). "The Sociological Movement in China." *Pacific Affairs* 4, no. 4 (1931): 283–307.

Hu Binxia (Pingsa). "Hutaoshan nüxiaozhang" (The female principals of the Walnut Hill School). *Liumie xuesheng nianbao* (1911).

———. "Jichu zhi jichu" (The foundation of foundation). *Funü zazhi* (Ladies' journal) 2, no. 8 (August 1916): 1–12.

———. "Meiguo jiating" (Families in America). *Funü zazhi* (Ladies' journal) 2, no. 2 (February 1916): 1–8.

Hu Guangbiao. *Bozhu liushinian* (Chasing the waves for sixty years). Taipei: Wenhai chubanshe, 1964.

Hu Shengwu, and Cheng Weikun. "Minchu shehui fengshang de yanbian" (Changes in social trends in the early republic). *Jindaishi yanjiu* 34, no. 4 (July 1986): 136–62.

Hu Shi. "Guiguo zagan" (The mischievous thoughts after returning to the country). In *Hu Shi wencun*, vol. 1, pp. 621–28.

———. *Hu Shi liuxue riji* (Hu Shi's diary during his student days in the U.S.). Shanghai: Shangwu yinshuguan, 1947.

———. *Hu Shi wencun* (The collected writings of Hu Shi). Taipei: Yuandong tushu gongsi, 1953.

———. "Lun zhencao wenti: Da Lan Zhixian" (On chastity: A reply to Lan Zhixian). In *Hu Shi wencun*, vol. 1, pp. 676–84.

———. "Meiguo de funü" (Women in America). In *Hu Shi wencun*, vol. 1, 648–64.

———. "Sishi zishu" (Autobiography at forty). In Chen Jingan, ed., *Hu Shi yanjiu ziliao* (Beijing: Shiyue wenyi chubanshe, 1989).

———. "Zhuidao Zhimo" (Mourning Zhimo). In *Xu Zhimo quanji* (Complete works of Xu Zhimo) (Taipei: Zhuanji wenxue chubanshe, 1969), vol. 1.

Hu Yi. "Beimei paihua liüshi" (Brief history of the anti-Chinese movement in North America). *Dajiang jikan* 1, no. 2.

Huang Chen-ch. "The Influence of an Educated Woman in the Home and Country." *World Chinese Students' Journal* (September 1912).

Huang Fu-ch'ing. *Chinese Students in Japan in the Late Ch'ing Period*. Tokyo: The Center for East Asian Cultural Studies, 1982.

Huang, Philip C. C. "Public Sphere/Civil Society in China?" *Modern China* (April 1993): 220–26.

Huang Wenzhong. *Zhongguo jinbainian tiyushi* (History of sports in China in the last hundred years). Taipei: Taiwan shangwu yinshuguan, 1967.

Huang Zhizheng. "Wusi shiqi liumei xuesheng dui kexue de chuanbo" (The spread of science by American-educated Chinese during the May Fourth period). *Jindaishi yanjiu* (February 1989): 17–40.

Hunt, Michael H. "The American Remission of the Boxer Indemnity: Reappraisal." *Journal of Asian Studies* 31, no. 3 (May 1972): 539–59.

———. "Chinese National Identity and Strong State: The Late-Qing Republican Crisis." In Lowell Dittmer and Samuel S. Kim, eds., *China's Quest for National Identity* (Ithaca, N.Y.: Cornell University Press, 1993).

———. *The Making of a Special Relationship*. New York: Columbia University Press, 1983.

Hunter, Jane. *The Gospel of Gentility*. New Haven, Conn.: Yale University Press, 1984.

Jiang Tingfu. "Jiang Tingfu huiyilü" (Reminiscence of Jiang Tingfu). *Zhuanji wenxue* 30, no. 3 (March 1977): 99–106.

Jiaoyu zazhi (Journal of education) (1916, 1918, and 1925).

Jin Shixuan. "Liumei sinian de huiyi" (Reminiscence of my four years in America). *Journal of Northern Transportation University* (November 1983).

Jindaishi yanjiu (Journal of modern history).

Johnson, Kay Ann. *Women, the Family, and Peasant Revolution in China*. Chicago: University of Chicago Press, 1983.

Johnson, Terence J. *Professions and Power*. London: MacMillan, 1972.

Jones, Dorothy B. *The Portrayal of China and India on the American Screen: The Evolution of Chinese and Indian Themes, 1896–1955*. Cambridge: Center for International Studies, MIT, 1955.

Judt, Tony. "The New Old Nationalism." *New York Review of Books* (26 May 1994): 44–51.

Kahn, Ida. Papers. General Commission on Archives and History, United Methodist Church, Madison, N.J.

Kallgren, Joyce K., and Denis Fred Simon, eds. *Educational Exchanges: Essays on the Sino-American Experience*. Berkeley: University of California Press, 1987.

Kang Youwei. "Qianguehui xu" (On the society of strengthening learning). *Buren zazhi* 8.

———. *Wuxu bianfa* (The One Hundred Days Reform). Shenzhou: Guoguang Press, 1954.

Kevles, D. J. *In the Name of Eugenics: Genetics and the Use of Human Heredity*. New York: Alfred A. Knopf, 1985.

Kexue jishu tuanti shiliao (Historical documents on the histories of science and technology societies). Vol. 2 (the republican period). Beijing: Zhongguo kexie, 1985.

Kin, Yamai (Jin Yunmei). "The Women of China." *Asia* (April 1917).

King Ya-mei (Jin Yunmei). "As We See Ourselves." *World Chinese Students' Journal* (January–February 1907).

Kirby, William. "Engineering China: Birth of the Developmental States 1928–37." In Yeh Wen-hsin, *Becoming Chinese: Passages to Modernity and Beyond 1900–1950* (Berkeley: University of California Press, 1999), pp. 137–60.

Ko, Dorothy. *Teachers of the Inner Chambers: Women and Culture in Seventeenth-Century China*. Stanford, Calif.: Stanford University Press, 1994.

Koo, Wellington (Gu Weijun). Interviews with Wellington Koo. Chinese Oral History Project, East Asian Institute, Columbia University, New York;

microfilm (Glen Rock, N.J.: Microfilming Corporation of America, 1978): film A219, Harvard University Widener Library microforms.

———. Memoirs. Columbia University Archives and Columbiana Library.

Kuang, Xinnian. "Xuehengpai dui xiandaixing de fansi" (Reflections on modernity by the Critical Review School). *Twenty-first Century* (April 1994): 46–55.

Kuper, Leo, ed. *Race, Science, and Society.* New York: Columbia University Press, 1975.

Kwok, Daniel W. Y. *Scientism in Chinese Thought, 1900–1950.* New Haven, Conn.: Yale University Press, 1965.

Kwok, Pui-lan. *Chinese Women and Christianity.* Atlanta: Scholars Press, 1992.

LaFargue, Thomas E. *China's First Hundred: Educational Mission Students in the United States, 1872–1881.* Pullman: Washington State University Press, 1987.

Lampton, David M., Joyce A. Madancy, and Kristen M. Williams. *A Relationship Restored: Trends in U.S.-China Educational Exchanges, 1978–1984.* Washington, D.C.: National Academy Press, 1988.

Lamson, Herbert Day. *Social Pathology in China: A Source Book for the Study of Problems of Livelihood, Health, and Family.* Shanghai: Commercial Press, 1935.

Lang, Olga. *Chinese Family and Society.* New Haven, Conn.: Yale University Press, 1946.

Larson, Magali Sarfatti. *The Rise of Professionalism.* Berkeley: University of California Press, 1977.

Latourette, Kenneth Scott. *A History of Christian Missions in China.* New York: Macmillan, 1929.

Lee, Alfred McClung. *Fraternities Without Brotherhood.* Boston: Beacon Press, 1955.

Lee, Leo Ou-fan. "The Cultural Construction of Modernity in Urban Shanghai." In Wen-hsin Yeh, *Becoming Chinese: Passages to Modernity and Beyond 1900–1950* (Berkeley: University of California Press, 1999), pp. 31–61.

———. *The Romantic Generation in Modern Chinese World.* Cambridge: Harvard University Press, 1973.

———. "In Search of Modernity: Some Reflections on a New Mode of Consciousness in Twentieth-Century Chinese History and Literature." In Paul A. Cohen and Merle Goldman, eds., *Ideas Across Cultures* (Cambridge: Harvard University Press, 1990).

———. *Shanghai Modern: The Flowering of a New Urban Culture in China, 1930–1945.* Cambridge: Harvard University Press, 1999.

Lee, Rose Hum. *The Chinese in the United States of America.* Hong Kong: Hong Kong University Press, 1960.

Levenson, Joseph R. *Confucian China and Its Modern Fate.* Berkeley: University of California Press, 1966.

Levine, Marilyn A. *The Found Generation: Chinese Communists in Europe During the Twentieth Century.* Seattle: University of Washington Press, 1993.

Levy, Marion J. *The Family Revolution in Modern China*. Ca. 1949. Reprint, New York: Octagon Books, 1971.

Lewis, Amy Gifford. "Dr.Ida Kahn—Nanchang, China." *Christian Advocate* (30 June 1930): 682–83.

Lewis, Ida B. *The Education of Girls in China*. New York: Teachers' College, Columbia University, 1919.

Li Jignhan. *Beijing jiaoqu xiangcun jiating shenghuo diaocha zaji* (The account of the survey on peasant families in the suburbs of Beijing). Beijing, 1981.

———. "Beijing renli chefu xianzhuang de diaocha" (An investigation of conditions among rickshaw pullers in Beijing). *Shehui xue zazhi* 2, no. 4 (April 1925).

———. "Beiping jiaowai zhi xiangcun jiating (The peasant families in the suburbs of Beiping). 1929.

———. *Dingxian shehui gaikuang diaocha* (Dingxian: A social survey). Beiping: Zhonghua pingmin jiaoyu cuojinhui, 1933.

———. *Shidi shehui diaocha fangfa* (Methods of social survey in China). Beiping: Xingyuntang shudian, 1933.

Li Jinghan and Zhang Shiwen. *Dingxian yangge xuan* (Dingxian plantation songs). Tianjin: Zhonghua pingmin jiaoyu cuojinhui, 1933.

Li Liangyu. "Cong xinhai dao wusi: Minzu zhuyi de lishi kaocha" (From the 1911 revolution to the May Fourth: A historical examination of nationalism). *Jianghai xuekan*, no. 172 (April 1994): 115–22.

Li Ping. "Xin qingnain zhi jiating" (The family of a new youth). *New Youth* 2, no. 2 (October 1916).

Li Wenhai. "Wuxu weixin shiqi de xuehui zuzhi" (Study societies during the One Hundred Days Reform period). In Gong Shuduo, ed., *Jindai Zhongguo yu jindai wenhua* (Modern China and modern Chinese culture) (Changsha: Hunan renmin chubanshe, 1988).

Li Xisuo. *Jindai Zhongguo de liuxuesheng* (Foreign-study students in modern Chinese history). Beijing: Renmin chubanshe, 1987.

Li Yu-ning, ed. *Hu Shi yu ta de pengyou* (Hu Shi and his friends). New York, 1990.

Li Yu-ning and Chang Yü-fa, eds. *Jindai Zhongguo nüquan yundong shiliao* (Documents on the feminist movement in modern China). Vol. 2. Taipei: Zhuanji wenxue chubanshe, 1975.

Liang Qichao. "Ji Jiangxi Kang nüshi" (On Miss Kang of Jiangxi). In *Yinbingshi heji* (Shanghai: Zhonghua shuju, 1936), *wenji*, vol. 1, no. 1, pp. 119–20.

———. "Kaiming junzhu lun" (On enlightened despotism). In *Yinbingshi heji*, *wenji*, vol. 6, 13–83.

———. "Lun nüxue" (On women's education). In *Yinbingshi heji*, *wenji*, vol. 1, no. 1, pp. 37–44.

———. "Lun xuehui" (On study societies). *Shiwu bao* 10 (Shanghai, 1896–98).

———. "Shuo qun xu" (The preface to a treatise on grouping). In *Yinbingshi heji*, *wenji*, vol. 2, pp. 3–7.

———. "Xin dalu youji" (Travel on the new continent). In *Yinbingshi cunzhu* (Shanghai, Shangwu yinshuguan, 1916), vol. 12.

———. "Xin dalu youji jielu" (Excerpts from "The Journey to the New Continent"). In *Yinbingshi heji, zhuanji*, vol. 5, pp. 127–31.

———. "Xinmin shuo" (On the New Citizen). In *Yinbingshi heji, zhuanji*, pp. 1–161.

———. "Xinzhongguo jianshe wenti" (On the building of new China). In *Yinbingshi heji, wenji*, vol. 10, pp. 27–47.

———. *Yinbingshi quanji* (Collected works of the ice-drinking room). Shanghai, 1924.

Liang Shiqiu. "Daonian Yu Shangyuan" (Commemorating Yu Shangyuan). In Liang Shiqiu, *Liang Shiqiu huairen conglu* (A collection of Liang Shiqiu's essays on reminiscence of old friends) (Beijing, 1991).

———. "Gongli" (Justice). *Dajiang jikan* 1, no. 1 (1925).

———. *Liang Shiqiu huairen conglu* (A collection of Liang Shiqiu's essays on reminiscence of old friends). Beijing: Zhongguo guangbo dianshi chubanshe, 1991.

———. *Liang Shiqiu sanwen* (Selected writings of Liang Shiqiu). Beijing: Zhongguo guangbo dianshi chubanshe, 1989.

———. "Qinghua banian" (Eight years at Qinghua]. In *Liang Shiqiu sanwen*.

———. "Tan Wen Yiduo" (On Wen Yiduo). In *Liang Shiqiu sanwen*.

———. "Tangren zi he chu lai?" (Where do you, Tangren, come from). In *Yashe xiaopin* (Essays of the house of elegance) (Taipei, 1982), pp. 79–81.

Lin Yü-sheng. *The Crisis of Chinese Consciousness.* Madison: University of Wisconsin Press, 1979.

Lin Zixun. *Zhongguo liuxue jiaoyushi* (History of the Chinese foreign-study movement). Taipei: Huangan chuban youxian gongsi, 1976.

Link, Perry. *Mandarin Duck and Butterfly: Popular Fiction in Early Twentieth-Century Chinese Cities.* Berkeley: University of California Press, 1981.

Liu, Lydia H. *Translingual Practice: Literature, National Culture, and Translated Modernity.* Stanford, Calif.: Stanford University Press, 1995.

Liu Mei Tsing Nien. 1914–17.

Liu Zhen, and Wang Huanchen, eds. *Liuxue jiaoyu* (Foreign education). Taipei: Guoli bianyiguan, 1980.

Liumei xuesheng jibao (The Chinese students' quarterly). 1914–22, 1926–28.

Liumei xuesheng nianbao (The Chinese students' annual). 1907–14.

"Liumei Zhongguo xuesheng chubanwu zhi jinbu" (The progress of Chinese students' publications in the United States). *Quarterly* (Spring–Summer 1922): 25–26.

"Liumei Zhongguo xuesheng zhi diaocha" (Survey of Chinese students in America). *Jiaoyu zazhi* (The journal of education) 17, no. 3 (March 1925): 13.

"Liumei Zhongguo xueshenghui xiaoshi" (A brief history of Chinese Students' Alliance). *The Eastern Miscellany* 14, no. 12 (December 1902): 172–76.

Loewen, James W. *The Mississippi Chinese.* Cambridge: Harvard University Press, 1971.

Long Fei, and Kong Yangeng. *Zhang Boling yu Zhang Pengchun* (Zhang Boling and Zhang Pengchun). Tianjin: Baihua wenyi chubanshe, 1997.

Lu Xun. *Lu Xun quanji* (Complete works of Lu Xun). Beijing: Renmi wenxue chubanshe, 1956.

———. "Suiganlu No. 40" (Miscellaneous thoughts no. 40). In *Refeng* (Hot wind) (Beijing: Renmin wenxue chubanshe, 1973).

———. "Tengye xiansheng" (Mr. Fujino). In *Lu Xun quanji*, vol. 2, pp. 273–75.

Luo Longji. *Renquan lunji* (Essays on human rights). Shanghai: Xinyue shudian, 1930.

———. "Wo de chubu jiaodai" (My preliminary confession). *Xinhua banyuekan*, no. 18 (1957). Reprinted in Xie Yong, ed., *Luo Longji wodebeipude jingguo yu fangan* (My arrest experience and my resentment) (Beijing: Zhongguo qingnian chubanshe, 1999), pp. 310–22.

Luo Xianglin. *Liang Cheng de chushi meiguo* (Liang Cheng's diplomatic mission to the United States). Taipei: Wenhai chubanshe, n.d.

Lutz, Jessie Gregory. *China and the Christian Colleges*. Ithaca, N.Y.: Cornell University Press, 1971.

Lyman, Stanford M. *Chinese Americans*. New York: New School for Social Research, 1974.

Ma, L. Eve Armentrout. *Revolutionaries, Monarchists, and Chinatown: Chinese Politics in the Americas and the 1911 Revolution*. Honolulu: University of Hawaii Press, 1990.

Ma Qianli. "Sishi niandai zhengzhi ziyou zhuyi zai Zhongguo" (Political liberalism in China in the 1940s). *Suzhou Daxue xuebao*, no. 1 (1995): 123–27.

Ma Yinchu. "Yi Kelunbiya Daxue guoji gongfa jiaoyuan Shiduoer xiansheng yanshuoci" (A translation of Columbia University international law Professor Shiduoer's speech). *Chinese Students' Quarterly* (June 1914): 85–88.

Mann, Susan. *Precious Records: Women in China's Long Eighteenth Century*. Stanford, Calif.: Stanford University Press, 1997.

Mao Yisheng. "Zhongguo gongchengshi xuehui jianshi" (Brief history of the Chinese Engineers' Society). In *Wenshi ziliao jingxuan* (Selected historical documents) (Beijing: Zhongguo wenshi chubanshe, 1990), vol. 13.

———. "Zhongguo jiechu de aiguo gongchengshi Zhan Tianyou" (China's patriotic engineer, Zhan Tianyou). In Gong Shuduo, ed., *Jindai Zhongguo yu jindai wenhua* (Changsha: Hunan renmin chubanshe, 1988).

Mao Zedong. "Tiyu zhi yanjiu" (The study of sports). *New Youth* 3, no. 2 (April 1917).

McGough, James P. *Fei Hsiao-tung: The Dilemma of a Chinese Intellectual*. New York: M. E. Sharpe, 1979.

McKee, Delber L. *Chinese Exclusion Versus the Open Door Policy, 1900–1906*. Detroit: Wayne State University Press, 1977.

Meng Chengxian. "Liumei xuesheng yu guonei wenhua yundong" (American-educated Chinese and the New Culture Movement in China). *Quarterly* (June 1920).

Meng, Chih. *Chinese American Understanding: A Sixty-Year Search*. New York: China Institute in America, 1981.

———. Papers. Mansfield Freeman Center for East Asian Studies, Wesleyan University, Middletown, Conn.

Miller, Stuart Creighton. *The Unwelcome Immigrant: American Image of the Chinese, 1785–1882*. Berkeley and Los Angeles: University of California Press, 1969.

Min Jie. "Jindai Zhongguo zuizao de zhenghun guanggao he xinshi hunli" (The earliest marriage ads and new-style weddings in modern China). *Bainain chao* (January 1999): 71–74.

Min Tu-ki. *National Polity and Local Power: The Transformation of Late Imperial China*. Ed. Philip A. Kuhn and Timothy Brook. Council on East Asian Studies, Harvard University Press, 1989.

Miner, Luella. "American Barbarianism and Chinese Hospitality." *Outlook*, no. 12 (1902): 984–88.

Mintz Steven, and Susan Kellogg. *Domestic Revolutions: A Social History of American Family Life*. New York: Free Press, 1988.

Nivard, Jacqueline. "Women and Women's Press: The Case of the *Ladies' Journal*, 1915–1931." *Republican China* (November 1984): 37–55.

Ono Kazuko. *Chinese Women in a Century of Revolution, 1850–1950*. Stanford, Calif.: Stanford University Press, 1989.

Orleans, Leo A. *Chinese Students in America: Policies, Issues, and Numbers*. Washington, D.C.: National Academy Press, 1988.

Oyang Yuqian. "Huiyi chunliu" (Reminiscences of Spring Willow). In *Zhongguo huaju yundong wushinian shiliaoji, 1907–1957* (Documentary history of fifty years of Chinese modern theater, 1907–57) (Hong Kong, 1978).

Pan Guangdan. "Jindai zhongzu zhuyi shilüe" (History of racism in modern history). *Dajiang jikan* 1, no. 2 (1925).

———. "Jinhou zhi jibao yu liumei xuesheng" (The future of the Quarterly and the Chinese students in America). *Quarterly* 2, no. 1 (March 1926).

———. *Minzu yanjiu wenji* (Selected works on ethnic studies). Beijing: Minzu chubanshe, 1995.

———. "Yousheng gailun" (Brief introduction to eugenics). *The Chinese Students' Quarterly* 11, no. 4 (May 1927): 51–70.

———. *Zhongguo zhi jiating wenti* (On Chinese family). Shanghai: Xinyue shudian, 1929.

Pan Naigu, and Pan Naihe, eds. *Pan Guangdan xuanji* (Selected works of Pan Guangdan). 4 vols. Beijing: Guangming ribao chubanshe, 1999.

Pan Naimu, ed. *Pan Guangdan wenji* (Collected works of Pan Guangdan). Vol. 1. Beijing: Beijing University Press, 1993.

Patterson's scrapbooks. Cornell University Archives, Ithaca, N.Y.

Paul, Diane B. *Controlling Human Heredity: 1865 to the Present*. Atlantic Highlands, N.J.: Humanities Press, 1995.

Peiwei. "Lianai yu zhencao de guanxi" (The relationship between love and morality). *Funü pinglun* (August 1921).

Perrot, Michelle. *From the Fires of Revolution to the Great War*. Vol. 4 of *A History of Private Life*. Cambridge, Mass.: Belknap Press, 1990.

Pleck, Elizabeth H., and Joseph H. Pleck. *The American Man*. Englewood Cliffs, N.J.: Prentice-Hall, 1980.

Porter, L. C. "The First Government Student Conference." *World Chinese Student's Journal* 1, no. 2 (November 1911): 607–8.

Pye, Lucian. *The Spirit of Chinese Politics: A Psycho-cultural Study of the Authority Crisis in Political Development*. Cambridge: MIT Press, 1968.

Qian Ning. *Liuxue Meiguo* (Studying in the U.S.A.). Nanjing: Jiangsu wenyi chubanshe, 1996.

Qinghua University History Project Office, ed. *Qinghua Daxue shiliao bianxuan* (Selected historical documentation of Qinghua University). Beijing: Qinghua University Press, 1991.

———. *Qinghua Daxue xiaoshi gao* (The history of Qinghua University: A draft). Beijing: Zhonghua shuju, 1981.

———. *Qinghua renwu zhi* (Biographical accounts of Qinghua people). Vols. 1–4. Beijing: Qinghua University Press, 1992–96.

———. *Qinghua tongxue lu* (Qinghua alumni registry). (Beijing, 1937).

Qiu Renzong. "Cultural and Ethical Dimensions of Genetic Practices in China." In *Ethical Issues of Human Genetics in Chinese and International Contexts* (Hamburg: n.p., 1999).

Quanguo fulian (All women's federation of China), ed. *Zhongguo funü yundongshi* (A history of the women's movement in China). Beijing: Chunqiu chubanshe, 1989.

Rankin, Mary. *Elite Activism and Political Transformation in China: Zhejiang Province, 1865–1911*. Stanford, Calif.: Stanford University Press, 1986.

Reardon-Anderson, James. *The Study of Change: Chemistry in China, 1840–1949*. Cambridge: Cambridge University Press, 1991.

"The Recent Examination in Nanjing." *World Chinese Students' Journal* (July–August 1907).

Ren Hongjun. "Jianli xuejie lun" (On the creation of the Chinese intellectual community). *Chinese Students Quarterly* (June 1914): 40–53.

———. "Jiaohui jiaoyu yu liuxuesheng" (Missionary education and foreign-study students). *Chinese Students' Quarterly*, no. 2 (Summer 1918).

"The Returned Students and the Peking Examination." *World Chinese Students' Journal* (July 1911).

Rhoads, Edward. *China's Republican Revolution: The Case of Kwangtung, 1895–1913*. Cambridge: Harvard University Press, 1975.

Riess, Steven. *Touching Base: Professional Baseball and American Culture in the Progressive Era*. Westport, Conn.: Greenwood Press, 1980.

Robert, Dana L. "The Methodist Struggle over Higher Education in Fuzhou, China, 1877–1883." *Methodist History* 34, no. 3 (April, 1996): 173–89.

Rockefeller Foundation Archives. Archive Center, Tarrytown, N.Y.

Saneto Keishu. *Zhongguoren liuxue reben shi* (History of Chinese studying in Japan). Trans. Tan Ruqian and Lin Qiyan. Beijing: Sanlian shudian, 1983.

Sang Bing. *Qingmo xin zhishijie de shetuan yu huodong* (Societies and activities of the new intellectual class in late Qing). Beijing: Sanlian shudian, 1995.

Sarri, Jon L. *Legacies of Childhood: Growing Up Chinese in a Time of Crisis*. Cambridge: Harvard University Press, 1990.

Saxton, Alexander. *The Indispensable Enemy*. Berkeley: University of California Press, 1971.

Schoppa, Keith R. *Chinese Elites and Political Change: Zhejiang Province in the Early Twentieth Century*. Cambridge: Harvard University Press, 1982.

Schwarcz, Vera. *The Chinese Enlightenment*. Berkeley: University of California Press, 1987.

———. *Time for Telling the Truth Is Running Out*. New Haven, Conn.: Yale University Press, 1992.

Schwartz, Benjamin. "Culture, Modernity, and Nationalism—Further Reflections." *Daedalus* (Summer 1993): 207–26.

———. "The Limits of 'Tradition vs. Modernity' as Categories of Explanation." *Daedalus* (Spring 1972): 77–88.

———. *In Search of Wealth and Power: Yan Fu and the West*. Cambridge: Harvard University Press, 1964.

———. "Themes in Intellectual History: May Fourth and After." In John K. Fairbank, ed., *The Cambridge History of China* (Cambridge: Cambridge University Press, 1983), vol. 12, pp. 406–50.

Seton, Grace Thompson. *Chinese Lanterns*. New York: Dodd Mead, 1924.

Shang Ding. "Luo Longji de shouzhang" (Lou Longji's walking stick). *Shanghai mengxun* (5 December 1986).

Shang Yanliu. *Qingdai keju kaoshi shulu* (An account of the examination system in the Qing dynasty). Beijing: Sanlian shudian, 1958.

Shen Shouze. "Meiguo xuesheng zhi shenghuo" (The lifestyle of American students). *Chinese Students' Quarterly* (September 1921): 50–55.

Shen Tsung-han (Shen Zonghan). *Autobiography of a Chinese Farmer's Servant*. Taipei: Linking Publications, 1981.

Shen Weiwei. "Hu Shi hunyin lüelun" (A brief study of Hu Shi's marriage). *Minguo dangan*, no. 1 (1991): 87–90.

———. *Hu Shi zhuan* (Biography of Hu Shi). Kaifen, Henan: Henan daxue chubanshe, 1988.

Shijie ribao (The world journal). New York: Shijie ribaoshe.

Shu Xincheng. *Jindai Zhongguo liuxueshi* (The history of China's modern foreign-study movement). Shanghai: Zhongguo shuju, 1927.

———. *Zhongguo jindai jiaoyushi ziliao* (A documentary history of education in modern China). Beijing: Renmin jiaoyu chubanshe, 1961.

Sia, Ruby. "Chinese Women Educated Abroad." *World Chinese Students' Journal* (November–December 1907): 27–32.

Skolnick, Arlene. *The Intimate Environment*. Boston: Little, Brown, 1987.

Solomon, Barbara Miller. *In the Company of Educated Women*. New Haven, Conn.: Yale University Press, 1985.

Spence, Jonathan D. *The Gate of Heavenly Peace*. New York: Viking Press, 1981.

———. *The Search for Modern China*. New York and London: Norton, 1990.

Stacey, Judith. *Patriarchy and Socialist Revolution in China*. Berkeley: University of California Press, 1983.

"Statement by the Critical Review." *Xueheng*, no. 13 (January 1923): 1–4.

Stepan, Nancy. *The Idea of Race in Science: Great Britain*. Hamden, Conn.: Archon, 1982.

Stone, Lawrence. *The Family, Sex, and Marriage in England, 1500–1800*. New York: Harper and Row, 1977.

Stone, Mary. Papers. General Commission on Archives and History. United Methodist Church, Madison, N.J.

Strand, David. *Rickshaw Beijing*. Berkeley and Los Angeles: University of California Press, 1989.

Stross, Randalle. *The Stubborn Earth*. Berkeley: University of California Press, 1986.

Su Yunfeng. *Jindai gaodeng jiaoyu yanjiu: Cong Qinghua Xuetang dao Qinghua Daxue 1911–1929* (A study of higher education in the modern period: From Qinghua College to Qinghua University 1911–1929). Taipei: Institute of Modern History Academic Sinica, 1996.

Sun Benwen. *Dangdai Zhongguo shehuixue* (Sociology in modern China). 1948. Reprint, Shanghai: Shanghai shudian, 1989.

———. *Shehuixue yuanli* (The principles of sociology). Shanghai: Shangwu yinshuguan, 1946.

Sun, E-Tu Zen. "The Growth of the Academic Community 1912–1949." In John K. Fairbank and Albert Feuerwerker, eds., *The Cambridge History of China* (Cambridge: Cambridge University Press, 1986), vol. 13, pp. 361–420.

———. *Ren Yidu jiaoshou fangwen jilu* (The interview of Professor E-Tu Zen Sun). Interviewers: Chang Peng-yuan, Yang Tsui-hua, and Shen Sung-chiao. Recorder: Pang Kuang-che. Taipei: Institute of Modern History, Academia Sinica, 1993.

Sun Longji. "Liangge geming de duihua, 1789 and 1911" (A dialogue between two revolutions, 1789 and 1911). *Twenty-first Century* (April 1994): 25–34; (June 1994): 42–63.

Sun Shangyang. "Zai qimeng yu xueshu zhijian: Chonggu xueheng" (Between enlightenment and scholarship: A reassessment of the Critical Review School). *Twenty-first Century* (April 1994): 33–45.

Sun Shiyue. *Zhongguo jindai nüzi liuxueshi* (A history of female foreign-study students in modern China). Beijing, 1995.

Sun Xiaoen, and Xiu Pengyue. "Xu Shou, Hua Hengfang yu jindai keji" (Xu Shou, Hua hengfang, and modern science and technology). In Gong Shuduo, ed., *Jindai Zhongguo yu jindai wenhua* (Modern China and modern culture) (Changsha: Hunan renmin chubanshe, 1988).

Sung, Betty Lee. *The Story of the Chinese in America*. New York: Collier, 1967.

A Survey of Chinese Students in American Universities and Colleges in the Past One Hundred Years. New York, 1954.

Tan Sheying. *Fuyun sishi nian* (Forty years' of women's movement). Taipei: n.p., 1952.

Tang Degang, trans. "Hu Shi de Zizhuan" (Autobiography of Hu Shi). In Cheng Jingan, ed., *Hu Shi yanliu ziliao* (Sources on the study of Hu Shi) (Beijing: Beijing shiyue wenyi chubanshe, 1989).

Tang Xiaobing. *Global Space and the National Discourse of Modernity: The Historical Thinking of Liang Qichao*. Stanford, Calif.: Stanford University Press, 1996.

Taylor, Charles. *Sources of the Self: The Making of the Modern Identity*. Cambridge: Harvard University Press, 1989.

Tcheng, Soumay. *A Girl from China*. New York: n.p., 1926.

Tian Benxiang. *Zhongguo xiandai bijiao xijushi* (Comparative history of Chinese modern theater). Beijing: Wenhua yishu chubanshe, 1993.

Ting, L. S. "Chinese Students in America." *World Chinese Students' Journal* (March–June 1907).

"To Learn, to Teach, to Serve, and to Enjoy." *World Chinese Students' Journal* (January–February 1907).

Topley, Marjorie. "Marriage Resistance in Rural Kwangtung." In Margery Wolf and Roxane Witke, eds., *Women in Chinese Society* (Stanford, Calif.: Stanford University Press, 1975).

Townsend, James. "Chinese Nationalism." *Australian Journal of Chinese Affairs* (January, 1992): 97–130.

Trachtenberg, Alan. *The Incorporation of America: Culture and Society in the Gilded Age*. New York: Hill and Wang, 1982.

Tsai, Shih-shan Henry. *China and the Overseas Chinese in the United States, 1868–1911*. Fayetteville: University of Arkansas Press, 1983.

———. *The Chinese Experience in America*. Bloomington: Indiana University Press, 1986.

Tyau, T. Z. "Educational Comments." *World Chinese Students' Journal* (July–August 1911).

Unger, Jonathan, ed. *Chinese Nationalism*. New York: M. E. Sharpe, 1996.

Varg, Paul. *Missionaries, Chinese, and Diplomats: The American Protestant Mission-*

aries Movement in China, 1890–1952. Princeton, N.J.: Princeton University Press, 1958.

Vollmer, Howard M., and Donald Mills, eds. *Professionalization*. Englewood Cliffs, N.J.: Prentice-Hall, 1966.

Walsh, Mary Roth. *Doctors Wanted: No Women Need Apply*. New Haven, Conn.: Yale University Press, 1977.

Wang Hui. "'Kexue zhuyi' yu shehui lilun de jige wenti" ("Scientism" and a number of social-theory questions). *Tianya*, no. 6 (June 1998): 132–41.

——. *Wang Hui zixuan ji* (The self-selected works of Wang Hui). Guilin: Guangxi Normal University Press, 1997.

——. "Weibo Yu Zhonggue de xiandaixing wenti" (Weber and the question of Chinese modernity). In *Wang Hui zixuan ji*.

——. "Yan Fu de sange shijie" (The three worlds of Yan Fu). *Xueren*, no. 12 (October 1997).

Wang Qisheng. *Zhongguo liuxuesheng de lishi guiji 1872–1949* (The historical trace of Chinese students abroad, 1872–1949). Hubei jiaoyu chubanshe, 1992.

Wang Tao. *Manyou suilu* (The record of my wanderings). Hunan: Yuelu chubanshe, 1985.

Wang, Y. C. *Chinese Intellectuals and the West, 1872–1949*. Chapel Hill: University of North Carolina Press, 1966.

Wang Zheng. *Women and Chinese Enlightenment: Oral and Textual Histories*. Berkeley: University of California Press, 1999.

Weber, Max. *The Theory of Social and Economic Organization*. Trans. A. M. Henderson and Talcott Parsons. New York: Oxford University Press, 1947.

Webster, John C. B., and Ellen Low, eds. *The Church Women in the Third World*. Philadelphia: Westminster, 1985.

Wei Shaochang. *Wo kan yuanyang hudiepai* (What I think of the mandarin-duck-and-butterfly school). Taipei: Taiwan shangwu yinshuguan, 1992.

Wen Liming. "Dajiang hui yanjiu" (On the Big River Society). Unpublished article.

Wen Liming and Hou Jukun, eds. *Wen Yiduo nianpu changbian* (The biographical materials of Wen Yiduo). Hubei renmin chubanshe, 1994.

West, Philip. *Yenching University and Sino-Western Relations, 1916–1952*. Cambridge: Harvard University Press.

Who's Who: American Returned Students. Tsinghua College, 1917. Reprint, San Francisco: Chinese Materials Center, 1978.

Williams, Raymond, *Keywords: A Vocabulary of Culture and Society*. New York: Oxford University Press, 1983.

Witke, Roxane Heater. "Transformation of Attitudes Toward Women During the May Fourth Era of Modern China." Ph.D. diss., University of California, Berkeley, 1970.

Wolf, Margery. *Women and the Family in Rural Taiwan*. Stanford, Calif.: Stanford University Press, 1972.

Wolf, Margery, and Roxane Witke, eds. *Women in Chinese Society*. Stanford, Calif.: Stanford University Press, 1975.

Woloch, Nancy. *Women and the American Experience*. New York: McGraw-Hill, 1994.

Wong, K. Chimin, and Wu Lien-teh. *History of Chinese Medicine*. Shanghai: National Quarantine Service, 1936.

Wong, Siu-lun (Huang Shaolun). *Sociology and Socialism in Contemporary China*. London: Routledge and Kegan Paul, 1979.

——. "Zhongguo jiefangqian shehuixue de chengzhang" (The growth of sociology in China before the liberation). In *Shehuixue wenxuan* (A collection of essays on sociology) (Hangzhou: Zhejiang renmin chubanshe, 1982).

Wu, Charles Ling. "Attitudes Toward Negroes, Jews, and Orientals in the United States." Ph.D. diss., Ohio State University, 1927. An abstract was published by the Ohio State University in 1930.

Wu, Cheng-tsu, ed. *"Chink": A Documentary History of Anti-Chinese Practice in America*. New York: World Publishing, 1972.

Wu Liming. *Liang Qichao he tade ernümen* (Liang Qichao and his children). Shanghai: Shanghai renmin chubanshe, 1999.

Wu Mi. "Lun xinwenhua yundong" (On the New Culture Movement). *Quarterly* (March 1921).

Wu Ruo and Jia Yili. *Zhongguo huaju shi* (History of Chinese modern theater). Taipei: Xingzhengyuan wenhua jianshe weiyuanhui, 1985.

Wu Wenzao. "Minzu yu guojia" (Ethnicity and nation). *Chinese Students' Quarterly* 11, no. 3.

——. *Renleixue shehuixue yanjiu wenji* (Research papers on anthropology and sociology). Beijing: Minzu chubanshe, 1990.

——. "Wu Wenzao zizhuan" (Autobiography of Wu Wenzao). In *Jinyang xuekan* (June 1982): 44–51.

Wu Wenzhong. *Zhongguo tiyu fazhanshi* (History of sports in China). Taipei: Sanmin shuju, 1981.

Wu, William. *The Yellow Peril*. Hamden, Conn.: Archon Books, 1982.

Wu Xiangxiang. "Chengzhi xuehui cujin Zhongguo xiandaihua" (CCH's promotion of China's modernization). In Wu Xiangxiang, *Minguo zongheng tan* (Reflections on the republican era) (Taipei: Shibao wenhua chuban shiye youxian gongsi, 1980).

Wu Zelin. *Xiandai zhongzu* (Modern races). Shanghai: Xinyue shudian, 1932.

Xia Jiashan, Cui Guoliang, and Li Lizhong, eds. *Nankai huaju yundong shiliao* (The documentary materials of Nankai drama activity). Tianjin: Nankai University Press, 1984.

Xiao Gongqin. "Cong kejiu zhidu de feichu kan jindai yilai de wenhua duanlie"

(The impact of the abolition of civil service examination: A case study of cultural rupture in the modern period). *Zhanlüe yu fangfa* (Strategy and Management) (April 1996): 11–17.

Xie Bingxin. "Wode laoban Wu Wenzao" (My husband, Wu Wenzao). In Wu Wenzao, *Selected Essays on Sociology and Anthropology by Wu Wenzao* (Beijing: Minzuo chubanshe, 1990).

Xie Yong. "Xinan lianda zhishi fenziqun de xingcheng yu shuailuo" (The formation and decline of the intellectual group at the Southwest United University). *Twenty-first Century* (December 1996): 57–65.

Xing Long. "Qingmo minchu hunyin shenghuozhong de xinchao" (New trends in marriage customs in the late Qing and early republic). *Jindaishi yanjiu* (April 1991): 169–83.

Xu Jiansheng. "Jindai Zhongguo hunyin jiating biange sichao shulun" (A review of the change of thinking on marriage and family in modern China). *Jindaishi yanjiu* (April 1991): 139–64.

———. "Wuxu nüzi jiefang xintan" (A new study of women's emancipation during the Wuxu period). *Shixue yuekan*, no. 5 (May 1989): 44–48.

Xu Jilin. "Zhongguo ziyou zhuyi zhishi fenzi de canzheng, 1945–1949" (The political participation of Chinese liberal intellectuals, 1945–49). *Twenty-first Century* (August 1991): 34–46.

Xu Jilin, and Chen Dakai, eds. *Zhongguo xiandaihua shi* (The history of Chinese modernization). Shanghai: Sanlian shudian, 1995.

Xu Shilian (Leonard Shih-lien Hsu). "Zhongguo shehuixue yundong de mubiao jingguo he fanwei" (The goal, history, and scope of sociology in China). *Shehui xuekan* 2 (1930): 1–29.

Xu Xianjia. "Youmei lüeshuo" (Brief account of traveling in America). *The Eastern Miscellany* 6, no. 2 (25 February 1909): 15–16.

Xu Yuzhai. *Xu Yuzhai zishu nianpu* (Self-account of autobiographical materials of Xu Yuzhai). Taipei, 1977.

Yan Dixun. "Shujia lüxing ji" (Travel in the summer). *Chinese Students' Quarterly* (March 1918): 136–39.

Yan Huiqing. *Yan Huiqing zizhuan* (Autobiography of Yan Huiqing). Trans. Yao Songling. Taipei: Zhuanji wenxue chubanshe, 1973.

Yan Zhengwu, ed. *Hu Shi yanjiu conglu* (A collection of studies on Hu Shi). Beijing: Sanlian shudian, 1989.

Yang Quan. "Tiyu pian" (On sports). *Chinese Students' Quarterly* (September 1914): 61–64.

Ye Duyi. "Wo de youpai zuizhuang" (My rightist "crimes"). *Bainian Chao* (Hundred year tide) (January 1999).

———. "Wo he Luo Longji" (Luo Longji and I). In Ye Duyi, *Bashi zishu* (Looking back at eighty years of my life) (Beijing: Qunyan chubanshe, 1994), pp. 66–76.

———. "Wo he Situleideng" (Leighton Stuart and I). *Wenshi ziliao*, no. 13 (1960): 57–83.

Ye Yonglie. "Bokai lishi de miwu: Luo Longji zhuan" (Clearing the mist of history: The biography of Luo Longji). In Ye Yonglie, *Chenzhong de 1957* (A heavy year: 1957) (Nanchang: Baihuazhou wenyi chubanshe, 1992).

Yen, W. W. "The Recent Imperial Metropolitan Examinations for Returned Students." *World Chinese Students' Journal* (September–October 1907).

Yi Gongcheng. "Jinxiandai de Zhongguo kexue jishu tuanti" (Science and technology organizations in modern China). *Zhongguo keji shiliao* (Historical materials of science and technology in China) 6, no. 5 (Beijing, 1985).

Yi Jiayue, and Luo Dunwei. *Zhongguo jiating wenti*. 1922. Reprint, Shanghai: Taidong shuju, 1936.

Yi Zhuxian. *Hu Shi zhuan* (Biography of Hu Shi). Hubei: Hupei renmin chubanshe, 1987.

Young, Ernest P. "Politics in the Aftermath of Revolution: The Era of Yuan Shih-k'ai, 1912–16." In John K. Fairbank, ed., *The Cambridge History of China* (Cambridge: Cambridge University Press, 1983), vol. 12, pp. 209–55.

Yu Shangyuan, ed. *Guoju yundong* (The national theater movement). Shanghai: Xinye shudian, 1927.

Yü Yingshih. "Zhongguo zhishi fenzi de bianyuanhua" (The marginalization of Chinese intellectuals). *Twenty-first Century* 6 (August 1991): 15–25.

Yuan, Tung-li. *A Guide to Doctoral Dissertations by Chinese Students in America, 1905–1960*. Washington, D.C.: Sino-American Cultural Society, 1961.

Yuan Xiaoming. "Qingmo shuxuejia Li Shanlan" (The late-Qing mathematician Li Shanlan). In Gong Shuduo, ed., *Jindai Zhongguo yu jindai wenhua* (Modern China and modern culture) (Changsha: Hunan renmin chubanshe, 1988).

Yun Zhi. "Hu Shi de liangshou qingshi" (Two love poems by Hu Shi). *Tuanjie bao* (31 July 1991).

Yung Wing. *My Life in China and America*. ca. 1909. Reprint, New York: Arno Press, 1979.

Zhang Chengyou. "Hunyin" (Marriage). *Chinese Students' Quarterly*, no. 3 (1916): 117–24.

Zhang Jianhua. "Cong Aobolin dao Mingxian" (From Oberlin to Mingxian). *Jindaishi yanjiu* (January 1995): 172–213.

Zhang Pengyuan. *Lixianpai yu xinhai geming* (The constitutionalists and the 1911 revolution). Taipei: Taiwan shangwu yinshuguan, 1969.

Zhang Ruohua. "Rujia zidi yangjiaotu" (A descendant of Confucius and a convert of Christianity). *Zhongwai zazhi* (February 1991): 17–19.

Zhang Xueji. "Minguo shiqide suosheng yundong" (The movement of merging provinces in the early republican period). *Twenty-first Century* (October 1994): 43–58.

Zhang Zhuo. *Xiandai Zhongguo shehuixue, 1979–1989* (Sociology in contemporary China). Chengdu: Sichuan renmin chubanshe, 1990.

Zhao Jiaming. "Jiang Tingfu de hunyin beiju" (Jiang Tingfu's tragic marriage). *Zhuanji wenxue* 57, no. 3 (September 1990): 21–27.

Zhong Beiying. "Liumei xuesheng ying ruhe fuzhu huaqiao" (How the Chinese students in America should help the Chinese immigrants). *Quarterly*, no. 1 (Spring 1921): 27–33.

Zhong Shaohua. "Zhongguo gongchengshi xuehui" (The Chinese Engineers' Society). *Zhongguo keji shiliao* (Historical materials of science and technology in China) 6, no. 3 (Beijing, 1985): 36–43.

Zhongguo da baike quanshu (The Chinese encyclopedia). Vol. on sociology. Beijing: Zhongguo da baike quanshu chubanshe, 1991.

Zhongguo huaju yundong wushinian shiliaoji, 1907–1957 (Documentary history of fifty years of Chinese modern theater, 1907–57). Hong Kong: 1978.

Zhongguo jindai tiyushi jianbian (A brief history of sports in modern China). The Research Center for the History of Sports at Chengdu Sports Institute. Beijing: Renmin tiyu chubanshe, 1981.

Zhou Gu. "Kong Xiangxi Fei Qihe fumei liuxue beiju rujing jingguo" (How Kong Xiangxi and Fei Qihe were refused entry to the United States). *Zhuanji wenxue* 47, no. 6 (December 1985): 72–79.

Zhou Zhiping. "Chuibusan de xindou renying" (A shadow in the heart that can not be blown away). In *Hu Shi Conglun* (On Hu Shi) (Taipei: Sanmin shuju, 1992).

———. *Hu Shi yu Weiliansi* (Hu Shi and Williams). Beijing: Beijing University Press, 1998.

Zhu Jineng. "Jiawu zhanqian siwei nüliuxuesheng" (Four returned female students in the 1890s). *The Eastern Miscellany* 31, no. 11 (June 1934): 10–14.

Zhu Kezhen. *Zhu Kezhen riji* (Zhu Kezhen's diary). 5 vols. Beijing: Renmin chubanshe, 1984.

Zhu Kezhen zhuan (The biography of Zhu Kezhen). *Zhu Kezhen zhuan* Editorial Board, comp. Sponsored by the National Natural Science Foundation. Beijing: Kexue chubanshe, 1990.

Zhu Qizhe. "Meiguo nüzi zhi jiaoyu." (Female education in America). *Chinese Students' Quarterly* (June and September 1914): 69–74.

Zweig, David, and Chen Changgui. *China's Brain Drain to the United States: Views of Overseas Chinese Students and Scholars in the 1990s.* Berkeley: Center for Chinese Studies, Institute of East Asian Studies, University of California, 1995.

Character List

Cai Yuanpei　蔡元培

Cao Yunfang　曹云芳

Cao Yunxiang (Y. S. Tsao)　曹云祥

Chen Da　陳達

Chen Guangfu　陳光甫

Chen Hengzhe　陳衡哲

Chen Heqin　陳鶴琴

Chen Yinke　陳寅恪

Ding Wenjiang (Ting Wen-chiang)
　丁文江

Duan Fang　端方

Fang Xianting (H. D. Fong)　方顯庭

Fei Xiaotong　費孝通

Gao Zi　高梓

Gu Yuxiu　顧毓秀

Gu Weijun (Wellington Koo)
　顧維鈞

Guo Bingwen (Kuo Ping-wen)
　郭秉文

Hao Gengsheng　郝更生

He Haoruo　何浩若

He Lian (Franklin Ho)　何廉

Hong Shen　洪深

Hong Ye (Hung Yeh, William Hung)
　洪業

Hu Binxia　胡彬夏

Hu Shi (Hu Shih)　胡適

Jiang Dongxiu　江冬秀

Jiang Menglin (Chiang Monlin)
　蔣夢麟

Jiang Tingfu　蔣廷黻

Jin Shixuan　金士宣

Jin Yunmei (Yamei King)　金韻梅

Kang Aide (Ida Kahn)　康愛德

Kong Xiangxi (H. H. Kung)　孔祥熙

Li Anzhai　李安宅

Li Jinghan (Franklin C. H. Lee)
　李景漢

Li Pinghua (Mabel Lee)　李平華

Liang Cheng　梁誠

Liang Dunyan　梁敦彥

Liang Qichao　梁啓超

Liang Shiqiu　梁實秋

Lin Shu　林抒

Liu Jingshan　劉景山

Luo Jialun　羅家倫

Luo Longji　羅隆基

Ma Yinchu　馬寅初

Mei Guangdi (K. T. May)　梅光迪

Meng Zhi (Chi Meng, Paul Meng)　孟治

Pan Guangdan　潘光旦

Pu Xuefeng　浦薛鳳

Qu Qiubai　瞿秋白

Ren Hongjun (Jen Hung-chün)　任鴻雋

Shen Zonghan (Shen Tsung-han)　沈宗瀚

Shi Meiyu (Mary Stone)　石美玉

Song Ailing (Ailing Soong)　宋靄齡

Song Qingling (Rosamunde Soong)　宋慶齡

Song Ziwen (T. V. Soong)　宋子文

Sun Benwen　孫本文

Tan Sitong　譚嗣同

Tang Yongdong　湯用彤

Yan Fu (Yen Fu)　嚴复

Yan Huiqing (W. W. Yen)　嚴惠慶

Yan Yangchu (James Yen)　晏陽初

Yang Buwei　楊布偉

Yang Quan　楊銓

Yu Shangyuan　余上沅

Yuan Shikai　袁士凱

Wang Chonghui　王寵惠

Wang Qingchun (Jing-chun Wang, C. C. Wang)　王景春

Wang Zhengting (C. T. Wang)　王正廷

Wen Yiduo (Wen I-to)　聞一多

Wu Jingchao　吳景超

Wu Mi　吳宓

Wu Wenzao　吳文藻

Wu Zelin　吳澤霖

Xie Bingxin　謝冰心

Xiong Foxi　熊佛西

Xu Jinhong (Hü Kingeng)　許金芺

Xu Zhimo　徐志摩

Zhan Tianyou (Jeme Tien Yau)　詹天佑

Zhang Boling　張伯苓

Zhang Jiazhu　張嘉鑄

Zhang Pengchun　張彭春

Zhang Taiyan　章太炎

Zhang Zhidong　張之洞

Zhao Taimou　趙太侔

Zhao Yuanren (Yuen Ren Chao)　趙元任

Zhu Kezhen (Chu K'o-chen, Coching Chu)　竺可楨

Zhu Tingqi (T. C. Chu)　朱庭祺

Index